VON DER HEYDT-MUSEUM
WUPPERTAL

MUSEUM BARBERINI
POTSDAM

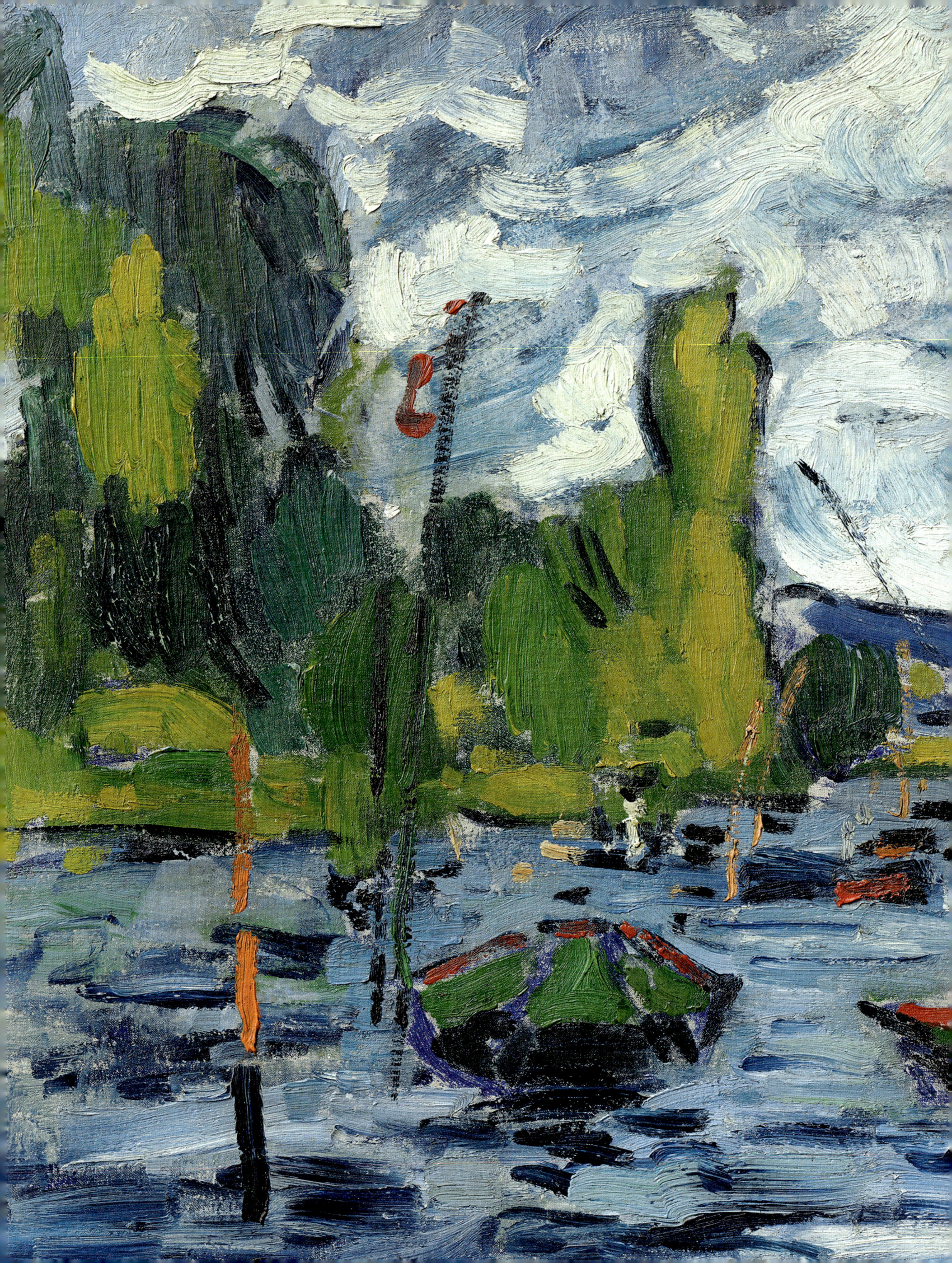

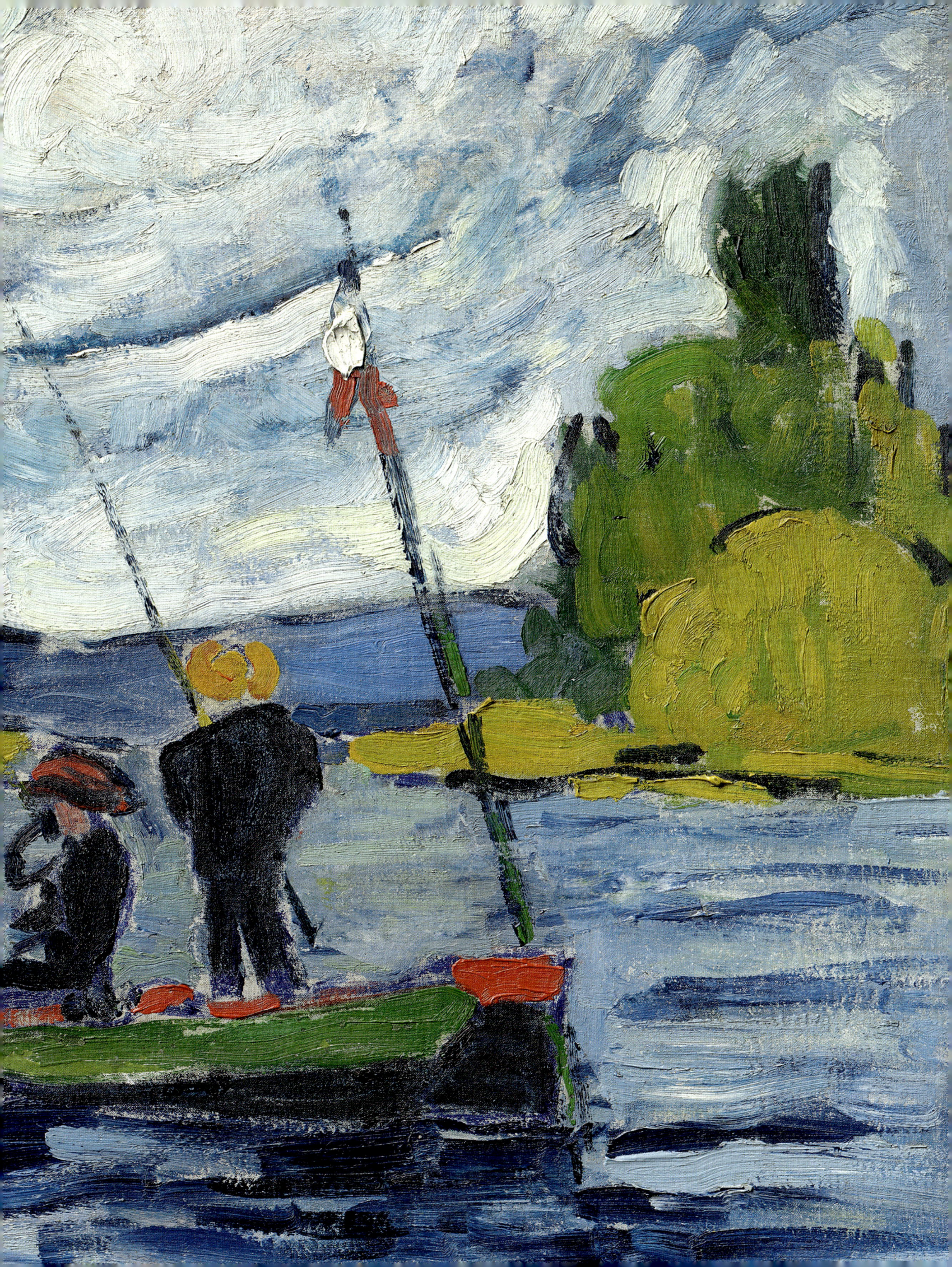

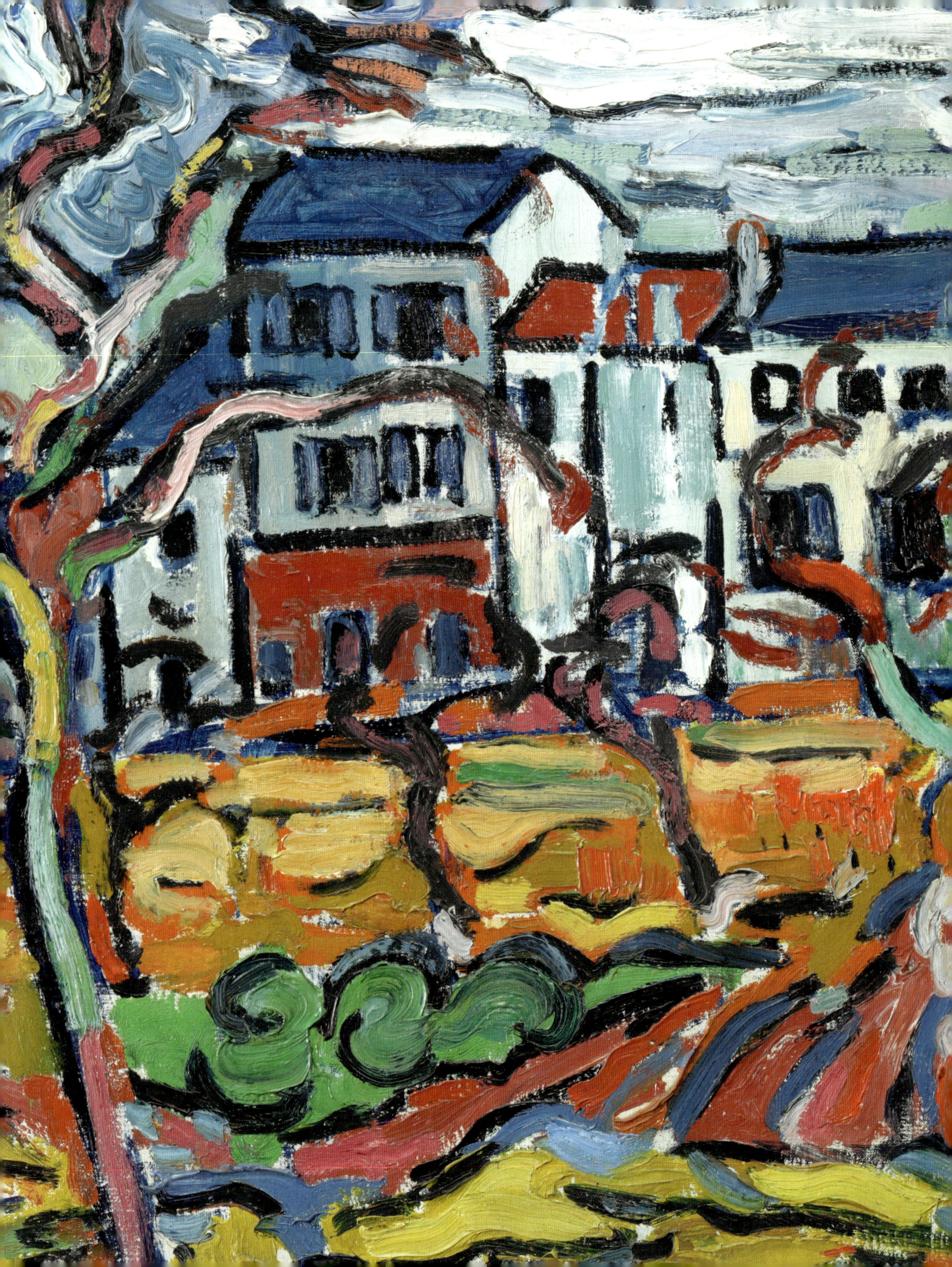

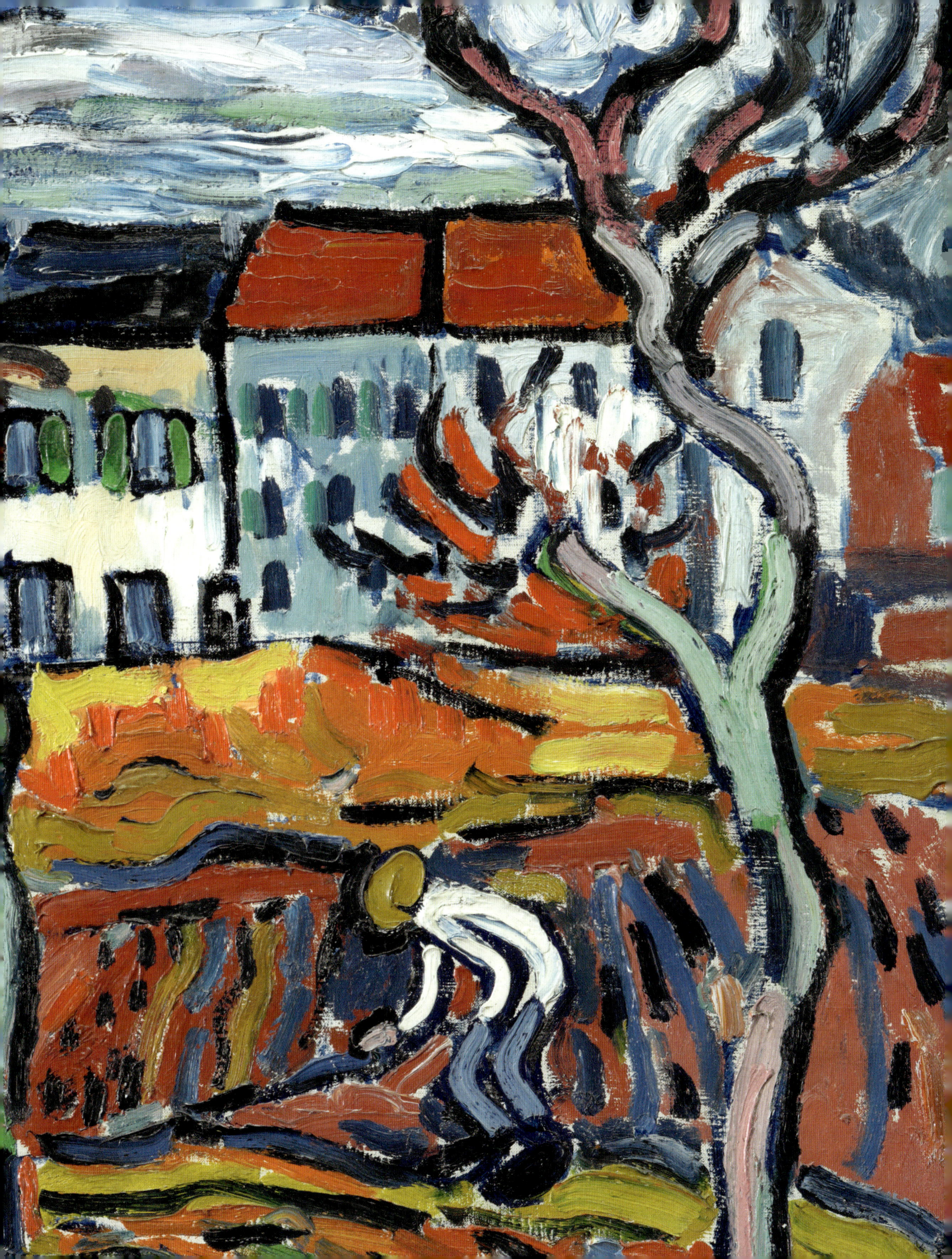

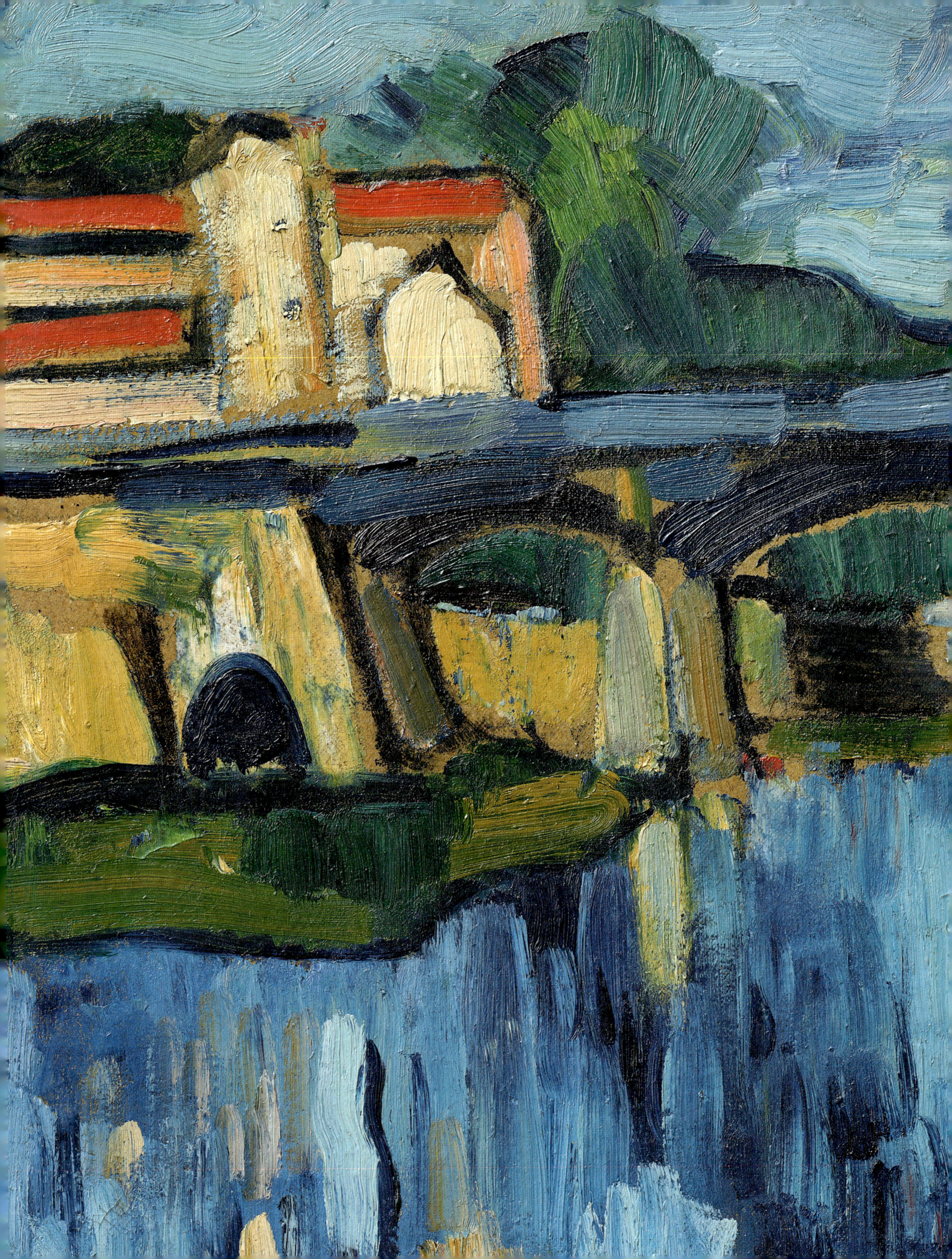

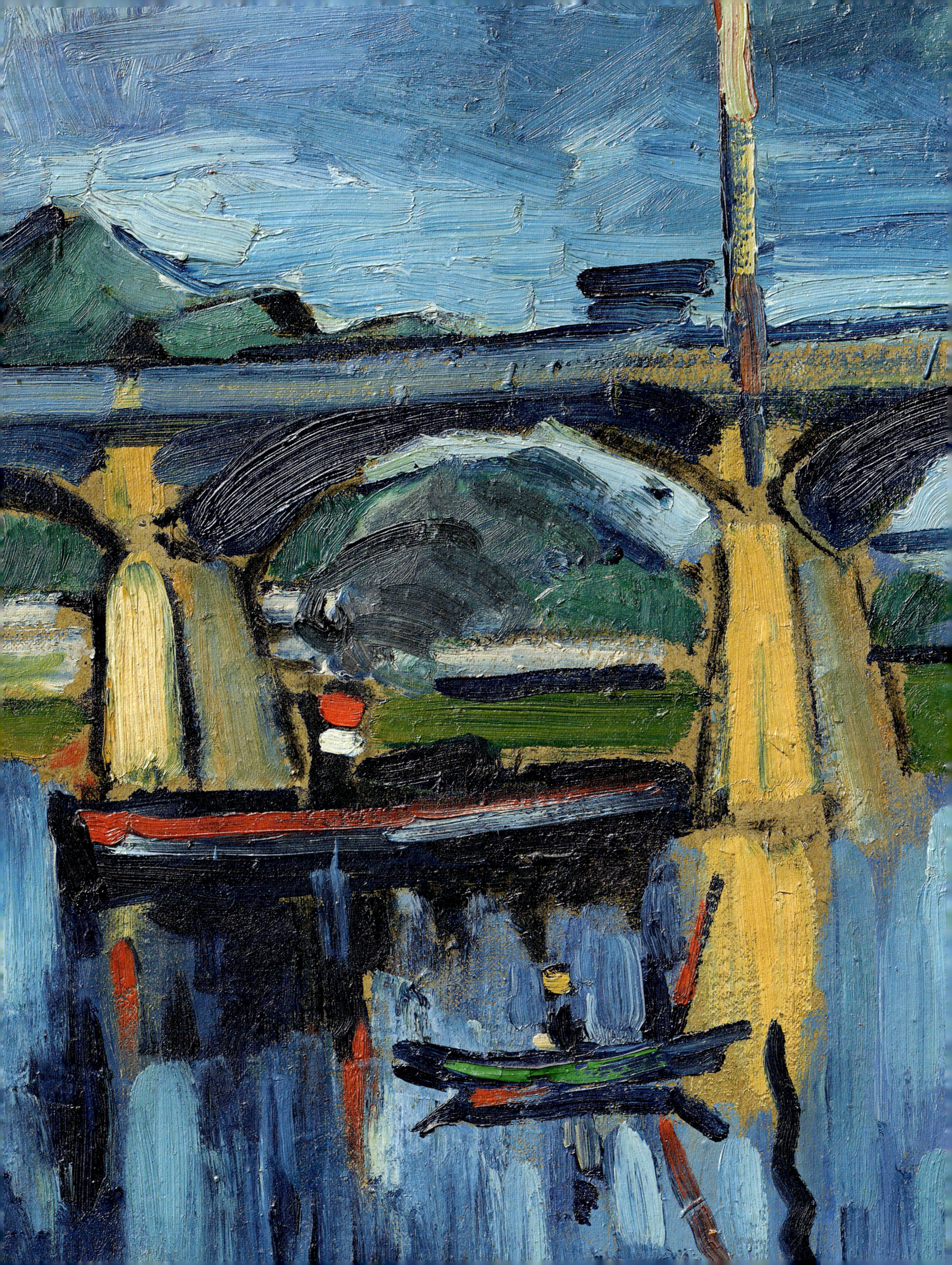

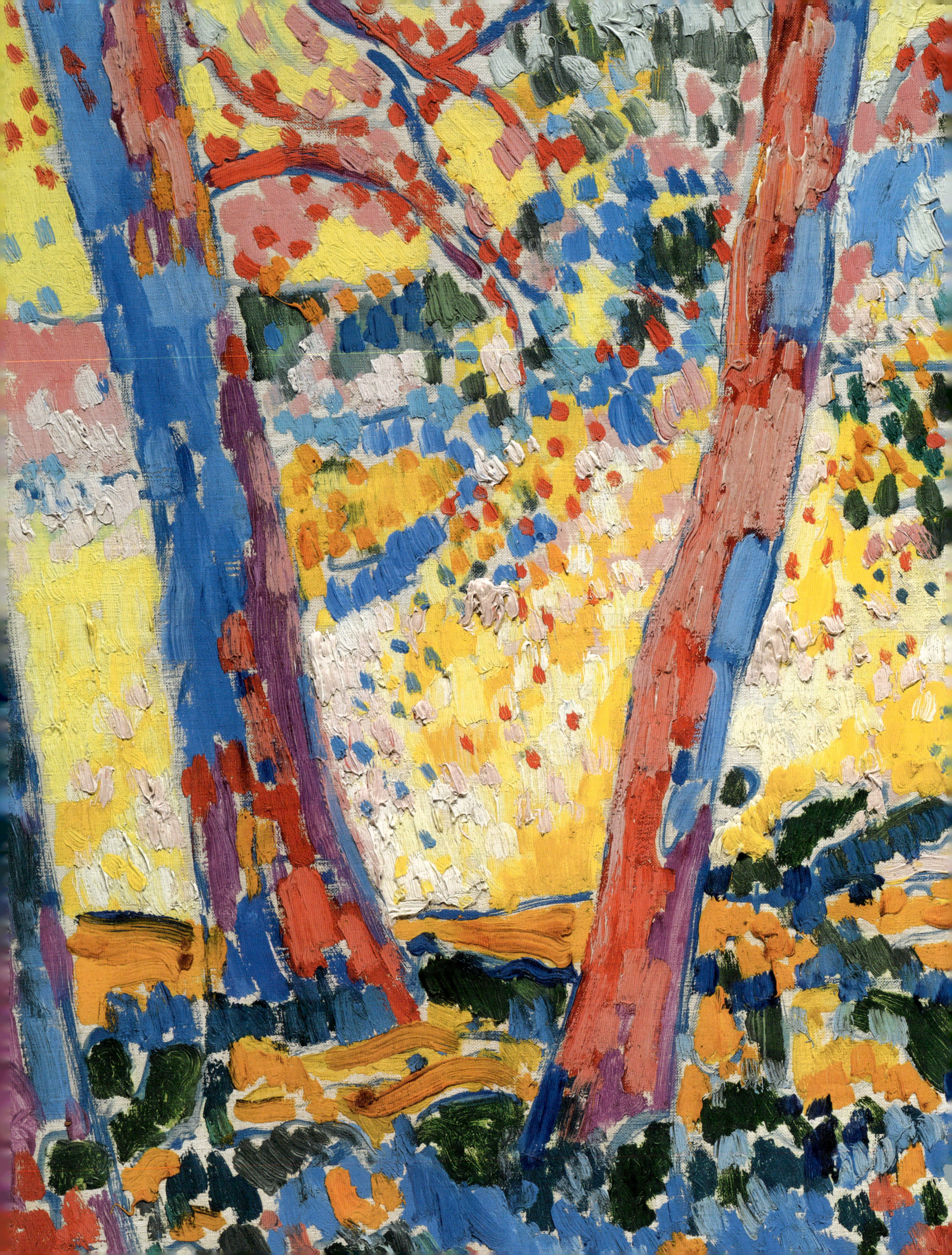

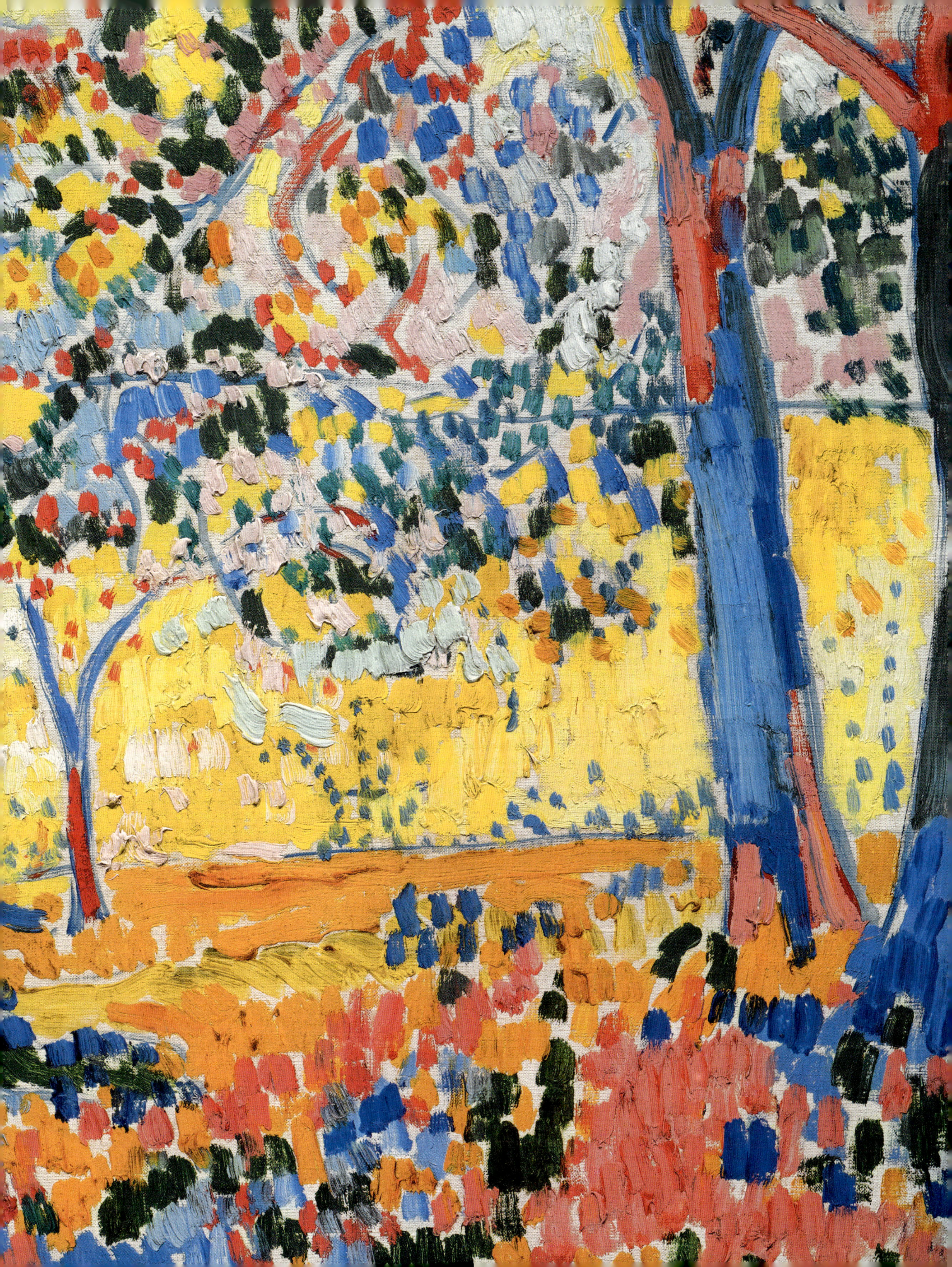

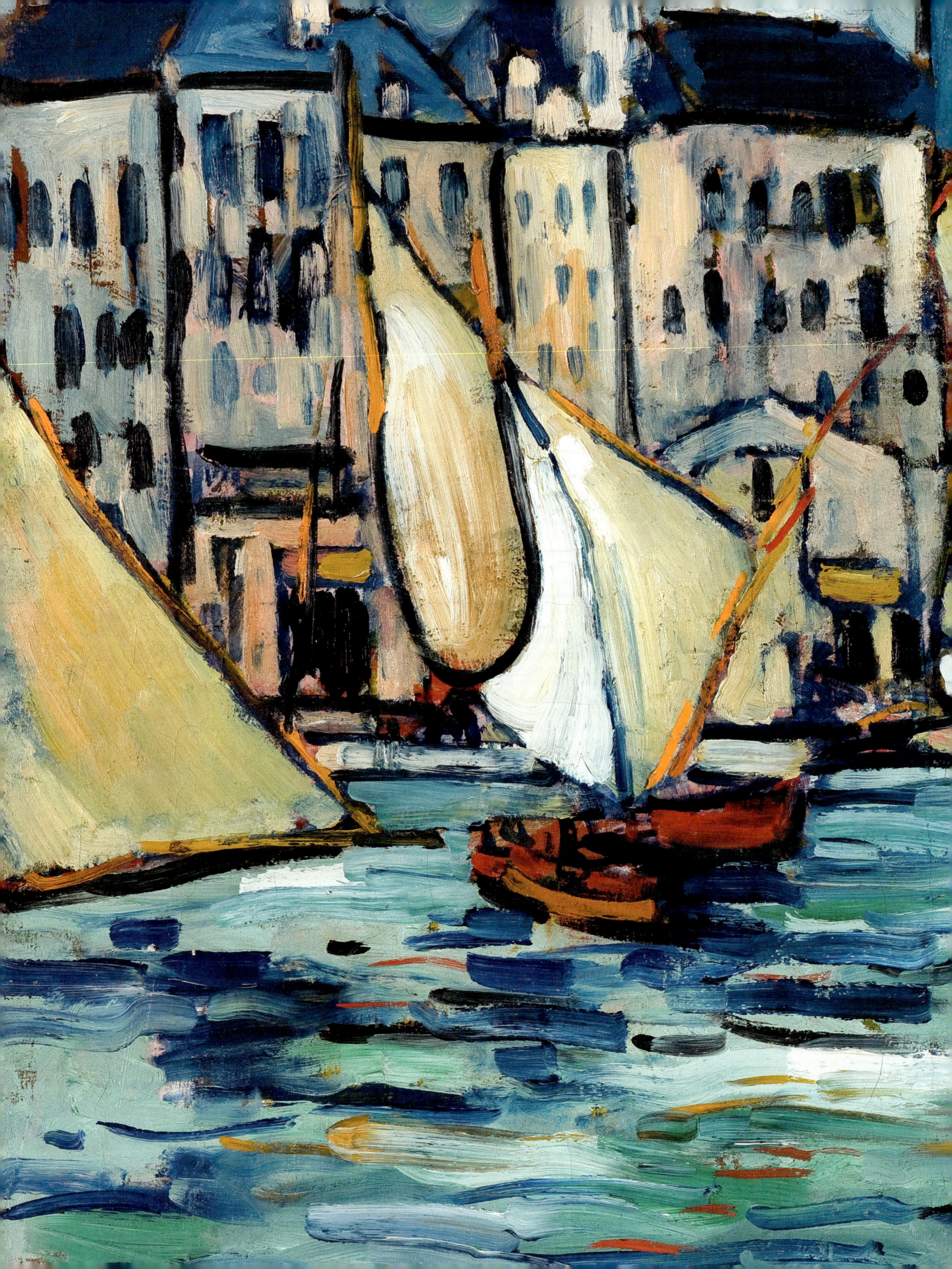

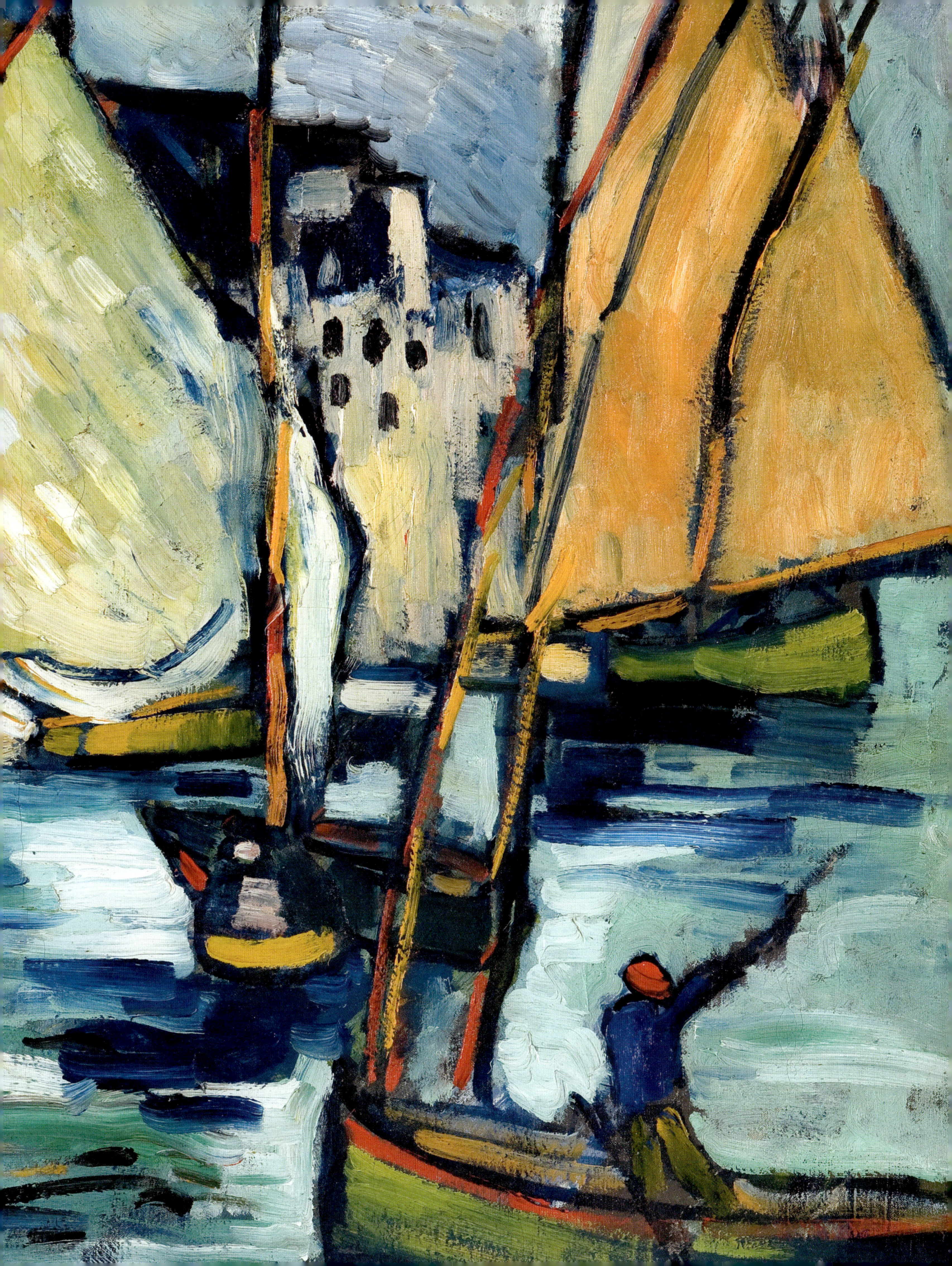

Maurice de

Vlaminck

Modern Art Rebel

Exhibition and catalog
Anna Storm and Daniel Zamani

Edited by
Roland Mönig
Michael Philipp
Anna Storm
Ortrud Westheider

With contributions by
Sterre Barentsen
Jacqueline Hartwig
Matthias Krüger
Valentina Plotnikova
Lisa Smit
Anna Storm
Heinz Widauer
Daniel Zamani

PRESTEL Munich · London · New York

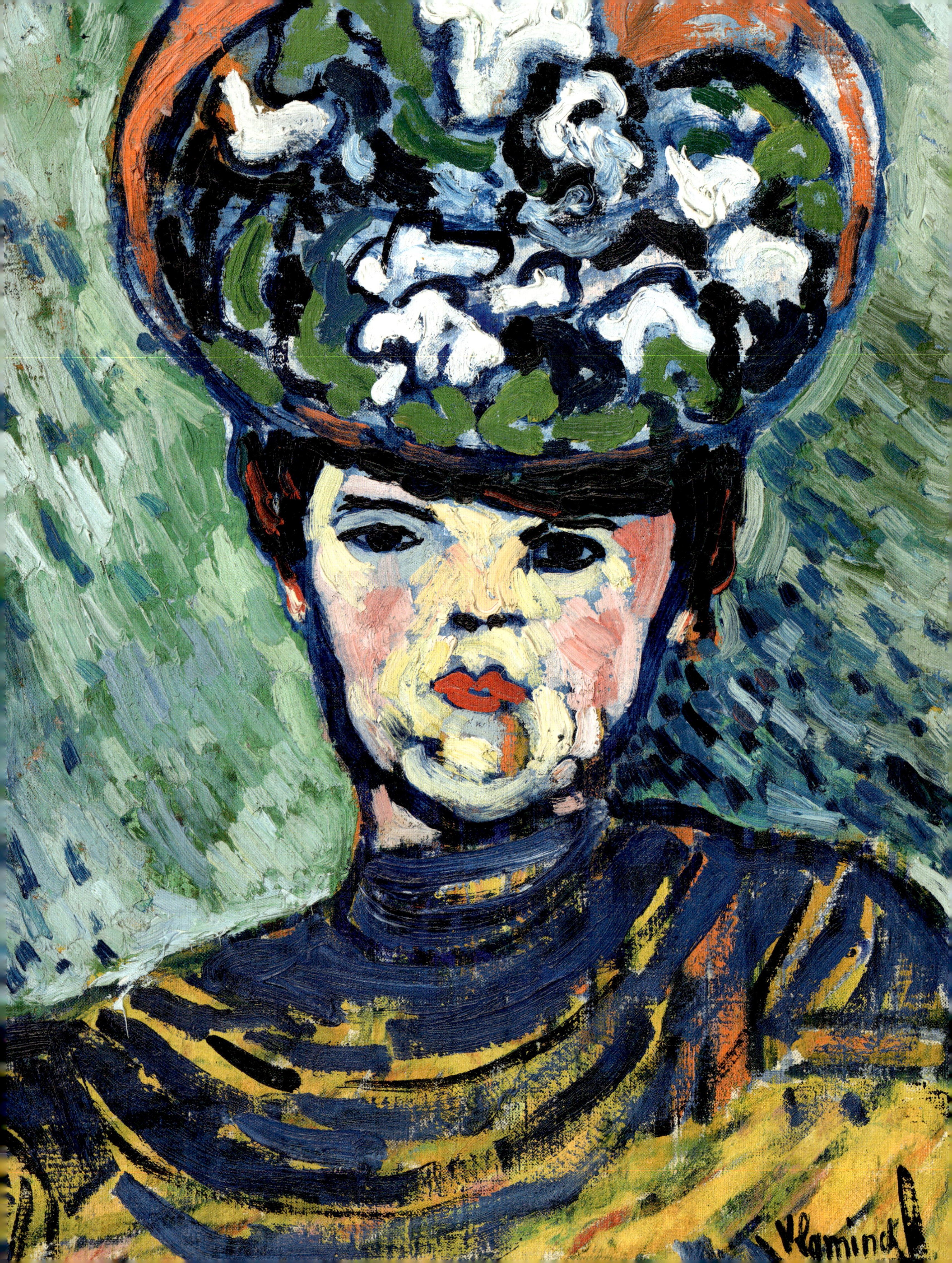

Contents

Essays

Catalog of Exhibited Works

Appendix

Foreword

At the Salon d'Automne in Paris in 1905, a number of young artists burst onto the scene with provocative paintings. Concurrently with the rise of Expressionism in Germany, they focused on the expressive power of color to an unprecedented degree. Critics perceived their vehement colorism as brutish and disparaged the group as "wild beasts" (*fauves*). Along with André Derain, Henri Matisse, and Kees van Dongen, the group of innovators included Maurice de Vlaminck, a passionate racing cyclist who at the time was supporting himself as a musician. He considered himself an autodidact, an outsider, and an artistic rebel. Art dealer Ambroise Vollard, however, who had acquired works by Vincent van Gogh, Paul Cézanne, and Pablo Picasso at a time when they were still controversial, bought most of the holdings in Vlaminck's studio as early as 1905. From then on, the artist was able to concentrate on painting and produced an extensive oeuvre within a few years. His works are now found worldwide in the most important museums and collections of early-twentieth-century modern European art.

Vlaminck had developed an eye for the topography of the Seine Valley through lengthy cycling tours and participation in water sports. He soon began exhibiting his landscapes internationally, showing works that combined the spontaneity of Impressionist plein-air painting with the intense colorism of brilliant, unmixed hues. In 1912 he was represented with six paintings at the pioneering Sonderbund exhibition in Cologne, and the following year his work was included in the Armory Show in New York. Berlin art dealer Herwarth Walden, who, like Vollard, was open to all that was innovative, exhibited Vlaminck's work in 1912, the first year of his gallery Der Sturm.

Vlaminck's rebellious spirit was reinforced by the anarchist authors he had read during his three years of military service around 1900, who confirmed his rejection of militarism and raison d'état. As the father of three daughters, Vlaminck was not sent to the front during World War I but deployed in an arms factory near Paris. This experience led to existential disillusionment and gave rise to a caesura in the artist's work. In 1929 he wrote, "The war taught me a great lesson. All my confidence in civilisation, science, progress, socialism has been destroyed. Even the confidence I had in friends of twenty years' standing. I don't believe in anything any longer. I only have confidence in myself. I don't even believe in the war of 1870, the war of our fathers. I don't believe in history at all, not even the history of art."

As early as 1907–08, Vlaminck had increasingly turned away from the intense color of his Fauvist phase and had instead experimented with the Cubist fragmentation of form. His new,

Cézanne-inspired landscapes and still lifes continued to garner recognition for him in France, and in 1919 a solo exhibition of his work was mounted at the important Galerie Druet in Paris. Ten years later, his international reception expanded to include a first retrospective in Germany at the Düsseldorf gallery of Alfred Flechtheim—the only major exhibition of Vlaminck's work in Germany until now. Thus it is high time to once again offer an extensive presentation of the artist's work, a task that the Museum Barberini and the Von der Heydt-Museum have embraced with the exhibition *Maurice de Vlaminck: Modern Art Rebel.*

With nine paintings by Vlaminck, the Hasso Plattner Collection holds the largest group of the artist's works in Germany. In the context of the Potsdam collection, viewers can experience Vlaminck as a creator who carried the painterly approach and motifs of Impressionism into the twentieth century and reinterpreted them in bold color. It was Daniel Zamani, curator of the collection at the Museum Barberini since 2018, who first proposed the idea of devoting an exhibition to this focus of the collection.

Anna Storm, deputy director of the Von der Heydt-Museum, also participated in the development of the project. For this museum, too, the context and history of the collection are of particular importance, since it was one of the first institutions in Germany to exhibit works by Vlaminck early on. The first piece to enter the collection was *Still Life* (before 1911, cat. 66). It was acquired at the 1911 Salon d'Automne in Paris by August Freiherr von der Heydt, an influential banker, diplomat, and art collector, as a gift for the Städtisches Museum Elberfeld (as it was then called). Von der Heydt had provided extensive support for the founding of the museum in 1902 and, as chair of the museum association from 1906 on, played a decisive role in its development into a singular venue for European avant-garde art. To this day, the Von der Heydt-Museum is known for its impressive collection of Impressionist, Postimpressionist, Cubist, and Expressionist works amassed during those years.

In 1912 the museum acquired another painting by Vlaminck, *River Landscape;* in 1937, however, the work was confiscated by the Nazis as "degenerate" and is now lost. The painting *Riverbank* entered the museum as a gift in 1913 but was destroyed during an Allied air raid in 1943. Today, thanks to gifts from private collections donated to reconstitute the museum's holdings after World War II, the Von der Heydt-Museum once again possesses three works by Vlaminck: the *Still Life* acquired in 1911, the painting *Three Houses* (1910, cat. 58), and *Sailboats* (before 1918, cat. 63). *Sailboats* came from the collection of Eduard von der Heydt, son of August von der Heydt.

We are grateful to Daniel Zamani and Anna Storm for their curatorial work. Together, they have organized the first solo exhibition devoted to Vlaminck in Germany since 1929. Its accent lies on the artist's enormously productive phase prior to World War I, augmented by a selection of later works. We would also like to thank the many national and international lenders who were won over by the arguments of our curators and made their works available to us. Without their support, the project would not have been possible. We are also grateful to our sponsors: the Museum Barberini with its ambitious exhibition program is supported by the Hasso Plattner Foundation, while the presentation of *Maurice de Vlaminck: Modern Art Rebel* in the Von der Heydt-Museum is made possible by the Dr. Werner Jackstädt-Stiftung, the Brennscheidt-Stiftung, the Rudolf-August Oetker-Stiftung, and the Sparkasse Wuppertal.

This exhibition catalog was preceded by a symposium in Potsdam on December 7, 2023. We are grateful to all the authors for their willingness to contribute to our project and provide texts exploring the oeuvre of Maurice de Vlaminck from a contemporary perspective. As the first extensive study of Vlaminck published in Germany, the catalog with its new insights can offer impulses for further research on the artist.

As a young man, Vlaminck had distanced himself from militarism and nationalism. In 1937 his works in German museums fell victim to the Nazi campaign against "Degenerate Art." Our exhibition shows Vlaminck's work from its beginnings to the late landscapes, independently of his political disposition during the German occupation of France. In November 1941, in the middle of World War II, Vlaminck traveled to Germany at the invitation of the German ministry of propaganda, together with fellow painters such as Othon Friesz, Kees van Dongen, and André Derain. He subsequently published two articles openly praising Nazi art and cultural policy, and in another text polemicized against avant-garde art in France as represented by the painting of Picasso. He had his portrait made by Arno Breker, a favorite artist of Adolf Hitler, and participated in a committee for an exhibition of Breker's work in Paris in 1942.

The fact that many of Vlaminck's works were confiscated from German museums by the Nazis in 1937 by no means exonerates him from the charge of propagandistic collaboration. Yet neither does it diminish the significance and standing of his early Fauvist painting, the primary focus of our exhibition. With his powerful, idiosyncratic works, this "modern art rebel" played a decisive role in defining the path of twentieth-century painting.

Ortrud Westheider
Director
Museum Barberini,
Potsdam

Roland Mönig
Director
Von der Heydt-Museum,
Wuppertal

Acknowledgments

We would like to thank the following for their support in making this exhibition possible:

Paloma Alarcó, Sylvain Amic, Augustín Arteaga, Ellen Arthur, Maria Balshaw, Jean-François Bélisle, Konrad Bitterli, Iphigenia Botzaki, Jeffrey N. Brown, Elizabeth Bruwer, Philippe Büttner, Florence Chibret-Plaussu, Françoise Chibret-Plaussu, Sally Choe, Tania Coen-Uzzielli, Marlies Cordia-Roeloffs, Martha Craig, Philippe David, Marcus Dekiert, Ann Demeester, Nadine Engel, Lucy Economakis, Kaywin Feldman, Roland Fox, Sandra Gianfreda, Keith Gill, Frédérique Girondeau, Ralph Gleis, Emilie Gordenker, Peter Gorschlüter, Grégoire Hallé, Caitlin Haskell, Anna Heling, Fabrice Hergott, Inge Herold, Karin Hindsbo, Johan Holten, Kyoko Kagawa, Lock Kesler, Min Jung Kim, Gisela Kirpicsenko, Alexander Klar, Gudrun Klemm, Sofia Komarova, Sophie Krebs, Christiane Lange, Isabella Lauder-Frost, Laurent Le Bon, Christophe Leribault, Dorotea Lorenz, Katherine Crawford Luber, Thomas Morel, Nicole R. Myers, Helly Nahmad, Hugo Nathan, Christian Ogier, Olga Osadtschy, Anne Pasternak, Romy Peires, Paul Perrin, Isolde Pludermacher, Marcelle Polednik, Sandra Poole, Xavier Rey, Sandra Richter, Penelope Riley, James Rondeau, Camille Roux dit Buisson, Barbara Schaefer, Karin Schick, Marie Schorlemmer, Klaus Albrecht Schröder, Simon Shaw, Ishibashi Shojiro, Lisa Small, Lisa Smit, Guillermo Solana, Oliver Tostmann, Giulia Trabaldo Togna, Maïthé Vallès-Bled, Julia Wallner, Emily Whittle, Nancy Whyte, and Ric Wilding.

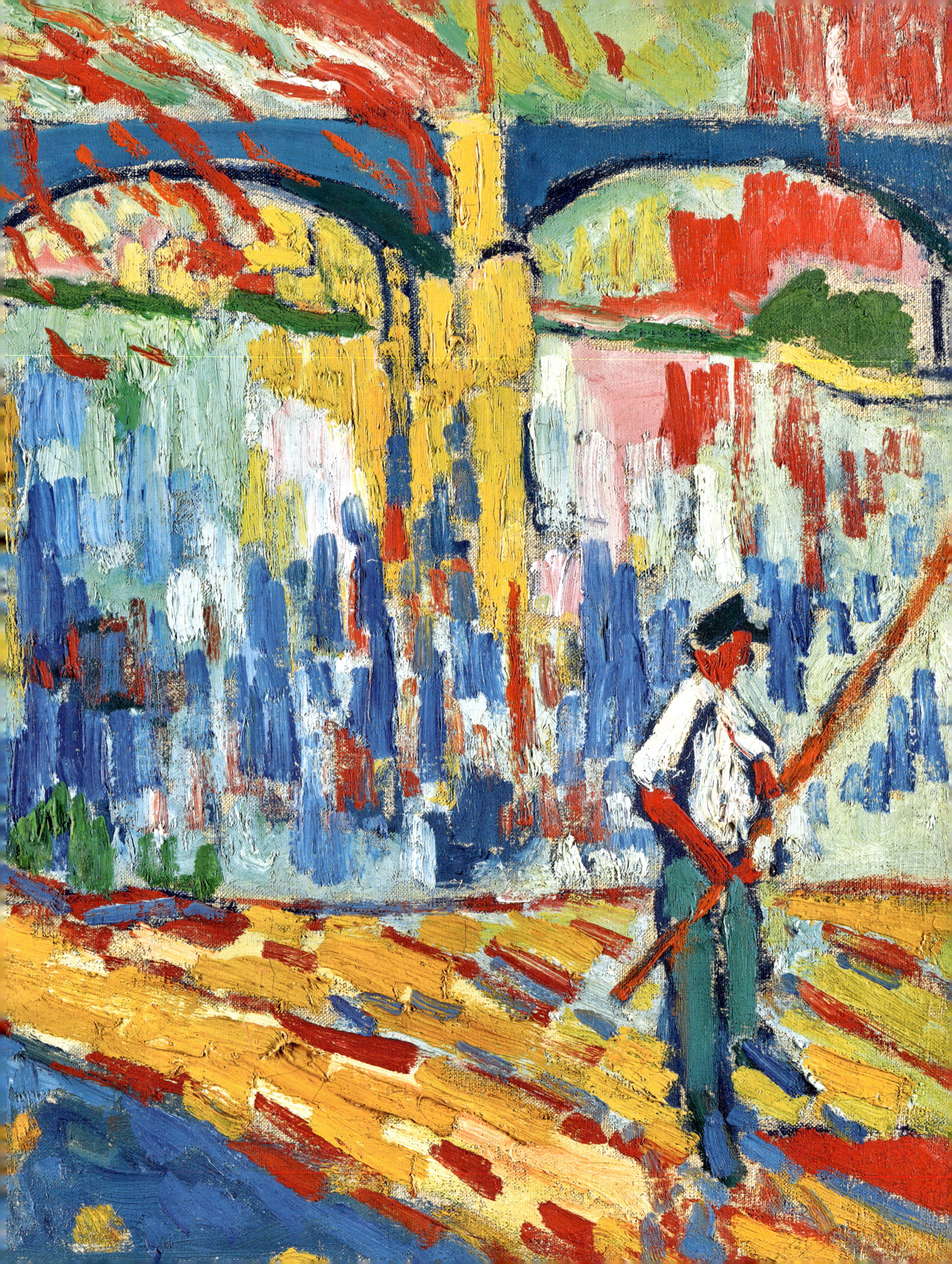

Lenders

Van Gogh Museum, Amsterdam
Musée Calvet, Avignon
Staatliche Museen zu Berlin, Nationalgalerie
Museum of Fine Arts, Boston
Musée des Beaux-Arts de Chartres
Art Institute of Chicago
Museum Ludwig, Cologne
Wallraf-Richartz-Museum & Fondation Corboud, Cologne
Dallas Museum of Art
Hugh Lane Gallery, Dublin
Museum Folkwang, Essen
Hamburger Kunsthalle
Wadsworth Atheneum Museum of Art, Hartford
Tate, London
Kunsthalle Mannheim
Milwaukee Art Museum
Minneapolis Institute of Art
Nahmad Collection
Triton Collection Foundation, the Netherlands
Brooklyn Museum, New York
Metropolitan Museum of Art, New York
Centre Pompidou, Paris, Musée national d'art moderne/Centre de création industrielle
Galerie de la Présidence, Paris
Musée d'Art Moderne de la Ville de Paris
Musée d'Orsay, Paris
Arp Museum Bahnhof Rolandseck, Remagen
Virginia Museum of Fine Arts, Richmond
Saint Louis Art Museum
Musée de l'Annonciade, Saint-Tropez
Staatsgalerie Stuttgart
Tel Aviv Museum of Art
Carmen Thyssen Collection
Artizon Museum, Ishibashi Foundation, Tokyo
Musée d'Art moderne, Troyes
Albertina Museum, Vienna
Fonds de dotation Maison Vlaminck
National Gallery of Art, Washington, DC
Kunst Museum Winterthur
Kunsthaus Zürich

as well as numerous private collectors who wish to remain anonymous

"Destined by Fate"

Vlaminck and Fauvism

Heinz Widauer

A photograph from about 1904 shows twenty-eight-year-old Maurice de Vlaminck with his daughter Solange (fig. p. 186). His powerful stature marks him as a former athlete: he had supported himself and his family with prize money from bicycle racing, and later worked as a violinist in a restaurant and the Théâtre du Château-d'Eau. The son of a violin teacher and a pianist, he had married Suzanne Berly in 1896, with whom he would have three daughters. The look in his eyes seems to convey what his autobiographical writings also suggest: he was quite taken with himself. In the photo he wears the bourgeois men's fashion of the time; his elegant suit with vest, patterned tie, bowler hat, and mustache make it hard to believe that he could also, according to his contemporaries, cut an eccentric figure. On such occasions, he and his painter friend André Derain liked to dress *à l'américaine,* in colorful plaid tweed suits.[1] In place of the red scarf, Vlaminck sometimes wore a necktie he had carved out of wood and painted, which he would bang energetically on the table to underscore his wishes.[2] He could be temperamental, volatile, and impetuous, and was prone to outbursts if people laughed at his painting.[3] Or so he was described by art dealer Ambroise Vollard, who acquired the entire holdings of Vlaminck's studio in 1906 after having previously bought up Derain's works as well; his ongoing annual purchases enabled the artists to make a living.

In 1905 Derain painted a small portrait of Vlaminck as a token of friendship, which would remain in Vlaminck's possession for the rest of his life (fig. 1). With its broad, visible brushstrokes, seemingly dashed onto the canvas, and its unusual color contrasts, the work stood as a rejection of realistic portraiture. Vlaminck's face is shown at close range, giving him a strong sense of presence. Derain combined the pink of the skin with vivid ocher and green in the background, rendered the irises of the eyes in two different colors, and over-painted the originally black mustache with vermilion to achieve an effective contrast with the blue-black bowler hat and blue-green clothing. Vlaminck, too, made a portrait of Derain in 1906 (fig. 2), painting him in a white shirt with a flat cap, smoking a pipe and possibly standing at the easel. His twirled mustache seems to vibrate, while the concentrated expression in his eyes gives his face a sense of directness and vitality. The portrait is painted in pure, unmixed hues; the shaded side of the subject's countenance glows in vermilion red and is bounded by a black contour line.

In Vlaminck's view, the experience of painting together and sharing ideas was the seed of Fauvism. The two artists had joined forces in Chatou, a suburb of Paris where they both lived, painting landscapes along the Seine with no regard for academic rules. Later, critic Louis Vauxcelles saw their work along with that of a group of artists he designated as *fauves,* or "wild beasts."[4] Visitors to the 1905 Salon d'Automne were shocked not only by the aggressive, gestural brushwork, but also by the unprecedented brilliance of color. Among the artists were Henri Matisse and his former classmates from the studio of Gustave Moreau, including Henri Manguin, Albert Marquet, and Charles Camoin. They were inaccurately described as the "school of Moreau," although they did not view themselves as followers of any school or teacher. They saw Matisse as their mentor and, from the 1905 Salon d'Automne on, as the leader of Fauvism.[5] Later, Vlaminck may have implied the contrary in his memoirs, and may even have instrumentalized Vauxcelles to call special attention to his own role in Fauvism.[6] In the 1939 text *Le Fauvisme,* presumably written at Vlaminck's prompting, Vauxcelles not only devoted the first chapter to a treatment of the artist, but portrayed him as the quintessential Fauve: "He [Vlaminck] was a Fauve, destined by fate, a Fauve for all eternity; he was born a Fauve, he remains a Fauve, and as a Fauve . . . he will die."[7] The present essay sheds light on the genesis of Fauvism as well as Vlaminck's role in this loose network of artists.

Wild Beasts

Despite the fact that Vlaminck and his fellow artists were not seeking to invent a new style, let alone new rules, and in reality wanted to sidestep any art-historical canon, Fauvism quickly gained traction as a classificatory term. Following its initial use, the designation *Fauve* was used more and more frequently until it took on a life of its own and, from 1911 on, was integrated into art-historical texts as another "ism" that writers soon sought to distinguish from Cubism.[8] At first, the painters themselves rejected the term and considered it a mere label that had been attached

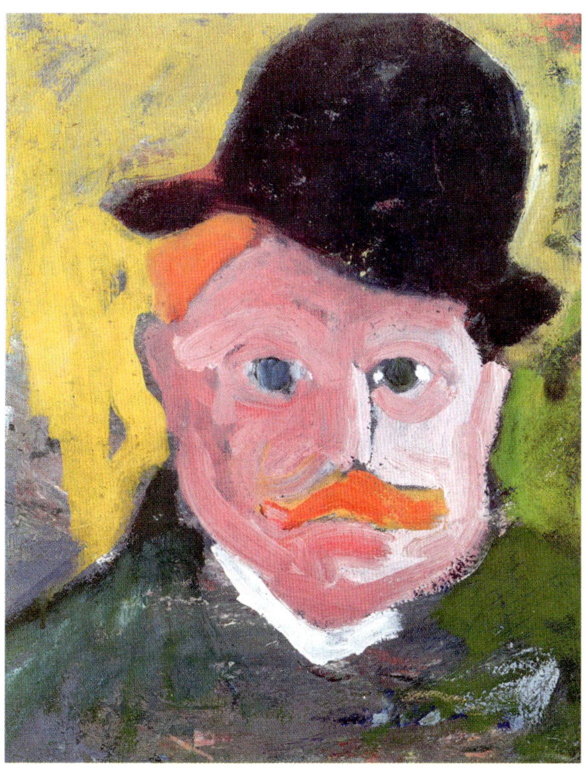

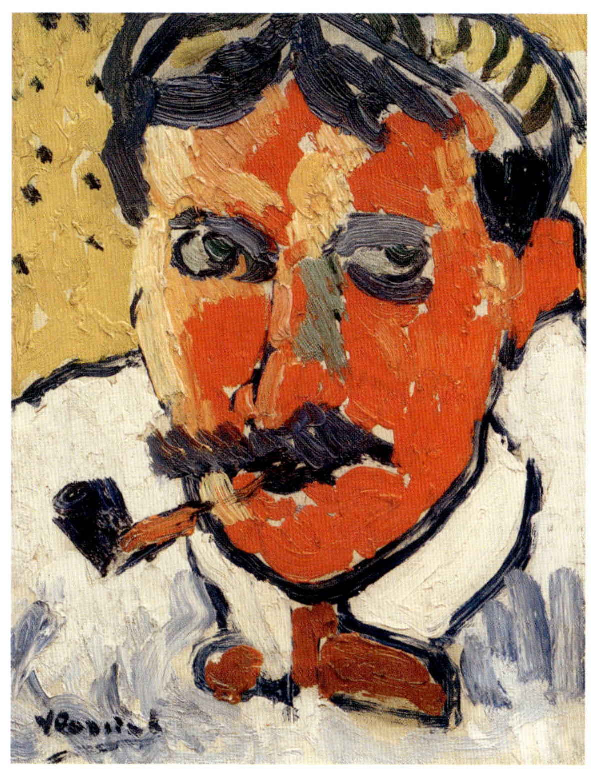

1
André Derain,
Maurice de Vlaminck, 1905,
Musée des Beaux-Arts de Chartres

2
Maurice de Vlaminck,
André Derain, 1906,
Metropolitan Museum of Art, New York

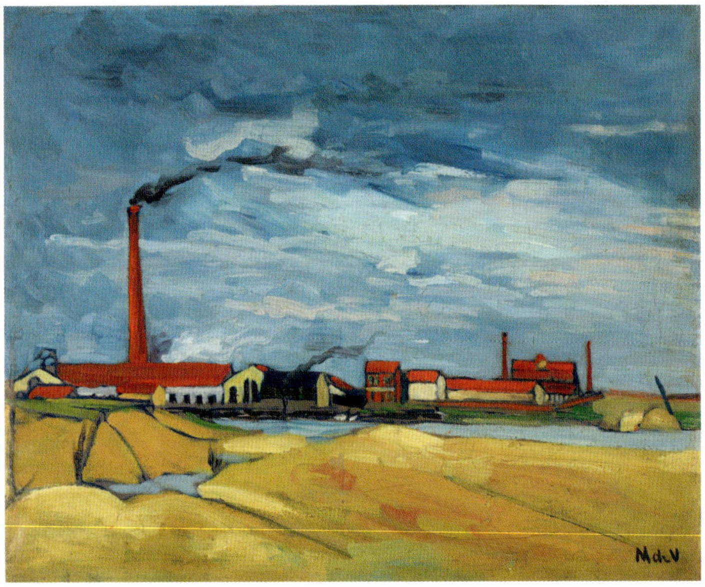

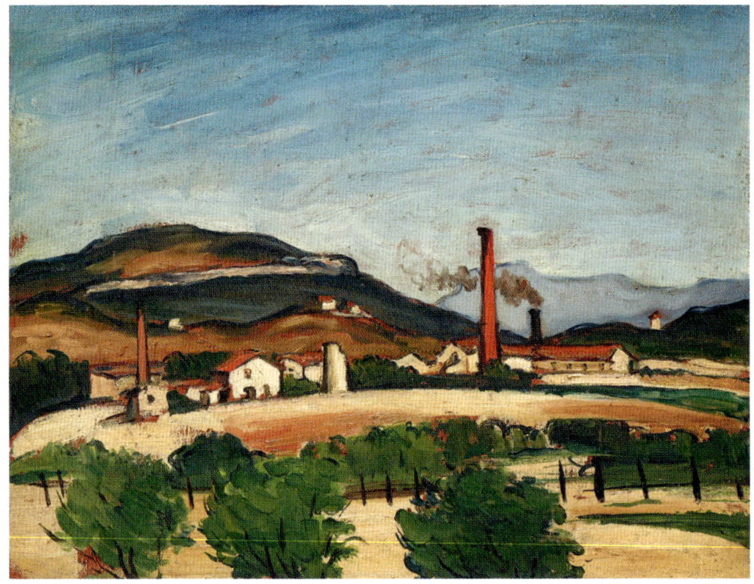

3
Maurice de Vlaminck,
The Factory, 1904,
Kunsthaus Zürich,
Emil Bührle Collection

4
Paul Cézanne,
Factories near Mont de Cengle, 1867–69,
Kunsthaus Zürich,
Emil Bührle Collection

to them.[9] Vlaminck, however, made reference to it and opined that Fauvism had already begun when he and Derain started painting together in Chatou around 1900, and that it was the two of them who had aroused Matisse's enthusiasm for their project in 1904.[10] Vlaminck's narrative, however, did not prevail, and he was deprived of his leading role in Fauvism.[11]

The word *fauve* appeared for the first time in a review published by Louis Vauxcelles in the journal *Gil Blas* on the opening day of the Salon d'Automne. The Salon d'Automne and its spring counterpart, the Salon des Indépendants, were two alternating exhibition venues for artists whose painting did not correspond to the taste of conservative and elite audiences. Being selected for the "academic" Salon de Paris by a jury whose members belonged to the École des Beaux-Arts promised prestige for the artists, but it also opened the door to favoritism and intrigue. Painters who ignored conventional academic rules or were not protégés of jury members were frequently excluded from participation. The Salon des Indépendants, which debuted in 1884, had no jury or medals and was open to all artists, especially the proponents of the trendsetting avant-garde. In 1905 the spring Salon featured 4,269 works by 669 artists. As art critic Charles Morice remarked, it was a "comprehensive homage to Cézanne"; in addition, considerable room was allotted to the Neo-Impressionists, who were still mocked as "confetti specialists."[12] Among the latter, Morice numbered Matisse, who had painted *Luxury, Calm, and Voluptuousness* (fig. p. 36) in 1904 during a visit to Paul Signac in Saint-Tropez. Reactions to the work were mixed: Morice called it a "confetti sketch,"[13] while Vauxcelles, who was otherwise well-disposed toward Matisse, claimed that it was contrary to the painter's temperament.[14] Signac, on the other hand, was enthusiastic and acquired the painting for himself. At that time, the critics of the Indépendants made hardly any mention of Vlaminck. It was the first time he and Derain had participated in a Salon; Matisse had urged them to do so in the winter of 1904–05 when he visited them in Chatou and noticed how stylistically similar their painterly experiments were to his own.[15] As noted earlier, Vlaminck would claim in retrospect that he and Derain had brought Matisse to Fauvism, and that the latter's visit to Chatou had made him ten years younger.[16]

Matisse and Vlaminck, however, were of different minds as to how the convictions they shared could best be promulgated. Matisse had studied the Old Masters in the Louvre and wanted to preserve the continuity of tradition.[17] Vlaminck, on the other hand, claimed to have never set foot in a museum. As he himself once declared, he wanted to "burn down the École des Beaux-Arts" with his vermilion[18] and follow only his own instinct in his painting.[19] In 1900 Vlaminck and Derain happened to be passengers on the same train when it was halted due to a railway accident. As they made their way home on foot, they conversed about their mutual passion for painting. Derain had received some training at the private painting school Académie Camillo, where he had met Matisse in 1898–99. Vlaminck had acquired rudimentary painting skills through his acquaintance with a well-known local painter, but it was not until after his military service and the meeting with Derain that he began to pursue art seriously. Both painters focused intensively on landscape, seeking out motifs in the environs of Chatou. In 1901 they attended the first Van Gogh retrospective at Galerie Bernheim-Jeune, where Vlaminck discovered Van Gogh's painting and made the acquaintance of Matisse.[20]

At the Salon des Indépendants in 1905, Vlaminck showed eight pictures, including a portrait and six landscapes from the period between 1902 and 1904.[21] Paul Cézanne, the Nabis, and even the already deceased Georges Seurat provided the vocabulary, which Vlaminck then translated into his own idiom with gestural brushwork and brilliant colors. His expressive application of paint is manifested in one his earliest works, *Portrait of Père Bouju* (cat. 1),[22] where the impetuous strokes point in the direction of French Expressionism.[23] His painterly approach appears with similar vehemence in *Woman in the Country* (fig. p. 187), where he allowed free rein to his irregular, visible brushstrokes and powerfully heightened the contrasts of subdued colors.[24] In his two landscape images of the paper mill at Nanterre, he prioritized the brilliance of the colors and employed loose brushstrokes, as if dashed onto the canvas: while working on *The Factory* (fig. 3), he stood at the edge of a sandpit from which he could view the factory grounds on the other shore. The picture shows striking affinities to Paul Cézanne's *Factories near Mont de Cengle* (fig. 4) and, with its harmony of flat areas of pure color, also recalls the painting of the Nabis associated with Édouard Vuillard and Paul Bonnard. The yellow of the sandpit almost directly meets the blue sky, which is enlivened with clouds; the Seine appears only as a delicate blue band beneath the row of buildings. In the smaller version entitled *The Banks of the Seine, Nanterre* (fig. 5), on the other hand, the

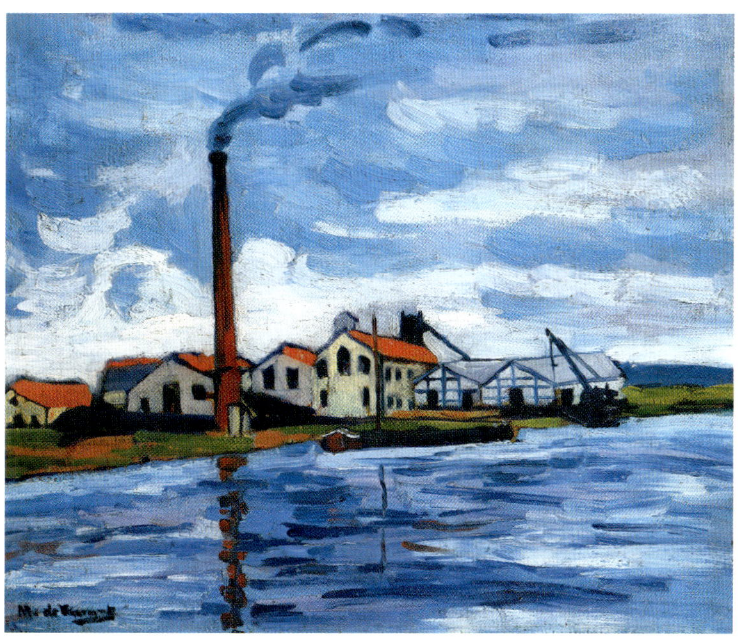

5
Maurice de Vlaminck,
The Banks of the Seine, Nanterre, 1904,
private collection

6
Maurice de Vlaminck,
Park in Carrières-Saint-Denis, 1904
(cat. 8)

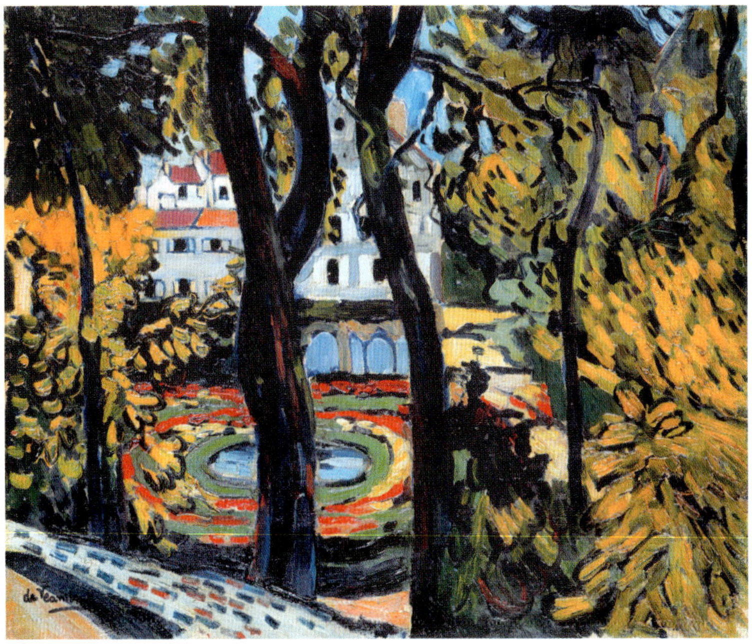

foreground is dominated by the river. Here, Vlaminck shows the scene from a nearer vantage point, apparently positioning himself directly on the banks of the Seine. In this way, he could more closely approach the row of buildings in the background; the composition recalls similar motifs in paintings and Conté crayon drawings by Georges Seurat. Vlaminck also incorporated Impressionist effects such as the smokestack reflected in the water.

It is surprising that Vlaminck showed two landscapes with such similar motifs, differing only in size, at one and the same Salon. Was he trying to appeal to the varying tastes and hanging options of different buyers, or was he exploring the different stylistic possibilities made available by the avant-garde? In any case, Vlaminck's contributions were scarcely noticed by the critics, nor does the public seem to have shown any appreciation for his painting. Although he managed to sell *The Banks of the Seine, Nanterre,* his joy at this success gave way to bitter disappointment when he discovered that the buyer had purchased what he considered to be the ugliest, most deranged picture at the Salon to present as a gift to his detested son-in-law.[25]

Breakthrough to the Avant-Garde

Despite his lack of success at the Salon des Indépendants, Vlaminck decided to participate in the Salon d'Automne several months later. In 1905 the Salon d'Automne, which had been founded in 1903 and took place annually, was strategically planned in advance. The intent was to present as many types of art as possible.[26] The plein-air painters were able to show the most recent works they had created only that summer. The most contemporary art was placed at the center of the Grand Palais: Vlaminck showed exclusively landscapes, while Derain's works included a port view; Manguin and Jean Puy each exhibited an Arcadian-seeming landscape with reclining female figures. Matisse's paintings showed the widest variety of motifs and bore witness to his gradual turn away from Pointillism. In the summer, he had gone to Collioure near the Spanish border to paint there independently of Signac; Derain had joined him, while Vlaminck had remained in the north for financial reasons.

Matisse now envisaged a freer brushstroke for his smaller works, while continuing to embrace the Pointillist method for larger canvases. In addition to paintings with loose daubs and free linear drawing, he also wanted to submit a large work in the Pointillist technique entitled *The Port of Avall* to the Salon d'Automne, but was unable to finish it in time. In great haste, he painted *Woman with a Hat* (fig. p. 31) after his return from Collioure and exhibited it along with other works. This portrait of a woman elicited the most heated criticism: in the academic hierarchy of genres, portraiture was near the top. This seeming image of a demimondaine—in reality, it was Matisse's wife, Amélie—was considered outrageous, its sketch-like brushwork and garish hues a coarse violation of all academic and Divisionist rules.

At the Salon d'Automne, Vlaminck exhibited five pictures that formed a counterpoint to the works painted by Matisse and Derain in the South of France, with colors informed by the cooler light of the north (see fig. 6). The reviews garnered him ridicule and incomprehension: he was accused of having painted *My Father's House* (fig. 7) by throwing small balls of color at the canvas.[27] The strokes of vermilion in the field in *The Valley at Port-Marly* (fig. 8) may have been similarly baffling to the critics. There, however, Vlaminck was probably following Matisse's advice that one color implied another and needed to be intensified by it in order to preserve the unity of the picture.[28] Appropriately for the Autumn Salon, Vlaminck rendered the wind-tossed treetop in loose, dynamic lines. The small red strokes on the ocher-yellow field sloping downward in the foreground create a harmonious transition from the warm colors of summer to the cooler hues of the background and the town in the valley.

The brilliantly colored paintings, hung in Room VII in the middle of the Grand Palais, were accompanied by two Neo-Renaissance busts by sculptor Albert Marque, displayed in the center of the room. It was this presentation that prompted Vauxcelles to coin the legendary term that gave the Fauvist style its name: in his review in *Gil Blas* on October 15, 1905, the critic wrote, "The candor of these busts is surprising, amid the orgy of pure tones: Donatello among the wild beasts [*fauves*]."[29] Unlike Impressionism, Pointillism, or Cubism, the word *fauve* was not a stylistic descriptor; here, Vauxcelles adopted a metaphor commonly used in nineteenth-century art and literature to symbolize the relationship between humans and animals, in both a literal and a figurative sense.[30] Vauxcelles's metaphor may also have been prompted by the

7
Maurice de Vlaminck,
My Father's House,
1904–05,
Pola Museum of Art,
Hakone

8
Maurice de Vlaminck,
The Valley at Port-Marly,
1904–05,
private collection

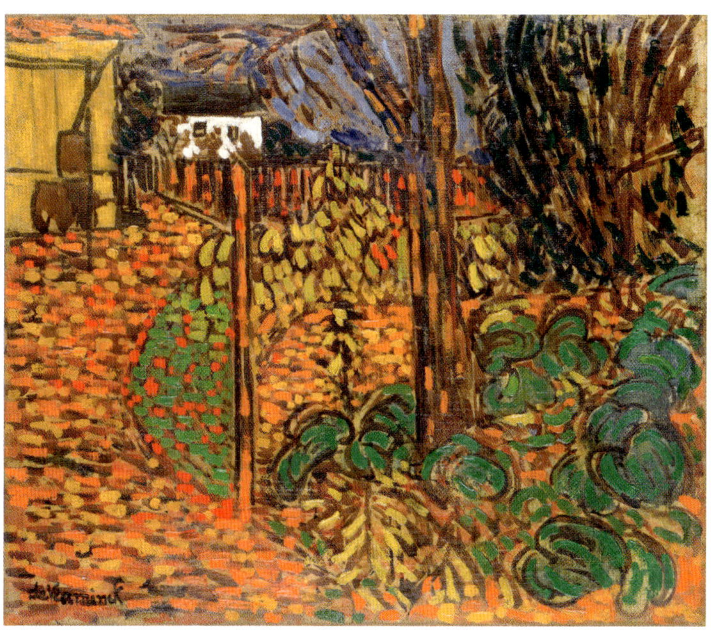

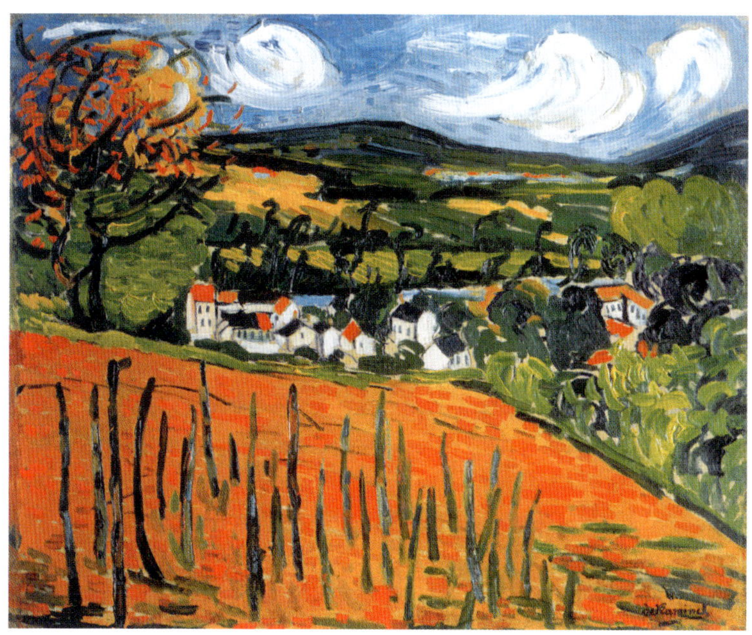

painting *The Hungry Lion Throws Itself on the Antelope* by Henri Rousseau (fig. 9), which was exhibited in the next room.

At the Salon d'Automne, Rousseau's work hung near Aristide Maillol's plaster model for *La Méditerranée,* which was executed as a limestone sculpture for Harry Graf Kessler in 1905–07 (Oskar Reinhart Collection "Am Römerholz," Winterthur). This and other juxtapositions were intended to bring to mind the motto promulgated by the organizers of the Salon: "The revolutionary of today is the classic of tomorrow." Maillol's sculpture was celebrated as the birth of a "new classicism," and the Fauves received the classicism of the Renaissance into their midst.[31] Two retrospectives, however, one devoted to classicist Jean-Auguste-Dominique Ingres and the other to revolutionary Édouard Manet, were the highlight of the Salon. The choice of the latter made sense: Manet had been the first of the avant-garde to reject the conventions of painting and provoke the Salon des Refusés in 1863. The focus on Ingres, however—whom critics dismissed as an "academician" and considered reactionary—came as a surprise.[32] The assessment of the allegedly bloodless classicist, however, changed with the debut exhibition of his painting *The Turkish Bath* (1862, Musée du Louvre, Paris), over forty years after its completion. Matisse marveled at the enigmatic spatial structure and the arabesques concealed behind the motif, which inspired him to paint *The Joy of Life* in 1905–06 (fig. p. 188); gestures and motifs from Ingres's painting likewise informed Pablo Picasso's *Les Demoiselles d'Avignon* (1907, Museum of Modern Art, New York). Vlaminck, on the other hand, resisted the novel fascination with Ingres; although he acknowledged his greatness, for him Ingres's line was marked by austerity and repressed sensuality.[33] Vlaminck was even more forthright in his rejection of Picasso, whom he accused of imitating Ingres.[34] Moreover, he also distanced himself from the emerging Cubism, which he viewed as an inhuman and mechanical formula.[35]

Vlaminck had a greater affinity to Manet. Vlaminck's *Reclining Nude* (fig. p. 34) was informed by impressions of Manet's *Olympia* (fig. p. 35), a work that had been completed in 1863 and rejected by the Paris Salon in 1865, combined with echoes of the *Naked Maja* by Francisco de Goya (1795–1800, Museo del Prado, Madrid). Vlaminck's brushwork is coarse and harsh; the face, marked by the burdens of life, is that of a garishly made-up prostitute from the nightclub Le Rat mort in Montmartre. There Vlaminck found his models for paintings such as *Nude with Black Stockings* (fig. p. 70) or *Reclining Nude* (cat. 20), where the faces, rife with suffering and distress, fix the viewer's gaze. As Vlaminck acknowledged, his concern was less to capture a likeness than to evoke "the black of the eyes, the red of the lips, in short, the whores"[36]—in order, like Henri de Toulouse-Lautrec, to express "with the portrait of a fallen woman the suffering of all humanity, the suffering of women, the suffering of Mary Magdalene. And his own!"[37]

Anarchical and Anarchistic

As vehemently as the progressive art critics rejected Ingres, so staunchly did their conservative counterparts denigrate Manet and the Fauves, referring to them as "anarchical," "hallucinating color workers" who practiced "splotch painting" and had "succumbed to ecstasy," expressing themselves in "gibberish." The critics spoke of an "anarchistic" "Salon of the Deluded" and called Manet its role model.[38] Although Vlaminck was not mentioned by name, the accusation was likewise directed at his style of painting and his participation in the Salon d'Automne.

Vlaminck had already grappled with social and political anarchism during his military service, and after his discharge wrote a number of articles in the magazine *Le Libertaire,* among other things criticizing the state- and church-supported exploitation of the dispossessed and the violence against striking workers.[39] In his writing, he openly professed anarchism; in his painting, on the other hand, he seems to have focused primarily on artistic interests and have been less concerned with anarchistic themes, even if the resemblance of paintings such as *Houses at Chatou* (cat. 31) or *Wheat Field and Houses with Red Roofs, Nanterre* (1906, private collection) to the 1887 Montmartre pictures of professed anarchist Maximilien Luce might suggest a similar social-utopian message.[40]

In the works of both artists, fields or vegetable gardens appear in front of a row of suburban houses. In the case of Luce, such images have been associated with the exemplary role of the vegetable gardeners to the north of Paris for the local supply of the metropolis, as described by writers such as French anarchist Élisée Reclus in the magazine *Nouvelle géographie universelle* in 1879.[41] For Vlaminck, painting seems to have served as a coping strategy, giving him the leeway to defy rigid rules and flout conventional norms. Here, color provided him with a release valve.[42] In typical self-stylization as a modern artist rebel, he declared to his friend Lieutenant Fernand Sernada, "What I could have done in life only as an anarchist, to throw a bomb—which would have sent me to the scaffold—I sought to realize in painting through the exclusive use of pure colors. In this way I yielded to my impulse to destroy old conventions, to disobey them, in order to once again create a sensual, vital, and liberated world."[43]

Translated from German by Melissa M. Thorson

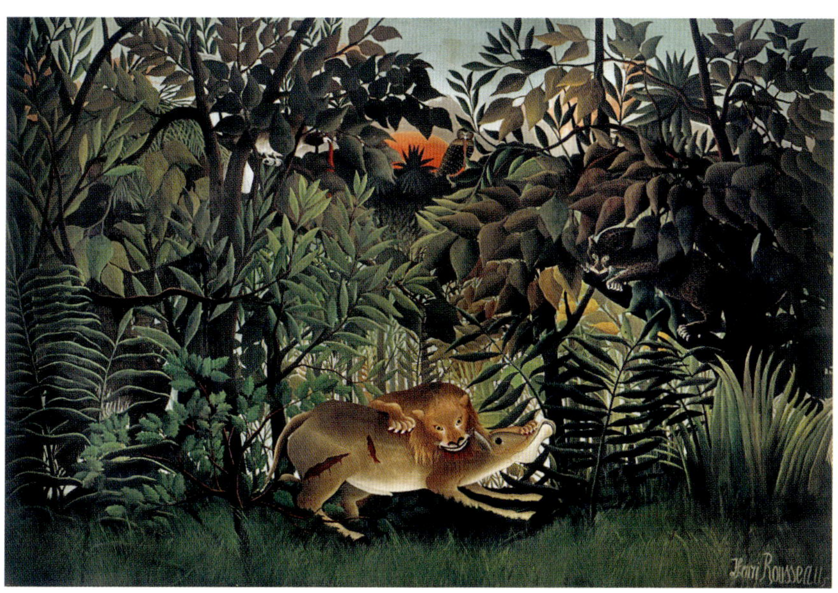

9
Henri Rousseau,
The Hungry Lion Throws Itself on the Antelope,
1898–1905,
Fondation Beyeler,
Riehen/Basel

Anarchy of Color

Vlaminck's Fauvist Painting

Daniel Zamani

While many of the Fauves rejected the attribute of wildness, Maurice de Vlaminck emphatically propagated the self-image of a social and artistic rebel. In his autobiographical work *Tournant dangereux* of 1929, which was later published in English as *Dangerous Corner,* he portrayed himself as a revolutionary individualist, emphasizing not only his youthful fascination with anarchistic ideas, but also his anti-intellectual attitude.[1] Vlaminck's claim to the reputation of a radical innovator is based primarily on his contribution to the development of Fauvist painting between 1904 and 1908—especially the brilliantly colored landscapes of the years 1905 to 1907, which distinguished him as a stylistic precursor of Expressionism. In his writings, Vlaminck never tired of reminding readers of his role as an outsider in the Paris art world. A proud autodidact, he downplayed both the influence of artistic models and the impulses and inspiration he had been able to glean from interactions with fellow artists. An exception was Vincent van Gogh, whose painting Vlaminck had discovered in 1901 at a solo exhibition at Galerie Bernheim-Jeune in Paris and whose growing renown as a misunderstood artistic genius clearly impressed him.[2] With regard to the influence of the Impressionists and Neo-Impressionists, however, whose visual language still served as an important reference point for many young artists around 1900, Vlaminck remained silent. The present essay examines Vlaminck's role as a pioneer and innovator in light of the significance of color as an expressive means for the Fauves. It also situates his painting within the broader context of the French avant-garde of his day and the many borrowings and reference points that fueled his Fauvist career.

Fortune's Chance

Before his participation in the Salon d'Automne of 1905, Vlaminck had exhibited paintings only twice before: at the up-and-coming Paris gallery of Berthe Weill in 1904, and at the Salon des Indépendants in 1905. In view of this fact, it is hardly surprising that the five landscapes he showed at the Salon d'Automne alongside paintings by Henri Matisse, André Derain, Kees van Dongen, and other artists who would soon become known as *fauves* attracted relatively little attention.[3] Reviews of the exhibition as a whole, however, which encompassed 1,625 works by 397 artists, focused disproportionately on the young painters in the seventh room—and mostly in a negative light.[4] By no means had the artists been thinking of themselves as a group or association, nor had they strategically planned or influenced the display of their work. It was only the organizing committee that had decided to show their paintings together in the same room, resulting in a concentrated presentation that invited visitors and critics to discover stylistic affinities. The common denominators were a decidedly antiacademic approach to composition and the seemingly unrestrained use of brilliant, pure color—even by Neo-Impressionist standards, still the dominant avant-garde movement at the time.

Influential critic Louis Vauxcelles identified Matisse as the ringleader of a new direction in French painting, one whose pictures seemed to him like orgies of color. In a review published in the journal *Gil Blas,* he described the aforementioned room in the exhibition as a "cage aux fauves" (cage of wild beasts) and joked about the incongruous impression of a classically modeled sculpture by Albert Marque amid the vividly colored paintings: "Donatello among the wild beasts."[5] In his article Vauxcelles, who was quite well-disposed toward Matisse, laid the cornerstone for the ambivalence that would continue to characterize reception of the Fauvist movement. While the attribute of wildness could be used pejoratively to dismiss their art as coarse and even barbaric, lacking in technical skill, it could also be understood in a positive sense as courageous innovation, a striving to replace sterile academic convention with a new emphasis on the emotional and instinctive. This reappraisal of the individual and the expressive was fomented by the pluralism of modern art currents in early-twentieth-century Paris, movements that simultaneously vied with each other for legitimacy—not only Impressionism and Neo-Impressionism, but also the Nabis, Symbolists, and isolated Postimpressionists such as Paul Cézanne and Vincent van Gogh, whose oeuvres slowly but surely gained entrance into an increasingly codified nineteenth-century canon.

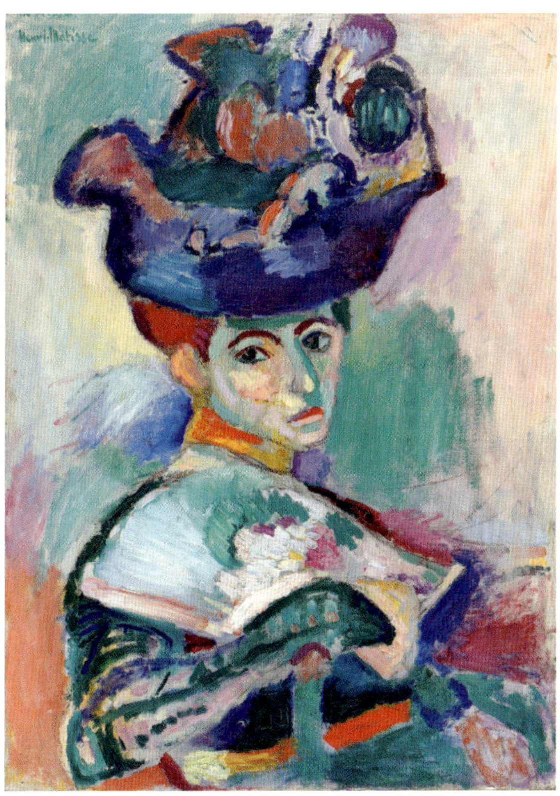

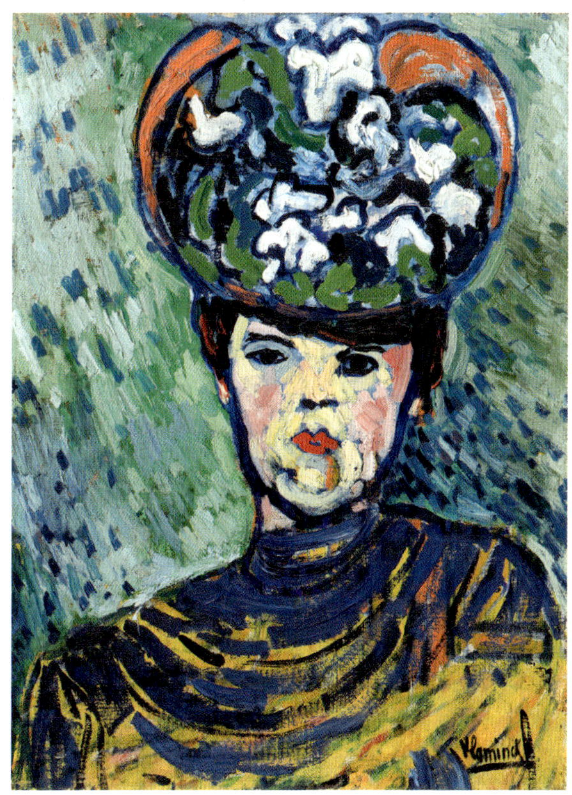

1
Henri Matisse,
Woman with a Hat, 1905,
San Francisco Museum
of Modern Art

2
Maurice de Vlaminck,
Woman with a Hat,
1905 (cat. 19)

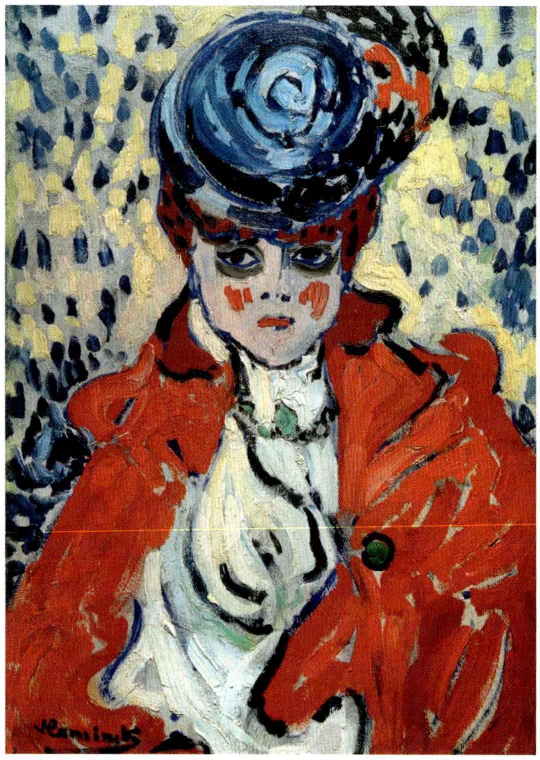

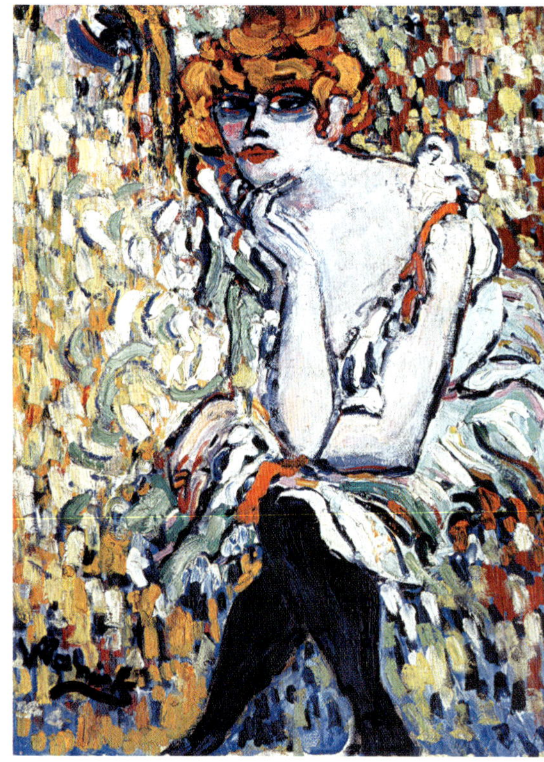

3
Maurice de Vlaminck, *Portrait of a Woman from the Rat mort,* 1905, private collection

4
Maurice de Vlaminck, *The Dancer from the Rat mort,* 1905, private collection

For Vlaminck, whose tenuous connection to the Paris avant-garde had resulted from his friendship with Derain and a rather fleeting acquaintance with Matisse, the association of his paintings with a movement perceived from the outside as a collective was a stroke of good luck. While artists such as Matisse had been classically trained as pupils of Gustave Moreau at the École des Beaux-Arts, Vlaminck had come to painting as an autodidact. Until the formation of Fauvism as a loose association of artists, he had earned his living as a bicycle racer, boxer, and violinist. Even after he temporarily moved into a studio with Derain in Chatou in 1900, he initially remained ambivalent toward painting as a profession: "I painted to restore my peace of mind, to calm my desires and, above all, to purify myself a little," he wrote in retrospect in *Dangerous Corner.* "I had no preconceived ideas. Make a career of painting! How I would have laughed if someone had talked to me about that! To be a painter is not a profession, no more than being an anarchist or a lover, a race-track rider, a dreamer or a boxer. It is just fortune's chance, just luck."[6]

The impressive journalistic echo elicited by the Fauvist works at the Salon d'Automne established a place for the young painters in the hotly contested Parisian art world, where they soon enjoyed the support of influential promoters such as art dealer Ambroise Vollard.[7] The perception of the art of Vlaminck and his colleagues as a radical break with the legacy of the nineteenth century—and thus also as avant-garde innovation—was based on more than just their unprecedented predilection for garish colors. Even more important was their often-arbitrary choice of hues, which were no longer intended to illustrate and imitate the motifs, but to transform them into a vehicle of subjective emotion—an anticipation of key premises of Expressionist painting. The popular association of their vibrant compositions with wildness and excess was anchored in an academic tradition that was beholden to doctrines handed down since the Renaissance and favored compositions with clear contours and harmoniously balanced tones. While form in the sense of *disegno* ("drawing" in Italian, as well as "pictorial invention" or "design") was primarily associated with the sublime world of the mind and the ideal, color *(colore)* was considered an expression of the corporeal and emotional.[8]

Moreover, many of the Fauves articulated the aims of their painting in language that suggested a deliberate attack on art-historical tradition. Derain, for example, described Fauvist color as “cartridges of dynamite,” intended to sensually embody the visual experience of pure light.[9] In retrospect, Vlaminck, who had become a fervent anarchist during his years of military service from 1897 to 1900, attributed his own penchant for boisterous color to a purely subjective and thus also antiacademic and anti-intellectual understanding of art. In one of the few passages of *Dangerous Corner* in which he discussed Fauvist painting at length, he wrote with unmistakable pathos, “My enthusiasm allowed me to take all sorts of liberties. I did not want to follow a conventional way of painting: I wanted to revolutionise habits and contemporary life, to liberate nature, to free it from the authority of old theories and classicism, which I hated as much as I had hated the general or the colonel of my regiment. . . . I heightened all my tonal values and transposed into an orchestration of pure colour every single thing I felt. I was a tender barbarian, filled with violence. I translated what I saw instinctively, without any method and conveyed it truly, not so much artistically as humanely.”[10] Vlaminck’s choice of terms such as *enthusiasm* and *tender* was intended to situate Fauvist color in the realm of the emotional and the instinctive—stylishly dramatized as the heroic rejection of academic rules.

Grotesque Exaggeration

Among the works exhibited at the Salon d’Automne that were most shocking in their brash approach to color was Matisse’s *Woman with a Hat* of 1905 (fig. 1), a portrait of the artist’s wife, Amélie, in flat pastel hues, which soon afterward was acquired by American collector Leo Stein. Presumably it was the media attention generated by Matisse’s picture that prompted Vlaminck to create his own version of the motif (fig. 2)—though he himself would certainly have denied any direct influence on the part of his Fauve colleagues, particularly Matisse. For his portrait of Amélie, Matisse chose a three-quarter profile view and introduced a dynamic element into the composition through the slight turn of her head. Vlaminck, on the other hand, presented his subject frontally, effectively dramatizing the flatness of the picture plane. Although the contours of the body stand out from the background in strokes of dark blue and black, the figure lacks volume; spatial depth is suggested only by the oval of the slightly forward-tilting hat. Vlaminck rendered the woman’s face in broad, coarse strokes of pink and cream, her cherry-red lips setting a pronounced accent in the center of the picture. The background is enlivened by energetic brushstrokes in white, green, and blue, whose diagonals contrast with the undulating horizontal strokes of the woman’s clothing. Even compared to other works by the Fauves, the seemingly unfinished, sketch-like quality of the painting seems jarring—the open structure of the visible, tactile brushstrokes flagrantly resists the academic ideal of the smooth, finished surface, known as *fini*.

While the social position of the subject in Vlaminck’s *Woman with a Hat* remains unclear, he produced a number of other figural paintings around the same time that unmistakably show women from the Paris demimonde. Many of them depict actresses from the infamous cabaret Le Rat mort, who often also earned their living as prostitutes. The theme of big-city sex work had already been explored in the late nineteenth century by artists such as Edgar Degas and Édouard Manet and was particularly associated with the work of Henri de Toulouse-Lautrec,

5
Maurice de Vlaminck,
Reclining Nude, 1905,
Museum of Fine Arts,
Houston

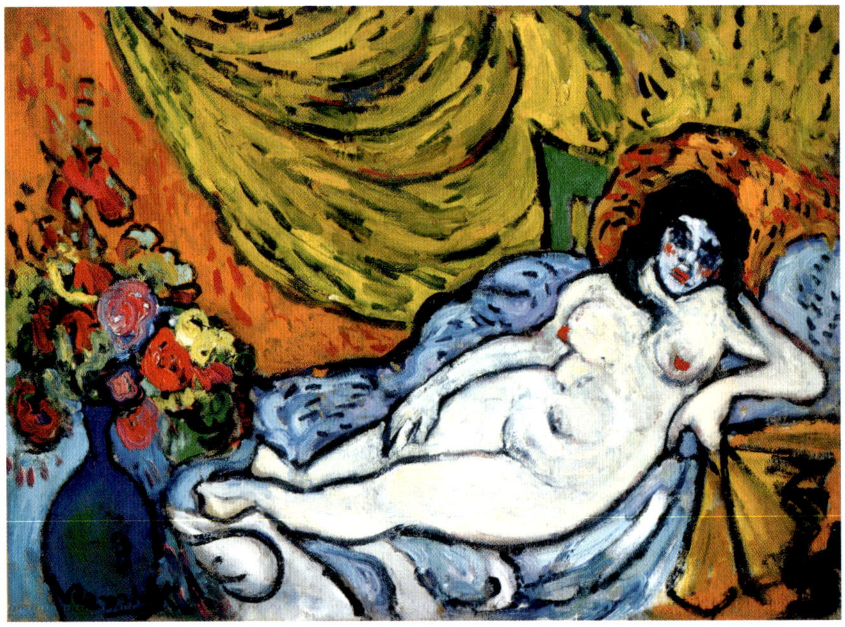

who also painted Le Rat mort in the 1890s. The many images devoted to the motif by Vlaminck and other Fauves such as Derain or Van Dongen thus followed a pictorial tradition already established in the fin de siècle.[11]

Vlaminck's *Reclining Nude* (cat. 20) of 1905 exemplifies the element of grotesque exaggeration characteristic of his female nudes. The flesh of the figure is rendered in vivid shades of pink, against which the bright red of her swollen nipples stands out disconcertingly. The white-powdered, heavily made-up face with its rigid expression seems strangely doll-like; the abstracted surroundings, marked by the complementary contrast of blue and orange tones, appear uninviting and garish. Notwithstanding her lascivious pose, the image of the naked woman refuses erotic appropriation by the male gaze. Vlaminck's Fauvist attack on nude painting, a genre dating back to the Venuses of the Renaissance, came to expression in similarly parodic manner in the painting *Reclining Nude* (fig. 5), also from 1905. Not coincidentally, the work echoes Manet's *Olympia* of 1863 (fig. 6), the nineteenth-century scandal painting par excellence that was closely associated with the avant-garde pursuit of stylistic and artistic innovation.[12] While Manet's image of nineteen-year-old Victorine Meurent had invoked the pictorial tradition of Old Masters from Titian to Francisco de Goya and Jean-Auguste-Dominique Ingres, Vlaminck quoted the great father of French modernism, to whom the Salon d'Automne also devoted a retrospective that same year with thirty-one works under the motto "The revolutionary of today is the classic of tomorrow." In the painting by Vlaminck, Olympia's cool complexion and youthfully appealing body yield to a dirty chalk white, whose sickly pallor is intensified still more by the contrast with the surrounding shades of red and black. Even more than in the other *Reclining Nude,* the body seems lifeless and clumsy, while the face turned challengingly toward the viewer appears inaccessible, stony, and rigid.

The ungainly limbs and masklike faces of Vlaminck's figural images were influenced by his interest in African statuettes, which he enthusiastically collected. Like works of "naïve" art or the nonperspectival painting of the Middle Ages—particularly the fifteenth-century works known as the *primitifs français*—the Fauves viewed non-Western artifacts as a source of inspiration for an emotionally charged renewal of modern painting.[13] In Vlaminck's Fauvist work, this process of cultural appropriation shows itself most clearly in the radically abstracted painting *Red Nude* (fig. p. 186), which once again suggests a stylistic dialogue with Matisse. The schematic head of the seated figure was probably inspired by a mask of the Fang people from Gabon in Central Africa, which Vlaminck acquired the year he made the painting.[14] As with his portrait of André Derain from the following year (fig. p. 23), here too Vlaminck may have chosen the dark red not only for its visual impact, but also to symbolize his programmatic affirmation of wildness and exoticism.

Explosive Visual Spaces

Although many of the Fauves joined Vlaminck in exploring figural representation, from the time of its christening at the Salon d'Automne in 1905 the movement was associated above all with landscape painting. Many of the artists drew inspiration from visits to the South of France, embracing the glittering light of the French Riviera as a catalyst for their dazzlingly colored images.[15] An important early work by Matisse is the ambitious painting *Luxury, Calm, and Voluptuousness* of 1904 (fig. 7), which stylistically is still informed by Neo-Impressionism. It shows a group of nudes gathered on a beach under the setting sun, decoratively assembled around a white picnic blanket. Glowing, jewel-like colors play about the figures, imbuing the southern evening scene with an enraptured atmosphere. Matisse's pictorial invention had been inspired by a visit to the French Riviera in the summer of 1904, where he interacted with fellow artists such as Paul Signac and Henri-Edmond Cross. Thus it is hardly surprising that both stylistically and compositionally, it resembles Cross's *The Evening Air* from around 1893 (fig. 8)—an homage to the enchantment of the South that Matisse could have seen at Signac's Villa La Hune in Saint-Tropez.[16]

Matisse returned to the theme of human leisure in a paradisical landscape in 1905–06, at the zenith of Fauvist experimentation. His monumental painting *The Joy of Life* (fig. p. 188) shows nude women and men dancing, making music, and lolling about, softly embedded in a sunlit landscape with pure, glowing colors. Themes such as the harmonious unity of

6
Édouard Manet,
Olympia, 1863,
Musée d'Orsay,
Paris

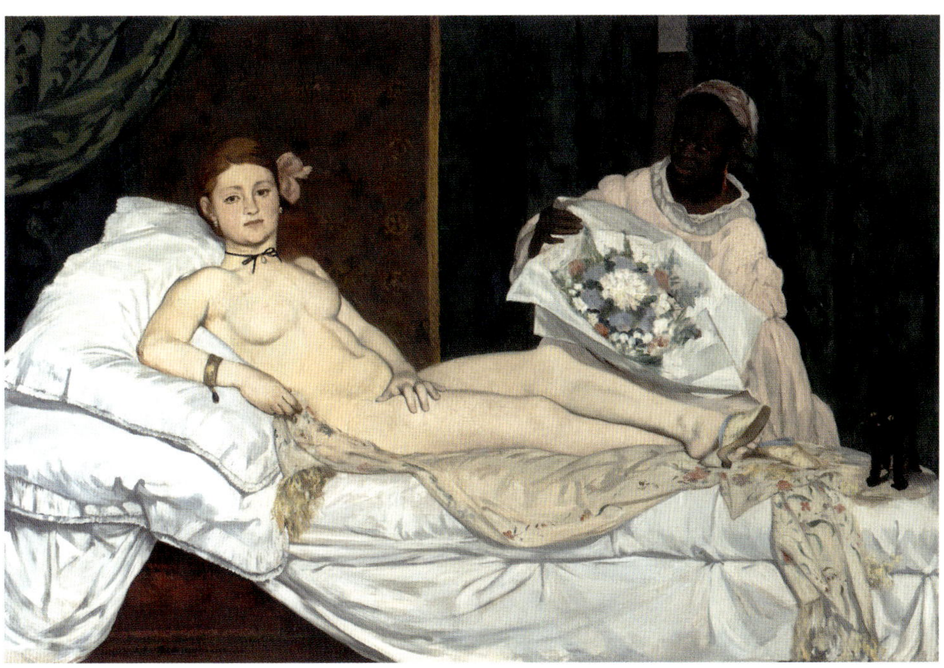

7
Henri Matisse,
Luxury, Calm, and Voluptuousness, 1904,
Musée d'Orsay, Paris

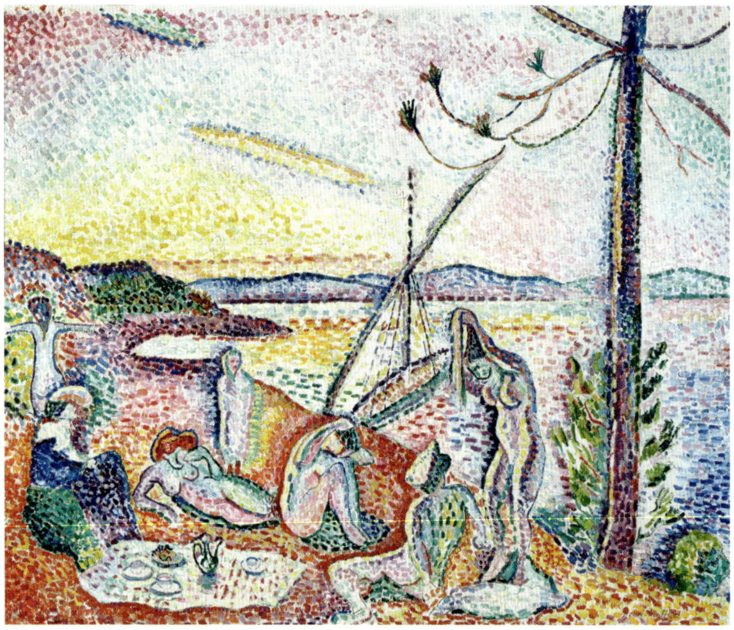

humanity and nature and the invocation of a Golden Age reflected the interest in nature utopias that had already characterized many of the pictorial inventions of the Neo-Impressionists. Iconographic references such as the ring of dancing figures in the center background strengthened the affinity to classical genres such as the *fête galante* or *déjeuner champêtre*—and, in a more general sense, alluded to the tradition of the pastorale.[17] The monumental composition, which was exhibited for the first time at the Fauve-dominated Salon d'Automne of 1906, was preceded by numerous preliminary studies in which Matisse meticulously developed the complex figural program.

In Vlaminck's Fauvist works as well, nature often seems symbolically charged with positive values such as vitality, nourishment, and human security. Yet the elegant spatial balance of Matisse's programmatic painting could not be further removed from the impetuously expressive approach that defines Vlaminck's mid-sized images of nature. Rather than conceiving an ideal landscape rich in art-historical and literary allusions, he turned his attention to his native Seine valley near Paris, painting numerous views of the landscape around Bougival, Rueil, Chatou, and Argenteuil.[18] In these depictions of real places, explored situationally and *sur le motif,* Vlaminck focused on the here and now of an unspectacular nature, from which he could elicit a veritably explosive spatial effect with his garishly exaggerated colors, pronounced tonal contrasts, and energetic, strongly textured surfaces.

The Legacy of Impressionism

In his painterly investigation of the Seine valley, Vlaminck devoted himself to a topography that was closely associated with the legacy of Impressionism and had already been explored by painters before him such as Claude Monet, Pierre-Auguste Renoir, and Gustave Caillebotte.[19] Like this older generation of artists, Vlaminck depicted different facets of the Seine, showing it both as the site of outdoor recreation and leisure and as a symbolic cipher for technological progress, modernization, and the rapid growth of industrialization in the region around Paris. Images of lonely rowers, sailboats gliding gently down the river, and summer regattas are found in his oeuvre alongside views of modern bridges and imposing industrial complexes. At times, the relationship to the artistic legacy of the late nineteenth century shows itself not only in the motifs, but also in the sketch-like approach to the subject matter, as well as in brushwork that recalls the *tache* of the Impressionists or the *pointillé* of the younger Neo-Impressionists.

A decisive departure from his older colleagues' choice of motifs becomes manifest in Vlaminck's rejection of middle-class subjects, themes that had defined the art of Impressionism. Monet and Renoir, for example, had repeatedly painted the Seine as a hotspot of bourgeois leisure activities, branding it as a motif for a particular class and, more broadly, for a particular clientele. A classic example is Renoir's *Luncheon of the Boating Party* from 1880–81 (Phillips Collection, Washington, DC), an important, large-scale work showing high-spirited vacationing urbanites at the Restaurant Fournaise—not far from Vlaminck's later atelier. While the fashionably elegant clothing of Renoir's figures clearly identifies them as middle-class excursionists, the bourgeoisie finds no place whatsoever in the landscape paintings of Vlaminck. A telling exception is the painting *The Rural Luncheon* (fig. 10), whose satirical elements verge on caricature: while the title of the picture awakens expectations of an idyllic scene of pastoral leisure à la Manet's *The Luncheon on the Grass* (fig. 9), the garish colors and distorted perspective produce a disconcerting, even dissonant atmosphere. The grim, apathetic-looking women in white dresses and straw hats are vaguely reminiscent of Edgar Degas's absinthe drinker, while the refreshments of the resting group are reduced to two wine bottles positioned in the center.[20]

While here the bourgeois figures seem like foreign objects in a tangled web of color, elsewhere Vlaminck shows nature as a vital, protective space in which human beings are peacefully and harmoniously embedded. Remarkably many of his paintings are devoted to fertility and agriculture—themes his great role model Van Gogh had also explored on multiple occasions. Van Gogh repeatedly painted luxuriant fields of wheat with bright golden heads of grain against the fresh blue of the summer sky, as well as reapers, sowers, and farmers toiling on the land in solitary tranquility (fig. 11).[21] Vlaminck embraced these subjects in compositions that echo Van Gogh stylistically as well, while the emphasis on rural labor also recalls the rustic landscapes of Realist painters including Jean-François Millet.

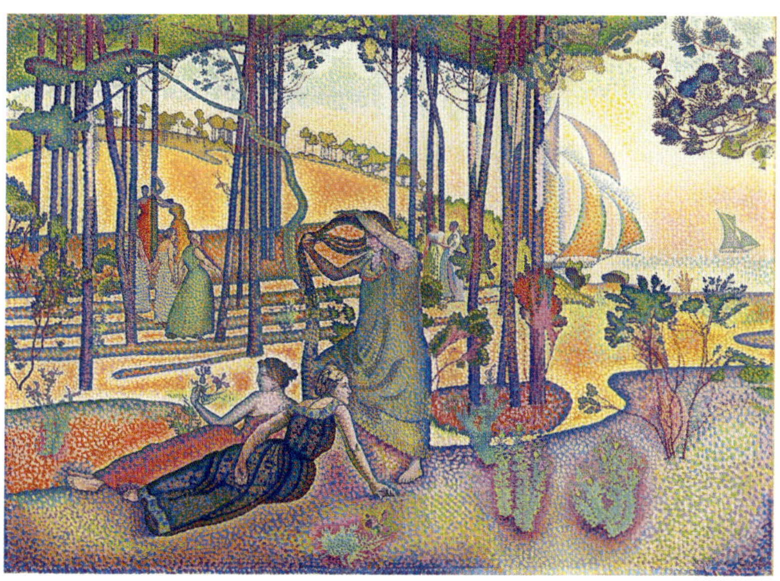

8
Henri-Edmond Cross,
The Evening Air,
ca. 1893,
Musée d'Orsay,
Paris

The intensive reception of Van Gogh's painting that began in early-twentieth-century France also focused on his pronounced interest in motifs of simple rural life.[22] Due to his numerous images of rustic subjects, Van Gogh was celebrated as a painter of the common folk and his art lauded as authentic and natural.[23] For Vlaminck, who presented himself as an artistic and social rebel throughout his entire life, this interpretation of Van Gogh's art may have offered an additional layer of identification, while his own interest in rural subjects far removed from Parisian high society may have provided a suitable outlet for his socially critical and decidedly anti-bourgeois mentality.

For Vlaminck, moreover, the work of Van Gogh was characterized by a "revolutionary sense" and "an almost religious feeling for the interpretation of nature."[24] This pantheistic conception of nature as a mysteriously animate force may also have informed Vlaminck's painting: in numerous landscape images, he employed a variety of stylistic means to create pulsating, highly charged visual spaces that evoke an immediate sense of unrestrained vitality—though often in complex compositions that belie the notion of a purely "instinctive," "barbaric," and thus unconsidered art. In his *View of Bougival* (cat. 15), for example, he chose a dramatic perspective looking down into the plain at the village, which appears strangely compact beneath the dynamic brushstrokes of the turbulent, cloud-filled sky. As in so many of his works, Vlaminck varied the direction of strokes and lines in the lush vegetation in the foreground. Together with the extreme complementary contrasts—red against green, blue against orange—the meticulously differentiated brushwork evokes the impression of an explosive spatial configuration in which the viewer's eye scarcely finds opportunity to rest.

The compositional scheme of Vlaminck's *Fishermen at Nanterre* (fig. p. 116) is similarly sophisticated: while the surface of the river, suggested in short strokes of glowing blue and white, recalls the mosaic texture of Neo-Impressionist painting, the turbulent sky in the upper half of the picture is more freely rendered. The smokestack of the factory in the center towers up dramatically like a blood-red spear, while its reflection on the surface of the river penetrates the cooler color scheme of the middle ground. In the foreground, the vegetation on the banks of the Seine serves as an echo and a visual parenthesis, shooting upward like bundles of licking,

9
Édouard Manet,
The Luncheon on the Grass, 1863,
Musée d'Orsay, Paris

10
Maurice de Vlaminck,
The Rural Luncheon,
1906
(cat. 34)

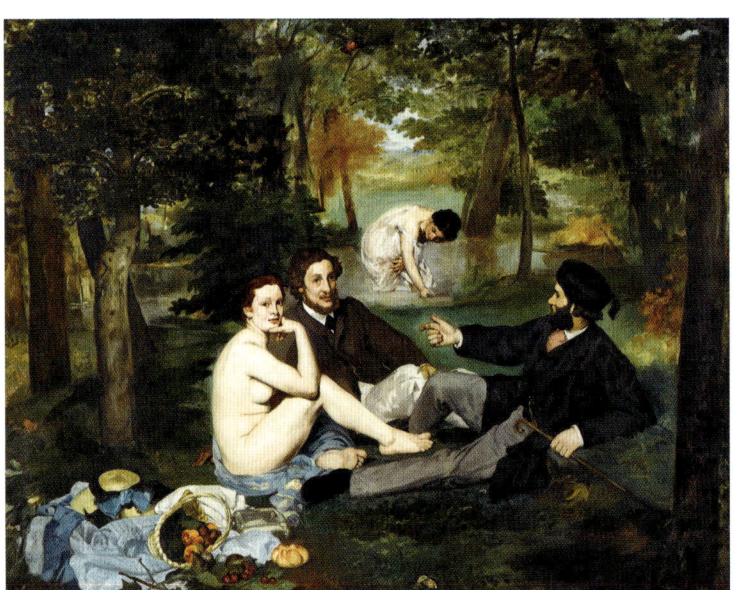

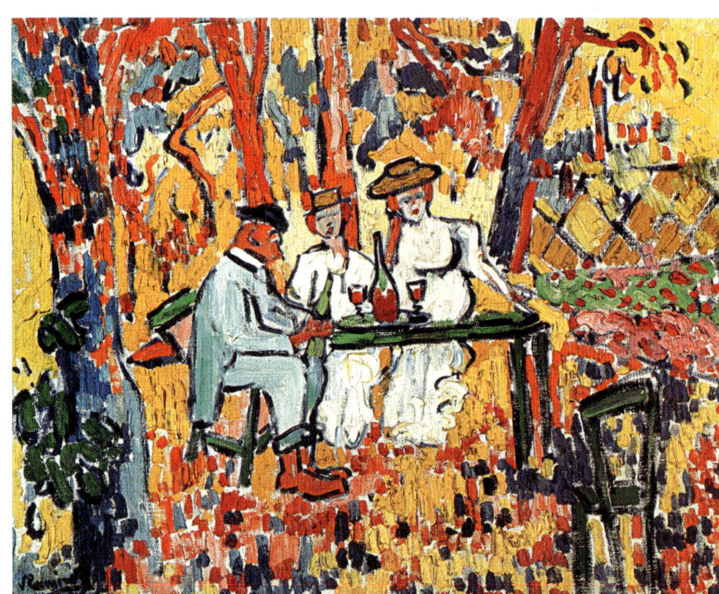

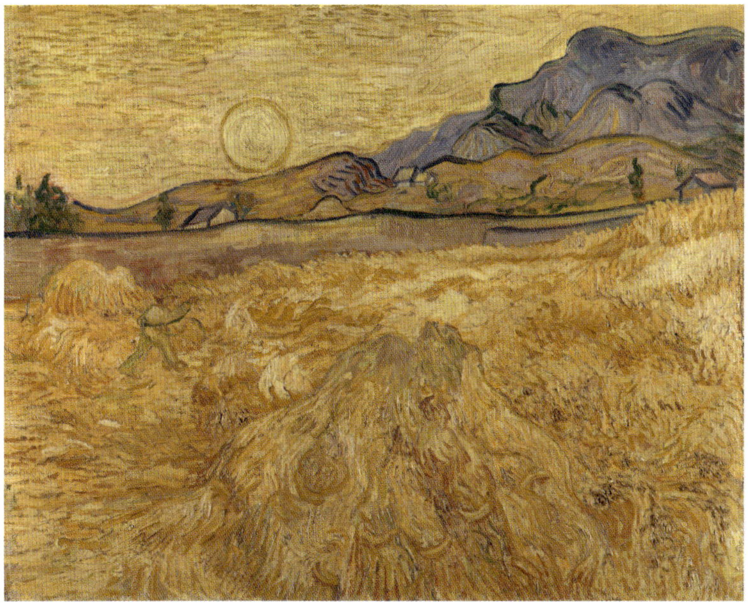

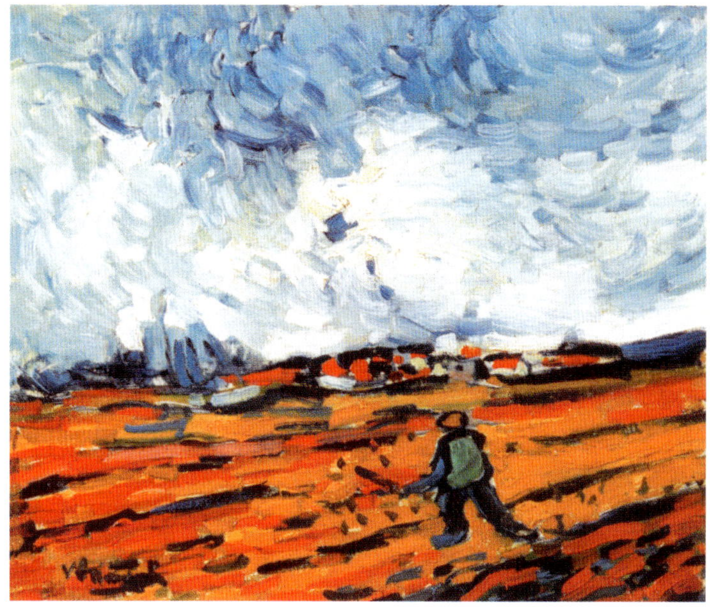

11
Vincent van Gogh,
Wheat Field with Reaper and Sun, 1889,
Kröller-Müller Museum, Otterlo

12
Maurice de Vlaminck,
The Peasant, 1905,
private collection

darting flames. The tonal intensity of the composition recalls Derain's aforementioned description of Fauvist colors as "cartridges of dynamite" intended to explode, as it were, on the canvas, discharging pure light.[25]

"With my cobalts and vermilions, I wished to burn down the École des Beaux-Arts and to render my impressions without any thought for what has been achieved in the past. . . . life and I, I and life."[26] In this retrospective statement from 1928, Vlaminck expressed the goals of his Fauvist painting, emphasizing his revolutionary embrace of pure color. His adroit use of anarchistic metaphor accorded with his lifelong self-stylization as an artistic subversive and revolutionary, steeped in the powerful visual language of Fauvism. Yet beyond his reception of Van Gogh, the examination of his painting within the context of late-nineteenth- and early-twentieth-century artistic currents reveals numerous points of reference that nourished his new and innovative form of expression. The struggle for technical skill, a patient persistence in the painter's craft, were of special importance for his Fauvist still lifes (cats. 21–27, 65)—studies in volume, spatial design, and color patiently executed in the studio, works that already anticipated the greater formal discipline he would embrace starting in 1907–08 under the influence of Paul Cézanne.[27] While Vlaminck himself always posed as a loner and an outsider, and although as a talented author he helped forge his own myth early on, as an artist he was inescapably a product of his time.

"My Inner Being Deeply Shaken" Vlaminck's Reception of Van Gogh's Art

Lisa Smit

In March 1901 Maurice de Vlaminck visited Galerie Bernheim-Jeune in Paris and was blown away by the art he encountered there. The bold brushstrokes and intense range of colors employed in the paintings by Vincent van Gogh had a profound and lasting impact on the aspiring young artist. Seeing this monographic exhibition of over seventy works would prove to be a key moment in the development of Vlaminck, who even went so far as to say, "On that day I loved Van Gogh more than my father."[1] Vlaminck clearly felt a deep sense of connection with Van Gogh's painting, which in turn became a catalyst for his own artistic maturation. This essay examines the role that Van Gogh's work played in the development of Vlaminck's art, both in terms of his painting technique and his choice of motifs. The analysis will focus on the artist's early years and how his reception of Van Gogh's art influenced the formation of his Fauvist idiom.

Encountering Van Gogh

At the time of his introduction to Van Gogh's art, Vlaminck had only been active as an artist for a short time. The previous summer, in July 1900, he had befriended André Derain and soon after began sharing a studio with him. In Vlaminck's own words, it was due to this interaction with Derain that he decided to fully devote himself to being an artist: "It's certain, in fact, that without this acquaintance . . . the idea would never have occurred to me to make 'Painting' my profession, to make a living from it."[2] It was also his friend Derain who took him to Galerie Bernheim-Jeune some nine months later to see the important Van Gogh retrospective that ran from March 15 to 31 with sixty-five paintings and six drawings listed in the catalog.[3] Moreover, this was the day that Vlaminck met Henri Matisse through Derain—which in itself made it a day of great historical importance for the early formation of Fauvism.

In his autobiographical *Portraits avant décès* (Portraits before Death) of 1943, Vlaminck states, "At that time Vincent van Gogh was known only by a few artists and by a very small number of collectors."[4] He then goes on to explain that the exhibition included marines, harvest scenes, Provence landscapes, a self-portrait, and versions of Van Gogh's portrait of *L'Arlésienne, Cypresses, Sunflowers, The Bedroom,* and *The Starry*

Night. By and large, this is an accurate description of the exhibited works. What is of great importance in view of the deep impression the selection of works made on Vlaminck—as well as Derain, Matisse, and other visitors to the exhibition—is the fact that most of the works on display were painted in Van Gogh's later years. Hardly any of the works were created in his Dutch years, which are characterized by a much more somber palette. First and foremost, the gallery was filled with the brightly hued paintings from Arles, as well as Saint-Rémy and Paris, supplemented by a few late compositions from Auvers-sur-Oise. That is, most of the works presented at Galerie Bernheim-Jeune were created in the South of France and Auvers, where Van Gogh had come into his prime as a painter.

The driving force behind the exhibition at Bernheim-Jeune was French poet and critic Julien Leclercq, a pioneering figure in the early reception of Van Gogh. He first encountered the art of Van Gogh in 1888 and once met the artist in person in 1890. Not only did Leclercq publish favorable critiques at a very early stage; he also had plans for a biography on the artist, acquired several works for his personal collection, including the iconic work *The Starry Night* (1889, Museum of Modern Art, New York), and organized several exhibitions, of which the one at Bernheim-Jeune in 1901 was the most important. In that show, he succeeded in bringing together a substantial number of Van Goghs from French collections. Among the collectors were artists such as Auguste Rodin, Camille Pissarro, and Émile Schuffenecker, and gallery owners including Ambroise Vollard, Eugène Blot, and Jos Hessel.[5] Leclercq formulated his hopes for the show in the foreword to the catalog, writing, "The present exhibition will allow those who are unaware of Vincent's work to render him justice," and concluding, "His name will always evoke ideas of the magnificence of colour."[6]

At Bernheim-Jeune, Vlaminck was faced with art that must have been nothing like he had ever seen before. In 1901 Van Gogh had yet to find peers in his radical treatment of paint and upscaling of colors. Take, for example, *Coal Barges* of 1888 (fig. 1), in which the blazing-bright yellow sky of the setting sun is reflected in the equally bright yellow

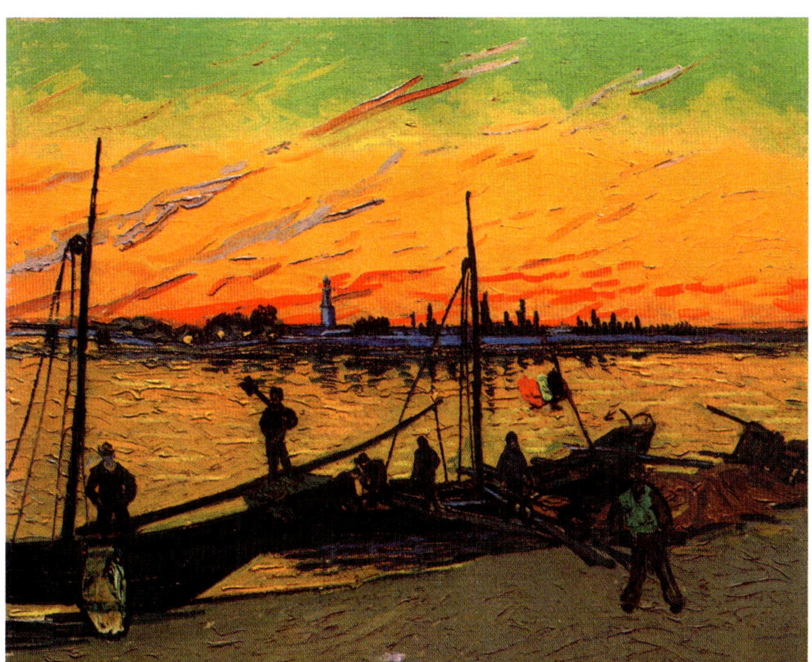

1
Vincent van Gogh, *Coal Barges,* 1888, private collection

surface of the water—a daring play with high-keyed colors that is dramatized by accents in fiery orange. The coal barges and workmen in the foreground stand out sharply in dark color against the brilliant evening light, a kind of pronounced tonal contrast that would become typical of Vlaminck's Fauvist period. Vlaminck's encounter with Van Gogh's art was an overwhelming experience, as the artist later frequently emphasized: "Coming away from an exhibition of Van Gogh in the Rue Laffitte I was so moved that I wanted to cry with joy and despair."[7] He instantly felt a profound connection with Van Gogh, in whom he found some of his own aspirations, as well as, "a revolutionary, almost religious feeling in the interpretation of nature."[8]

Violent Desire

Acting on his "violent desire"[9] to own one or more paintings by Van Gogh, Vlaminck contacted exhibition organizer Leclercq. His autobiography contains extensive quotes from their ensuing correspondence. Leclercq informed Vlaminck, "I personally possess five paintings by Vincent van Gogh. . . . None of these canvases are for sale. But one of my friends has entrusted four paintings to me that he would be willing to give up."[10] He also invited Vlaminck to come and see his own Van Goghs—an invitation that he eagerly accepted. Despite asking friends including Derain to pitch in, Vlaminck was unable to raise the necessary funds to acquire a painting. When Leclercq passed away unexpectedly in October 1901, his widow approached Vlaminck about her husband's collection, but unfortunately, again, no purchase resulted. He later recalled with evident frustration, "I would have had to be crazy to believe that I could acquire one or two paintings by Van Gogh!"[11]

About six months after the Van Gogh exhibition, Derain began his military service for a period of three years. During this time he stayed in touch with Vlaminck through a lively correspondence. Only Derain's letters are known today and have been published, but these are insightful about Vlaminck's development and vision as well. From his letters, it is clear that Derain, too, was deeply impressed by Van Gogh. About a year after seeing the exhibition he wrote to his friend, "Really, his memory haunts me to this day. More and more, I see the true meaning in him."[12] Interestingly, Derain's correspondence reveals that he was aware of Van Gogh's life story. With today's vast biographical knowledge of Van Gogh's life, it is immediately clear that Derain's description is full of inaccuracies, with a strong focus on his mental health issues ("He cut off his ears to prove that physical pain didn't exist"[13]) and suicide—a reading that was common in those days.[14]

At the time, the most important source of information about Van Gogh was the series of extracts from Van Gogh's letters that had been published in the French journal *Mercure de France* between 1893 and 1897 on the initiative of his artist-friend Émile Bernard (1868–1941). These letters became known to the progressive readership of the magazine, which included many artists, and reprints in other media soon followed.[15] Despite Vlaminck's later reputation as the "wildest" of the Fauves, he was in fact—like Van Gogh—very well read, in addition to being an articulate author of novels, plays, and autobiographical writings.[16] It can be assumed that he would have been interested in learning more about Van Gogh in the period following his meaningful first encounter with his paintings. Texts that would have been easily accessible to Vlaminck include the introduction by Leclercq in the catalog of the Bernheim-Jeune exhibition and an influential article by writer and critic Octave Mirbeau in *Le Journal*.[17]

In the years following Vlaminck's first encounter with Van Gogh's art and his fruitless attempts to acquire a painting by the artist he so admired, the impact on his own output seems to have been negligeable. The fact that Derain left for his military service in September 1901 put a temporary end to the fruitful collaboration between the two. Moreover, Vlaminck found himself facing financial difficulties, something that affected his young family and probably did not have a positive influence on his creative flow: "Colors and canvases were expensive and my financial means were more than limited."[18] Not many paintings are known for the period between 1901 and 1904.[19] Executed as they were by a largely self-taught artist, these radically anti-academic compositions already hint at the vigor of his Fauvist period, but in many ways constitute a prelude to his mature, much more expressive style. In fact, it was not until 1905 that Vlaminck's artistic practice really took flight. Not coincidentally, it was in the spring of that year that the artist had another opportunity to thoroughly familiarize himself with the legacy of his great role model.

The Salon des Indépendants of 1905

From March 24 to April 30, 1905, another sizeable retrospective of Van Gogh's work took place in Paris. This one was part of the twenty-first Salon des Indépendants, which included the huge number of nearly 4,300 works by 669 artists. Within the Salon, both Van Gogh and Georges Seurat were honored with exhibitions in spaces of their own. Like at Bernheim-Jeune in 1901, nearly all the forty-five works by Van Gogh had been created in the South of France and Auvers, and all were owned by Frenchmen, including three drawings in the possession of Matisse.[20] While some of the canvases had been part of the Bernheim-Jeune show, visitors were also presented with other top-quality paintings, including *Self-Portrait with Bandaged Ear* (1889, Courtauld Gallery, London) and *Doctor Paul Gachet* (1890, Musée d'Orsay, Paris), making the selection an incredibly fine show on the artist. Critic Louis Vauxcelles, who was to coin the term *fauves* later that year, emphasized this in his review of the event: "The retrospective exhibition of this mad genius is of the utmost beauty. The art lovers who have lent these masterpieces . . . will have caused one of the most intense joys that artists can feel."[21]

It is a fine coincidence that this new opportunity for Vlaminck to indulge in the art of the painter he admired so greatly was simultaneously accompanied by his own debut. Vlaminck exhibited eight paintings alongside the art of his peers Derain (also making his debut) and Matisse as well as others who would later come to be associated with the Fauves.[22] According to Vlaminck, their room caused a scandal on the opening day.[23] However, this seems rather exaggerated, since only Matisse, who was already much more established, received significant attention, while the others were largely neglected in the extensive press coverage of the Salon.[24] Interestingly, it was Derain who was qualified as a "bold follower of Van Gogh" by Vauxcelles, who dismissed Vlaminck with the harsh remark, "I disregard the foolish simplifications of Mr. Vlaminck". [25] That being said, his debut did result in Vlaminck's first-ever sale.[26]

One of the paintings Vlaminck debuted with was *Rustic Setting, or Children in a Garden* of 1903 (fig. p. 187). This modest composition can already be considered a precursor of the artist's Fauvist style in which the indebtedness to Van Gogh is palpable, yet somewhat clumsily expressed. The boisterously painted sky is modeled around the tree too blatantly, and the awkwardly placed figures are rendered in a plump manner, while the filling-in of the different

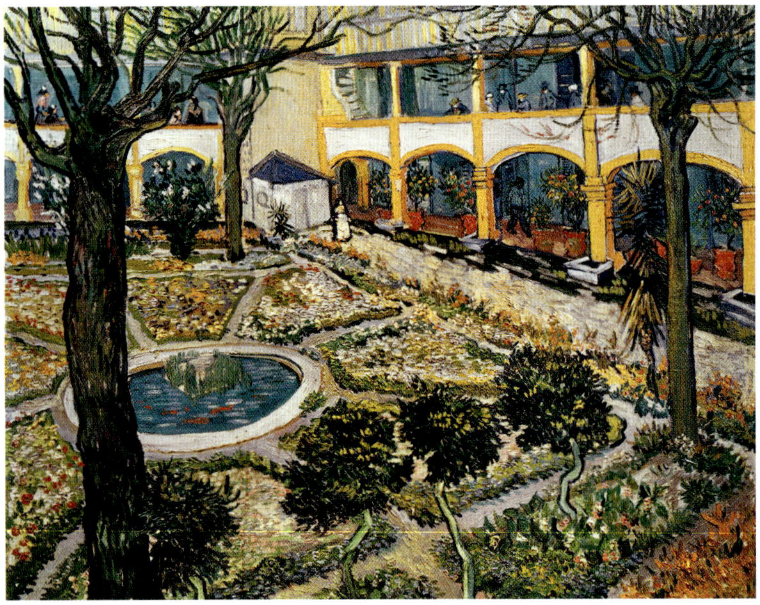

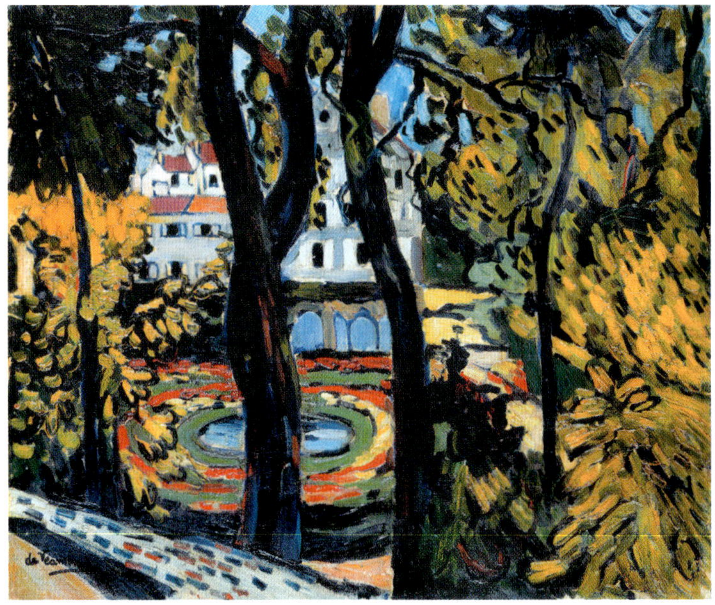

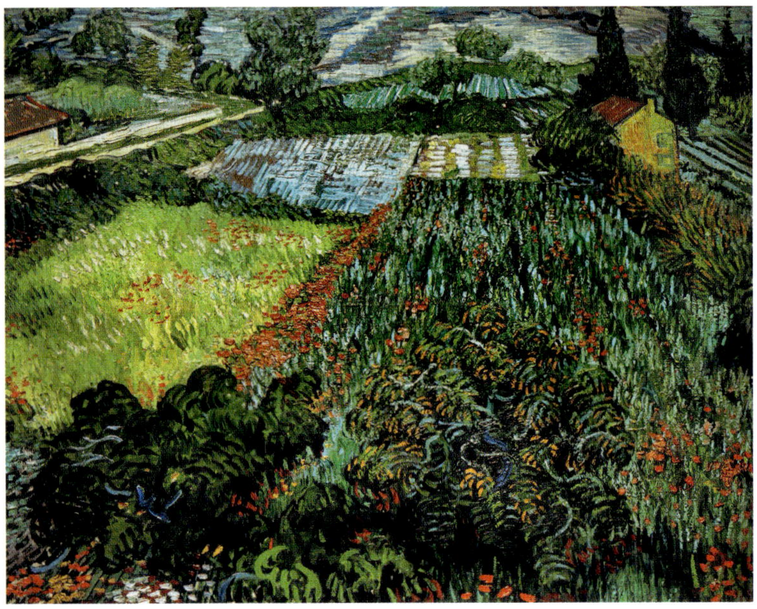

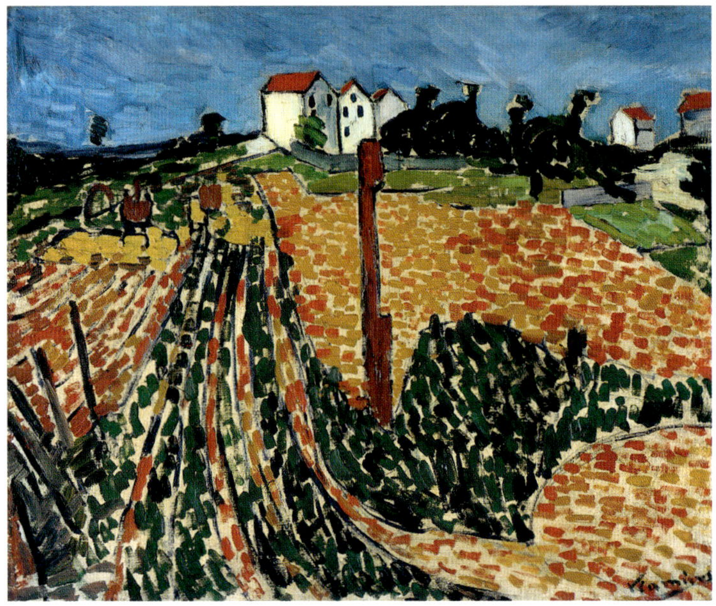

2
Vincent van Gogh,
The Courtyard of the Hospital at Arles, 1889,
Oskar Reinhart Collection "Am Römerholz," Winterthur

3
Maurice de Vlaminck,
Park in Carrières-Saint-Denis, 1904
(cat. 8)

4
Vincent van Gogh,
Field with Poppies, 1889,
Kunsthalle Bremen

5
Maurice de Vlaminck,
Route maraîchère, 1905
(cat. 14)

plains that together make up the garden is rather flat. Moreover, compared to Van Gogh or Vlaminck's own later works, the palette remains quite muted.

Jean-Paul Crespelle, an early biographer of Vlaminck, already noted that Van Gogh led him to profoundly modify his painting: "Vlaminck's palette was ignited by contact with Van Gogh's canvases."[27] That is exactly what happened in 1905. Now that he had had the opportunity to develop as an artist since the Van Gogh exhibition of 1901, his renewed intensive acquaintance with Van Gogh's paintings fell on fertile ground. An extremely creative period followed in which Van Gogh's influence is patently obvious. This was clearly visible at the next occasion where Vlaminck had the opportunity to present his art: the now legendary Salon d'Automne of 1905.

At the third Salon d'Automne, which took place in Paris from October 18 to November 25, 1905, Vlaminck exhibited five paintings alongside those of his peers Derain, Matisse, Charles Camoin, Henri Manguin, and Albert Marquet.[28] Despite the crude tone of many critics, the joint display of their works in the seventh room of the show was a great success. The term *fauves* was coined in a review by Vauxcelles in *Gil Blas,* and Vlaminck did not go by unnoticed this time.[29] Although his paintings were mockingly described as "small balls of color thrown at the canvas," he presented a cohesive selection that truly showed his latest development.[30] His colors had intensified immensely, his brushstroke had become bolder and more confident in handling, and his modulation and organization of the picture plane more skillfully self-assured.

Van Gogh's influence is evident in all the works that Vlaminck chose to submit to the salon. Most striking in this regard is *Park in Carrières-Saint-Denis* (fig. 3). This painting is closely related to Van Gogh's *The Courtyard of the Hospital at Arles* (fig. 2), inviting a closer comparison. Each depicts a circular basin surrounded by a greenery and flanked by a colonnade that is hidden from view by tree trunks claiming a prominent place in the foreground. The palettes used are of a similar range, Vlaminck's leaning slightly more to the green and Van Gogh's tending more toward the yellow. The loose handling of the paint for the trees, plants, and flowers versus the somewhat flatter execution of the architectural elements also breathes the same atmosphere. While *The Courtyard of the Hospital at Arles* had been exhibited neither at Bernheim-Jeune nor at the Salon des Indépendants, it passed through several Parisian galleries before it ended up in Berlin in 1904.[31] Given Vlaminck's deep commitment to Van Gogh during this period, it is possible that he actually saw it at one of these galleries and that it was a direct source of inspiration for *Park in Carrières-Saint-Denis.*

After this important year in which Vlaminck debuted and truly started to thrive as a painter, success did not seem to cease. In April 1906 influential art dealer Ambroise Vollard bought up the entire contents of his studio, just like he had done with Derain some months earlier, and asked Vlaminck to reserve for him whatever he painted.[32] In *Recollections of a Picture Dealer,* Vollard remembered with relish, "The landscapes covering the walls of the studio were so many challenges to the *bourgeois* whose idea of nature is of something tame and tidied up. Far from being put off by this *outrance,* I bought everything Vlaminck showed me."[33] The following year he gave him his first solo show.

Interestingly, Vlaminck claims to have had the opportunity to see what seems to be an abundance of Van Gogh works at Vollard's: "I recognized them all, having had them in front of me at Vollard's for months and years, and having been able to look at them at my leisure."[34] This is hard to square with the facts. Vollard's involvement with Van Gogh was very substantial in the 1890s as one of the very first to deal extensively in the artist's works.[35] Vollard, however, was not very active as a dealer of Van Gogh's works in the early twentieth century. Regardless of exactly how much of Van Gogh's work Vlaminck was able to see at Vollard's, it shows that his gallery allowed a younger generation of artists a type of exposure that went beyond that of the larger exhibitions. This certainly was an added benefit to Vlaminck's stylistic maturation at this critical juncture in his career.

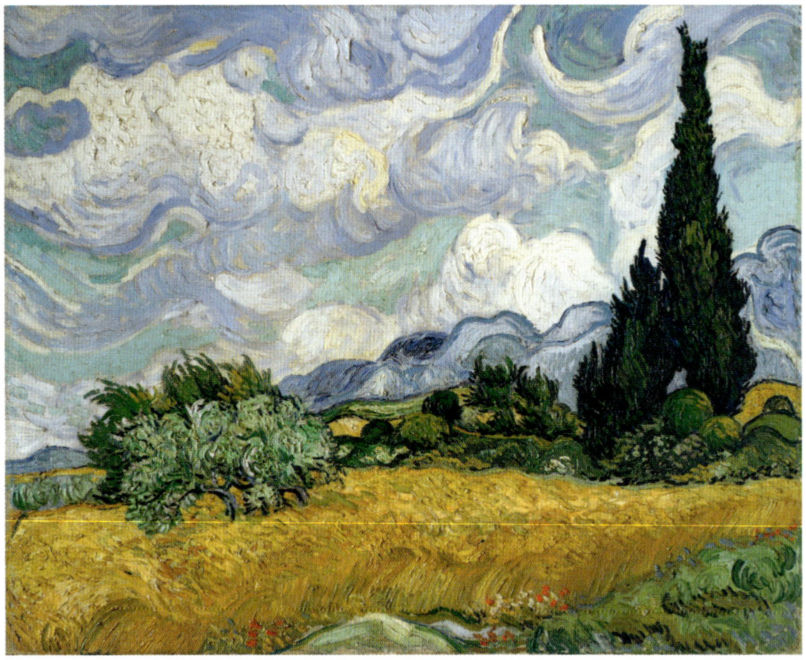

6
Vincent van Gogh, *Wheat Field with Cypresses*, 1889, Metropolitan Museum of Art, New York

Artistic Affinities

The years between 1905 and 1907 marked a period of enormous creativity for Vlaminck during which he produced his now most-prized paintings. With the exception of Derain, Van Gogh's influence on the other Fauves, despite their admiration for his work, was not as substantial. Among them, Vlaminck was certainly most strongly influenced by Van Gogh. Although he would paint several homages to Van Gogh much later, the Fauvist paintings of 1905 to 1907 are the paintings in which Vlaminck—albeit in his own idiosyncratic way—was stylistically most directly engaged with his great role model. Of course, there were other sources of influence, principally Cézanne, and obviously other Fauves, primarily his dear friend Derain. But in Van Gogh, Vlaminck seemed to recognize a like-minded spirit like no other: an artist with what he considered "Nordic affinities" like himself, and with—in Vlaminck's eyes—a highly personal and instinctive artistic response to his surroundings.[36]

Consider the obvious affiliation between Van Gogh's *Wheat Field with Cypresses* (fig. 6), exhibited at Bernheim-Jeune in 1901, and Vlaminck's *The Wheat Field (Champs de Blé)* of about 1906 (fig. 7). Both paintings offer sweeping vistas of the French countryside; in Vlaminck's case, houses are visible in the far distance. The artist simplified the landscapes to their most essential components, omitting figures and anecdotal details. The different planes of the landscape are dominated from foreground to background by the colors green, yellow, green, and blue. Both painters enlivened the composition with notes of red. Taking into account the discoloration of the Van Gogh, the sky will originally have been more pink in hue (Vlaminck's sky also has pink notes), and the mountains more contrasting in view of the waving wheat.

Both artists had a preference for painting outside, working from nature like the Impressionists had already done before them. Inspired by Van Gogh, Vlaminck focused purely on his personal response to the scenery before him, translating his lyrical enthusiasm for the environment into a symphony of pure colors and savage, strongly textured strokes. In *The Wheat Field (Champs de Blé),* each brushstroke is loaded with paint. His multicolor palette takes

Van Gogh's incandescence a few shades higher. Particularly for the air, Vlaminck clearly worked in the swirling brushstrokes of Van Gogh. The rounded shapes of the greenery in the foreground are also modeled similarly. What both works transmit with great success, is a profound delight in the sensory experience of nature.

Another striking comparison is that of Van Gogh's *Field with Poppies* (fig. 4), also exhibited at Bernheim-Jeune, and Vlaminck's *Route maraîchère* (fig. 5). In both canvases, the various pieces of farmland extend across the canvas like a patchwork; in *Field with Poppies,* the horizon is absent altogether. The painting was briefly owned by Leclercq, so it is possible that Vlaminck would have been able to see it more than once. The prominent diagonal design of each composition immediately draws the viewer into the fields. The similar use of green and red is intriguing, as is the naive yet apt rendering of the houses. Yet the paintings primarily exude the same look and feel through the multitude of firmly painted yet separately placed touches, modeling each plot in a different direction to add texture to the painting. The major difference here is that Van Gogh completely covered the canvas, while with Vlaminck the canvas is still clearly visible, except for the houses and the sky, and his approach is thus closer to the Divisionists.

Vlaminck painted innumerable scenes of the river Seine, including *Tugboats on the Seine, Chatou* (cat. 37), *Rowboat at Chatou* (cat. 47), and *The Seine at Nanterre* (cat. 43). It seems obvious to compare a painting such as *River Scene with Bridge* (cat. 40) to Van Gogh's river scenes, such as *Coal Barges* (fig. 1). Many of Vlaminck's river views feature a slight bird's-eye perspective, like this painting by Van Gogh. Both paintings are also characterized by a strong diagonal thrust, and each composition is divided into clear large areas for the water, sky, and quay. However, Van Gogh's influence should not be sought only in obvious similarities. Vlaminck was able to admire *Wheat Field with Reaper and Sun* (fig. p. 39) in both 1901 and 1905. As was their habit, both men richly applied their paint and exploited the expressive possibilities of powerful, dynamic brushstrokes as well as thickly set outlines. The color yellow dominates much of Van Gogh's landscape, whereas Vlaminck mainly chose marine and azure blue for his *River Scene with Bridge*. Diagonals are formed by the long wall that surrounded the asylum where Van Gogh was living in Saint-Rémy-de-Provence, and in

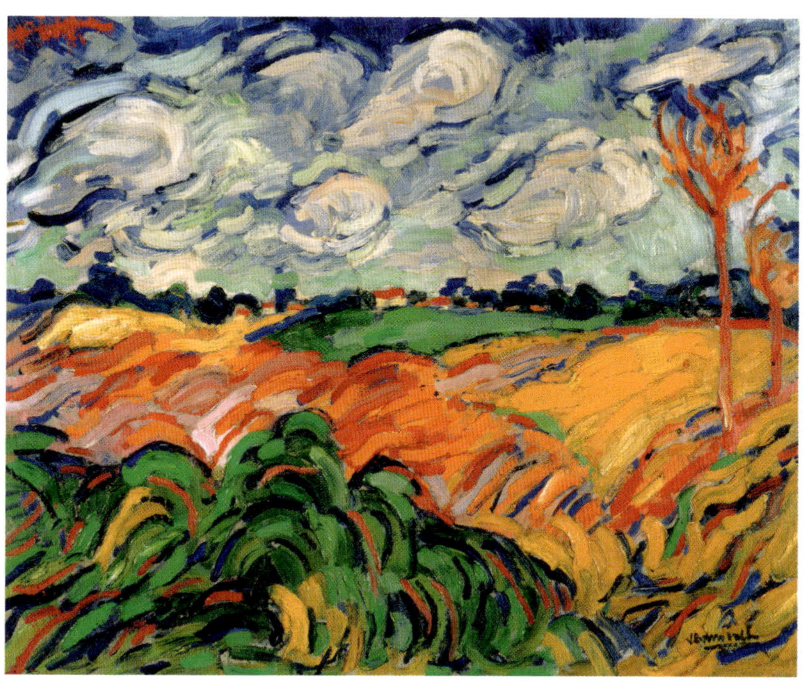

7
Maurice de Vlaminck,
The Wheat Field
(Champs de Blé),
ca. 1906
(cat. 33)

Vlaminck's case by the sturdy red ship. The appeal of both paintings, however, lies in the undulating surface of the water and the large field of waving wheat, which take up more than half of each canvas. Both Van Gogh and Vlaminck succeeded very well in creating spatiality and movement. Above all, both surfaces transmit a sense of pleasure in the physical act painting itself.

A Lasting Influence

Van Gogh was well aware that it would take a long time for his art to be understood, let alone appreciated. He was simply too far ahead of his time. However, he had firm convictions about what modern art should be: "As for me, I'll work, and here and there some of my work will last . . . . But the painter of the future is a *colourist such as there hasn't been before.*"[37] It was right around the time the Fauves appeared on the scene that Van Gogh made his big breakthrough.[38] Given their interest in pure, wild colors, it should come as no surprise that they had a hitherto unprecedented appreciation for the artist. Among the Fauves, as well as many other artists of that generation, Van Gogh found like-minded spirits posthumously, as it were.

However, from 1907, Vlaminck took a different direction, away from Fauvism. After exploring its full potential for several years, he felt he had reached its limits: "It was fun to work in pure colour and tone, a game into which I had thrown myself heart and soul, but it was not enough for me."[39] Vlaminck's palette became much darker and his volumes much more geometric with far less impasto. That he took a different path certainly did not mean that his appreciation for Van Gogh had lessened. He later resided in Auvers-sur-Oise, the last place where Van Gogh lived and where Vlaminck was to visit his grave in the 1920s: "When I arrived in the countryside, I went to the cemetery to pay a posthumous visit to Van Gogh, who was sleeping his last sleep there," he later wrote, and dramatically added, "Swarms of crows circled the sky . . . ."[40]

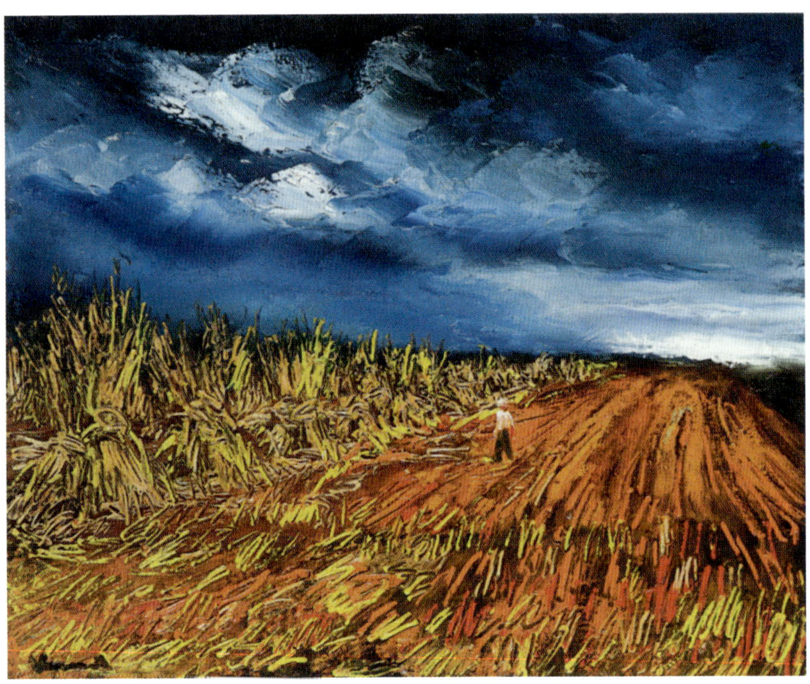

8
Maurice de Vlaminck,
Harvest during Approaching Thunderstorm, 1950
(cat. 79)

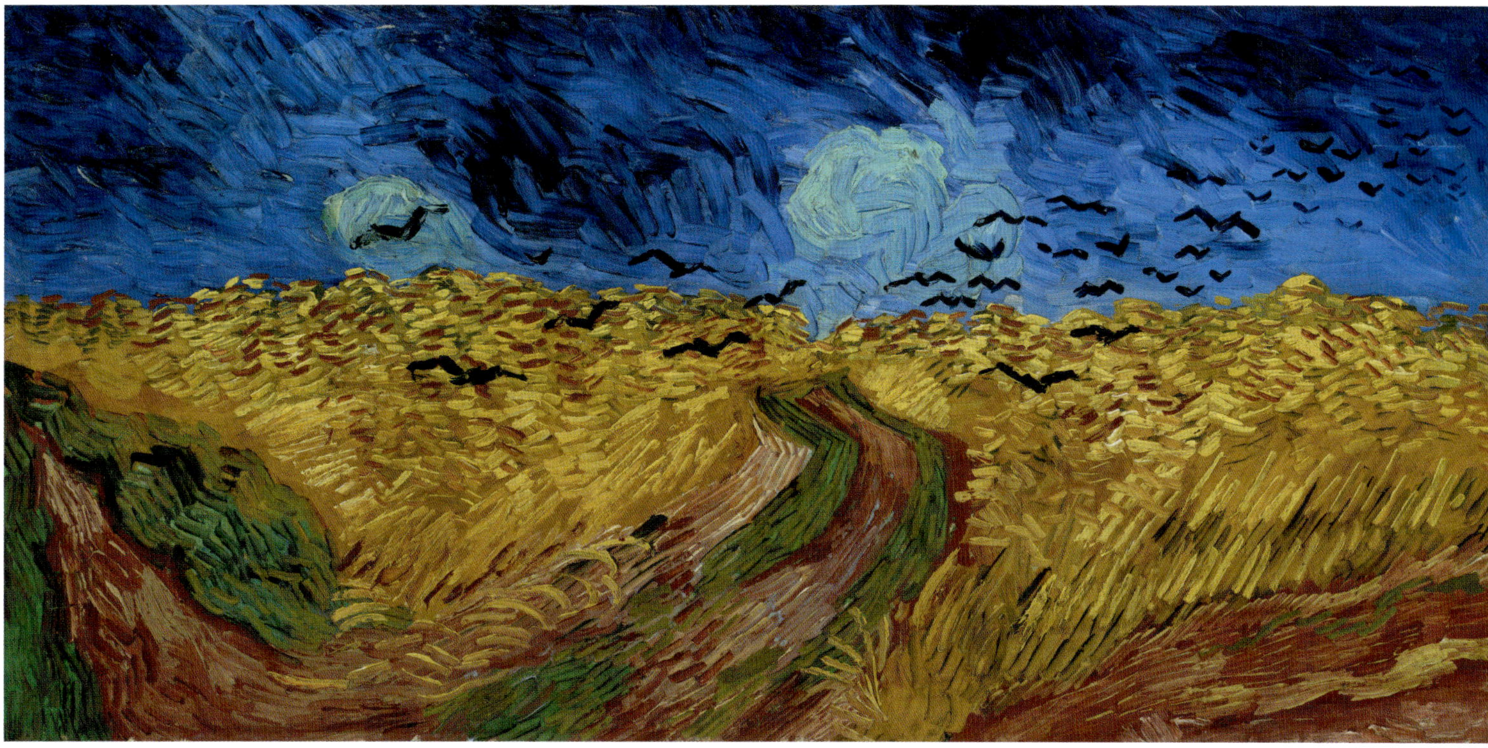

9
Vincent van Gogh,
Wheatfield with Crows,
1890, Van Gogh Museum,
Amsterdam (Vincent van
Gogh Foundation)

In the 1940s Vlaminck once again returned to the art of Van Gogh. His late depictions of fields of wheat are clearly related to *Wheatfield with Crows* (fig. 9). This famous painting, often inadvertently thought to be the last picture Van Gogh ever executed, was exhibited in Paris on several occasions, which makes it likely that Vlaminck was able to see it with his own eyes.[41] The stormy sky and coarsely painted sheaves of wheat in *Harvest during Approaching Thunderstorm* (fig. 8) recall the haunted atmosphere of this painting. The color scheme is also strikingly similar, with its intense deep blue, sunburnt yellow, and orange-brown. The crows are absent, but it is possible that the desolate figure references Van Gogh. For him, harvesting symbolized the end of the life cycle: in *Harvest during Approaching Thunderstorm,* the wheat has been cut and tied in sheaves. The painting can be seen as paying homage to Van Gogh, who meant so much to Vlaminck throughout his artistic career and about whom he later claimed: "Van Gogh's art is human, sensitive, and full of life."[42]

Kinship of Forms — Cézanne, Picasso, Vlaminck

Anna Storm

> "As far as possible I avoided meeting artists and painters. I wanted to keep intact the confidence and love which I had for my own painting, and deliberately I closed my eyes and blocked my ears to outside influences."[1]

With these words from his autobiography *Dangerous Corner* (1929), Maurice de Vlaminck described his detachment from the Paris art scene. Yet Vlaminck's painting was by no means so unaffected by external influences as his later self-portrayal might suggest. It is not unusual for an artist's work to be informed by promptings and inspirations; the practice of copying was an element of academic training, though Vlaminck never studied at an academy. His desire for autonomy was intense, perhaps also as a way of distancing himself from academic practice. Moreover, the image of the independent artist rebel is associated with this attitude. Yet even so, Vlaminck's paintings are characterized by motifs and formal means that show parallels to those of his precursors and contemporaries. The influence of Vincent van Gogh is especially notable and left its mark on Vlaminck's early, Fauvist phase.[2] Vlaminck clearly articulated his admiration for Van Gogh, and at first even allegedly emulated the latter's signature.[3]

Seldom, however, has Vlaminck's interest in Paul Cézanne been investigated, as will be addressed in the following discussion. The still lifes of Vlaminck can be fruitfully compared to those of Cézanne regarding aspects such as pictorial structure.[4] Instead of defining Vlaminck's artistic development in terms of influence or the appropriation of formal or motivic means, the purpose of this essay is to sketch out important lines of development and present them for discussion relating to a kinship of forms. As Peter Geimer has observed, no one can look at a painting without thinking of other works that have previously been viewed, and the practice of binary juxtaposition is dominant in art history as well.[5] Yet formal similarities do not always indicate an explicit reference or the result of direct inspiration. In many instances, artists working independently of each other in varying contexts have arrived at similar pictorial solutions. The similarities between Vlaminck and Cézanne as well as between Vlaminck and the Cubists around Pablo Picasso that will be outlined in the following are not intended to prove a direct connection in terms of the aesthetics of reception. Rather, the objective is to trace Vlaminck's artistic development and situate it within its historical context.

The works by Vlaminck in which motivic, formal, and aesthetic parallels to Cézanne can be identified were created primarily between 1905 and 1911—partly during, but to a greater extent after his Fauvist phase. At this time, especially between 1905 and 1907, a genuine "Cézanne fever" broke out in Paris, a circumstance that, as Peter Kropmanns has noted, also contributed to Fauvism's lack of enduring success.[6] In 1907, a year after Cézanne's death, four exhibitions with a total of 146 works by the painter were shown in Paris.[7] Cézanne was thus omnipresent in the art metropolis, and although Vlaminck, like many of his fellow artists, had shown some interest in Cézanne's art—Matisse had already purchased a painting by Cézanne in 1899—that interest now began to intensify. Vlaminck reported that he regularly visited Ambroise Vollard and sometimes accompanied the dealer to see collectors who owned numerous works by Cézanne.[8] Not only Vlaminck and Matisse, but all the other Fauves except for Kees van Dongen studied the painter's work.[9] As influential American critic Clement Greenberg observed, they "filled in what Cézanne . . . had outlined."[10] The Cézanne retrospective mounted in Paris in September 1907 was apparently a revelation for Georges Braque, Raoul Dufy, and Pablo Picasso as well.[11] The still lifes of André Derain, who stood in close contact with Vlaminck and shared a studio with him in Chatou in 1900–01,[12] also show parallels to Cézanne, and Derain repeatedly traveled to L'Estaque, where Cézanne had worked on multiple occasions.

Still life holds a position of fundamental importance in the art of the Fauves. It stands at the beginning of the work of Matisse and Derain, and the other Fauves, as well, explored the genre in depth.[13] The high value these artists attributed to still life as a pictorial type is associated with two specific role models: Jean Siméon Chardin and, not surprisingly, Paul Cézanne. Matisse's interest in Cézanne is of particular significance: between 1898 and 1900, he intensively studied the work of Cézanne and Chardin in addition to the color theory of Paul Signac.[14] The Cézanne retrospective at the second Salon d'Automne in 1904 also represented an important event for the Fauves' reception of Cézanne.

1
Maurice de Vlaminck, *Still Life with Books and Fruit Bowl,* 1906 (cat. 21)

2
Paul Cézanne, *Still Life with Fruit Dish,* 1879–80, Museum of Modern Art, New York

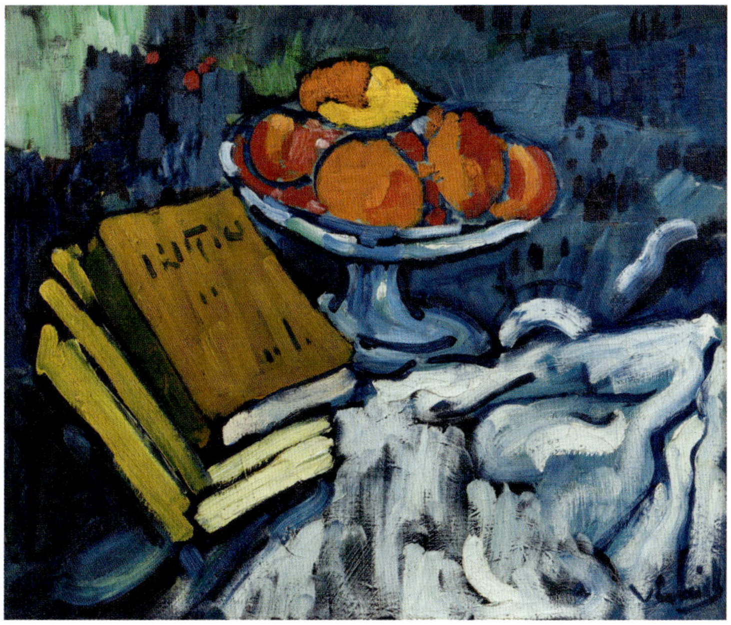

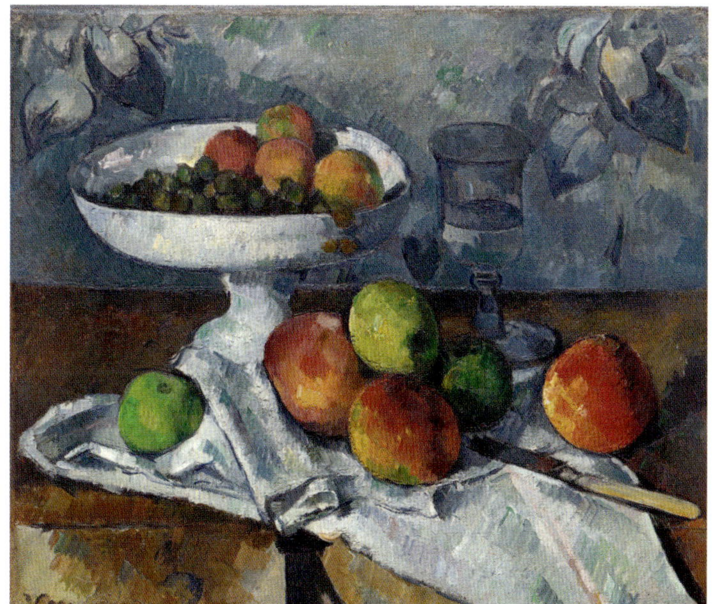

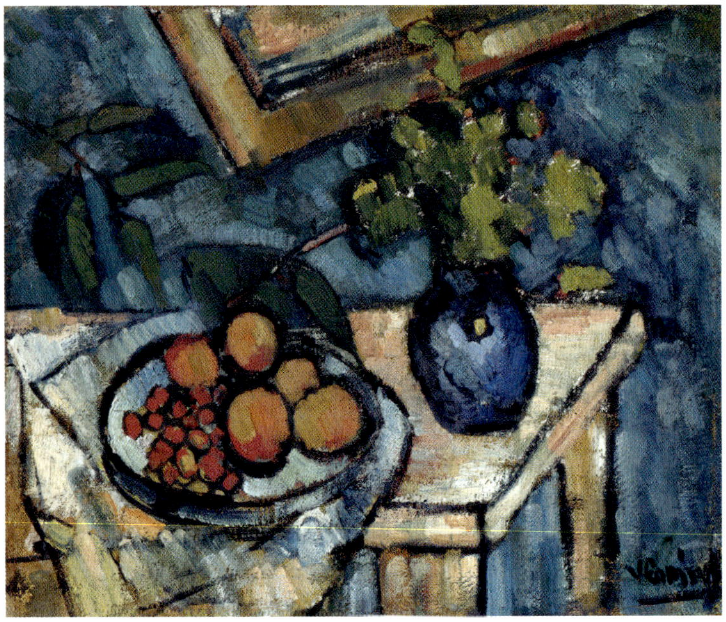

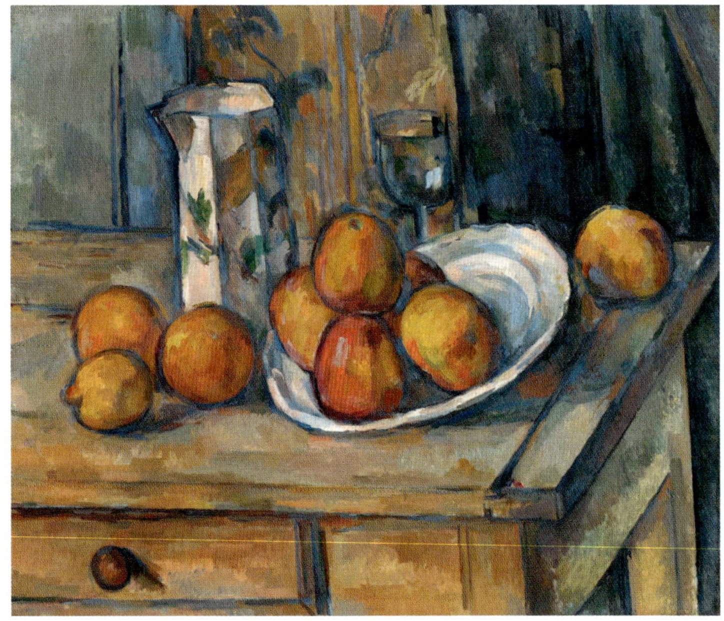

3
Maurice de Vlaminck,
Still Life, 1907
(cat. 65)

4
Paul Cézanne,
Still Life with Milk Jug and Fruit, ca. 1900,
National Gallery of Art,
Washington, DC

The Still Life as an Arena of Experimentation

Vlaminck produced only a limited number of still lifes during his Fauvist phase, which instead was dominated by landscapes, most of which included rivers. Nonetheless, he repeatedly returned to still life, a genre that more than any other is predestined for formal experimentation. Here he tested new spatial solutions and compositional approaches. During the dark winter months, he focused his attention on still lifes that, unlike his landscapes, were painted in the studio rather than *en plein air,* though admittedly it is difficult to determine the chronological order of the works created in the winters of 1905–06 and 1906–07.[15] The genre of still life plays a prominent role in Cézanne's oeuvre as well, encompassing around two hundred paintings and eighty watercolors.[16] As such, it reflects a general development of the nineteenth century, a period in which still life painting flourished.[17]

Vlaminck's painting *Still Life with Books and Fruit Bowl* (fig. 1) was probably created in the winter of 1906. The arrangement consists of a few objects viewed at close range: books are stacked next to a fruit bowl with a slightly raised foot; in front and to the side is a white tablecloth, which Vlaminck rendered in coarse, broad brushstrokes. The painting is predominantly blue, with bright yellow and red also used for the fruit. The objects are portrayed in a simple, abbreviated, almost symbolic manner; the composition acquires dynamism through the agitated and at times very rough brushwork. Vlaminck developed neither the three-dimensionality of the table, which is indicated by the tablecloth, nor the spatial context of the arrangement. There is no sense of illusionism: the artist worked the entire surface of the painting in a unified way, avoiding any impression whatsoever of depth and space. The stack of books at the left, with only the hint of a title visible on the top book, seems to tilt slightly forward, eliciting a feeling of perspectival disorientation. Compared to the artist's Fauvist landscapes, the most noticeable difference is the approach to space and pictorial depth. While in his landscapes Vlaminck still evoked spatial illusionism through methods such as the horizontal staggering of pictorial levels, the overlapping of objects, or the suggestion of perspective through paths leading from the foreground to the background, such devices are entirely absent here. The still life is oriented to the picture plane, an effect that is reinforced by the close-up view. In its refusal of illusionistic depth and space, Vlaminck's work also resembles contemporaneous compositions by Matisse.

While the still life by Vlaminck also finds striking parallels in Cézanne's *Still Life with Fruit Dish* (fig. 2), this is not to say that the latter work could have directly inspired Vlaminck's painting. Vlaminck did nevertheless employ formal means that are also observable with Cézanne. In this painting from 1879–80, Cézanne shows a white fruit bowl, also footed, standing on a dark table next to a glass. Atop a tablecloth arranged in folds in front of the bowl and glass lie several apples and a knife. This type of still life, in which the objects are shown in a close-up view and consist of a limited number of basic geometric forms, is characteristic of Cézanne's oeuvre and was further developed by Braque, Derain, and Picasso.[18] Vlaminck, too, can be included in this company. Another striking feature developed in Cézanne's still lifes that Vlaminck employed as well is the white tablecloth. This element, which has a long tradition in European still life painting, was reinterpreted by Cézanne.[19] He adopted the topos of the draped cloth not in order to emphasize the materiality, surface, or specific character of the fabric,[20] but as a means of accelerating or decelerating the rhythm of the pictorial structure and providing a neutral (white) foil for the objects.[21] Compared to the aforementioned painting by Cézanne, the repertoire of items in Vlaminck's *Still Life with Books and Fruit Bowl* is even more starkly reduced, with a focus on the painterly means. The broad, sweeping brushwork gives dynamism to the image, like the cloth in Cézanne's still life. Vlaminck, too, seems to have been concerned not with the material quality of the fabric, but with the materiality of the paint, which he emphasizes. In this sense, the cloth can be read as a reference to the canvas, that is, to the physical support on which the picture is painted. Thus for Vlaminck, the tablecloth serves not as a foil for the objects, but as a means of making the painter's practice the focus of the image.

The motif of the draped cloth is even more dominant in *Still Life with Fruit and Vase* (fig. p. 144). Here Vlaminck modeled the folds in blue; contrasting with the white, they appear almost sculptural and object-like as they tower up to the top edge of the picture. Rounded fruits lie amid the folds of the fabric. As with Cézanne, the cloth evokes an intriguing visual rhythm of rest and dynamism. Vlaminck used the paint to intensify this rhythmic effect, applying it not only in different hues, but also in energetic patches. In addition, the sculptural quality of the cloth calls attention to the surface by both distorting the illusionistic sense of space and emphasizing the picture plane. Although a dark blue stroke next to the vase at the far left suggests the edge of the table, the planes are inseparably connected with each other through the application of paint.

In *Still Life* (fig. 3) from 1907, Vlaminck adopted a different approach. Here, the objects—a bowl with fruit, a tablecloth, and a vase—are arranged on a wooden table positioned parallel to the picture plane. Against a blue background, a branch with dark green leaves juts into the scene from the left, while a wooden frame hanging at a slant is cut off by the top edge of the picture. The tablecloth, which does not cover the entire table but is gathered only around the fruit bowl, seems stiff and bulky; it appears not fabric-like, but flat and solid. Comparison with the two earlier still lifes by Vlaminck clearly shows the difference in the approach to space. Here, too, broad, rough brushstrokes uniformly cover the various surfaces of cloth, table, and background; yet Vlaminck uses the shape of the

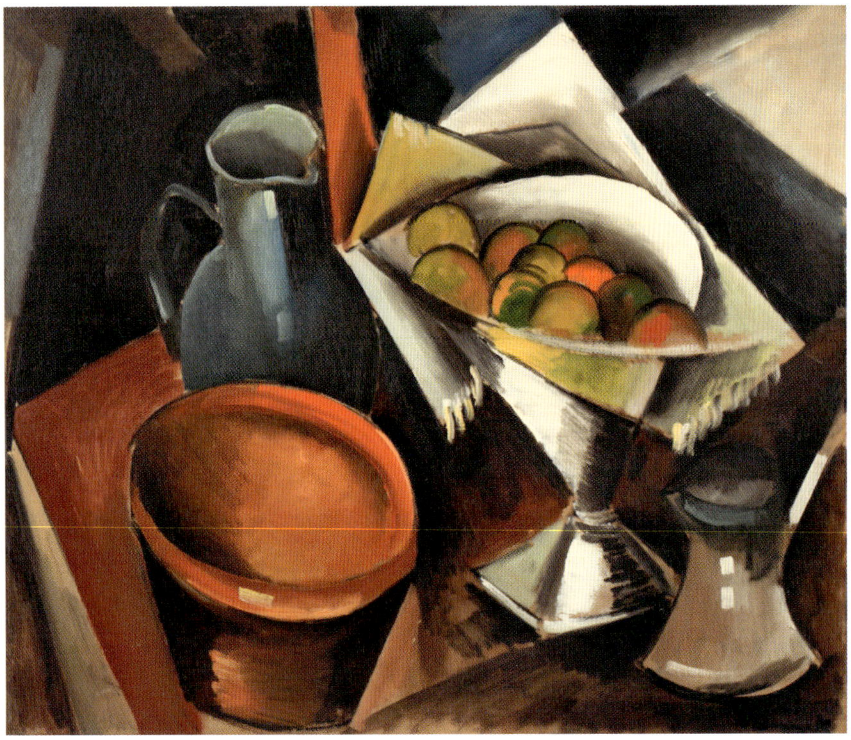

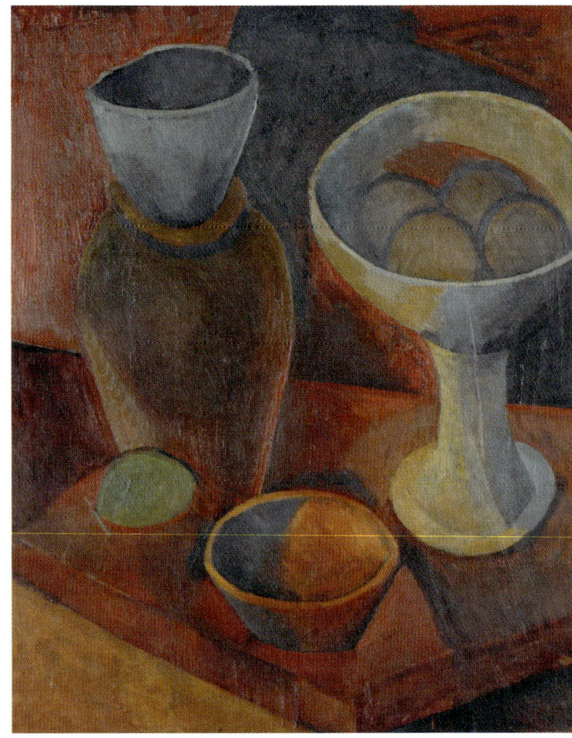

5
Maurice de Vlaminck,
Still Life, 1910–11
(cat. 68)

6
Pablo Picasso,
Still Life with Bowls and a Jug, 1908,
Philadelphia Museum of Art

table and the blue behind it to give this still life a clear sense of (surrounding) space. Once again, the composition is viewed from close up, and the demarcated space remains flat, with little recession in depth. The table defines the scale of the room. A similar approach characterizes Cézanne's *Still Life with Milk Jug and Fruit* (fig. 4), which also shows parallels to Vlaminck's work.[22] Here, too, Cézanne arranged his objects—this time without a tablecloth—on a wooden table running parallel to the edge of the picture. Behind the table, which fills the entire width of the painting, a curtain is discernable, its floral pattern echoed in the pitcher. Direct comparison of the two still lifes reveals that Vlaminck adopted a steeper view from above. In both images, the tables function as isolated surfaces that are depicted at close range and tightly cropped, without chairs. In the truest sense of the word, they constitute *tableaux* for the still lifes arranged on them, and in each case the depth of the table defines the depth of the space. Although in both paintings the tables are three-dimensional objects that suggest spatiality, the two scenes nonetheless remain confined to the surface—the surface of the table. The pictorial space is flat and remains essentially undefined.

The motif of the table in a close-up view recurs in various other paintings by Vlaminck, including the *Still Life* acquired by August von der Heydt for the Von der Heydt-Museum in 1911 at the Salon d'Automne in Paris (cat. 66). In this image, the table is much more stylized, and is indicated only by multiple thick red strokes. A diagonal line at the upper edge of the painting recalls the crooked picture frame from the *Still Life* from 1907. In the work of 1911, which is quite dark on the whole, Vlaminck arranged a number of vessels, each of which are quite thoroughly modeled. The artist also seems to have been interested in exploring three-dimensionality and lighting. The blue pitcher is a motivic revenant that first occurs in *The Fruit Bowl* of 1905 (private collection); yet as this *Still Life* demonstrates, by now Vlaminck had left Fauvist painting far behind.

Although Vlaminck later expressed derogatory sentiments toward Cubism, from 1908 on he nonetheless experimented with forms and means that can be described as Cubist.[23] This was also the moment when he moved beyond Fauvism once and for all. Vlaminck's artistic development thus paradigmatically exemplifies a tendency of that period that has also been described by Philip Hook, in which Fauvism yielded to the onset of Cubism.[24] No longer did artists use patches of pure, brilliant color to construct their landscapes, but instead embraced blocklike forms from which the intensity of Fauvist color had begun to fade.[25] According to Hook, this shift was initiated by Cézanne, or rather by the momentous rediscovery of his work after his death. Cubism, and with it the waning of Fauvist painting, would thus never have occurred without the influence of Cézanne.[26] As Brigitte Leal likewise observes, Cubist painting was shaped not only by "Primitivism," but also by "Cézanne's famous geometry lesson."[27] Moreover, as Ariane Coulondre notes with reference to Daniel-Henry Kahnweiler, even the term *Cubism* coined by Charles Morice reflected the collective admiration of artists for Cézanne, whom Picasso once glorified as his only true master.[28] Vlaminck's experimentation with cubistic, blocklike forms likewise echoes the Cubist works of Picasso and Braque. His interest in Cubist pictorial solutions is evident in *Still Life with Flowers and Fruit* of 1911 (cat. 67), where he once again turned to the motif of the table. It now appears in a distorted perspective, as if tilted upward, a palpable demonstration of the intensity with which Vlaminck explored the theme of space during these years. That he engaged in this practice in the context of still life rather than landscape is remarkable, and once again shows the importance of the genre as an arena of formal experimentation.

7
Maurice de Vlaminck,
Opium, ca. 1910
(cat. 64)

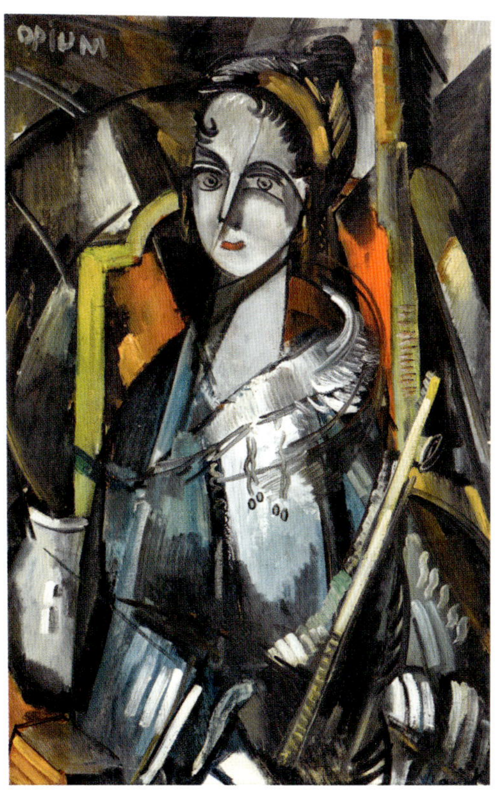

8
Pablo Picasso,
Nude in an Armchair, 1909,
Metropolitan Museum
of Art, New York

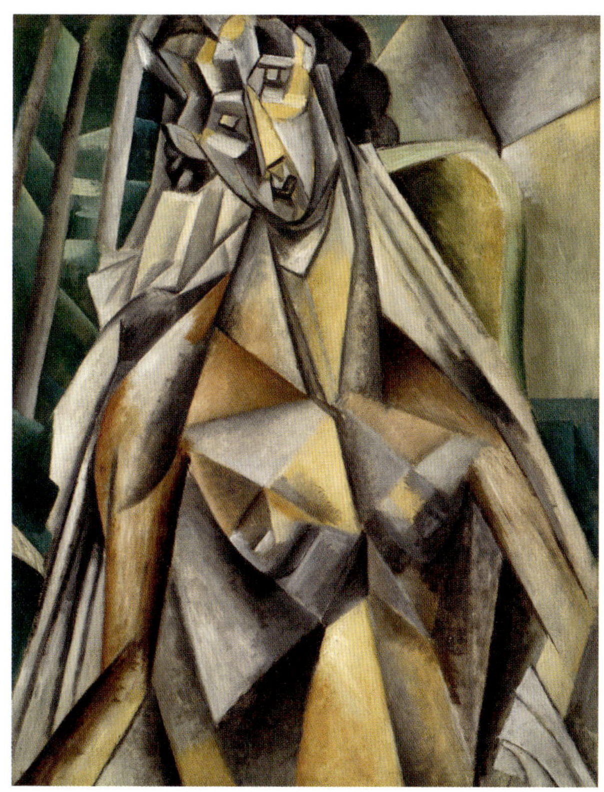

The cubistic forms are even more pronounced in the painting *Still Life* from 1910–11 (fig. 5). Now the angle of view is steeper, and the color palette, application of paint, and organization of forms are developed further. Yet the spatial means are the same: as already in the Cézannesque still lifes, here too there is an emphasis on the surface and a lack of spatiality. Vlaminck thus maintained the approach to spatial design he had learned from Cézanne, but varied the formal elements, which now resemble Cubism. Comparison with Picasso's early painting *Still Life with Bowls and a Jug* from 1908 (fig. 6) reveals a similar handling of both the pictorial space and the forms themselves, which are geometric and tapering. Vlaminck's application of paint has become smoother, in notable contradistinction to his Fauvist paintings. Whether it was specifically the work of Picasso that introduced Vlaminck to such forms during those years, however, is a question that cannot be unequivocally answered—the thesis articulated by Peter Geimer once again comes to mind. In any case, Picasso's Cubist paintings were little known and were not exhibited at the Salons.[29] Cubist elements also appear in works by Derain from 1910, indicating that a number of former Fauvists—not only Braque, but also Vlaminck and Derain—experimented with the new pictorial language. By 1911, as Hook observes, Fauvism had been eclipsed by Cubism.[30]

The painting *Opium* from ca. 1910 (fig. 7) is one of the most impressive examples of Vlaminck's exploration of Cubism and his only figural image in this style.[31] The approach to both figure and space and the interrelationship of these two elements show similarities to Picasso's works from the same years. Moreover, Vlaminck may also have been inspired by African masks, which were a subject of interest to the Fauves as well as to other contemporaries. In 1905 Vlaminck was the first of the Fauves to acquire a Fang mask from Gabon, which he later sold to Derain,[32] and Matisse purchased a similar mask in 1906. The object may have provided inspiration for Vlaminck's abstract-seeming painting *Red Nude* (fig. p. 186).[33] Like Vlaminck and Matisse, Picasso was also fascinated by African masks and drew artistic inspiration from them, as has been broadly discussed in reference to his Cubist works.[34]

Vlaminck's partly intuitive, partly direct emulation of Cézanne is manifested not only in his still lifes, but also in his post-Fauvist landscapes. The new forms and visual approaches rehearsed in his still life painting found entrance, in varied and adapted ways, into his preferred motif—as demonstrated, for example, by the painting *Landscape near Martigues* from 1913 (fig. 9). Vlaminck composed the scene of undulating horizontal planes articulated by thin black contour lines. The staggered effect evokes a feeling of spatial depth, which is reinforced by the horizon on the right and the small area of water beneath it. Examples of a similar pictorial construction occur in landscape paintings by Cézanne from the 1880s such as *On the Plain of Bellevue* (fig. 10). The cubic forms of the buildings in Cézanne's work are striking, and on the whole his forms and planes are more geometric than Vlaminck's. Once again, the color palette is similar. Now, however, Vlaminck applied the paint more thinly, in glazes, no longer using it as a three-dimensional formal element as previously in his Fauvist pictures. Despite the staggered structure of the composition, Cézanne's works seem planar; this emphasis on flatness is one of the significant artistic characteristics of his work, which was considered innovative already by his contemporaries. Greenberg later described it as a "vibration from front to back and back to front,"[35] while also noting that Cézanne simultaneously desired to "to give Impressionism a solid aspect."[36] Vlaminck, too, integrated the surface of the canvas into the composition of the motif as a fundamental component of the picture. This approach was already discernable in elements such as

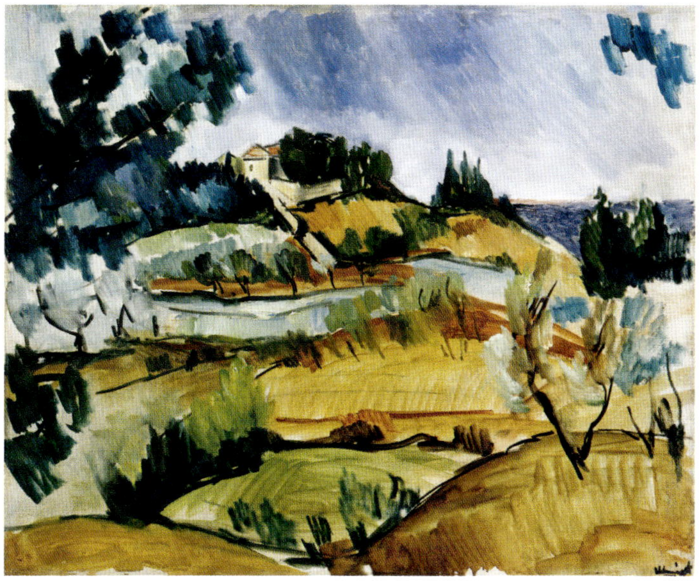

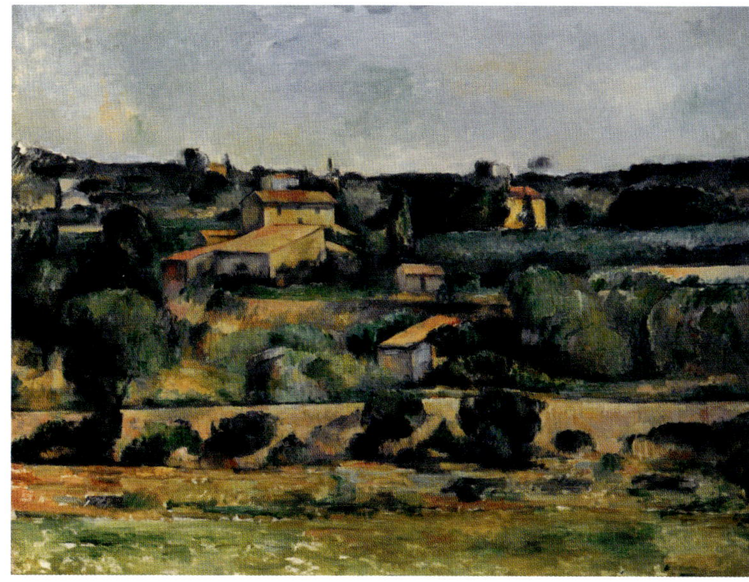

9
Maurice de Vlaminck,
Landscape near Martigues,
1913
(cat. 59)

10
Paul Cézanne,
On the Plain of Bellevue,
1885–88,
Wallraf-Richartz-Museum &
Fondation Corboud,
Cologne

the stiff tablecloths in his still lifes and now became an essential element in his landscapes of the 1910s. In contrast to the early Fauvist works, which were still inspired by Van Gogh, here the forms seem solidified and imbue the scenes with a sense of visual calm.

From 1906 on, the work of Vlaminck was marked by a shift, associated on the one hand with the waning of Fauvism and on the other with the rise of "Cézanne fever." The rediscovery of Cézanne after his death not only accelerated the decline of Fauvist painting, but also fueled the parallel advance of Cubism, which found a stylistic echo in Vlaminck's oeuvre from around 1908 to 1911. His artistic development thus reflects broader processes and changes that can be observed in the painting of those years. The role of Cézanne in Vlaminck's career is of particular importance: the work of Cézanne informed the handling of pictorial space, perspective, and surface that, hand in hand with changes in the approach to color and painting technique, characterized Vlaminck's post-Fauvist phase. The resulting formal kinships to Cézannesque cubes as well as to the Cubist and geometric forms of Picasso and Braque bespeak not only the parallelism of artistic developments, but also the artistic networks and the vital, adventurous avant-garde spirit of early-twentieth-century Paris.

Translated from German by Melissa M. Thorson

The Expressive Power of Pure Color

Vlaminck and Painting from the Tube

Matthias Krüger

"What is Fauvism? It is me; it was my style of that time,
my way of combined revolt and liberation,
my self-chosen alienation from schools or anyone else;
my blues, my red, my yellows,
my pure colors and unmixed tones."[1]

Vlaminck saw Fauvism as the translation of his anarchistic ideals into the realm of art. Radically rejecting all theoretical systems and ideologies, all tradition and authority, he equated Fauvism with absolute individual freedom; unconstrained by any method, he sought only to follow his instinct.[2] And so for Vlaminck—unlike his fellow Fauves—it was not a deficit, but rather an advantage to have never received professional artistic training. In his mind, it was this very thing that had preserved his primal, barbaric wildness. And for precisely the same reason, he claimed to embody Fauvism more purely than the other Fauve artists (from the French word *fauves,* meaning "wild beasts"), whose primal instincts had already been curbed to some extent by their academic training.[3] His own savagery, on the other hand, was still untamed and expressed itself in the "pure," unadulterated colors of his works.

In this context, the phrase "pure colors" ("couleurs pures") does not constitute a specialized term in color theory. For Vlaminck, "pure colors" were nothing other than colors "as they come from the tube" ("telles qu'elles sortent du tube")[4]—that is, paint that the artist neither thinned nor mixed with other hues after squeezing it out. Such pure colors from the tube are generally characterized by a high level of saturation and are especially intense in their effect. Not only did Vlaminck often work with unmixed, unthinned paint from the tube, he sometimes squeezed the tube directly onto the canvas.[5] Painting with unmixed colors from the tube, however, is not the same thing as painting with the tube: the former has to do with the color scheme of a painting, the latter with the application of the paint. Tube paints are the artist's material; the paint tube is his utensil, one that for Vlaminck served not only as a container, but also as a tool for applying the pigment to the canvas. Both of these features of his painting—the use of pure colors from the tube and the act of painting with the tube—were viewed already by contemporaries as primary hallmarks of Fauvist painting. This essay will investigate these two aspects in light of both the history of technique and the art-critical and art-theoretical discourse of Vlaminck's day. Particular attention will be paid to the question of the significance attributed to painting with colors straight from the tube, as well as to the use of the tube itself as an artist's implement.

Vlaminck was not the only artist of his time who experimented with pure color from the tube and at times applied the tube directly to the canvas. Both techniques were also practiced by a number of his contemporaries. In the first decade of the twentieth century alone—at the same time the Fauves were provoking such an uproar in France—the artists working in this way included German late Impressionists such as Lovis Corinth, Max Liebermann, and Max Slevogt as well as numerous Expressionists including Edvard Munch and painters Erich Heckel, Ernst Ludwig Kirchner, Emil Nolde, and Karl Schmidt-Rottluff from the artists' group Die Brücke. Yet this painterly approach had its precursors even in the nineteenth century. Vlaminck had adopted the precept of using colors "as they come from the tube" from Paul Gauguin, who allegedly taught it to his artist friends in Pont-Aven as early as 1888.[6] The mere fact that Gauguin spent his final years in the South Pacific with an indigenous population that at the time was still described as "savage" by Europeans must have made him seem a suitable forefather to Vlaminck, who was fond of posturing as a wild man and a barbarian. For the use of the tube as a painting implement, on the other hand, the role model was Vincent van Gogh—not only for Vlaminck, but also for Munch and the German Expressionists.[7]

But even if a number of other avant-garde artists were already painting with pure colors from the tube, such a practice was—if Vlaminck is to be believed—still controversial, even among his Fauvist comrades-in-arms. As he recounted in *Portraits avant décès* (Portraits before Death) of 1943, one of his autobiographical writings, André Derain advised him, "If you rely solely on the brilliance of the color coming out of the tube, you'll never get away from it. It's a dyers' theory! You'll never be able to have a redder red, a bluer blue, than those manufactured by the color merchant."[8] It is doubtful whether Derain actually said anything like this, since he himself frequently employed pure colors.[9] If Vlaminck put these words in his mouth, he probably did so in an effort to differentiate himself from his colleague, since by that time Derain's supposed assertion was probably already considered "academic." In the letters of Belgian artist Henri Evenepoel, for example, we learn that this view was espoused by Gustave Moreau, professor at the École des Beaux-Arts and teacher of a number of later Fauves. According to Evenepoel, Moreau preached to his pupils that the color in a painting should be "thought, dreamed, reflected, and imagined"—a quality he apparently missed in a study by Evenepoel, upbraiding him for having merely treated the canvas with dye.[10] Apparently, Evenepoel had not succeeded in transcending the materiality of the paint in the way that Moreau required.

Derain's alleged pronouncement in fact represents a school of thought that had developed already in the Renaissance in reaction to excessive colorism—at a time when pigment was stored not in tubes, but in boxes as powder. In the fifteenth century, the artistic excellence of a work had increasingly gained in importance over its material value.[11] By the mid-sixteenth century, the brilliance and purity of the colors—core values of medieval painting—were dismissed by art theorists as subordinate, not to say trivial qualities. As Paolo Pino explained in his *Dialogo di pittura* of 1548, for example, beauty (*vaghezza* in Italian) consisted neither in ultramarine blue for sixty scudi an ounce nor in a lovely colored lacquer; after all, such colors were as beautiful in the box in which they were stored as they were in the finished painting.[12] Similarly, Venetian artist Jacopo Tintoretto is said to have downplayed the importance of color: "He also said that beautiful colors were sold in the shops of the Rialto."[13]

In this conception, color could not be considered an achievement of the artist—unlike *disegno,* drawing, which was seated in the artistic *ingenium* and, as Tintoretto emphasized, could only be learned with great effort.

At that time, the market in the Campo di Rialto was the leading hub for the trade in dyes and pigments arriving in Europe from the Middle East through Venice. With the Industrial Revolution, however, fundamental changes in the production of colorants began to occur. By the early twentieth century, almost all colors were synthetically manufactured: what was formerly a costly import had now become a relatively cheap product of the chemical industry. Moreover, in contrast to the nineteenth century, when paint was often mixed and filled into tubes by local druggists, its production now passed into the hands of large companies such as Winsor & Newton in Great Britain, Schmincke in Germany, and Lefranc, Bourgeois, Sennelier, and Blockx in France.[14]

This radical transformation in the production of paint gives a new twist to Derain's criticism of Vlaminck's use of pure color from the tube, one that sets it apart from any Renaissance censure of overly splendid color. Unlike the pigments acquired by Venetian Renaissance painters in the Campo di Rialto, which still had to undergo elaborate procedures to make them usable for artists, tube paints were an industrially manufactured product. They were, in fact, *readymade,* a term that at the same time invokes a category invented by Marcel Duchamp. For Duchamp, readymades were objects, usually industrially manufactured, that were appropriated by an artist—either as is, or at the most with minimal alteration—and designated as a work of art, simply and without further ado. As Duchamp explained in a 1961 lecture at the Museum of Modern Art in New York, paintings created with tube paints should also be considered readymades[15]—a bold thesis that he reiterated in a 1967 interview: "A readymade is a work of art without an artist to make it, if I may simplify the definition. A tube of paint that an artist uses is not made by the artist; it is made by the manufacturer that makes paints. So the painter really is making a readymade when he paints with a manufactured object that is called paints."[16]

Duchamp's assertion can be understood as provocatively reductive. As a rule, tube paint serves merely as the raw material that the artist already transforms on the palette by mixing the colors together. Only when such mixing does not occur does it seem justified to call, if not the work of art as such, then at least the paint, a "readymade" obtained from the tube. In the 1960s it was considered a virtue for painting to expose its own materiality, at least in avant-garde circles. Only a year before Duchamp declared paintings made with tube colors to be readymades, American art critic Clement Greenberg argued for a development within modern painting in which increasing emphasis was placed on the material qualities of the work. In his influential essay "Modernist Painting," Greenberg described it as a historical achievement of the Impressionists to have been the first to reject "underpainting and glazes, to leave the eye under no doubt as to the fact that the colors they used were made of paint that came from tubes or pots."[17] In fact, however, there is little to suggest that the artists of Impressionism pursued such a goal. Rather, it seems far more justified to credit Vlaminck and the Fauves with this achievement when they embraced the maxim of painting with colors "as they come from the tube."

This programmatic aim, at least, makes them the precursors of a conception of art that was propounded in the 1960s in New York not only by art theorists, but also by avant-garde artists such as Frank Stella, a painter associated with Minimalism. In a 1964 interview, Stella explained: "I wanted to get the paint out of the can and onto the canvas. . . . I tried to keep the paint as good as it was in the can."[18] As obvious as these parallels to Vlaminck's fondness for pure color from the tube may be, the differences in the painterly approach are equally evident. While Stella strove to avoid any hint of expression by applying the paint as evenly as possible, Vlaminck's unmixed tube color served precisely to heighten the expressive content of his paintings. Ultimately, he even saw tube paints as placing limits on his power of expression; as he acknowledged in *Dangerous Corner,* "I worried because, confined to the blue and red of color merchants, I was not able to be more forceful, and I had reached a maximum degree of intensity."[19]

The Ostentatious Autodidact

Art historians have repeatedly emphasized the importance of the invention of tube paint in 1841 for the development of plein-air painting.[20] Attention is seldom paid, however, to the fact that the availability of paint in tubes also made painting accessible as a hobby to broader echelons of society.[21] Not only did tubes make it easier to store paint: they also made the activity of painting a clean and nearly odorless affair, significantly elevating its attractiveness for laypersons. For as a handbook on painting published in 1877 observed, ordinary people did not like to concern themselves with the "tedious, sometimes dangerous, and often very dirty procedures" required to mix paint.[22] The availability of readymade paint in tubes gave amateurs easier access to painting: rather than slaving away with lengthy preparations, they now needed only apply gentle pressure to a tube with their fingers in order to garnish their palette with color and begin painting. Often, substances were even added to the tubes with the sole intent of giving the paint a more homogeneous, supple consistency. As a color merchant noted with consternation, for his clientele—in which amateur painters increasingly wielded more influence than professional artists—the ease with which the paint could be squeezed out of the tube was often more important than the quality of the paint itself.[23]

Detail from cat. 37

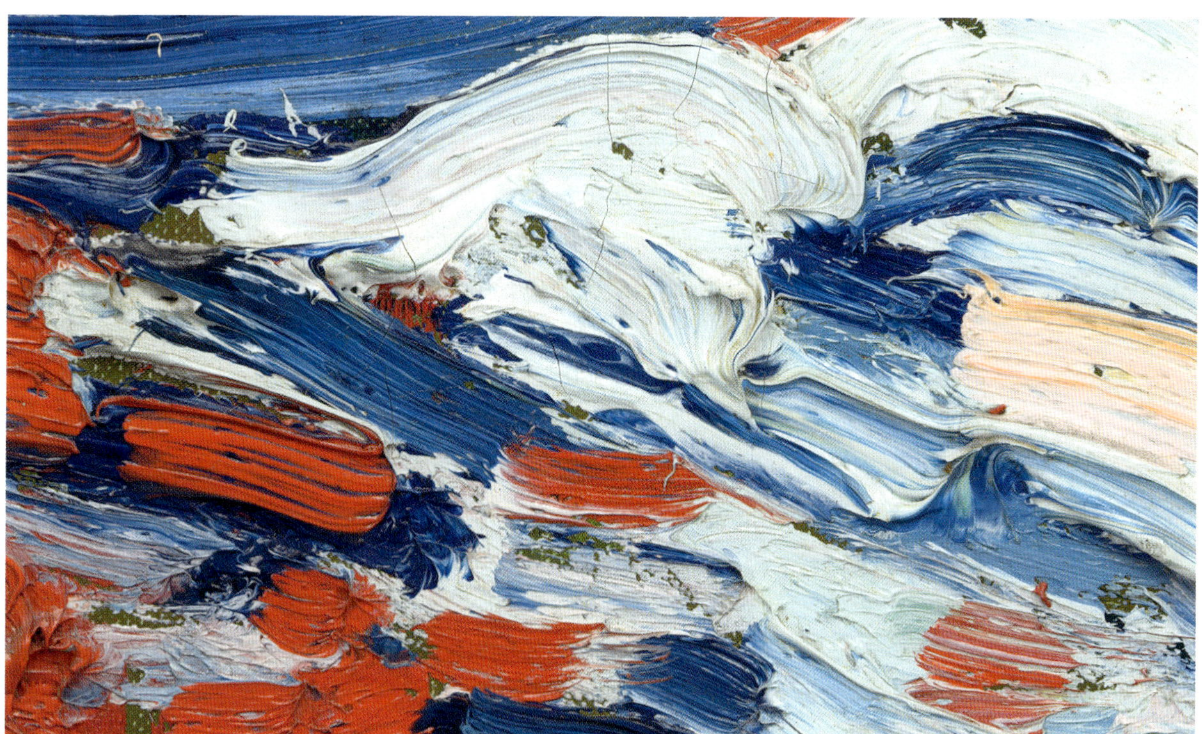

Naturally a host of amateur painters of both sexes had existed before this point, but for the most part they had opted for the more easily practicable medium of watercolor. Paint in tubes now made it easier to work as autodidacts in the more prestigious medium of oils. Like Paul Gauguin, Vlaminck spent years pursuing painting as a leisure activity before deciding to make it his profession; he was, so to speak, a career jumper. To describe Vlaminck as an autodidact, however, is not to say that his knowledge of painting was acquired entirely on his own. Ever since the major school reform of 1881 in France, instruction in drawing and modeling had been an established part of the educational curriculum; furthermore, Vlaminck had also received private instruction in drawing and painting from artist Jules Robichon in 1893. In this context, therefore, the term *autodidact* simply means that unlike his fellow Fauves, Vlaminck had not enjoyed professional training as a fine artist. There are a variety of reasons why, in the late nineteenth and early twentieth centuries, it became increasingly possible for independent artists to establish themselves without having studied at an art school or academy; certainly, however, the availability of tube paint was one of the technical prerequisites.

Not only did Vlaminck repeatedly emphasize his status as autodidact in his autobiographical writings; he also made it the program of his painting. It is precisely in this context that his use of unmixed tube paints as well as his practice of painting with the tube should be viewed. He himself asserted that the use of pure tube colors served him as a weapon against academic doctrine: as he later wrote, he wanted to "burn down the École des Beaux-Arts" with his "cobalts and vermilions."[24] And in fact the Fauves seem to have had no problem using paint as a readymade, ostentatiously presenting it as a manufactured product from the tube. In so doing, they also sacrificed a number of venerable and longstanding principles of European painting. In the first place, the limiting of the palette to hues that were prefilled in tubes and purchased at the color shop signaled a break from the ideal of the precise imitation of nature. Artists who refused to mix their paint robbed

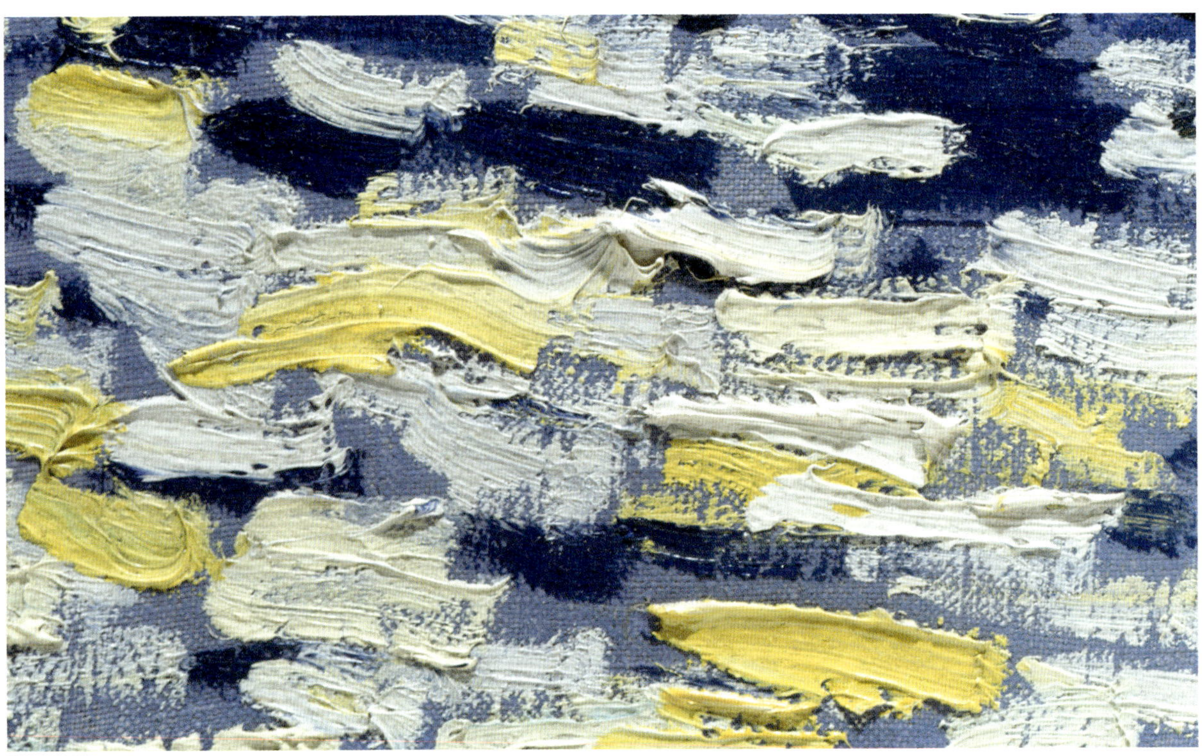

Detail from cat. 51

themselves of the ability to attune the colors on their palette as closely as possible to those observed in nature. Furthermore, the Fauves showed no interest in the illusion of depth and space, whether through linear perspective or through atmospheric perspective, achieved through the gradation of color in different pictorial zones. They also abandoned chiaroscuro, the contrast of light and dark, and with it the ability to model in three dimensions through lighter and darker shades of color. And since the consistency of unmixed tube paint meant that it could only be applied impasto, painting with colors "as they come from the tube" also meant a rejection of glazing.

Thus it comes as no surprise that art criticism would take exception to the Fauves' nonobservance of fundamental principles of painting. The critics interpreted this deficit, however, not as a voluntary choice on the part of the painters, but as evidence of a lack of skill. The artists' alleged nonmastery of even elementary techniques of drawing and painting also provoked comparison with the art of children: in reviews of the Salon d'Automne in 1905, the paintings of those artists who would later become known as Fauves were reviled as "childish scrawls."[25] Marcel Nicolle fell into the same vein when he described the Fauvist works as a "formless confusion of colors; blue, red, yellow, green; some splotches of pigment crudely juxtaposed; the barbaric and naïve sport of a child who plays with the box of colors he just got as a Christmas present."[26] As polemical as such criticism may be, it nonetheless operated with a series of terms used by the Fauves to characterize themselves and their art: Vlaminck described himself as an instinct-driven "barbarian," while Matisse emphasized even into old age how important it was for artists to maintain a childlike naiveté.[27]

From Ex-pressing to Expression

What Nicolle and other critics failed to recognize was that the Fauves were not the least bit interested in the faithful imitation of nature. Rather, in their works they sought to give expression to the feelings they experienced in front of the motif—a significant step in the direction of an Expressionist conception of art. As discussed earlier, Vlaminck claimed it was only possible to achieve this aim by relying solely upon instinct. In his view, acquired knowledge or learned techniques were not only useless, but downright counterproductive, since they hindered the free play of instinct.

With the rejection of the simulation of nature and the turn toward expressive painting, the function of color changed as well: its purpose was now no longer to *imitate,* but to *express.* The intensity of the color was directly proportionate to the feeling to be conveyed: the more intense the color, the greater the expressive power. This equation was why the Fauves insisted upon pure, unmixed colors from the tube. But the manner in which the paint was applied also stood in the service of expression. Vlaminck primarily used broad bristle brushes; the impasto color, seemingly applied in rapid, spontaneous strokes, gives his paintings an often agitated, relief-like surface—a quality that in the Expressionist period was generally considered a manifestation of the artist's inner turmoil. It is in this context that the squeezing of the tube directly onto the canvas should also be viewed.

When Nicolle accused the Fauves of not deploying the paint box in an appropriately professional way, his criticism was justified, at least with respect to the use of the paint tube. Like the Brücke artists, Vlaminck violated its actual function as a container and often squeezed the paint directly onto the canvas. This improper use of the tube also manifested itself in the way in which the color was extracted from it: for according to contemporaneous descriptions, at least, the action was frequently performed not through gentle pressure with the fingers, but by wantonly squashing the paint from the tube—often in excessive amounts, at times even emptying it onto the canvas in its entirety.[28] This behavior was imagined and described as an act of violence not only by critics, but by the artists themselves. Georges Rouault, one of the painters christened *fauves* by the critics in 1905, is alleged to have said of squeezed-out paint tubes, "I assassinate them."[29] Vlaminck, too, described his own approach to the painting materials during his Fauvist years as violent, ruthless, and wasteful: "I was a tender barbarian, filled with violence. I translated what I saw instinctively, without any method, and conveyed truth, not so much artistically as humanely. I squeezed and ruined tubes of aquamarine and vermilion which, incidentally, cost quite a lot of money at the paint shop at the Pont de Chatou where I used to be given credit."[30]

The squashing of the tube onto the canvas may be considered the trademark of the autodidact who, ignorant of the rules and conventions of the profession, sets to work with little knowledge, but all the more freedom. In this context, it seems no coincidence that the Brücke artists, of whom none but Max Pechstein ever studied at an art academy, also often applied the paint directly from the tube. In the reception of Van Gogh—the great role model not only of Vlaminck, but also of the Brücke artists—painting with the tube was likewise associated with a lack of artistic training. A review of a 1904 Van Gogh retrospective in Groningen, for example, mentions "barbaric streams of color," "squeezed from the tube with feverish fingers, without method, without manner, and in complete disregard for the 'chemistry of painting.'"[31] Similarly, in a text published in 1910, art historian Werner Weisbach attributed Van Gogh's tube painting to his lack of training, which forced him to invent a painting technique entirely his own: "For the tallest protrusions," he writes, Van Gogh "sometimes squeezed the tubes onto the canvas. He never learned to paint in a systematic way. And he is proud of the fact that as an autodidact, he was able to create an entirely independent method for himself."[32]

Vlaminck turned this into a requirement: unlike the craftsman who learns his trade from a master, in Vlaminck's view every artist should develop his own technique—for only in this way could he express his individuality in his works.[33] Such expression, however, should not be equated with the ex-pressing of a tube—a confusion to which German gallerist and art critic Herwarth Walden ironically alluded in 1917. When the magazine *Das neue Deutschland* claimed to be able to identify a transition from Impressionism to Expressionism in recent works by Max Liebermann, Walden printed a response in his own magazine, *Der Sturm.* According to Walden, the new quality in Liebermann's paintings was attributable solely to "a copious pressing out [*Ausdrücken* in German] of paint tubes." Full of scorn, he added, "Dear man [*Lieber Mann* in German] from *Das neue Deutschland:* pressing out [*Ausdrücken*] is not expression [*Ausdruck*]."[34] Though Walden may have had a point, it still seems to be anything but a coincidence that painting with the tube enjoyed such tremendous popularity among both the Fauves and the Expressionists—in other words, two artistic currents committed to expressive painting. Ultimately, the greatest power of expression was attributed to the paint as it came out of the tube; yet the furious squeezing of the tube itself was also a direct reflection of the artistic will to expression.

The Impressionists had already been compelled to paint rapidly in order to capture the fleeting impressions of nature on their canvases.[35] If descriptions of the creative act of Expressionist artists are to be believed, the latter were subject to even more powerful urges.

Driven by wild instinct, consumed by an irrepressible passion that could seize them without warning, they were forced quite literally to "put the squeeze on." For Gerarda Hermina Marius, such was the case with Van Gogh; in her treatise on nineteenth-century Dutch painting, first published in 1903, she wrote: "The well-considered mixing of paint on the palette seemed to him too long a journey. . . . In full creative passion he flung the unmixed paint onto the canvas in commas, dashes, or dots . . . sometimes straight from the tube."[36] Similarly, in an essay published in 1908 in *Velhagen und Klasings Monatshefte,* Max Osborn asserted that Van Gogh "often allowed the paint to flow directly from the tube onto the canvas, without the mediation of the brush, which was too time-consuming for him. For his painting now becomes ever more agitated, more rapid, more devouring."[37] And in his 1910 novella "Nimführ und Willenius," Jakob Wassermann writes of an artist named Willenius, who is modeled so closely on Van Gogh that in the end he too cuts off his ear: "Willenius didn't paint his pictures, he flung them out of himself. . . . Often he did not take time to put the colors on the palette, but let them flow directly from the tube onto the canvas, for fear that the vitality of his inner vision would become clouded before he had obtained the hue that he saw and felt."[38]

Such notions were also propagated by Vlaminck and his milieu, among others by Ambroise Vollard, one of the painter's most important supporters. When Vollard encountered Vlaminck for the first time, the artist was carrying a large painting under his arm: "As far as I remember, the picture in question represented a sunset which appeared to have been squeezed out of tubes of paint in a fit of rage."[39] In this interpretation, Vlaminck's wild, creative frenzy found a suitable release in the "ex-pressing" of the paint tube. Although such descriptions are probably closer to imagination than reality, they nonetheless demonstrate the programmatic significance attributed by the Fauves to painting from the tube.

Translated from German by Melissa M. Thorson

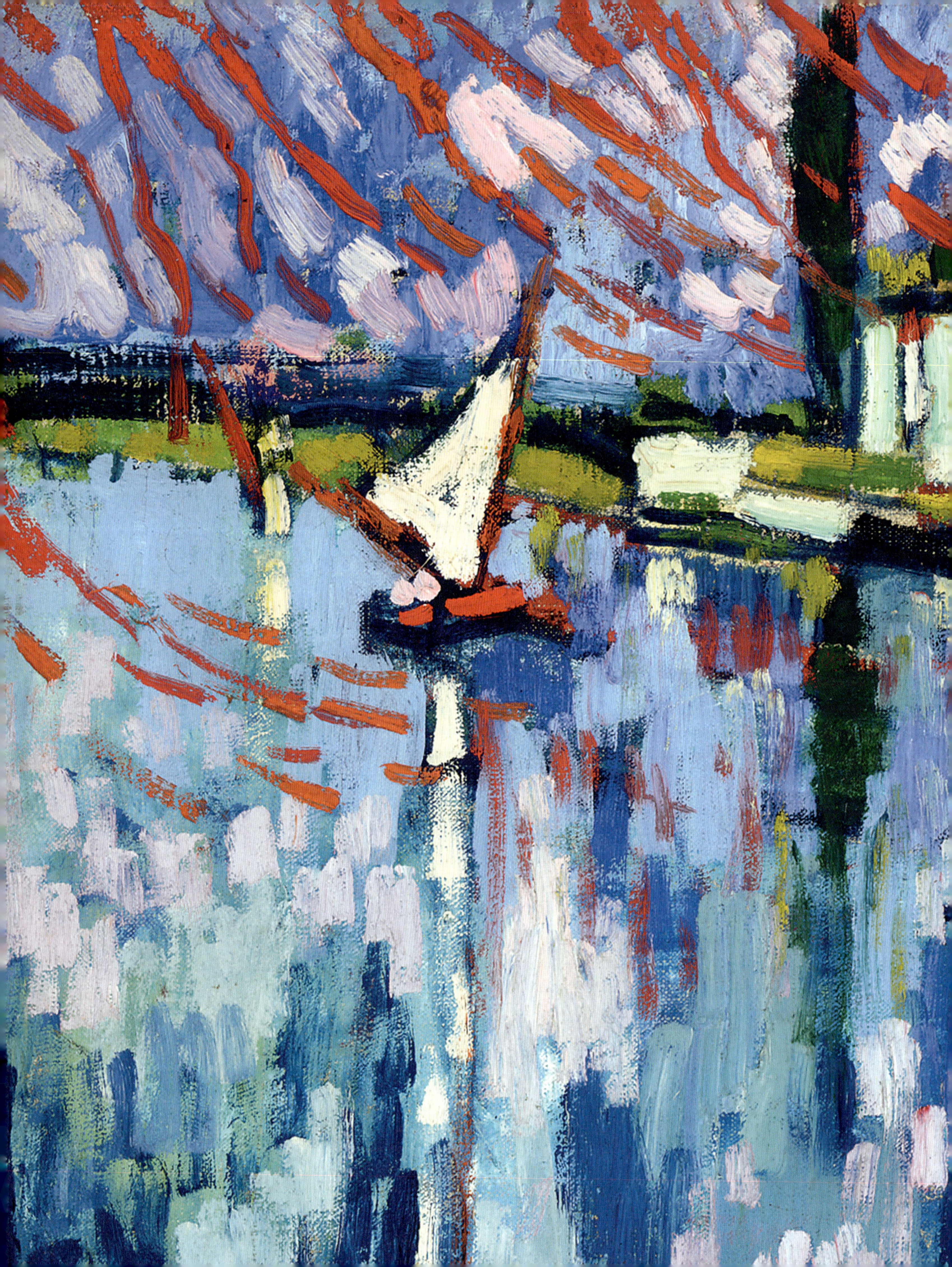

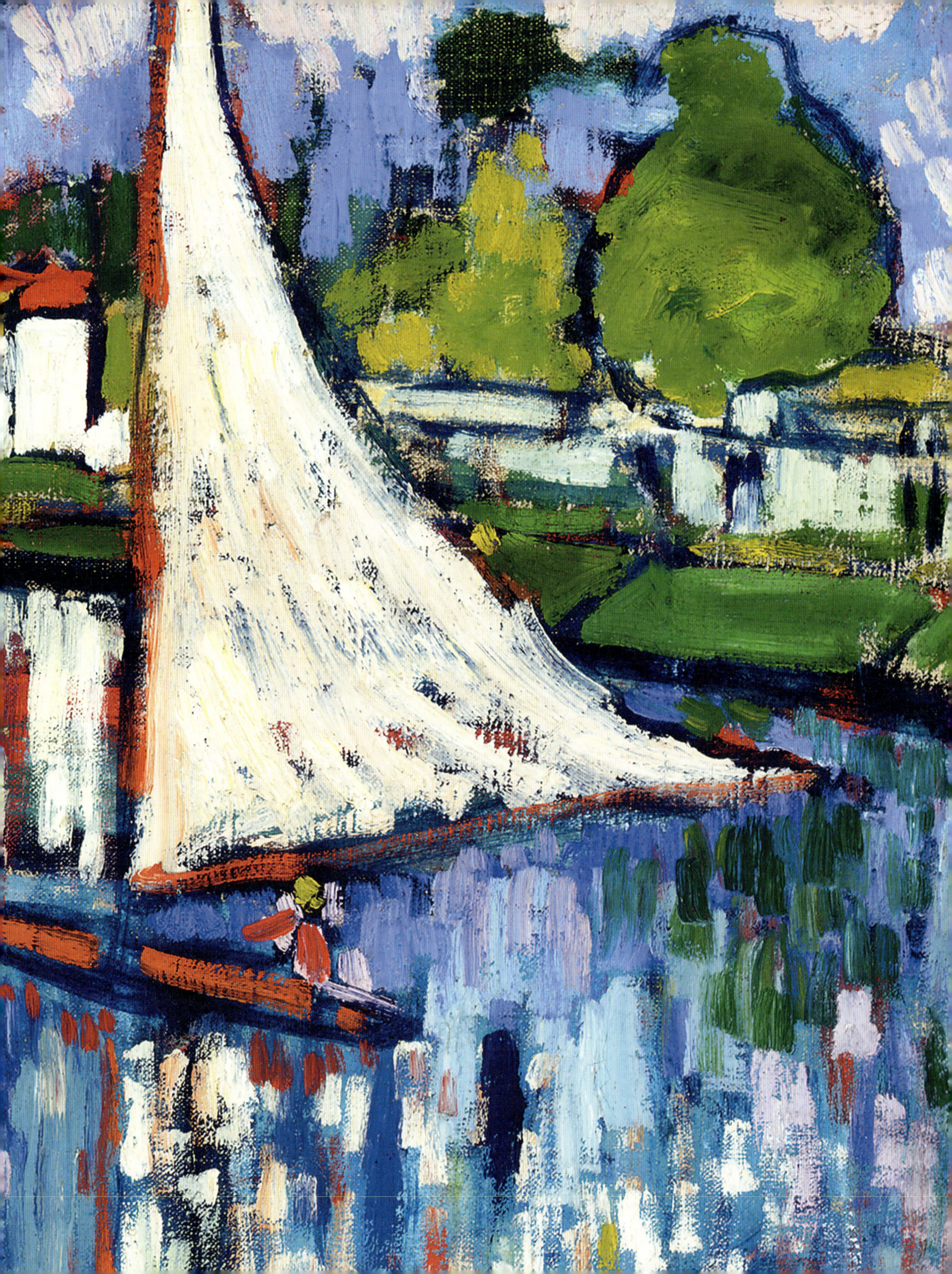

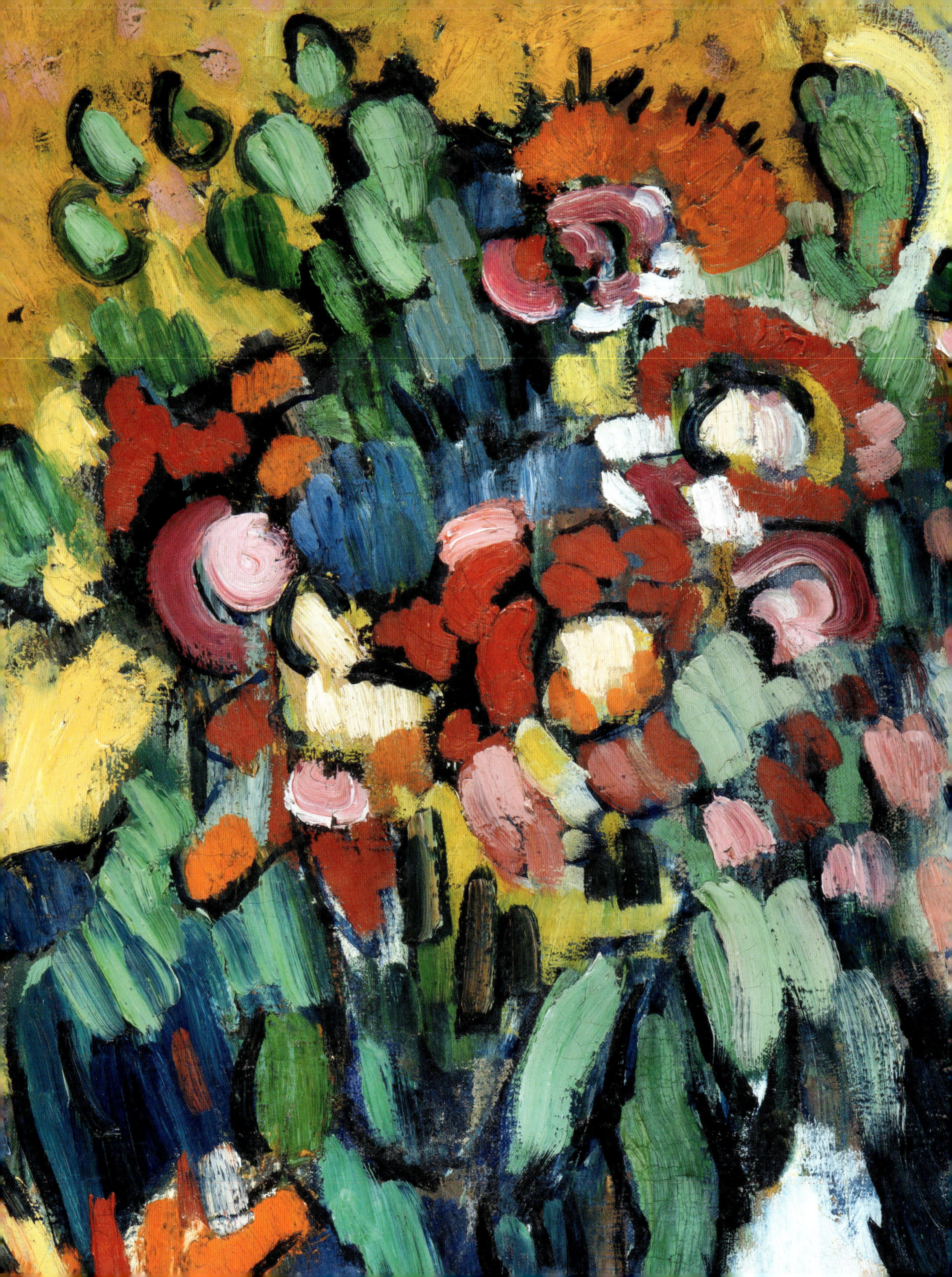

Intoxicated with Color — Fauvist Painting

Sterre Barentsen

In 1905 numerous works by aspiring artists such as André Derain, Henri Matisse, and Maurice de Vlaminck were shown together for the first time in one room at the Salon d'Automne in Paris. Critic Louis Vauxcelles was so shocked by the brash color of the paintings that he described their creators as "wild beasts" (*fauves*).[1] Although they were not an artists' group in the strict sense, the term *Fauvism* stuck and is now used to refer to the work produced by this loose collective between about 1904 and 1908—a phase that represented a decisive transition from late Impressionism to Expressionism. The painting of Fauvism is characterized by the use of pure, brilliant colors, often in pronounced tonal contrasts, as well as the absence of perspective or illusionistic space. Many of the compositions also show energetic brushwork and strongly textured surfaces. For Maurice de Vlaminck, who came to painting as an autodidact, Fauvism was both the most important and the most productive phase of his oeuvre. The years 1905 and 1906, in particular, were marked by an extraordinary creative energy that determinatively influenced the establishment of Fauvism as a new, trendsetting avant-garde movement.

Vlaminck was represented with five works at the Salon d'Automne of 1905. In these emphatically anti-academic compositions, he turned his back on the accurate, detailed rendering of nature in favor of an expressive pictorial effect. Both the free brushwork and exaggerated color scheme show the influence of Vincent van Gogh, whose art Vlaminck had encountered in 1901 at a retrospective at Galerie Bernheim-Jeune in Paris. In the painting *Twilight* (cat. 7), the garish yellow of a field in the background contrasts with the deep black of the two trees before it. Their bulky forms are coarsely modeled in multiple layers of paint, giving them a tactile quality that evokes the texture of the thick, rough bark. Behind them, the sky is freely rendered in energetic, clearly visible strokes of blue and white, while isolated accents of bright red lend freshness and dynamism to the dark, shadowed foreground. Like two other works from around the same time, *Park in Carrières-Saint-Denis* (cat. 8) and *My Father's House* (fig. p. 27), the painting deviates from the academic ideal of a finished, finely detailed surface. The agitated brushwork and impasto application of paint emphasize the expressive power of color as an autonomous aesthetic value.

Most of Vlaminck's Fauvist paintings show landscapes from the region around Chatou, a village on the Seine that is now a suburb of Paris. For a time, Vlaminck shared a studio in

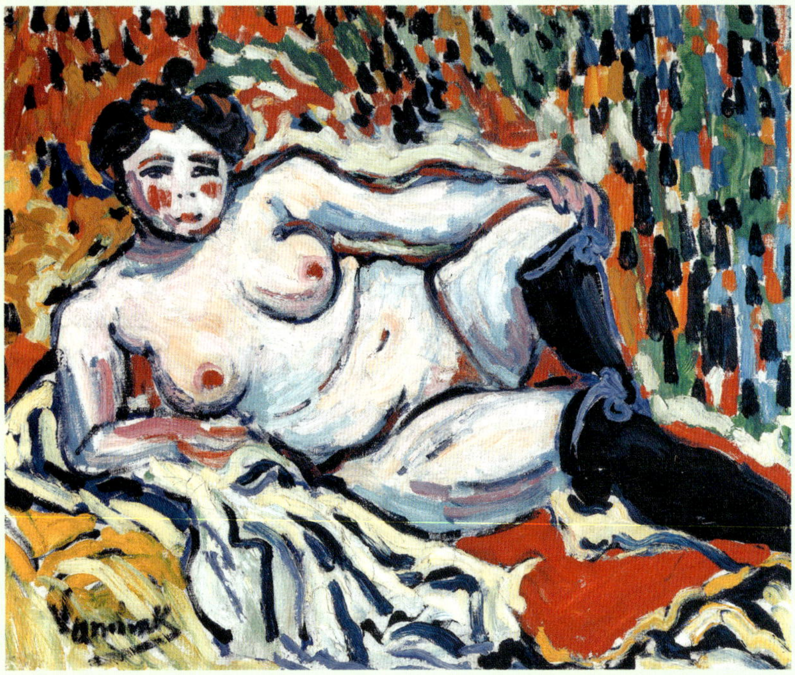

Maurice de Vlaminck,
Nude with Black Stockings, 1905,
private collection

Chatou with Derain, with whom he enjoyed a lively exchange during the early days of Fauvism. In *Houses at Chatou* (cat. 31), Vlaminck shows a field of luxuriant vegetable gardens as an abstract tangle of pure, brilliant colors, a horizontal web filling the lower two thirds of the composition. Above it is a row of houses, schematically rendered in white, blue, and red. Three graceful tree trunks serve as connecting elements, their vertical, upward thrust articulating the composition and giving it a sense of rhythm. Discernable between the two trees on the right is the figure of a gardener, working the fertile soil in solitary labor. As in many of Vlaminck's landscape pictures, the figure, suggested with only a few brushstrokes, is peacefully integrated into the surrounding scenery—a symbolic cipher for the harmony of man and nature.

While Vlaminck remained in Chatou during the summer of 1905, Derain traveled to the French Riviera together with Matisse. There, in the glittering light of the South, he created several sun-drenched landscapes, setting pure, unmixed colors against the white of the canvas. In *Mountains at Collioure* (1905, National Gallery of Art, Washington, DC), the individual slopes are rendered as broad areas of orange, red, and blue, while the lime green of the summer sky finds an echo in the color of the dense growth of trees in the middle ground. Probably that same year, Vlaminck painted a view of the Seine village of *Bougival* (cat. 17) with a similar composition, in which the carmine and vermilion of the foreground vegetation effectively contrast with the cobalt and navy blue of the sky and river. Although Vlaminck took the motifs for his Fauvist landscape paintings exclusively from the region of the Seine Valley and in so doing limited himself to the cooler light of the North, the exuberant color of his images is remarkably akin to the brilliant hues of Derain's and Matisse's views of the French Riviera. In his painting *Underbrush* (cat. 36), Vlaminck shows a sun-drenched patch of forest as a mosaic of daubs of pure color—probably a reaction to *Luxury, Calm, and Voluptuousness* (fig. p. 36), a major early work by Matisse that was exhibited for the first time at the Salon des Indépendants in 1905.

Unlike many of his fellow artists, Vlaminck never lived in the French capital and rarely depicted urban subjects. An important exception is a group of paintings from 1905 in which he focused his attention on the Paris nightclub Le Rat mort (cat. 18; figs. pp. 32, 70) in the entertainment district of Montmartre. Vlaminck was a regular at the caberet and created several images of the actresses there, who often also worked as prostitutes. In the portraits, the poses of the models oscillate between cool composure and lascivious display. In their brash, expressive application of paint, the compositions echo Vlaminck's figural works from around 1900, *On the Counter* (cat. 3) and *Portrait of Père Bouju* (cat. 1). But while his early portraits were executed in darker colors, the nudes and images of women from his Fauvist phase are distinguished by brighter hues and glowing tonality. The sometimes garishly exaggerated faces of the women often serve as eye-catching focal points in the composition. In *Reclining Nude* (cat. 20), the striking green eye shadow as well as the saturated red of the cheeks and lips stand out prominently against the thick white makeup. Makeup was commonly worn by women of all social classes in early-twentieth-century France, but its excessive use was considered offensive and vulgar.[2] In his images of the Parisian demimonde, Vlaminck rejected any element of idealization whatsoever; the garish colors, often hulking bodies, and thickly applied, grotesque-seeming makeup appear as an intentional violation of bourgeois *bon goût,* or good taste.

In addition to landscapes and figural images, Vlaminck also explored still life painting during his Fauvist period. Like the Impressionists and Postimpressionists before him, he used the genre as his preferred vehicle for experimentation with form, color, and spatial structure. In *Blue Vase with Flowers* (cat. 27) from around 1906, Vlaminck placed the red, orange, and green of a luxuriant bouquet against a yellow background in a play of tonal contrasts similar to that seen in his landscape pictures. In the painting *Blue Still Life* (cat. 22) from around 1907, on the other hand, the artist confined himself to a largely monochromatic palette. The dish of oranges in the center and the lemon lying next to it offer the only color contrast to the dominant blue and white, modeled in finely nuanced gradations. Rather than hanging downward, the left-hand corner of the tablecloth seems to ascend, a device that cloaks the entire canvas in blue, while the still life itself appears strangely compact and perspectivally distorted. A similarly sophisticated play of spatial perception informs the composition *The Table (Still Life with Almonds)* (cat. 25), in which the viewer's eye is led horizontally through the picture along clearly defined paths rather than into illusionistic depth. These carefully considered, spatially complex works already bear witness to Vlaminck's interest in the legacy of Paul Cézanne, whose flat, abstracted pictorial language would prove a definitive source of inspiration for Vlaminck's post-Fauvist career.[3]

Translated from German by Melissa M. Thorson

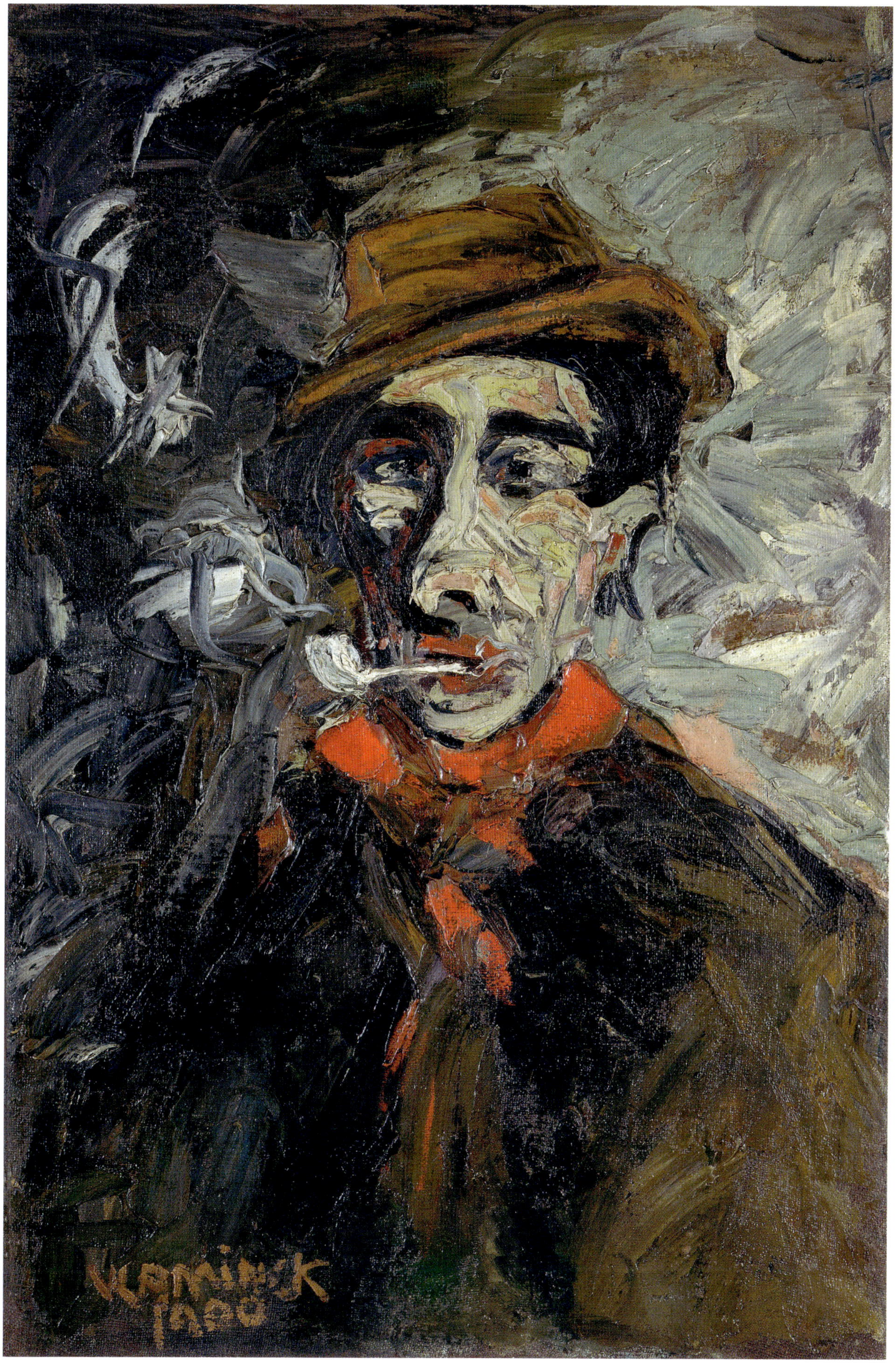

1
Portrait of Père Bouju, 1900

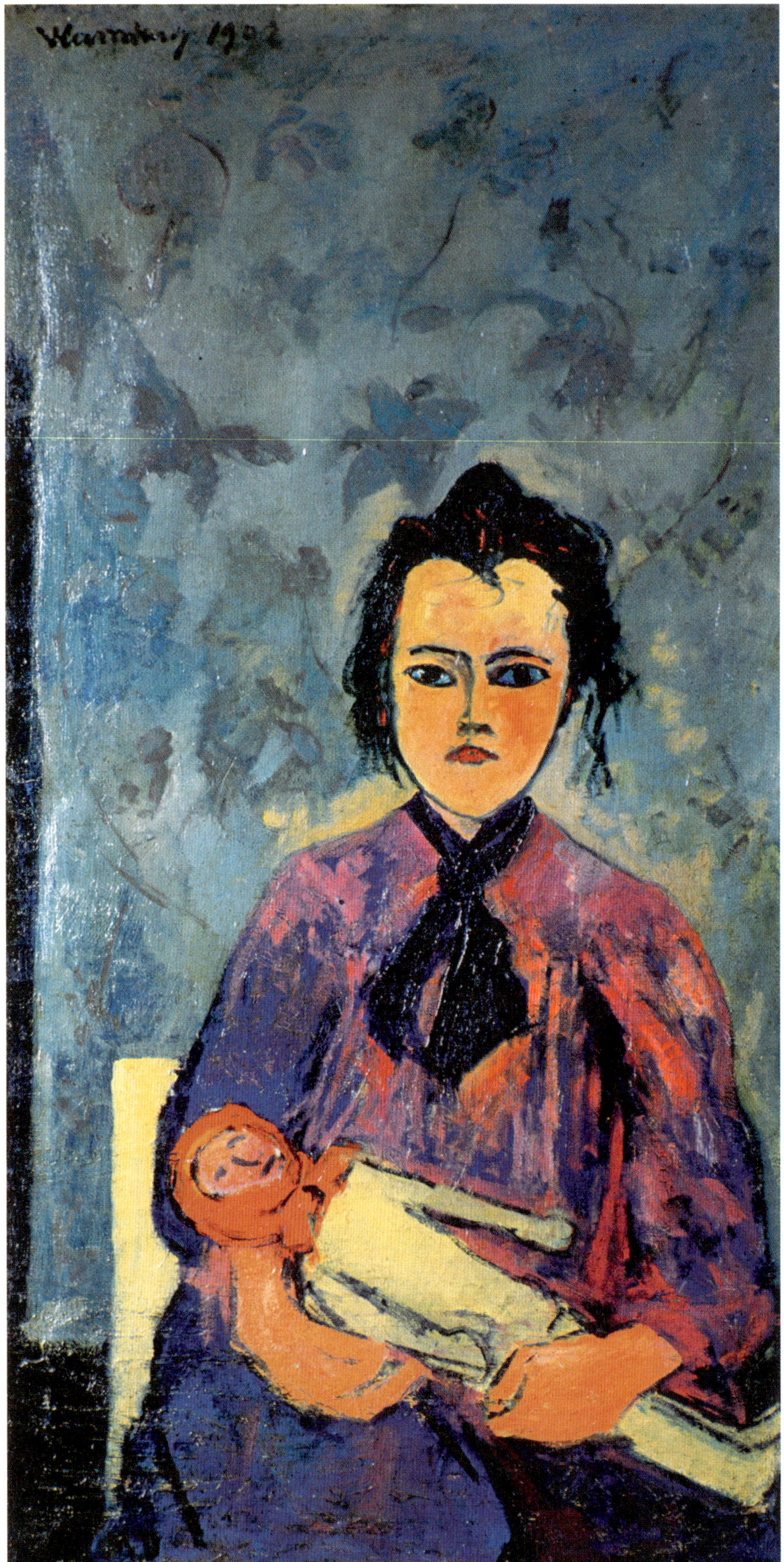

2
Young Girl with Doll, 1902

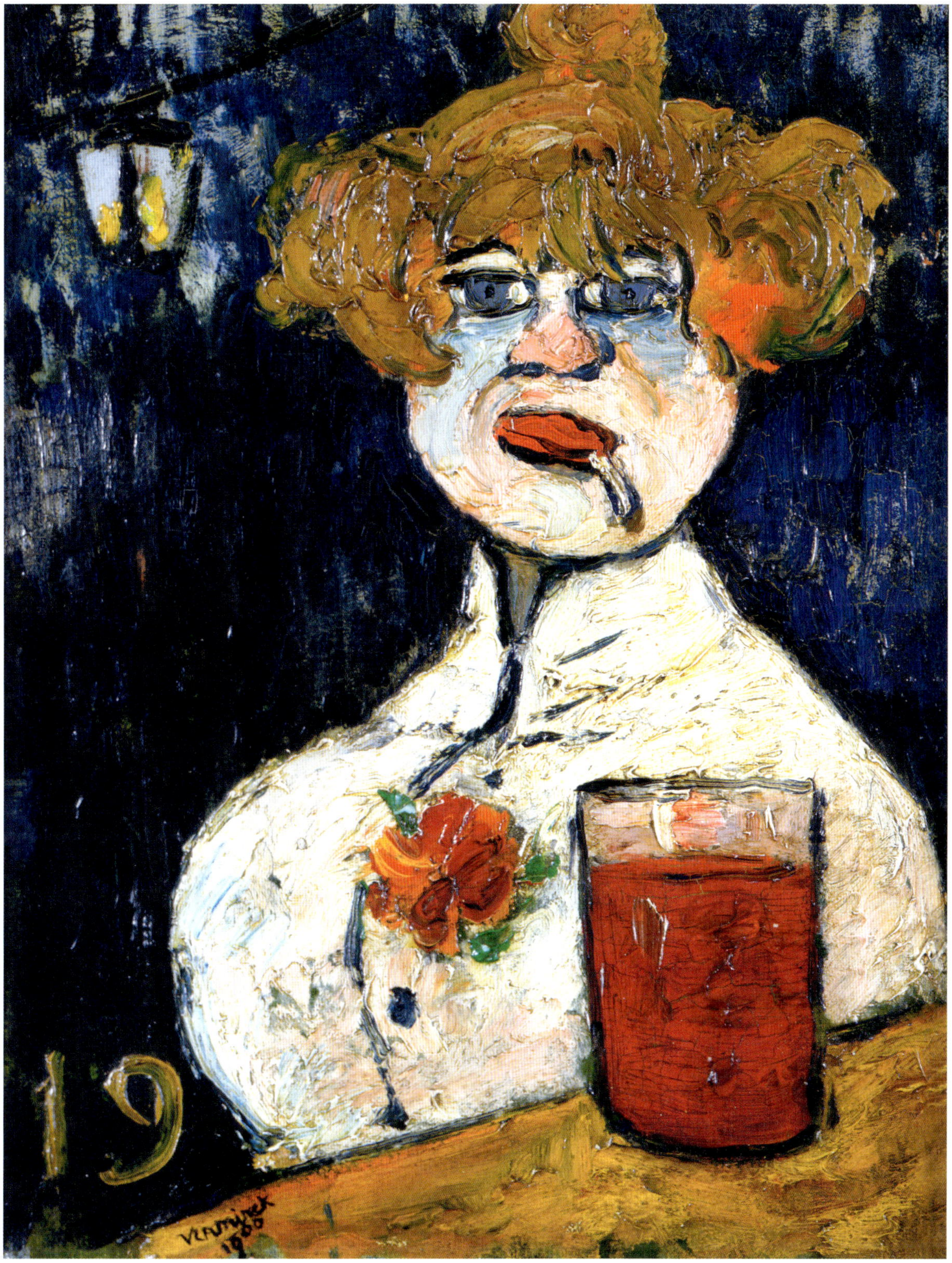

3
On the Counter, 1900

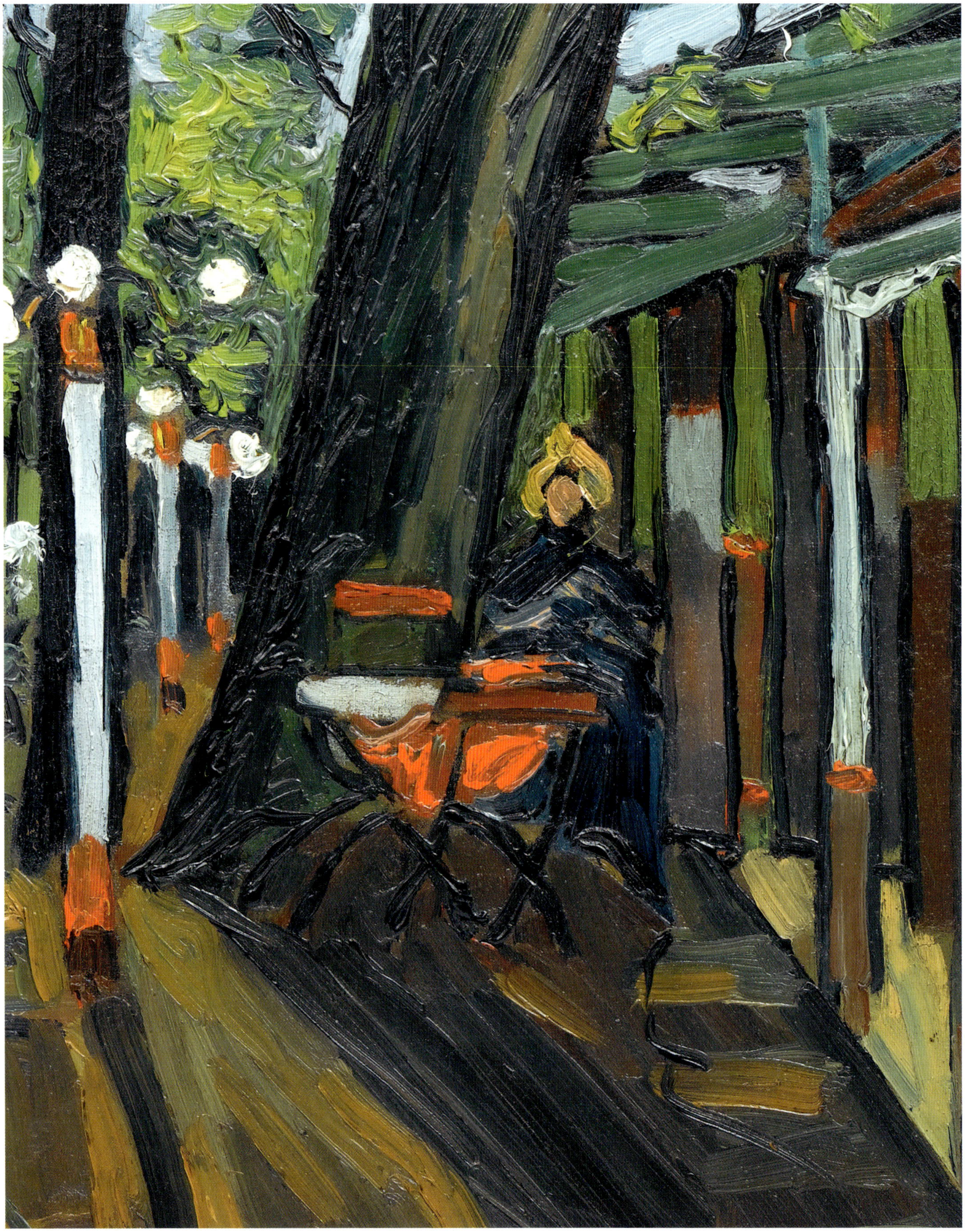

4
La Grenouillère, ca. 1905

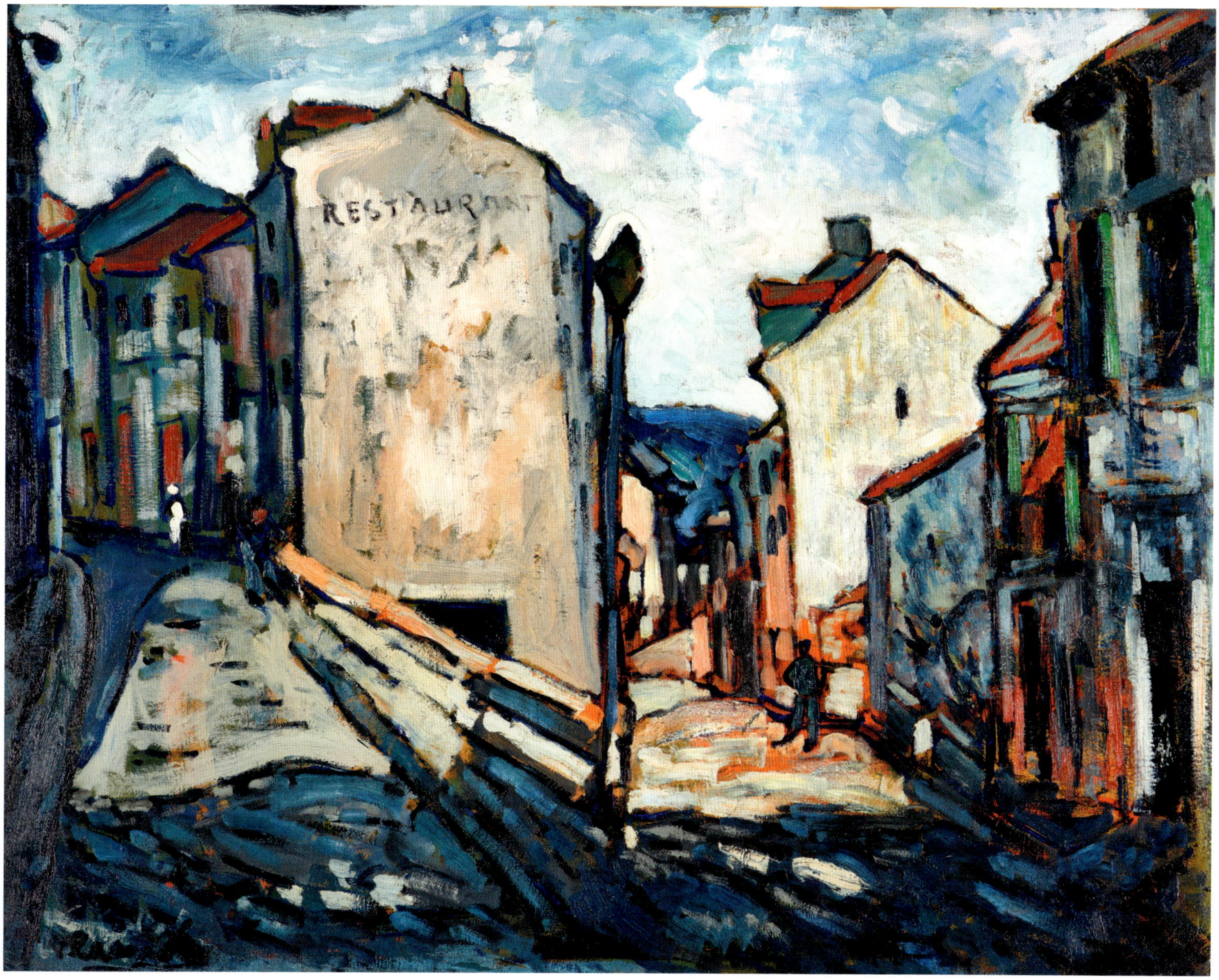

5
Carrières-sur-Seine, or The Village, 1905

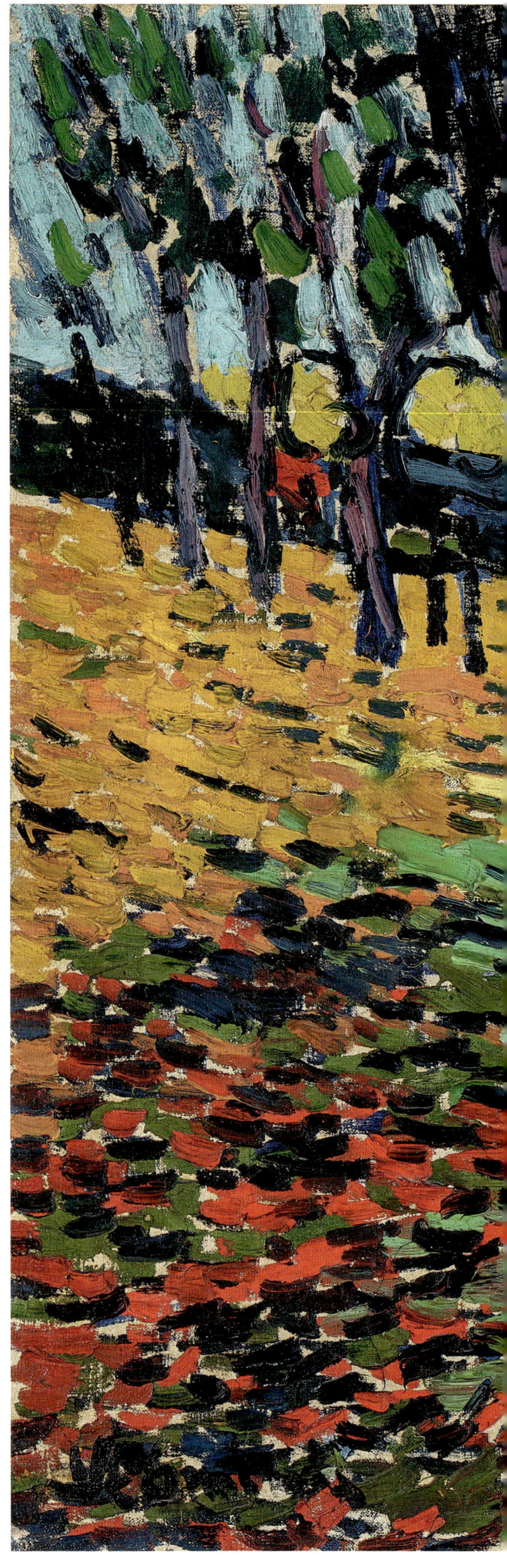

6
Chestnut Grove in Chatou, 1905

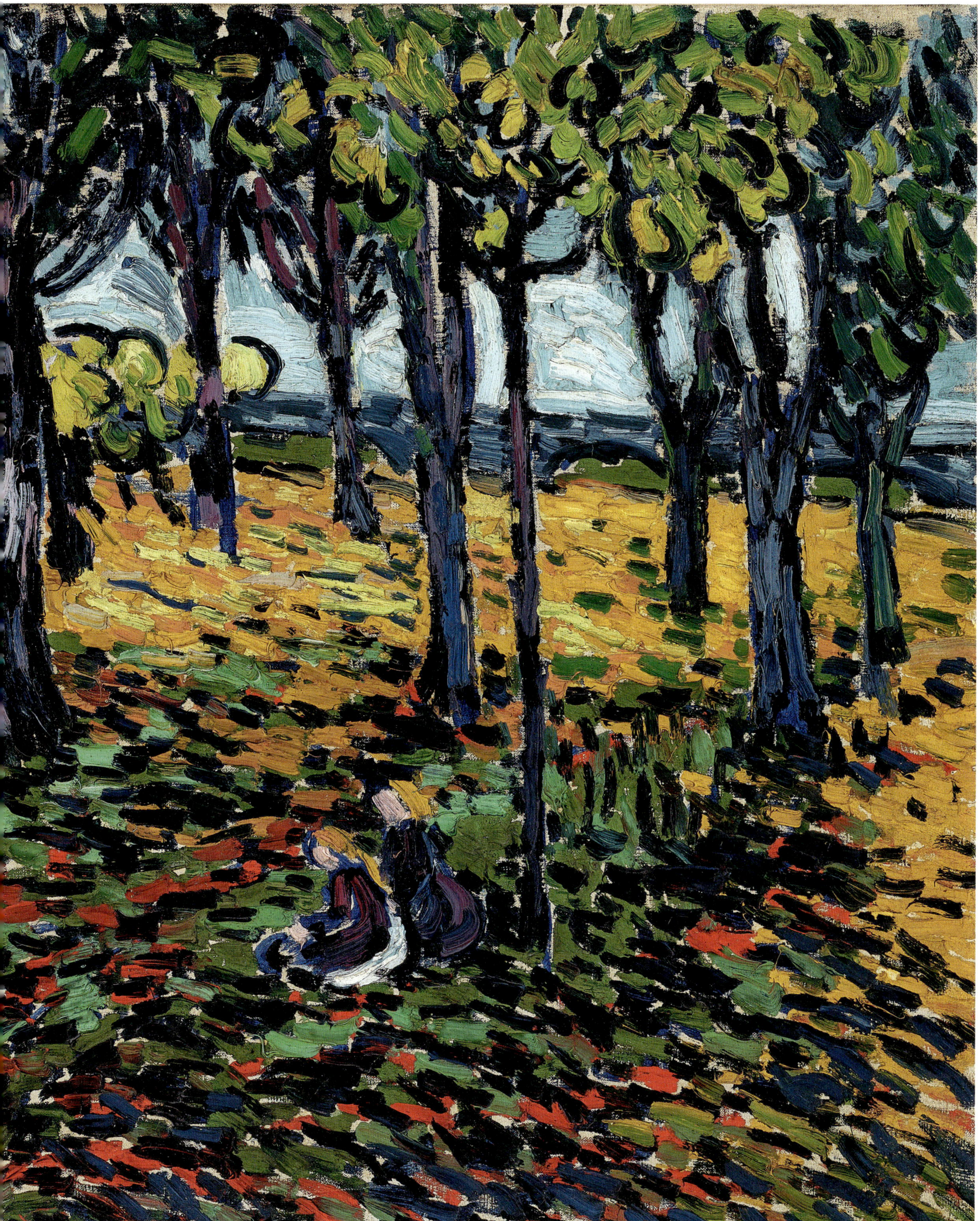

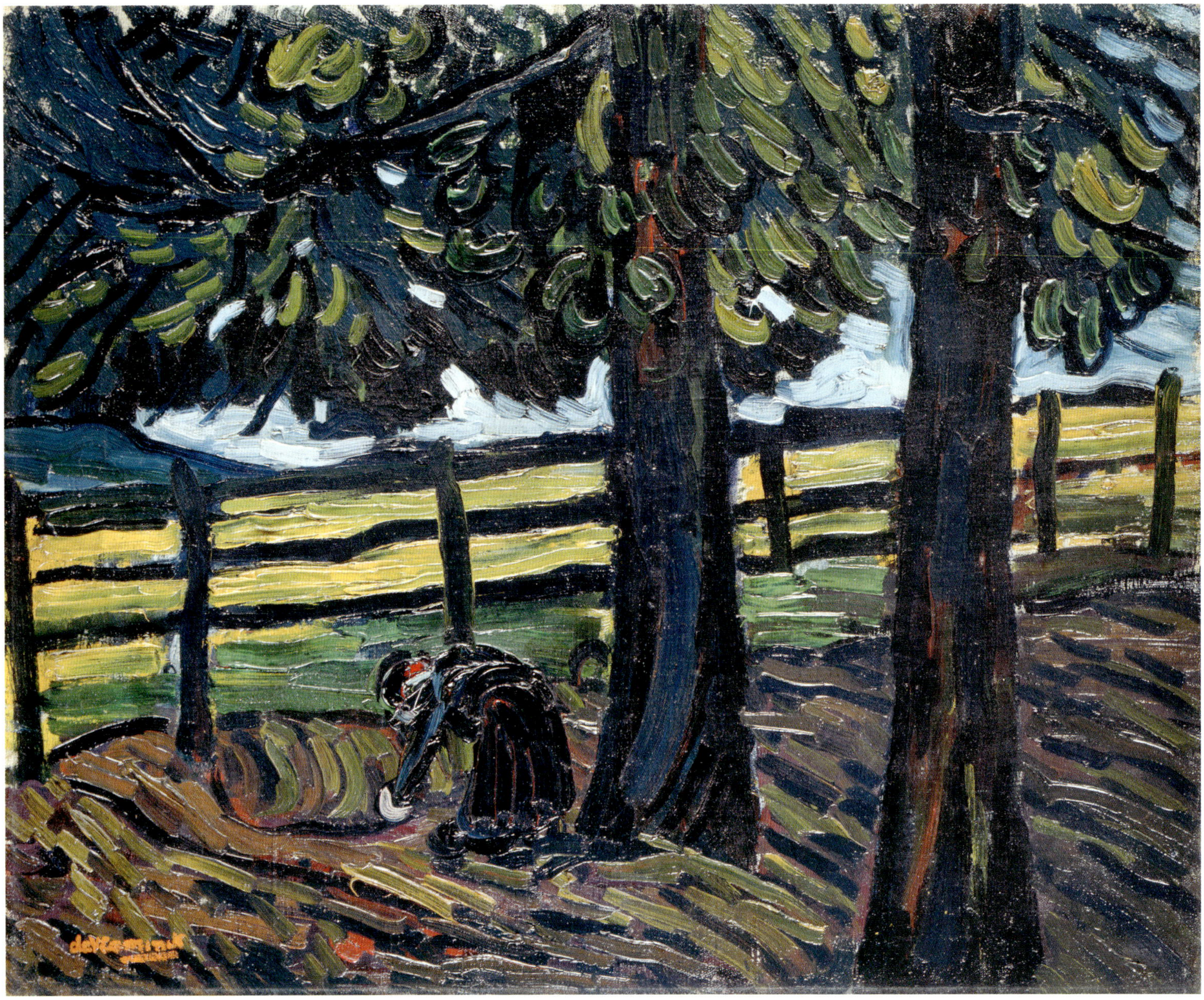

7
Twilight, 1904–05

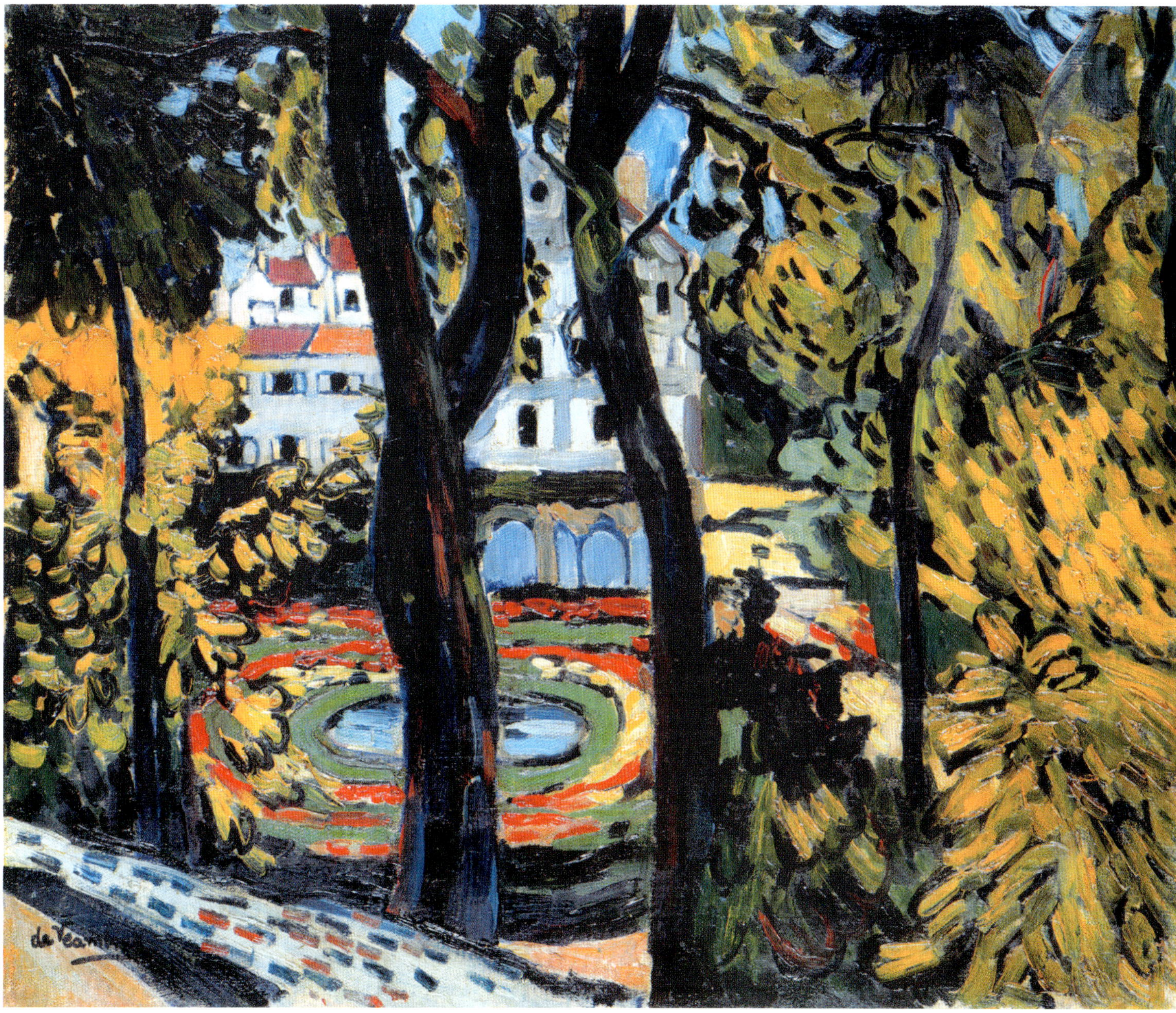

8
Park in Carrières-Saint-Denis, 1904

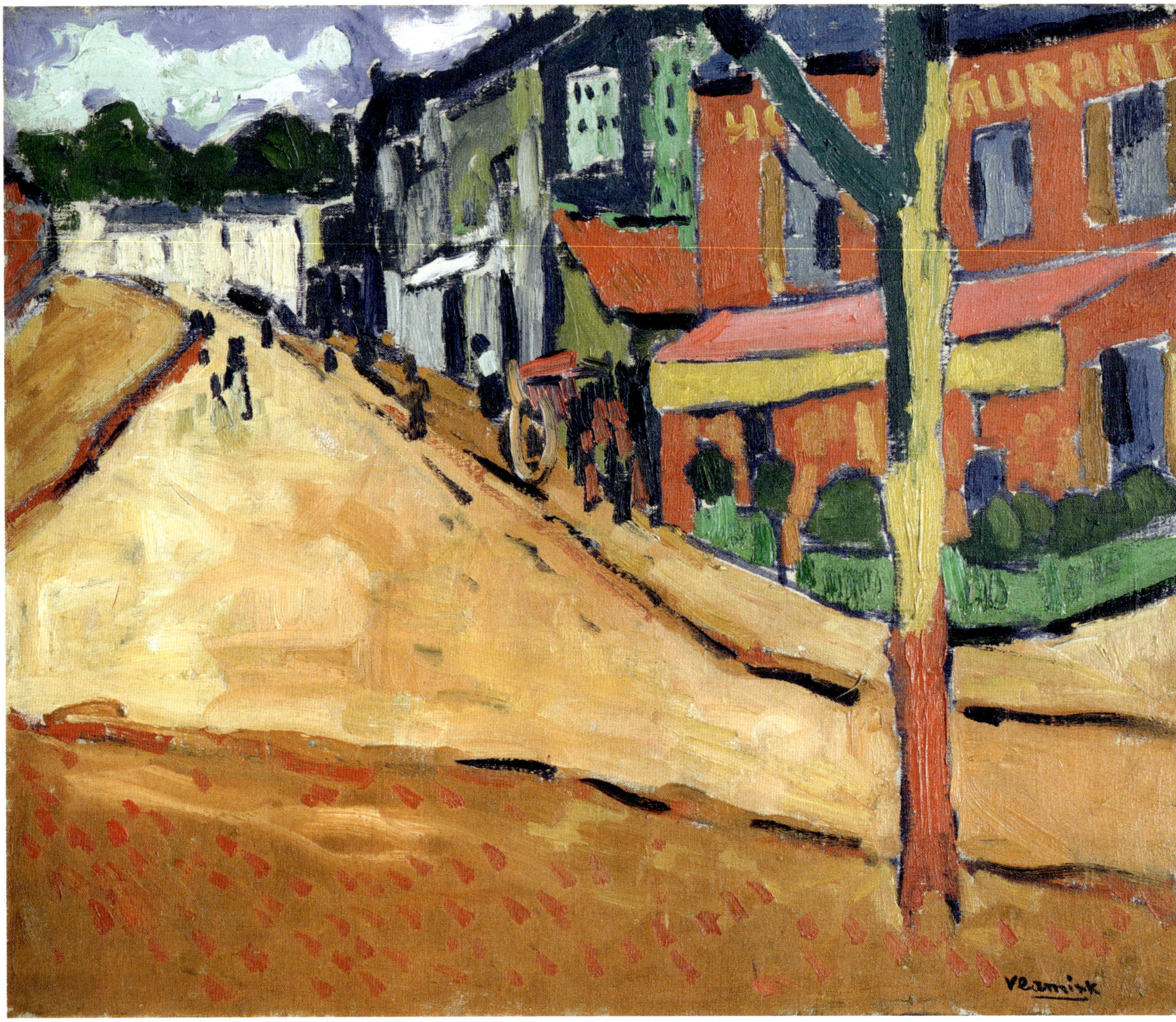

9
A Street in Marly-le-Roi, 1905–06

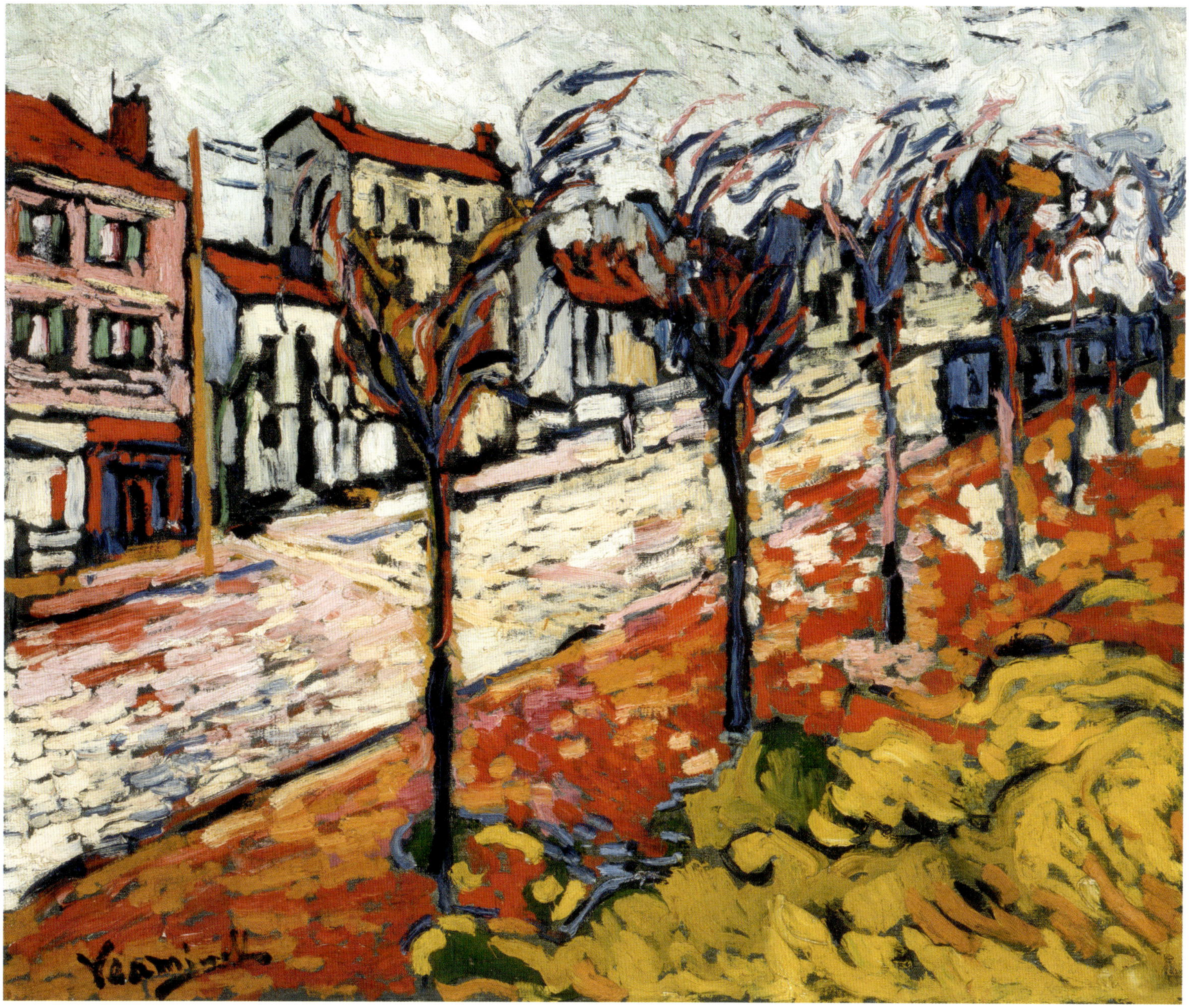

10
Suburban Landscape, 1905

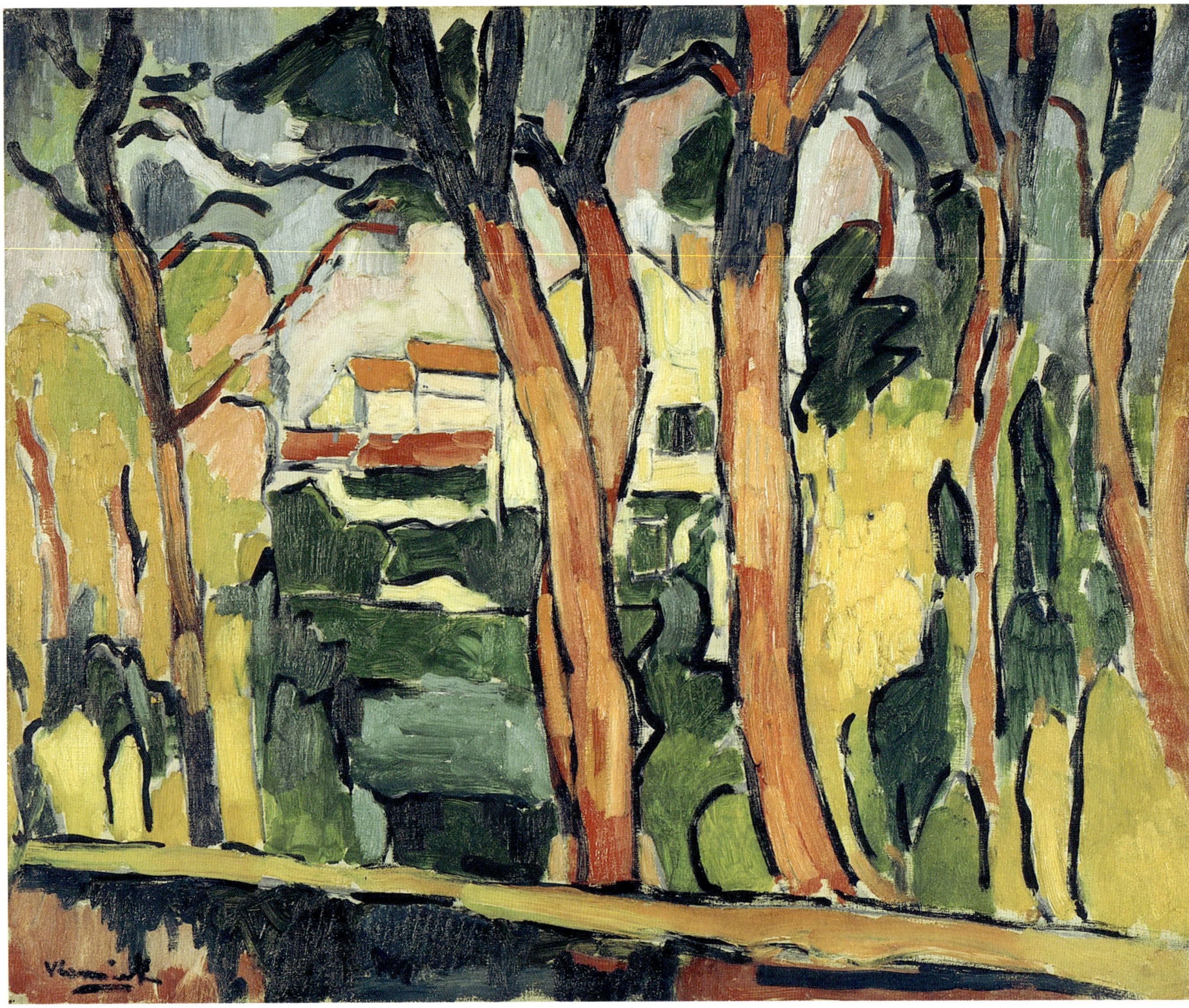

11
The Red Trees, 1906

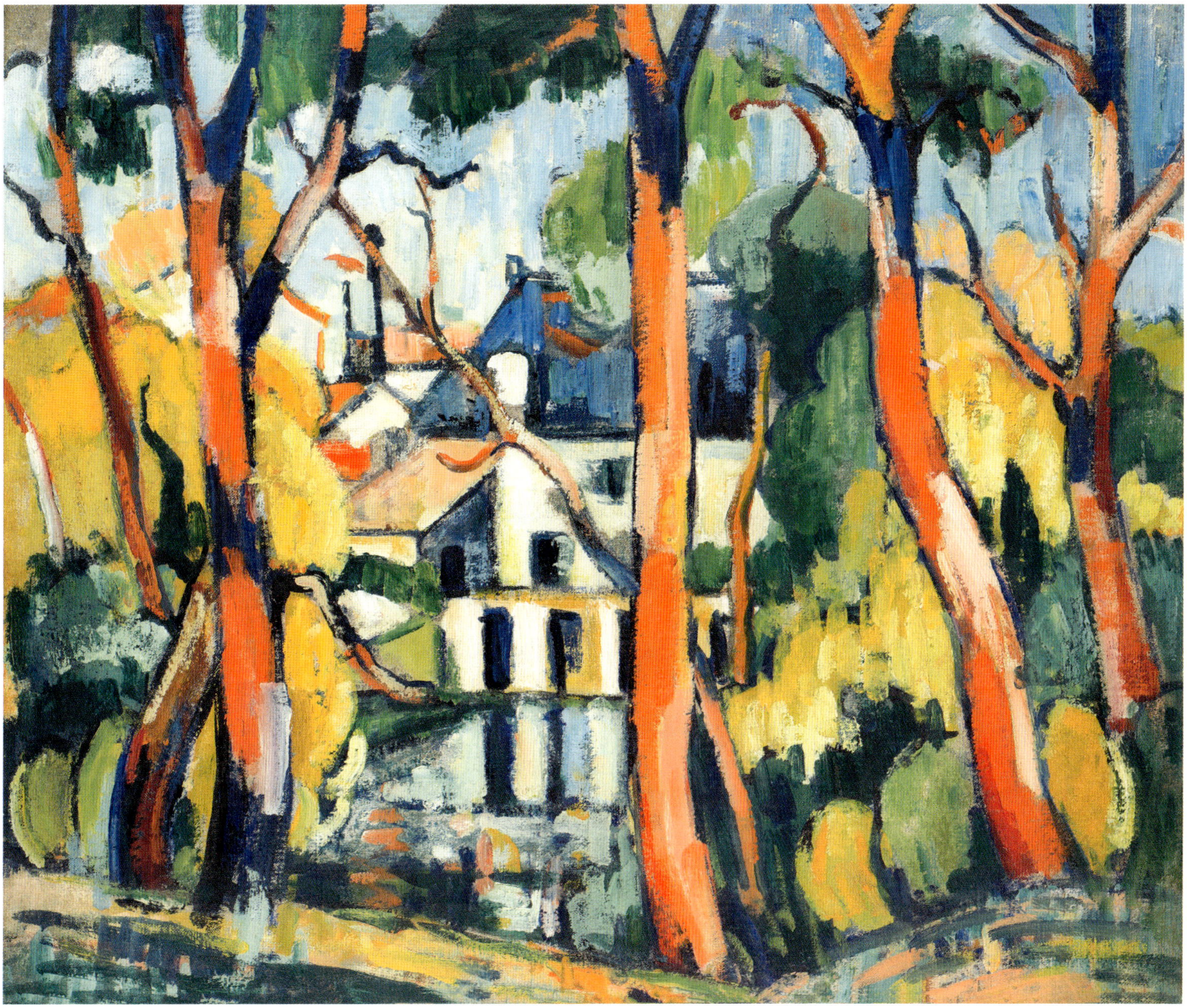

12
Trees at the Blue House, 1906

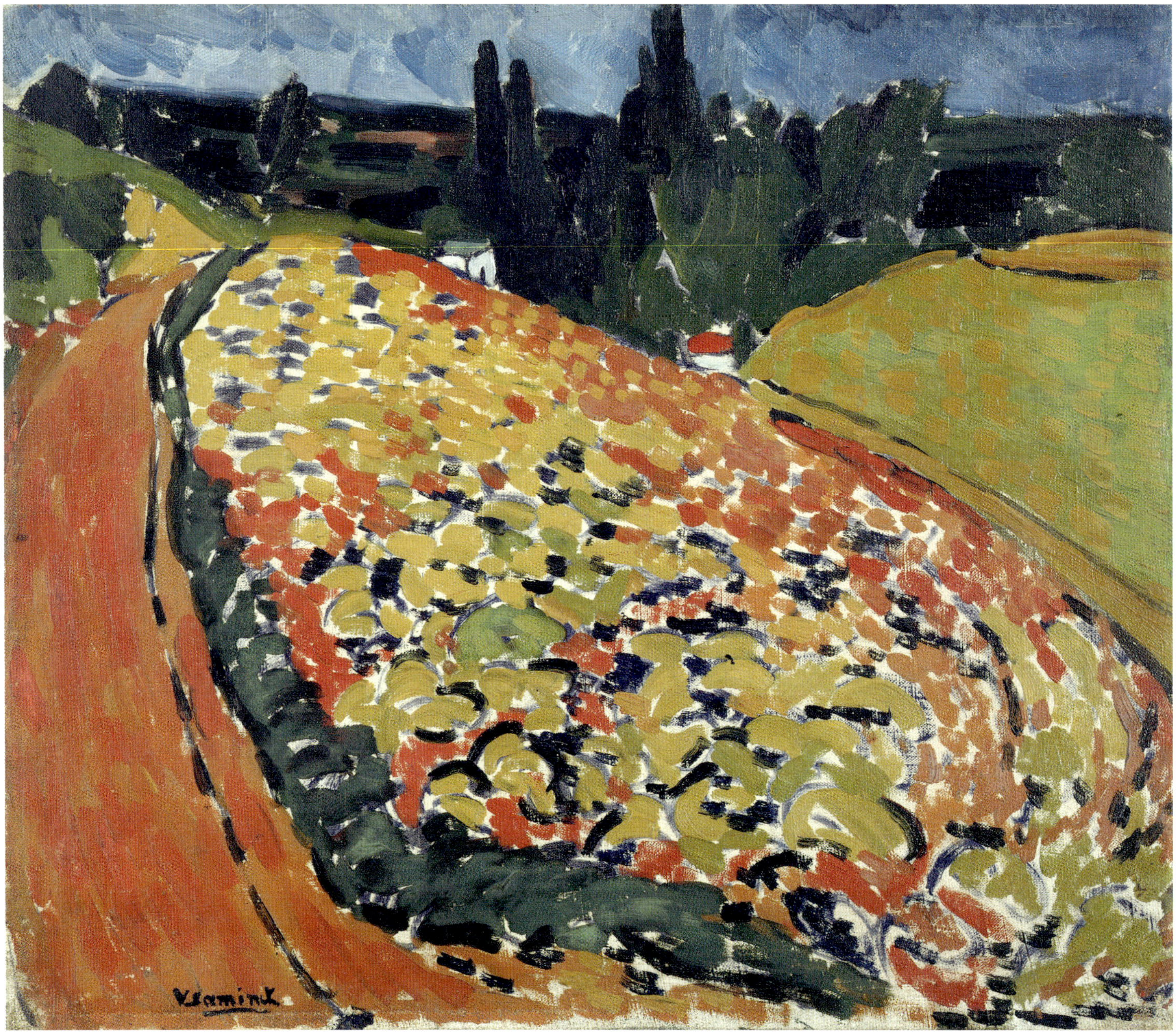

13
The Hills at Rueil, 1906

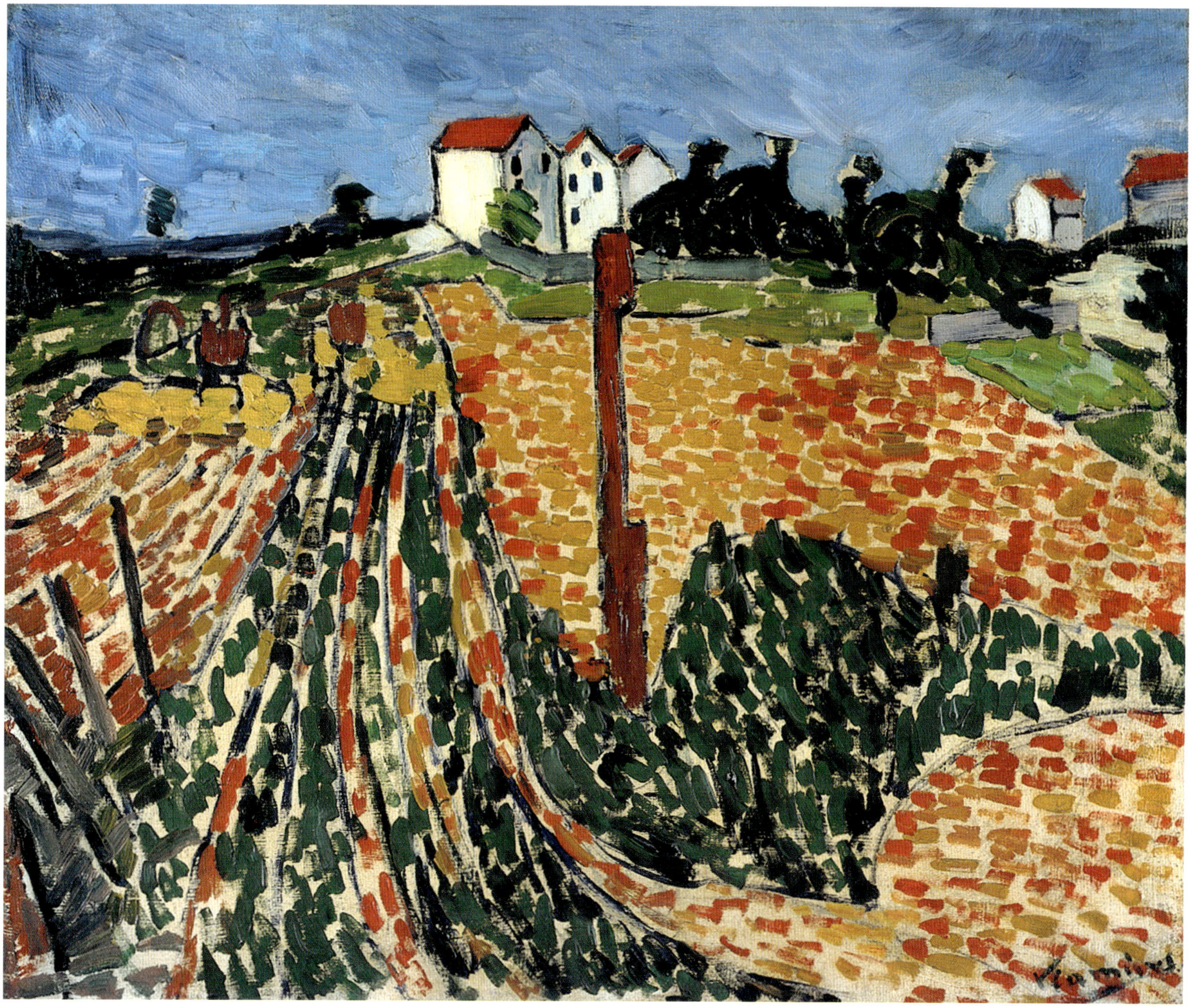

14
Route maraîchère, 1905

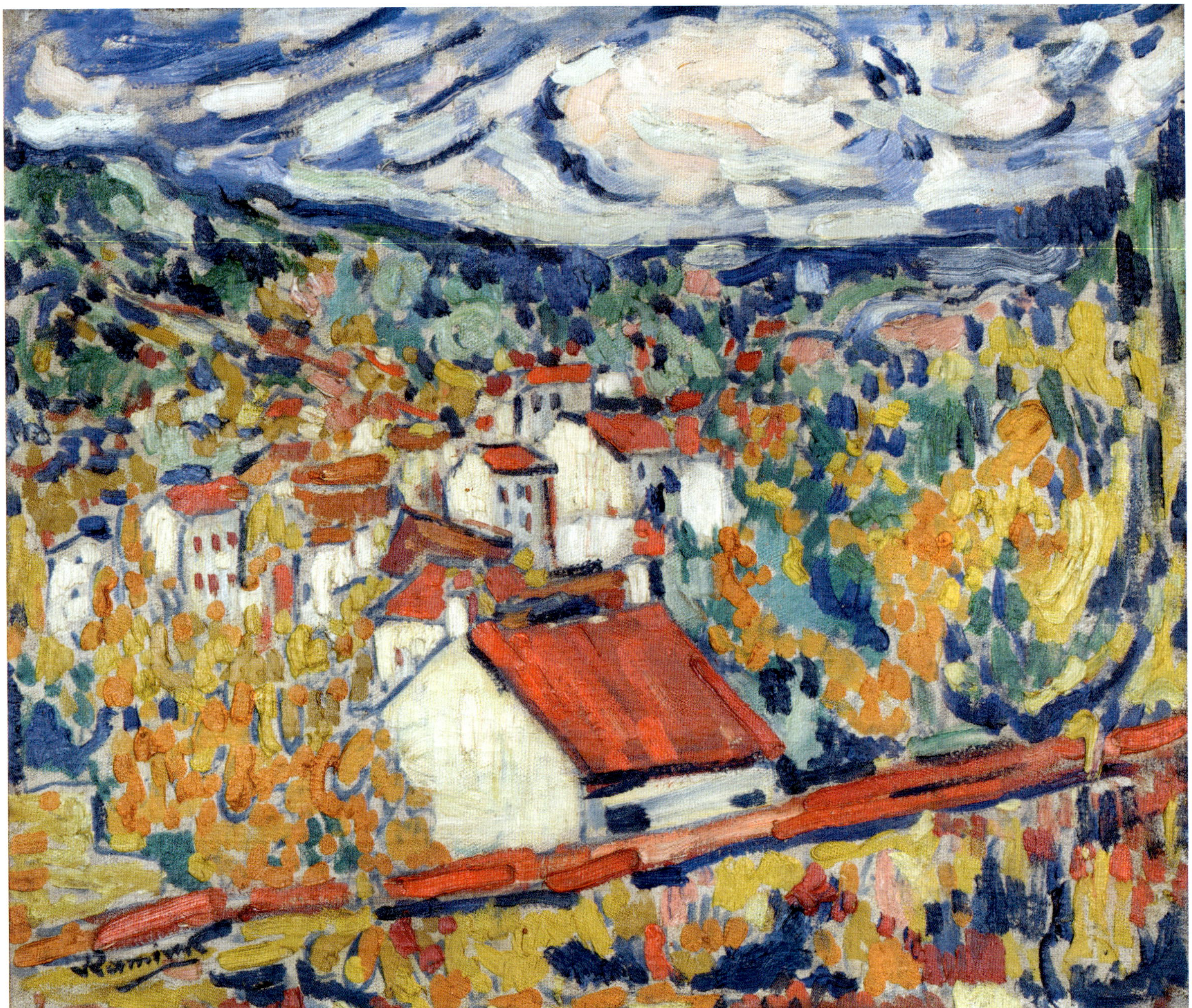

15
View of Bougival, 1906

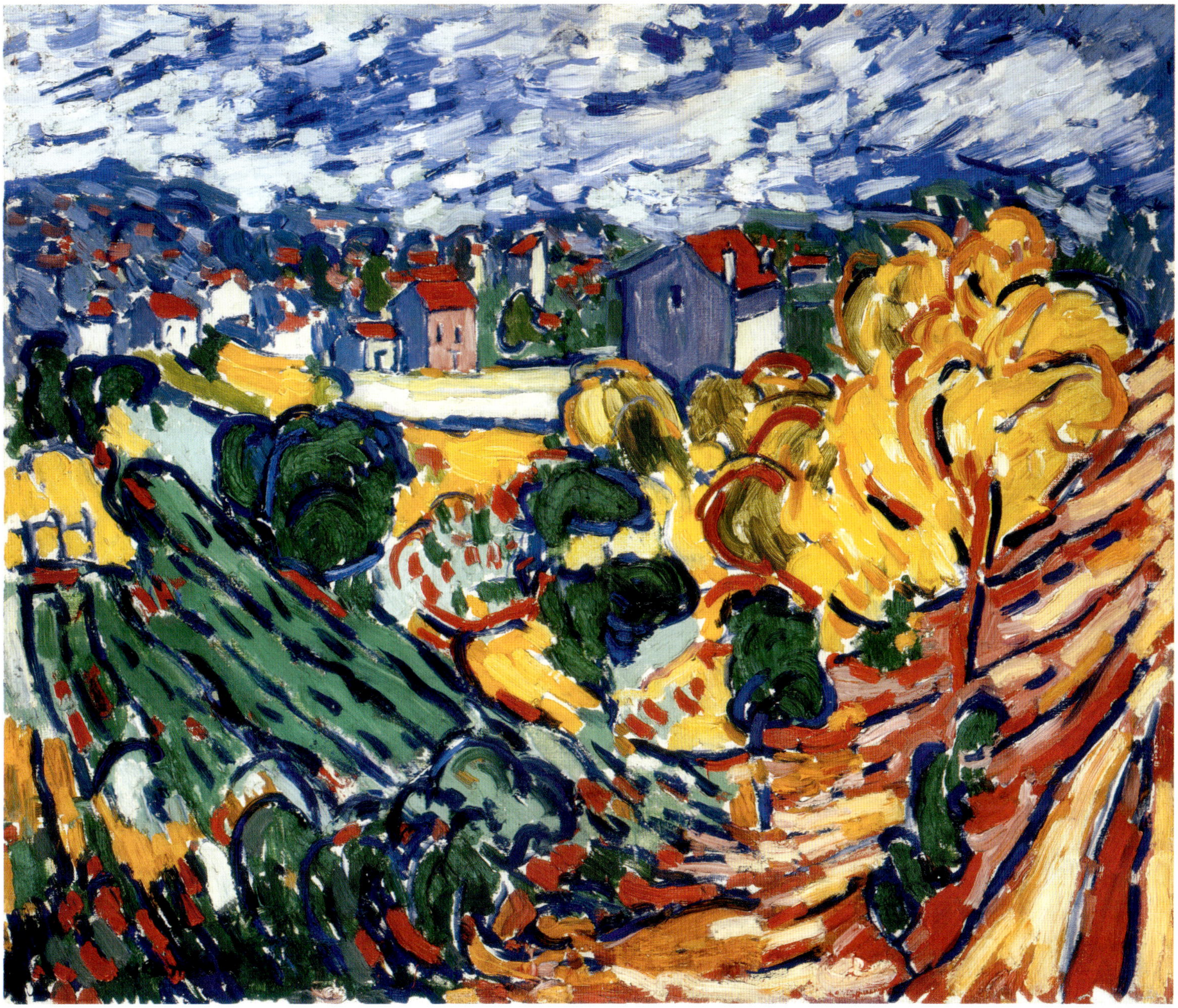

16
Landscape at Bougival, 1906

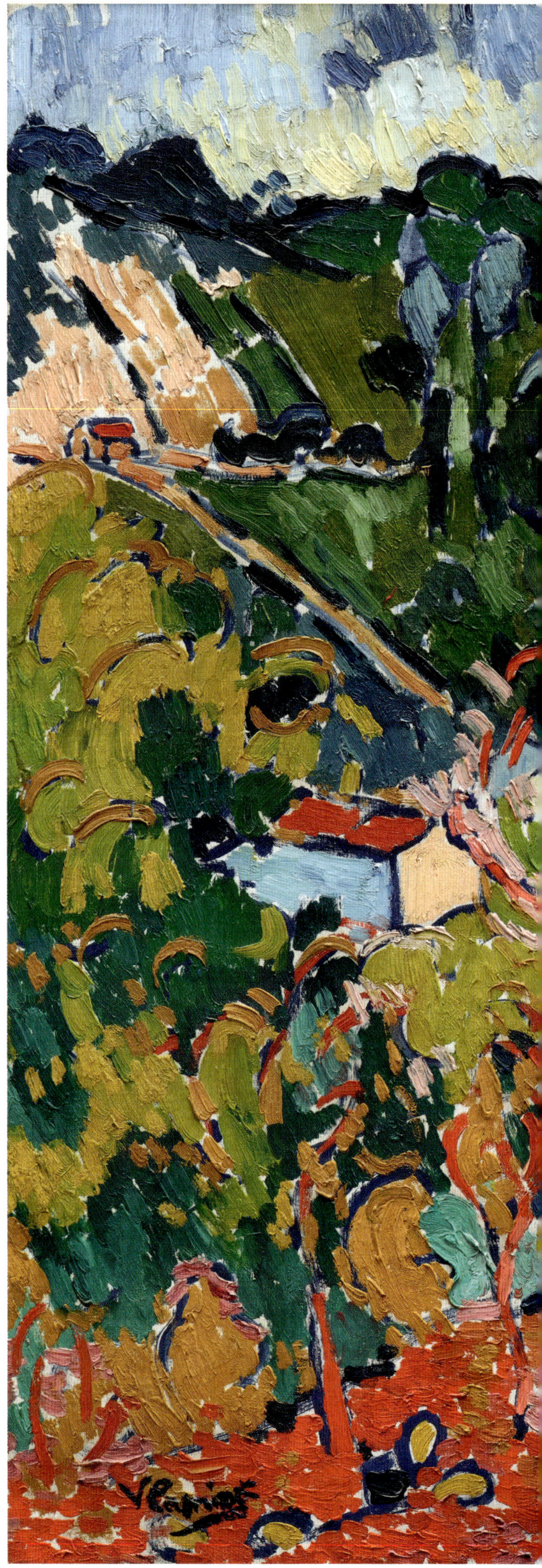

17
Bougival, ca. 1905

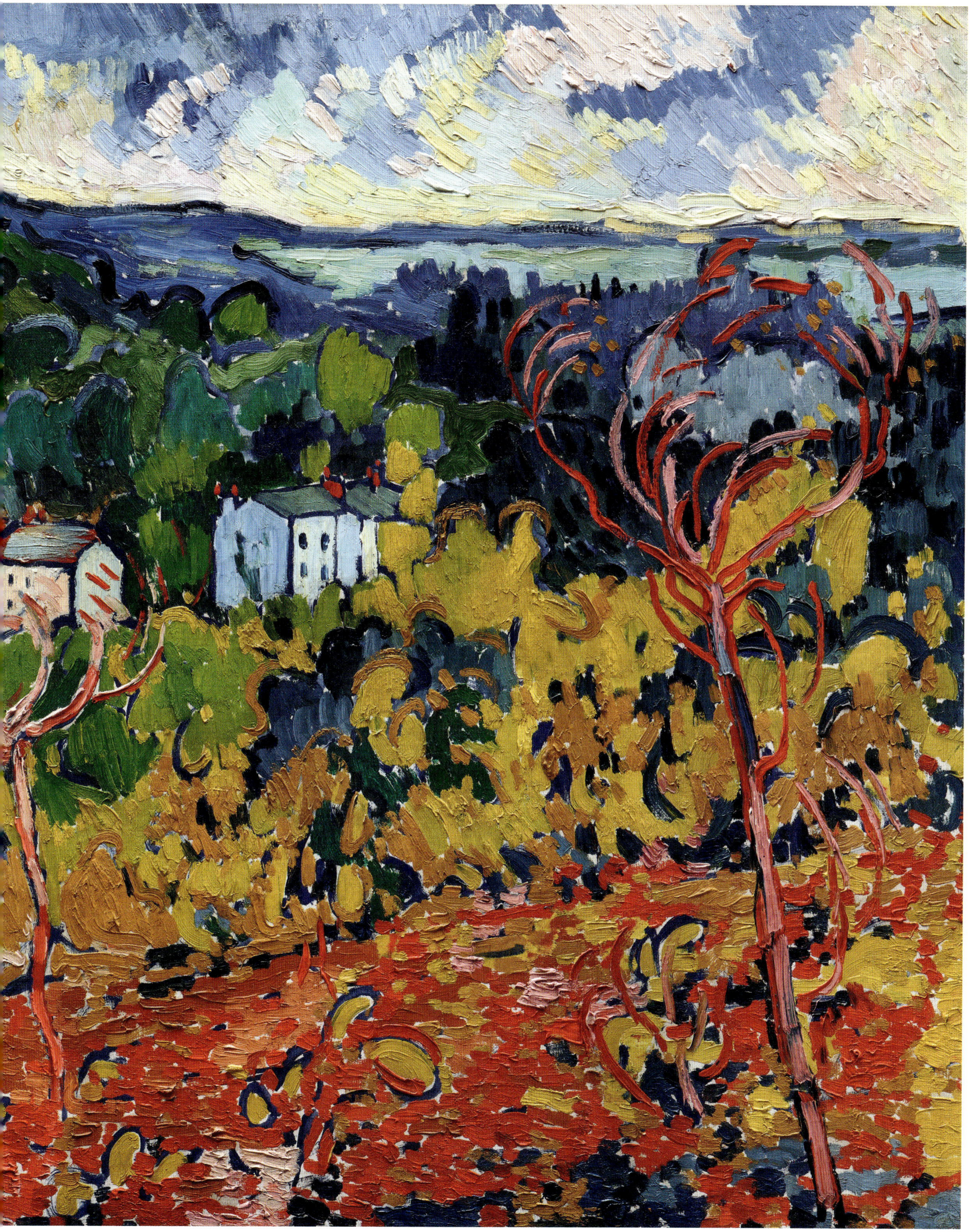

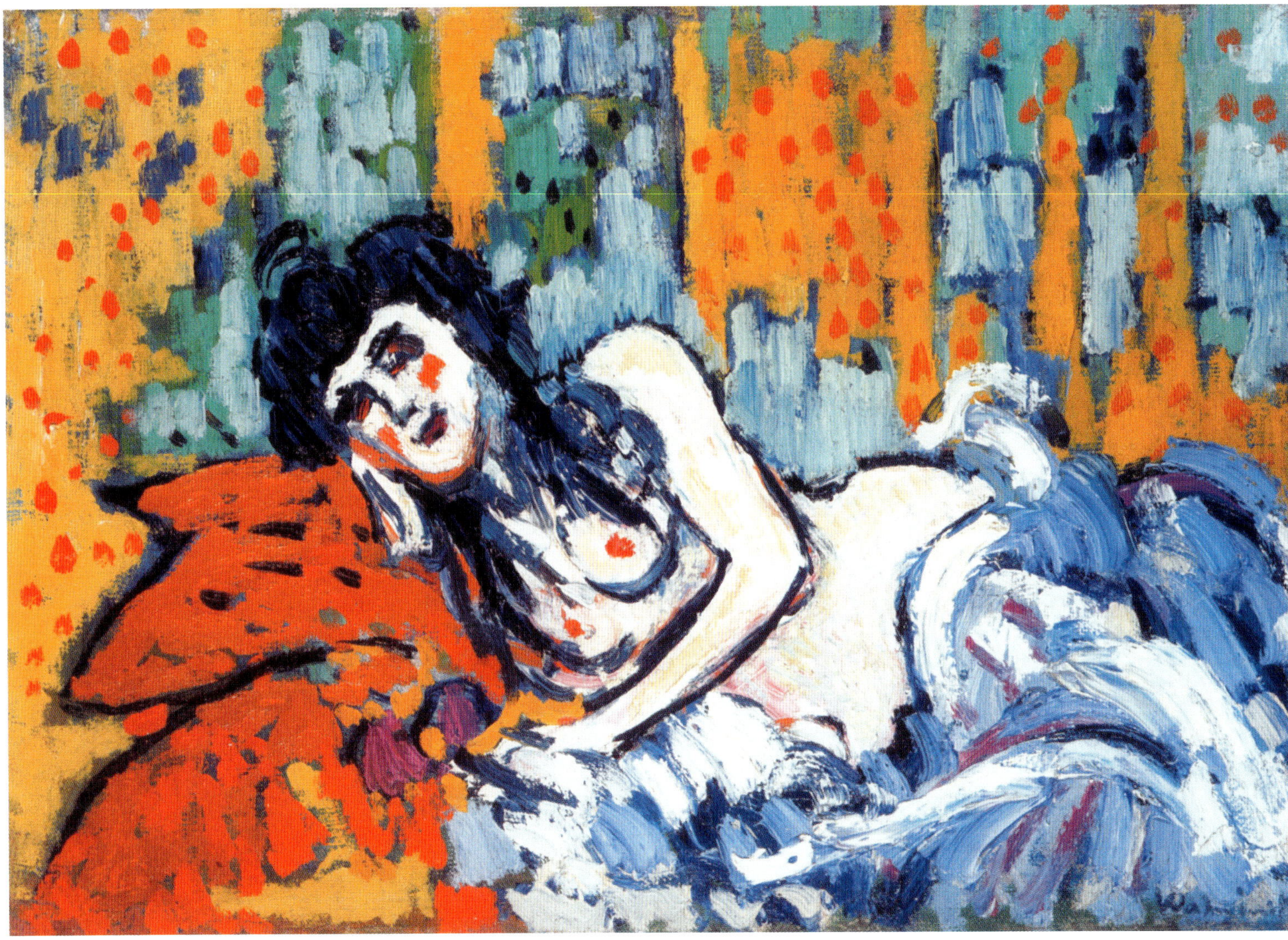

18
The Girl from the Rat mort, 1905

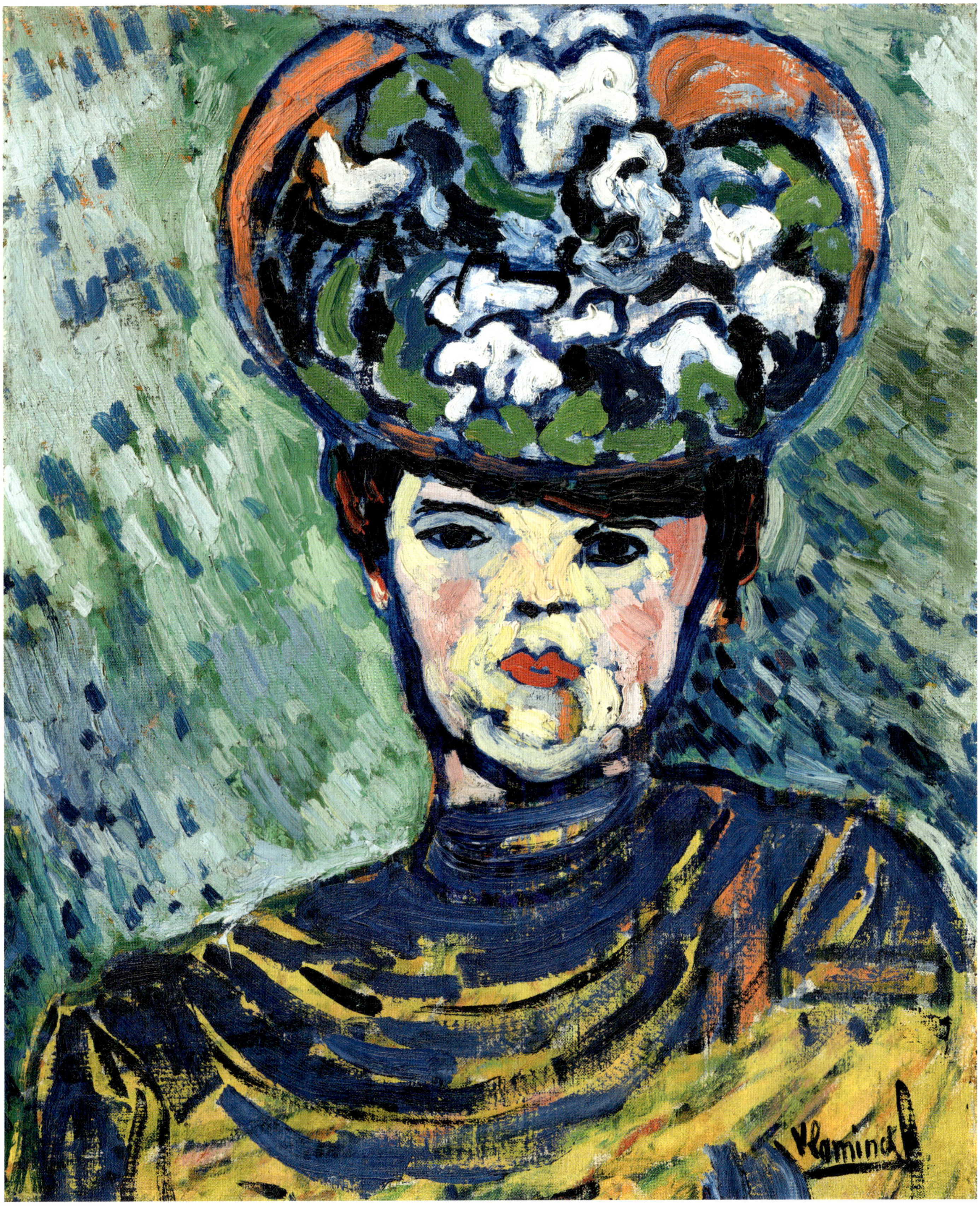

19
Woman with a Hat, 1905

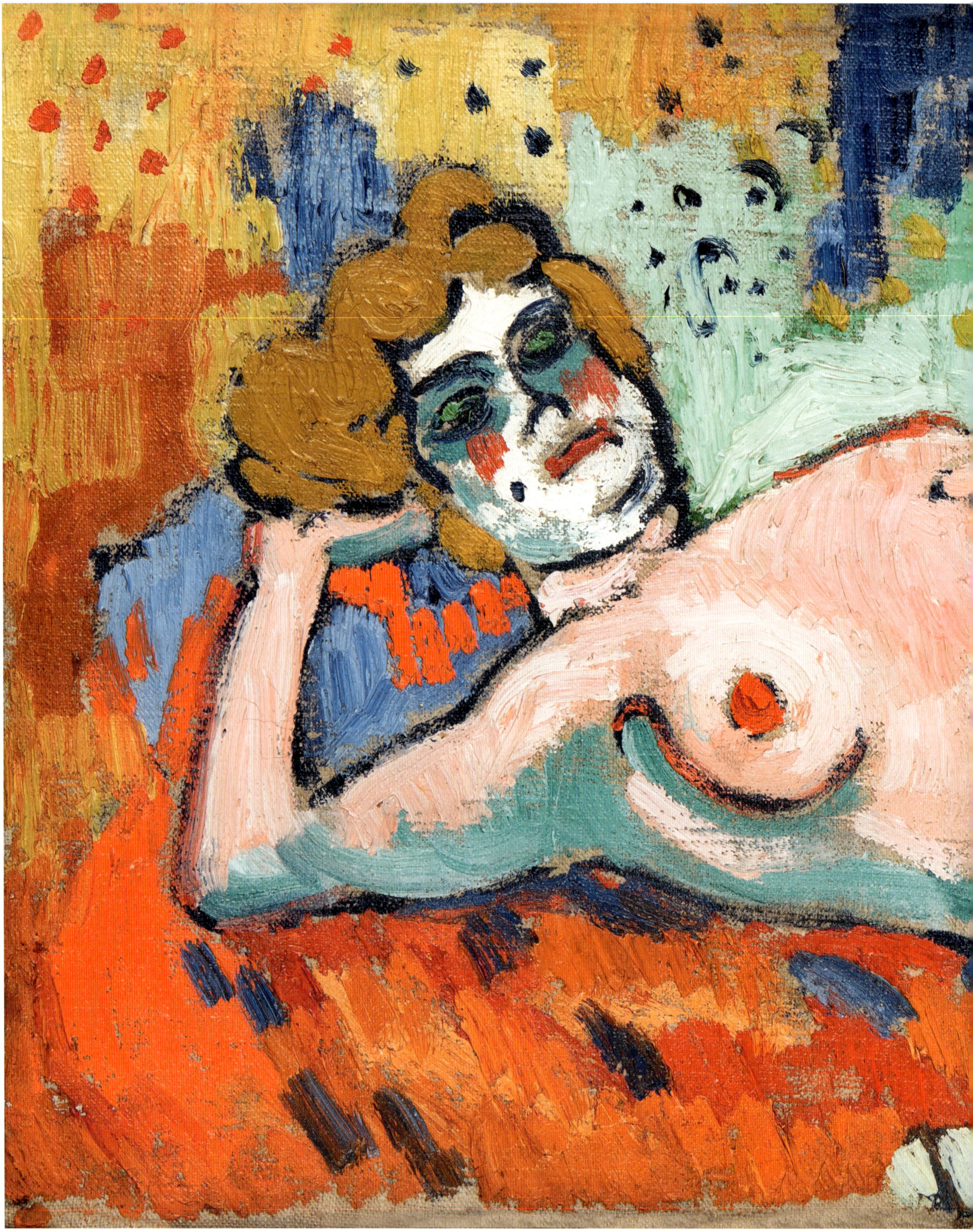

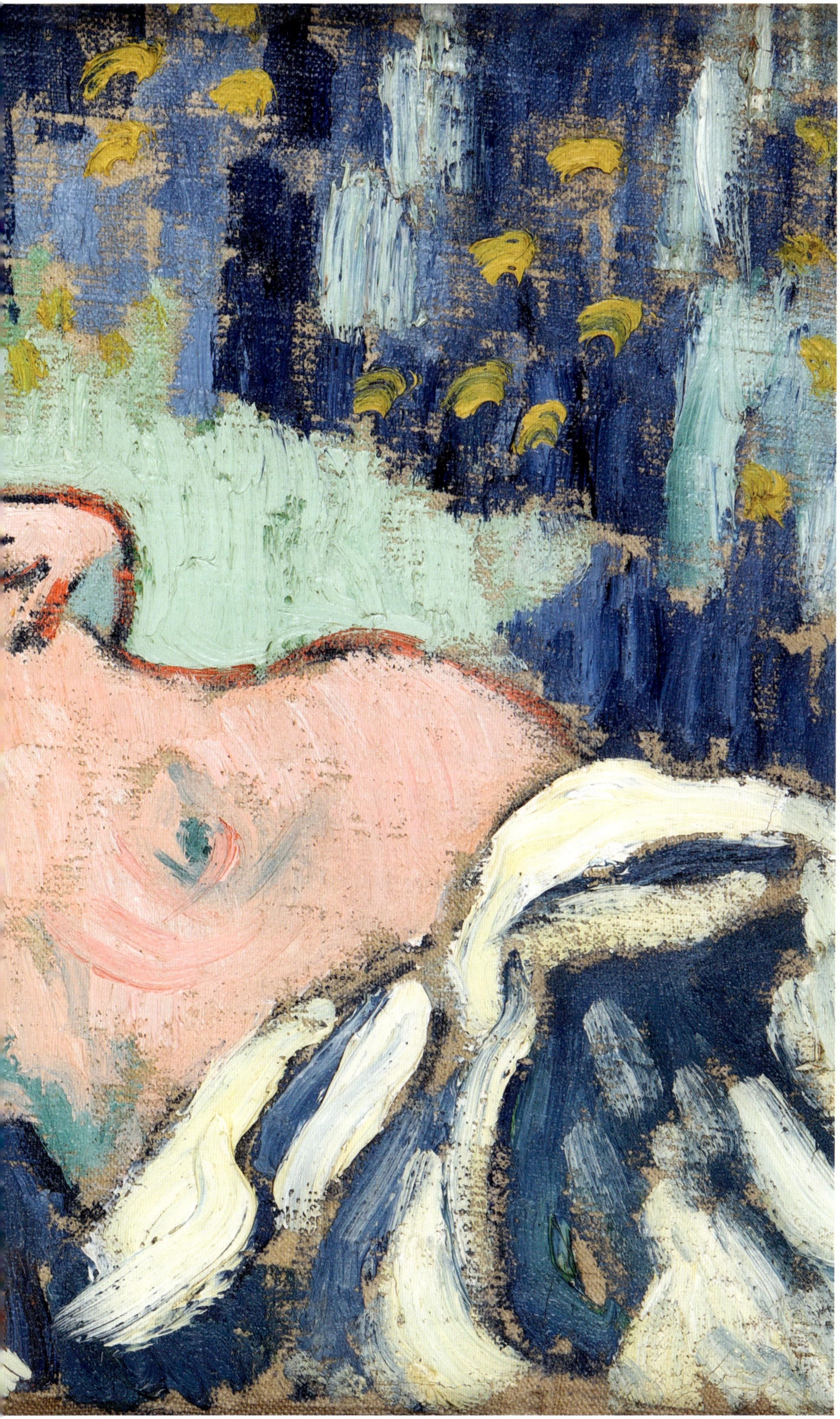

20
Reclining Nude, 1905

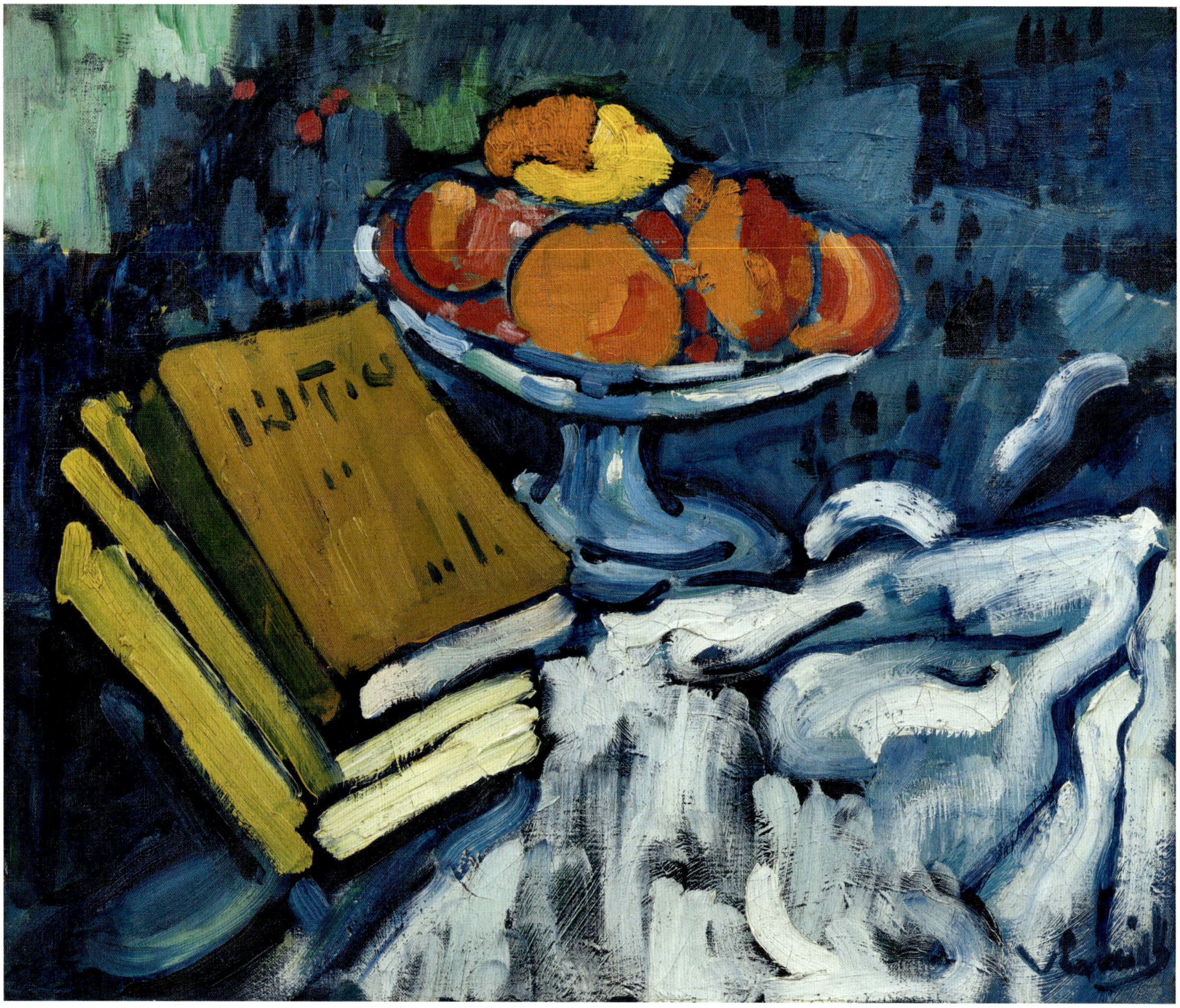

21
Still Life with Books and Fruit Bowl, 1906

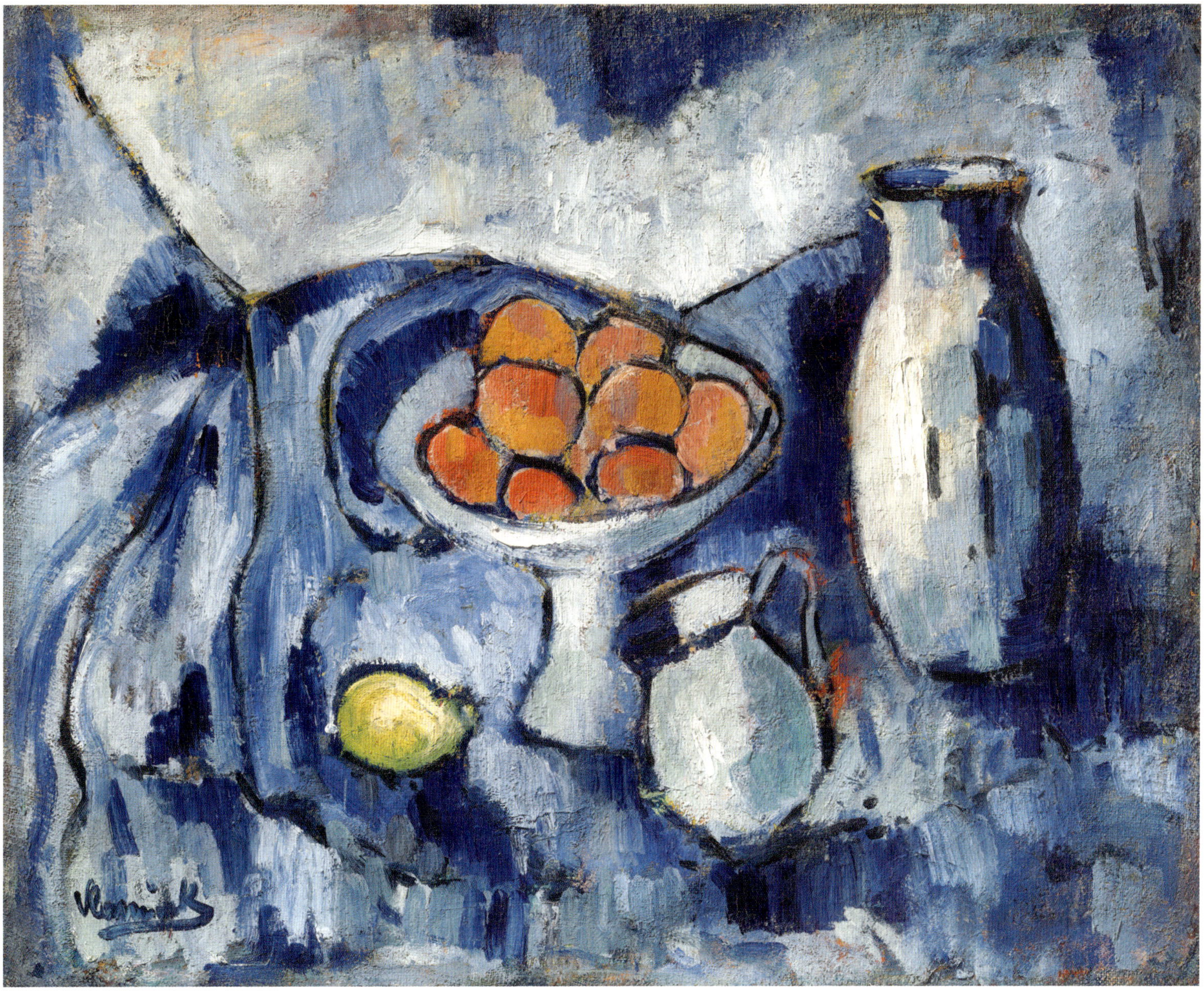

22
Blue Still Life, ca. 1907

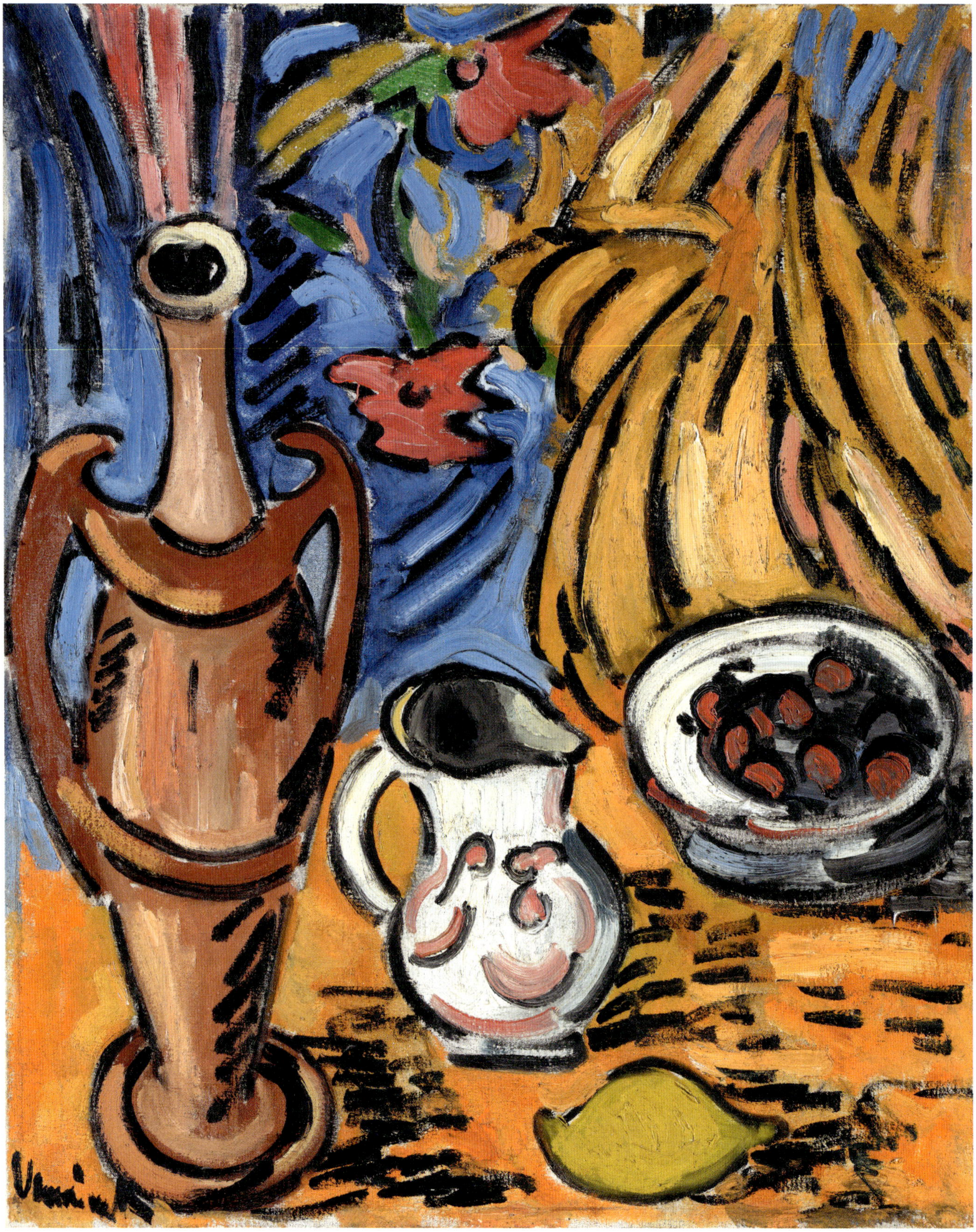

23
Still Life with Vase, Pitcher, and Fruit Bowl, 1907

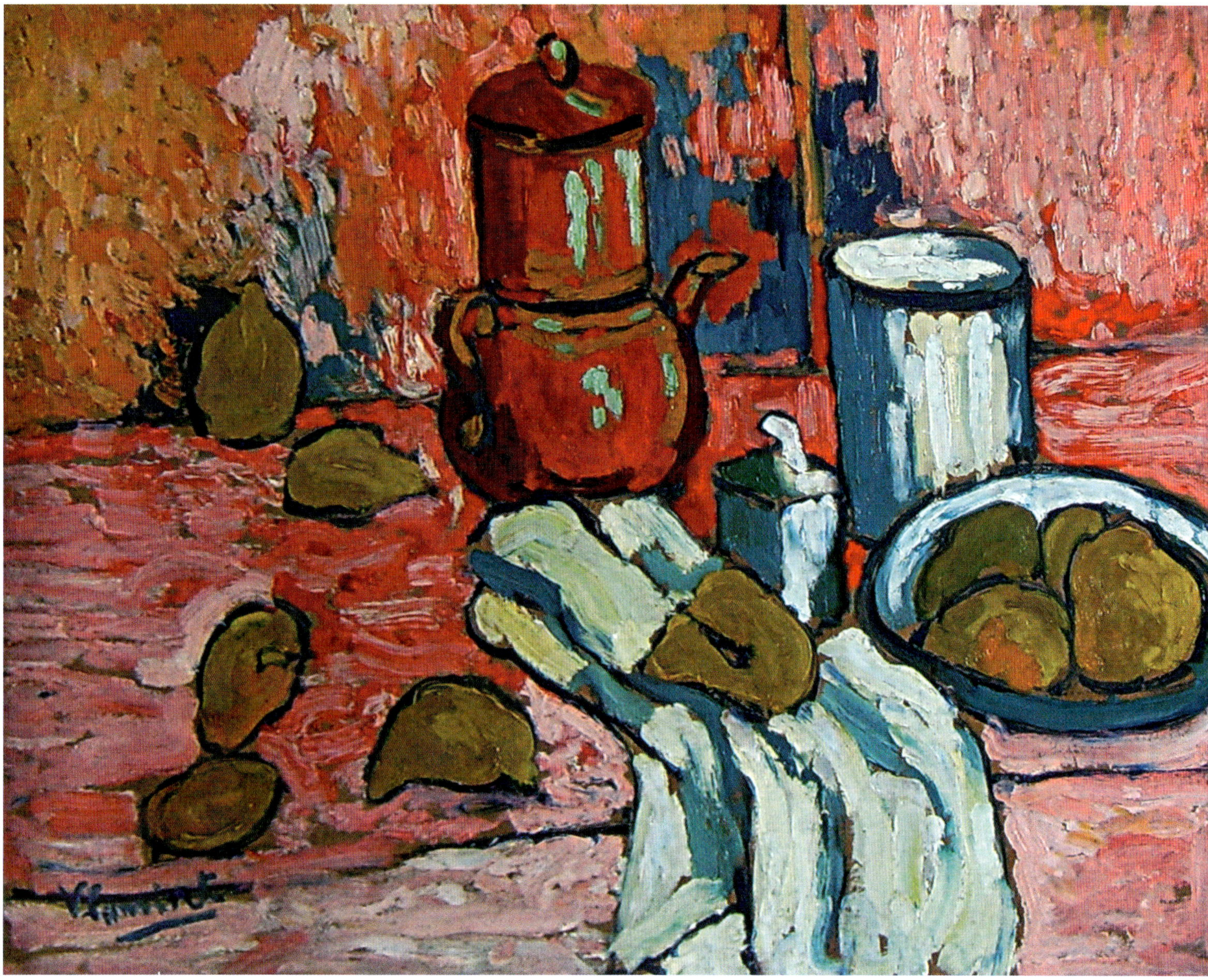

24
Still Life, 1907

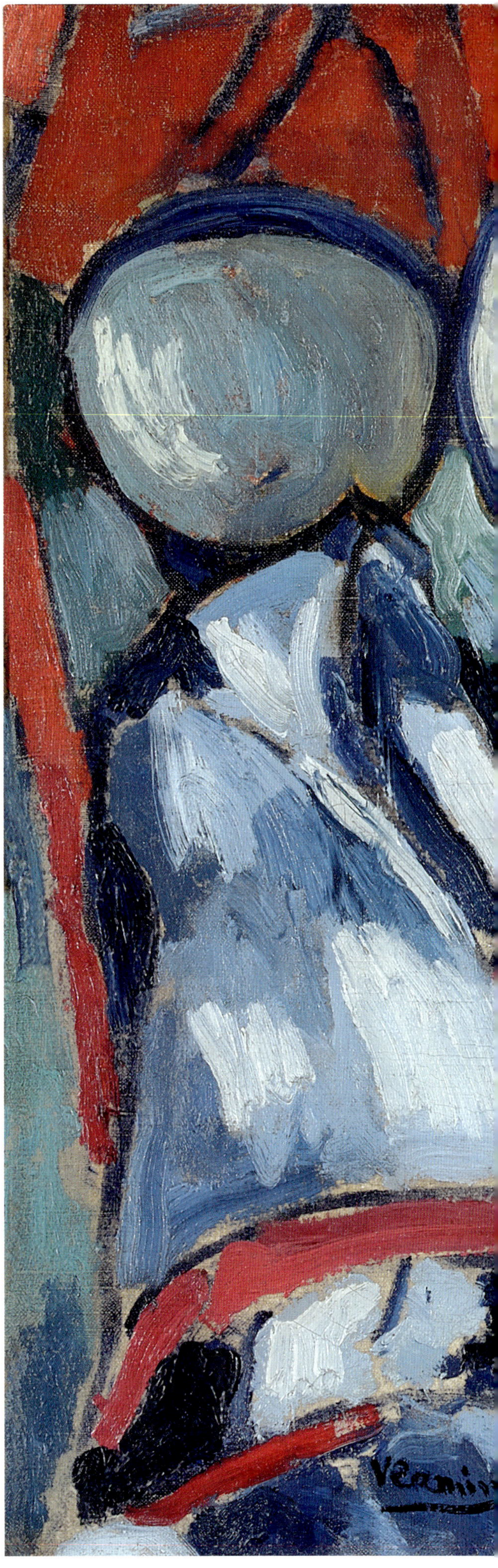

25
The Table (Still Life with Almonds), 1907

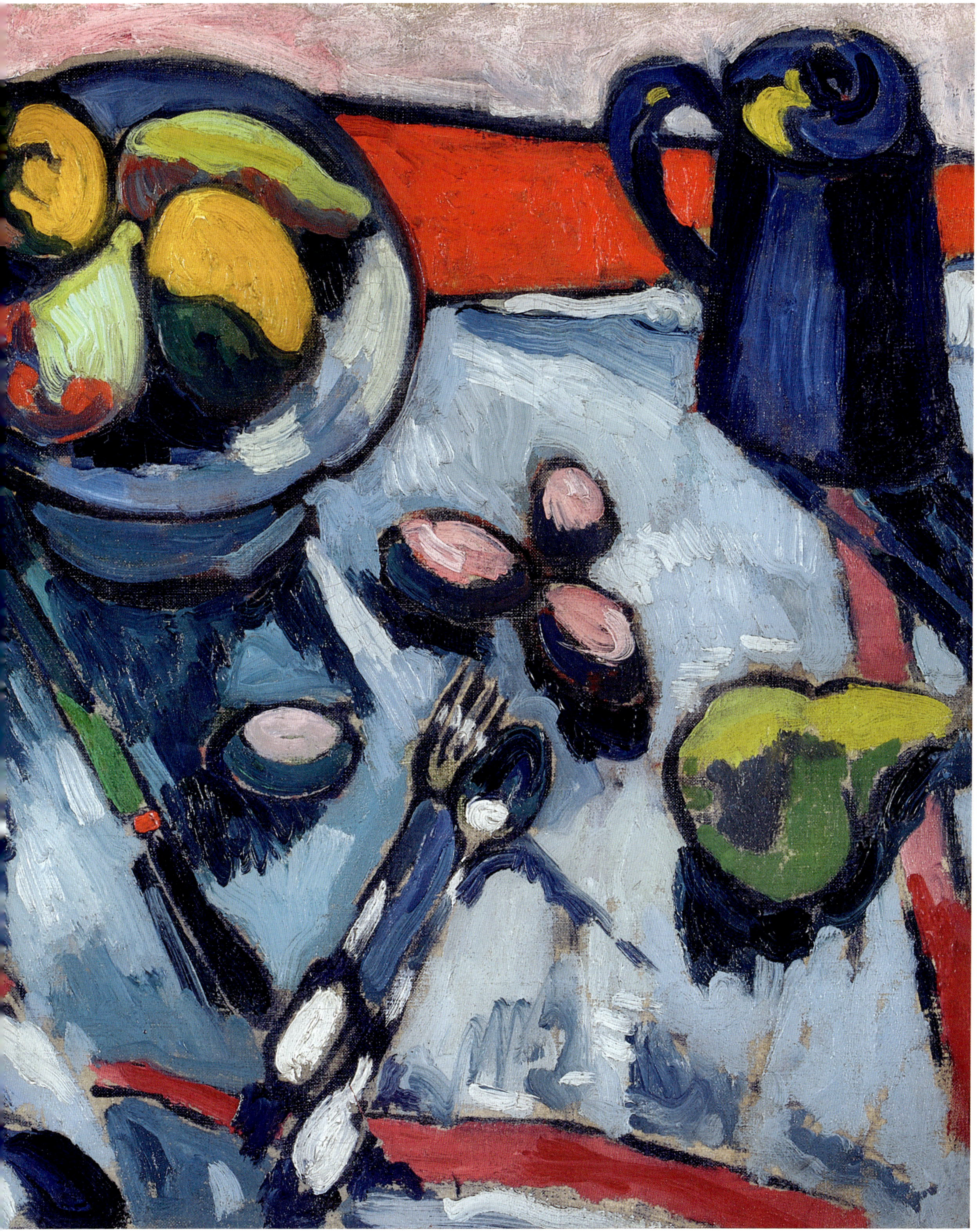

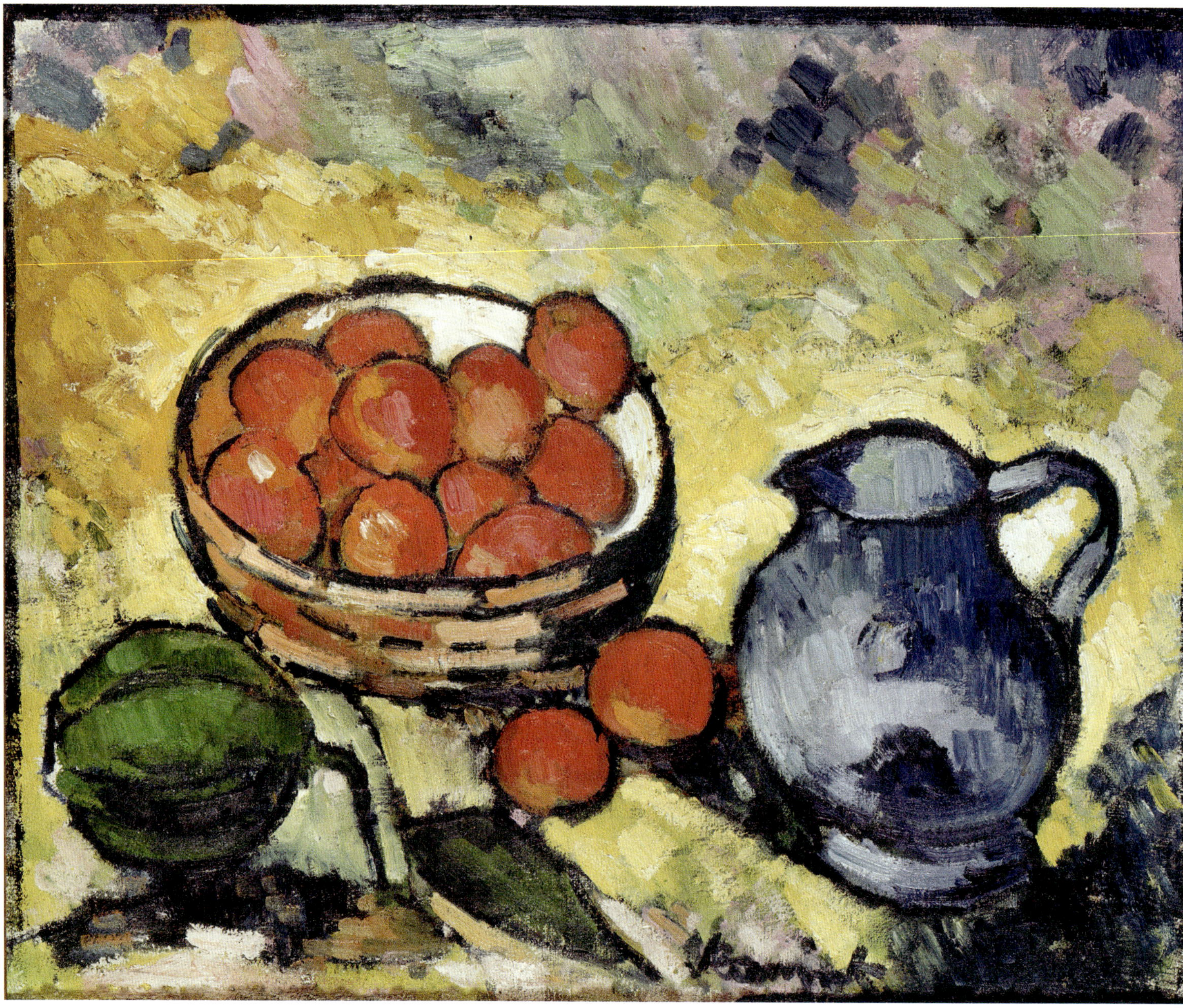

26
Still Life, 1907

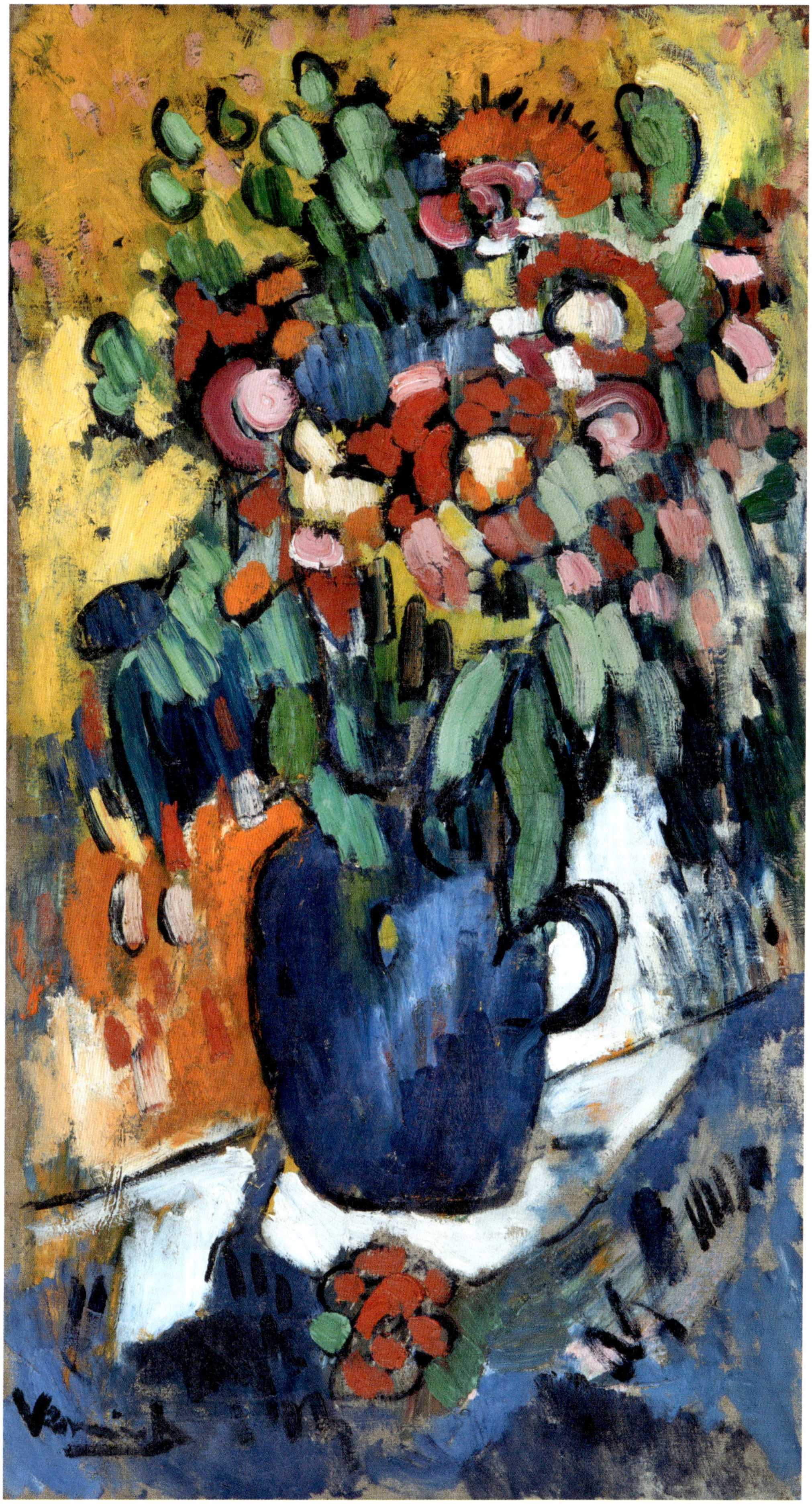

27
Blue Vase with Flowers, ca. 1906

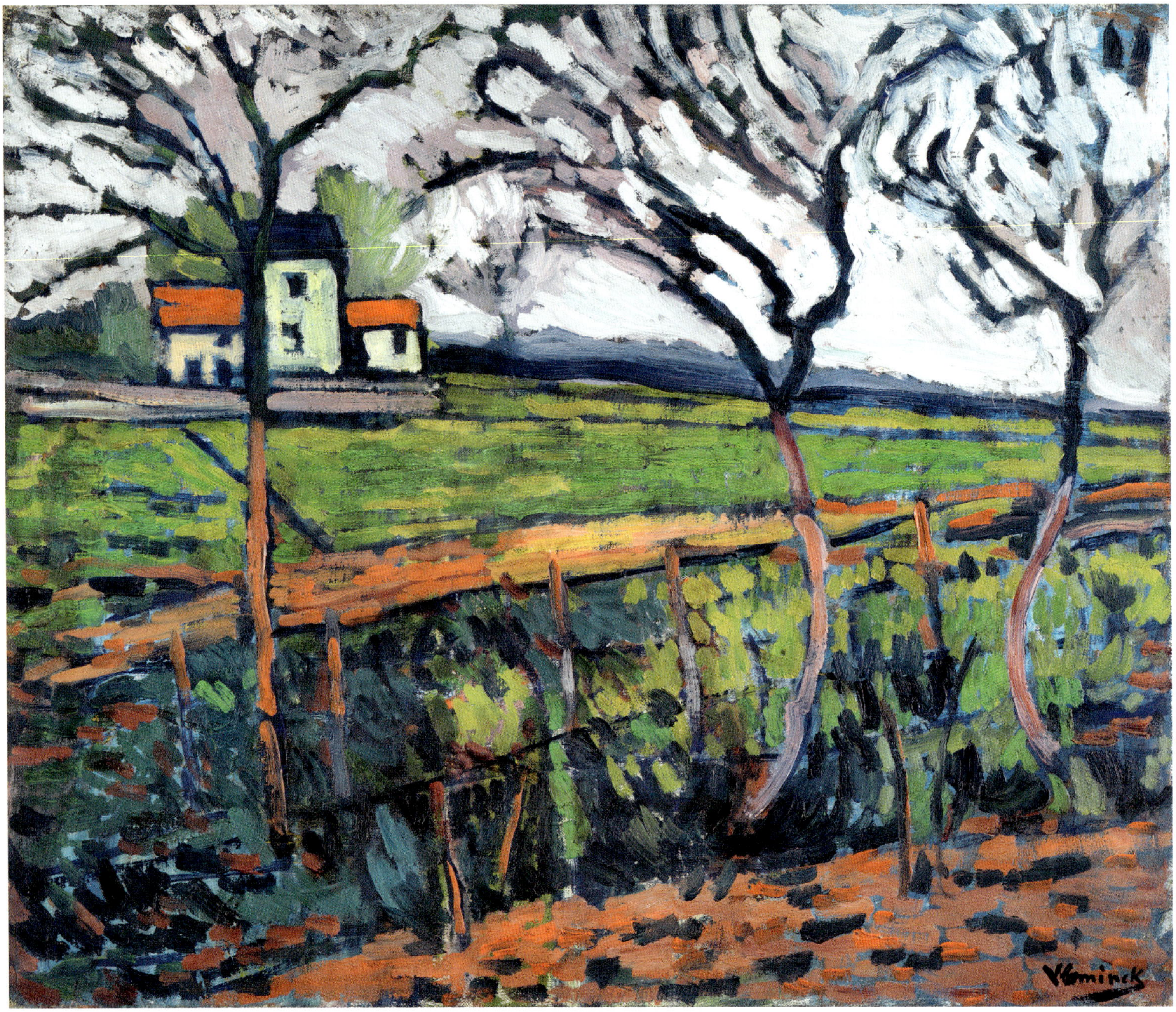

28
Fields, Rueil, ca. 1906–07

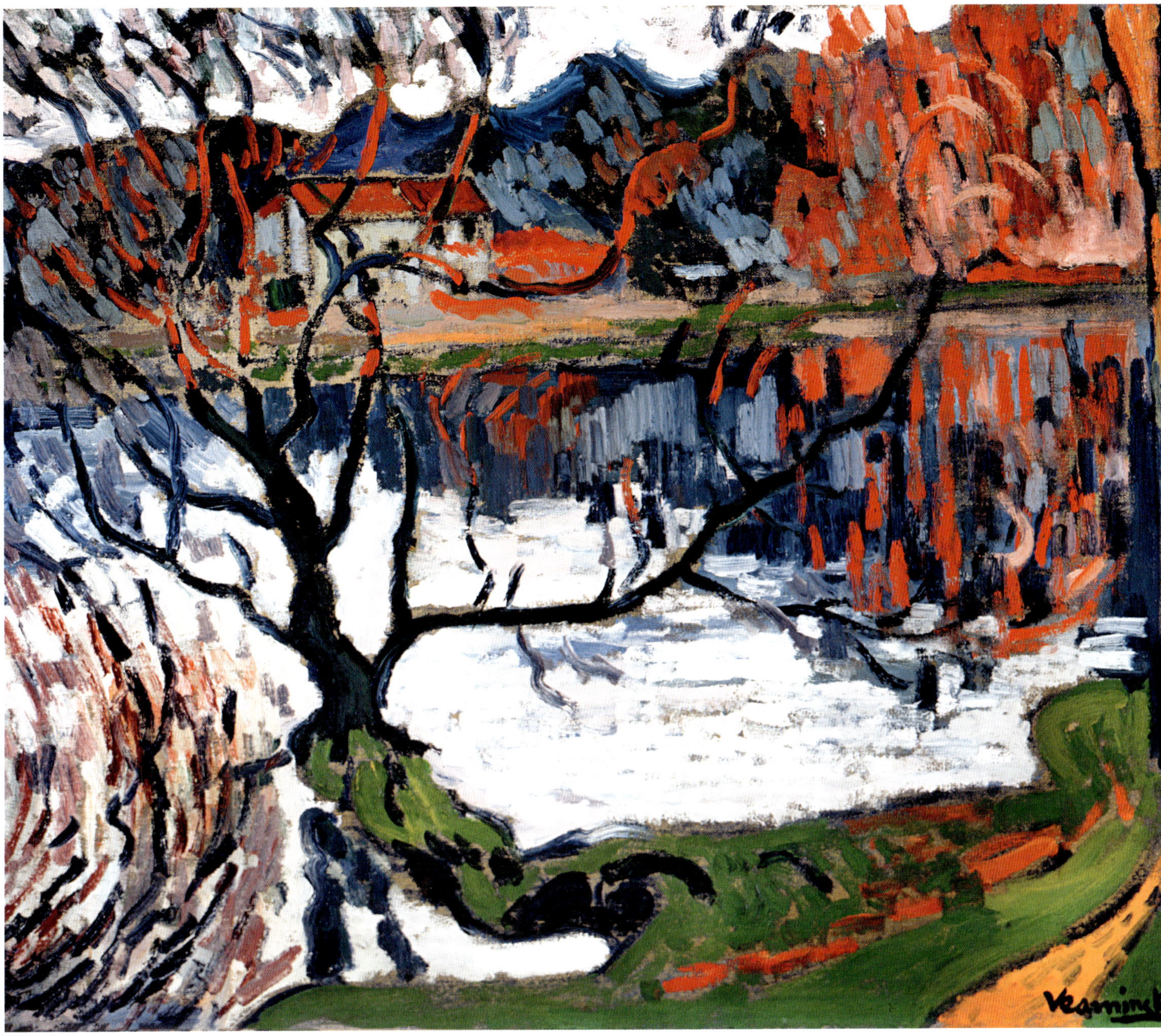

29
Pond at Ursine near Chaville, 1905

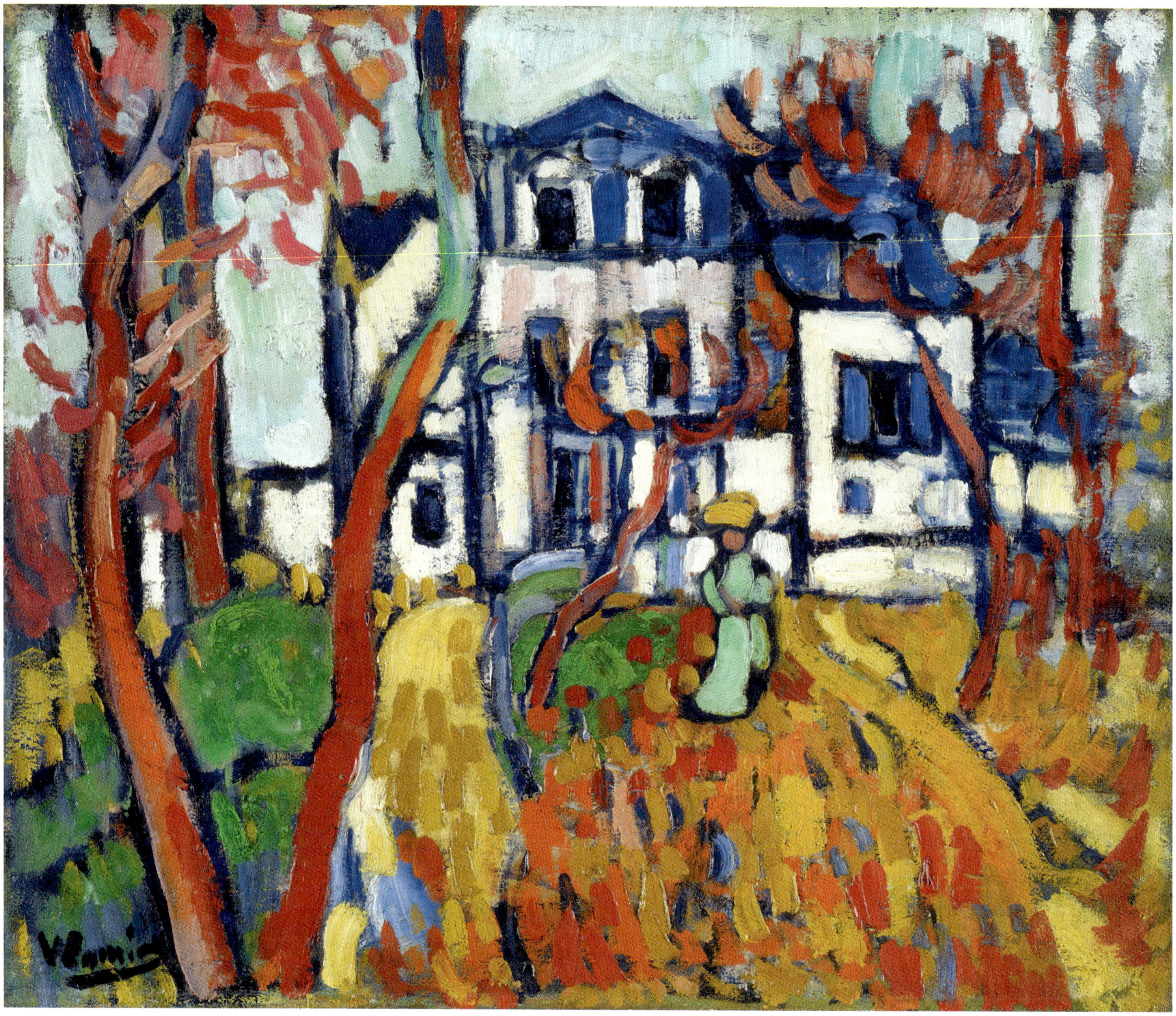

30
The Blue House, 1906

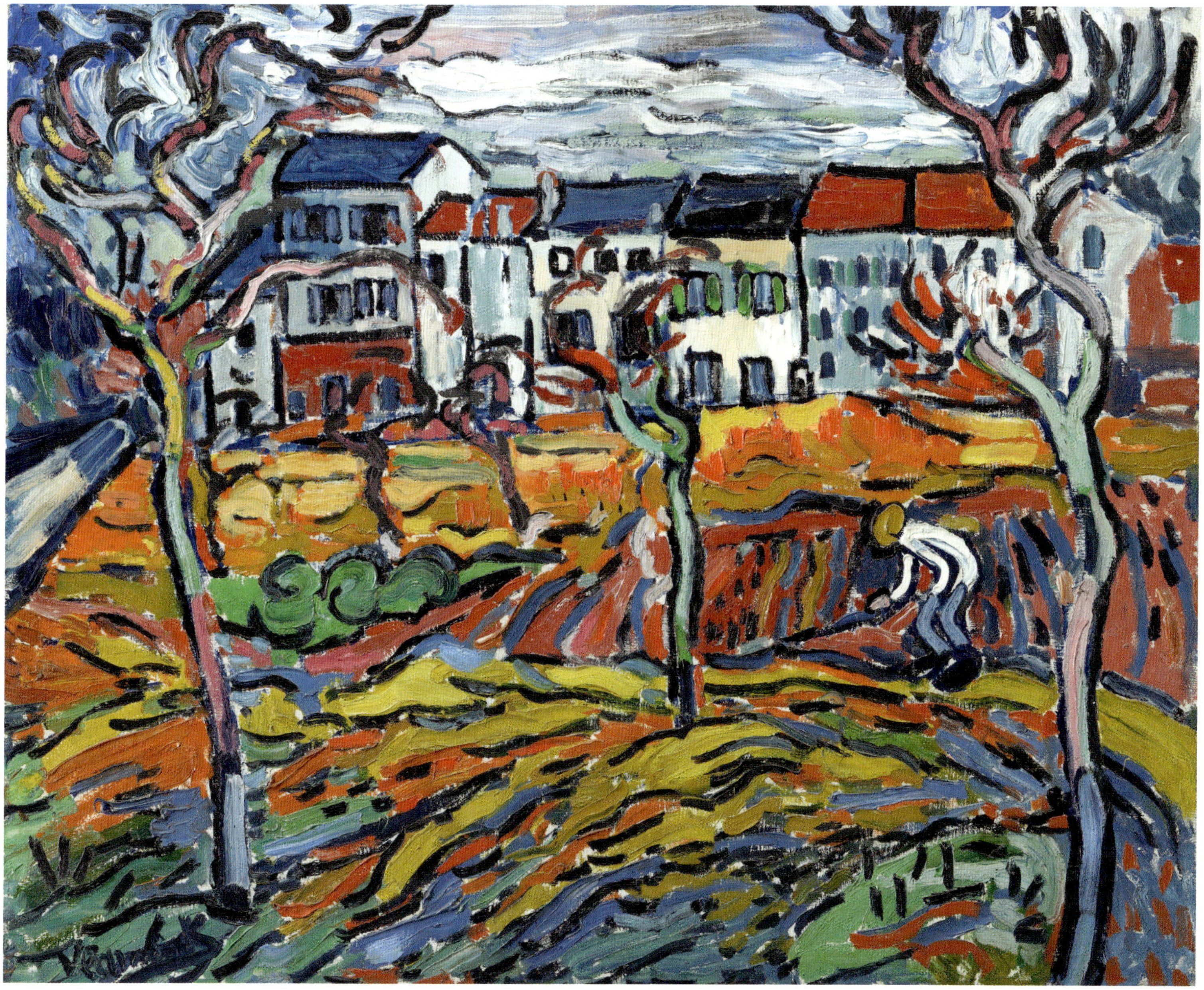

31
Houses at Chatou, ca. 1905

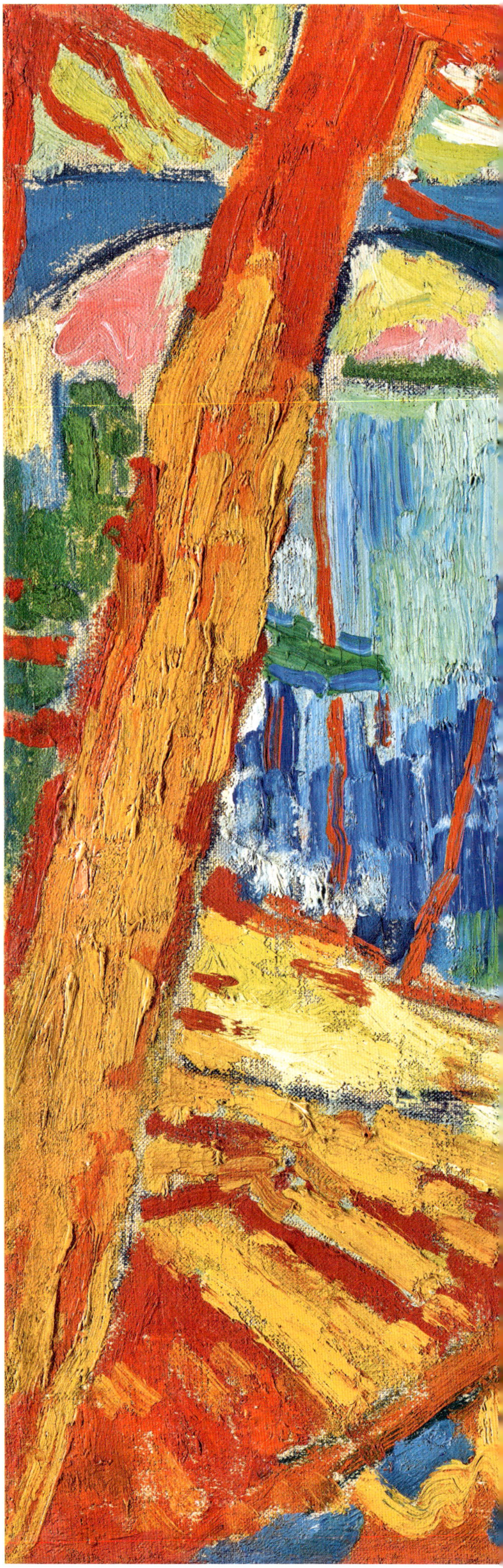

32
Fisherman in Chatou, 1906

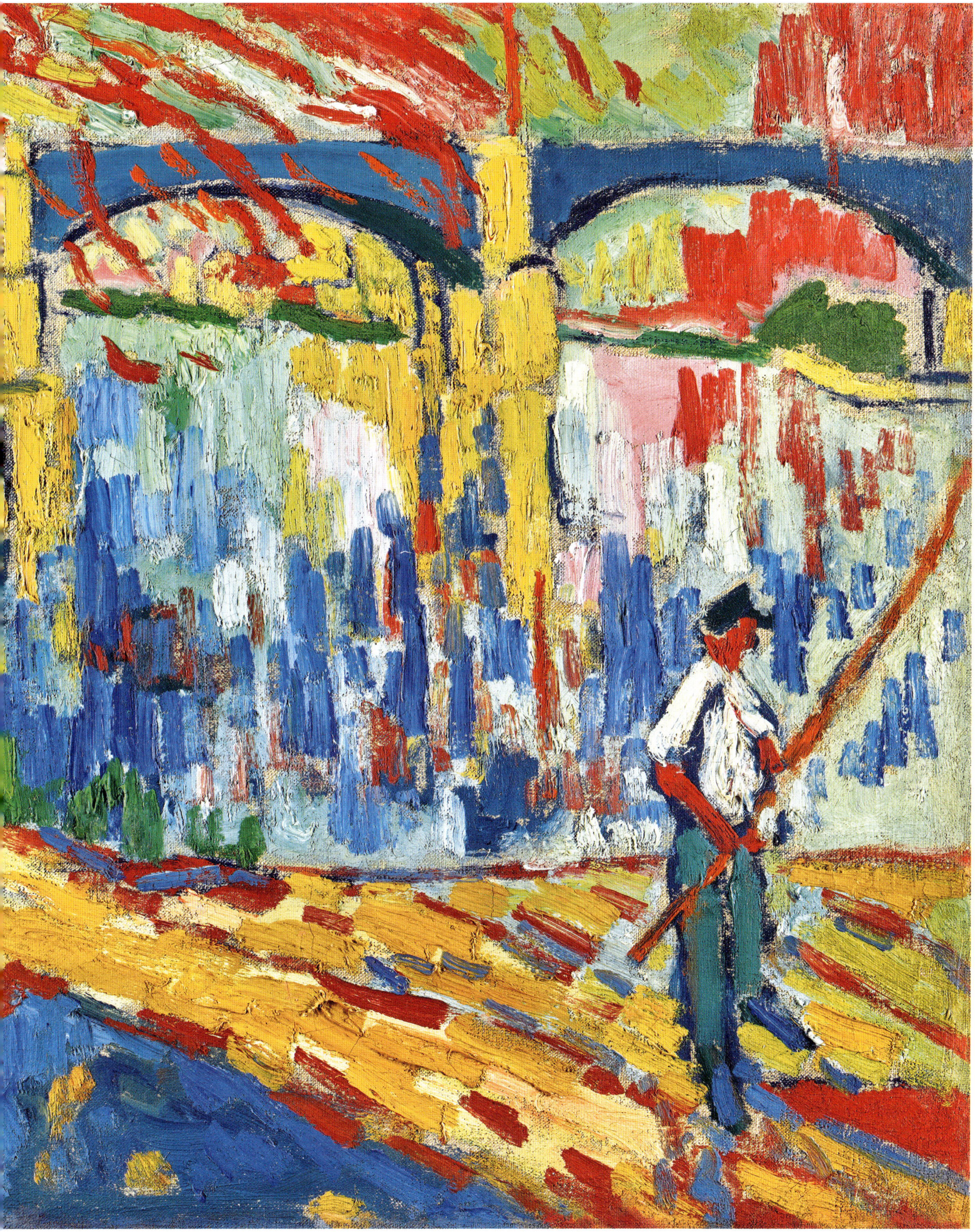

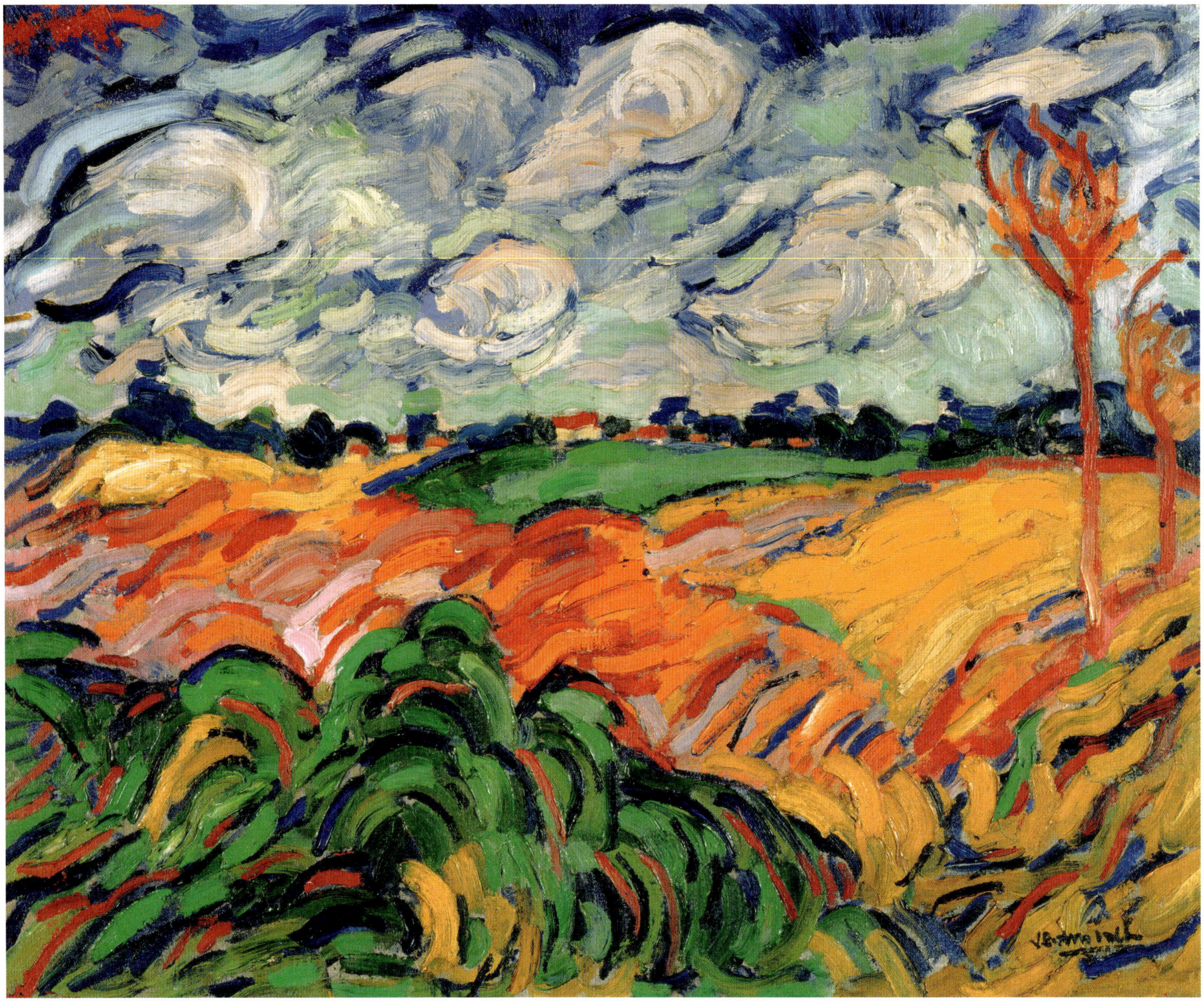

33
The Wheat Field (Champs de Blé), ca. 1906

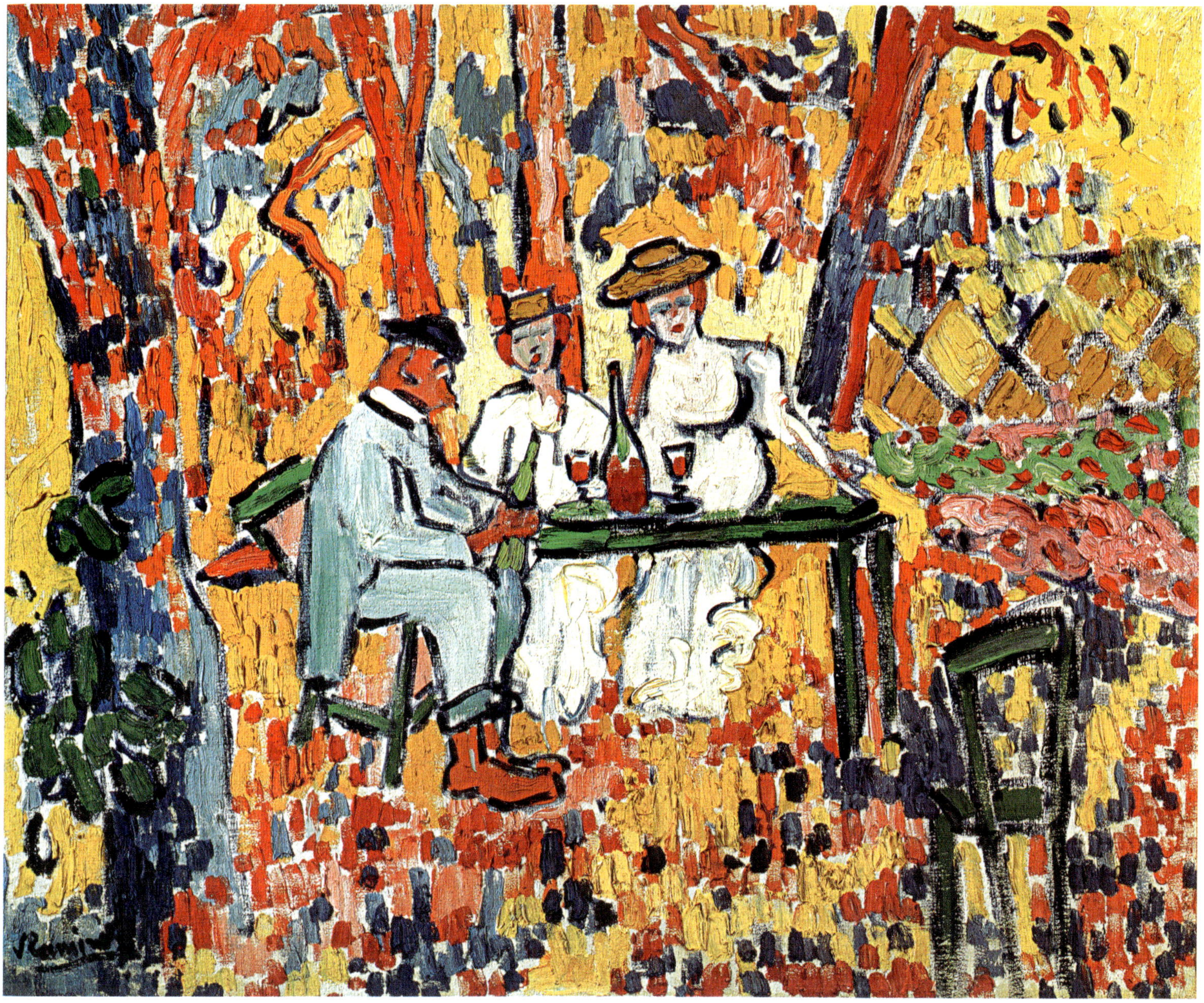

34
The Rural Luncheon, 1906

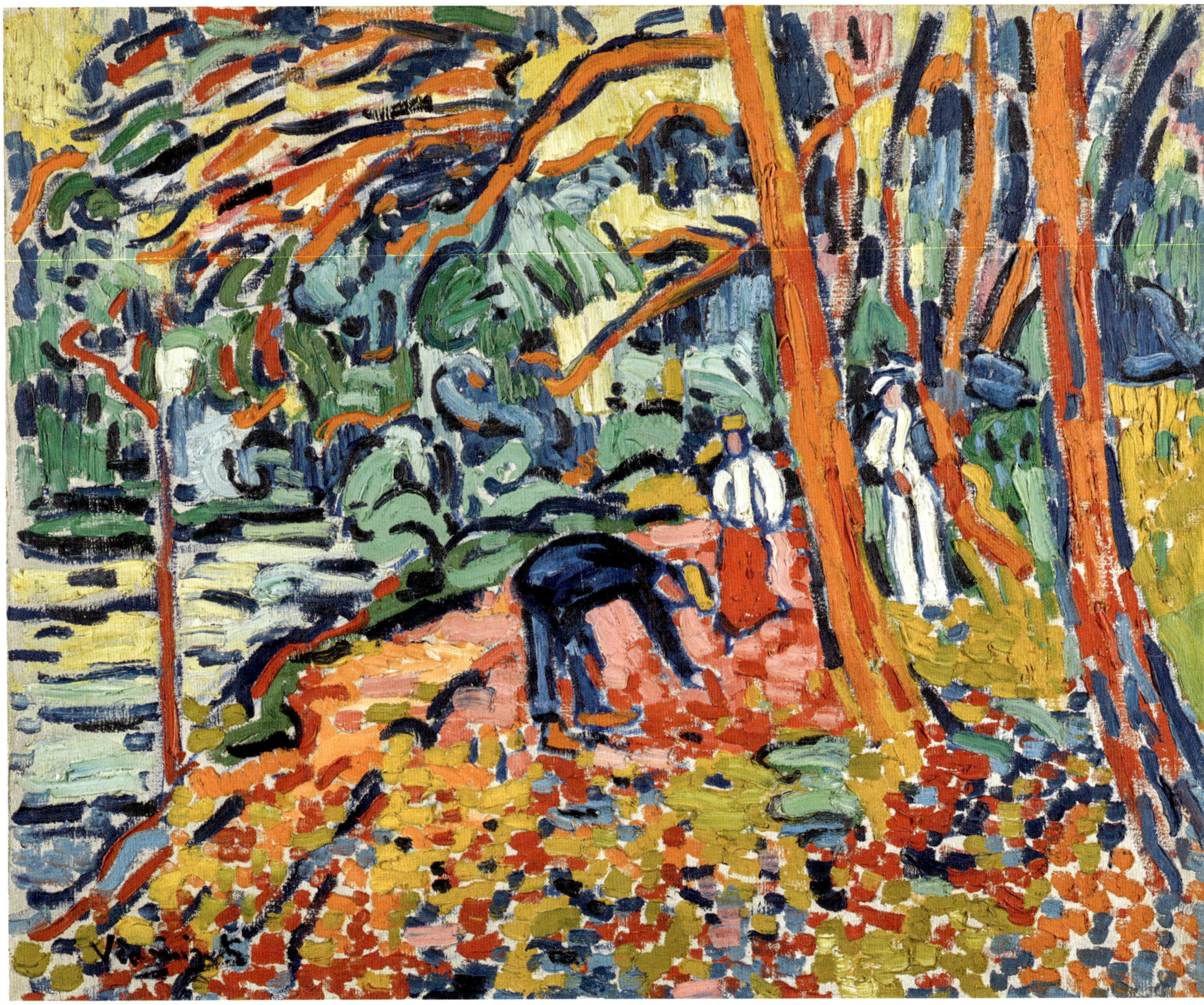

35
Forest Scene with Deadwood (Deadwood Collectors), 1906

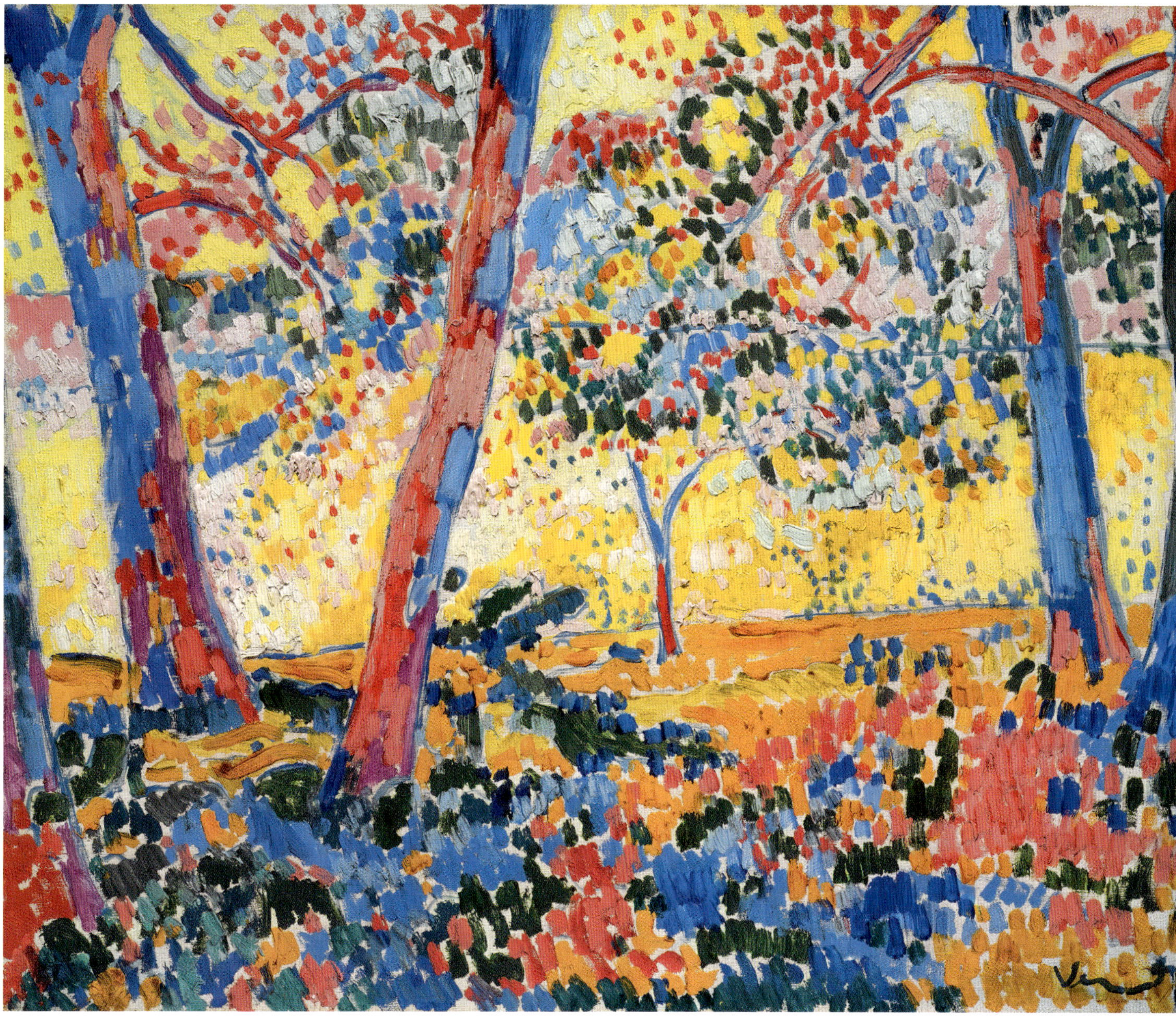

36
Underbrush, 1905

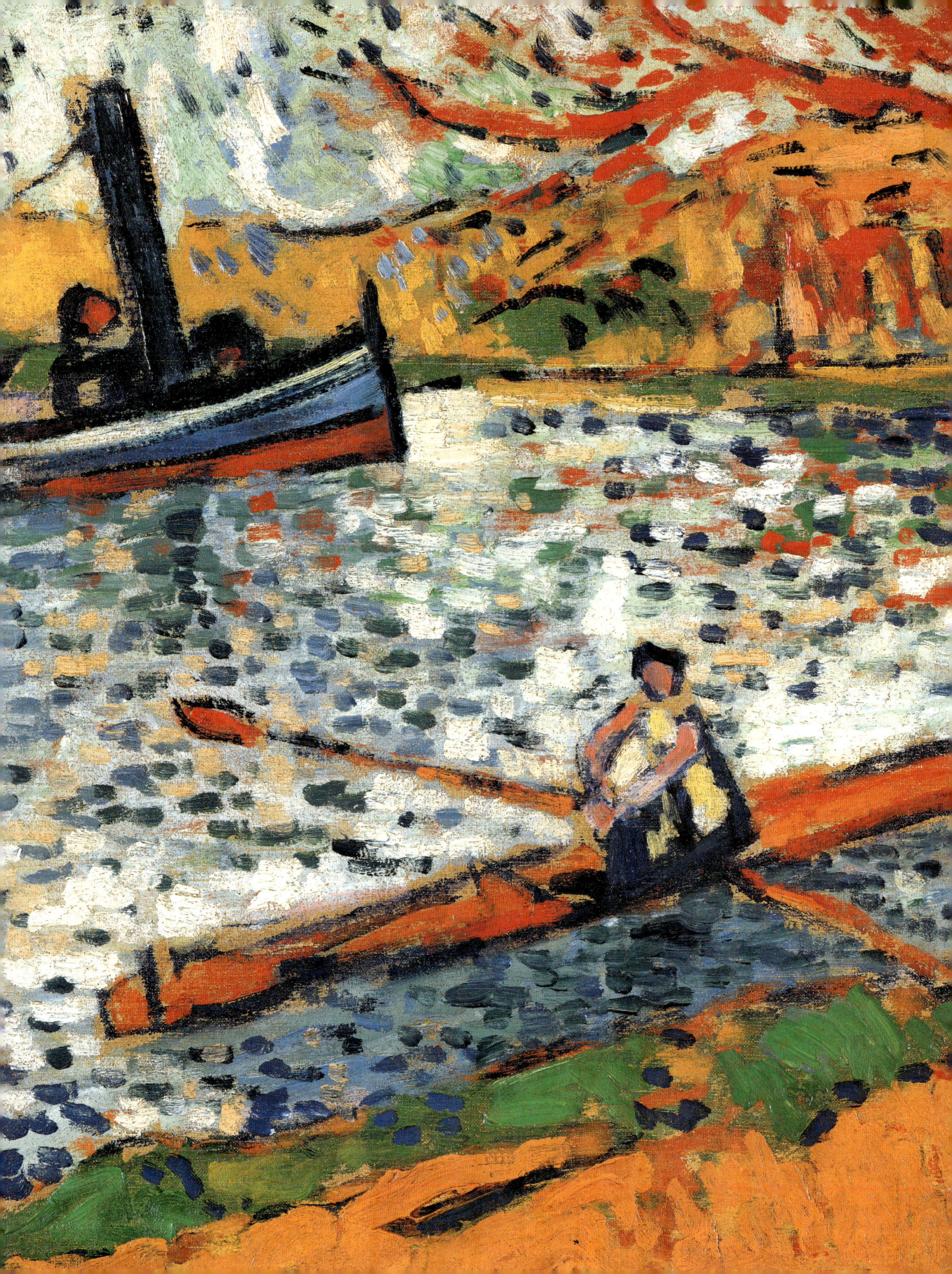

Impressionist Motifs

Painting along the Seine

Jacqueline Hartwig

In the early years of the twentieth century, Vlaminck rented a studio in Chatou together with fellow Fauvist painter André Derain. Although he also created figural images and still lifes, his artistic interests revolved primarily around the landscape of the Seine Valley. In his painting he followed the practice of the Impressionists, rendering his motifs in the open air and from direct observation. Between 1904 and 1908, he painted numerous views in the environs of villages such as Poissy, Bougival, Rueil, Nanterre, and Argenteuil—idyllic locations that were all situated along the three wide bends of the Seine west of Paris. With the choice of this landscape, Vlaminck devoted himself to a topography that had already been explored by Impressionist painters such as Claude Monet and Pierre-Auguste Renoir in the late nineteenth century.[1] In both technique and motif, his Fauvist compositions stood in the same tradition as the works of this older generation of artists. The subject matter is captured in a sketch-like, abstracted manner with forceful, clearly visible brushstrokes, while tonal contrasts serve to heighten the chromatic intensity. The chosen vantage points frequently show views of bridges or factories—imposing witnesses of French engineering prowess that connoted progress and modernization. The idyllic river landscapes are often enlivened with sailboats, rowboats, or steam-powered tugboats; along with the cropped compositions and focus on the play of colored reflections, they lend the images a sense of immediacy and dynamism.

For Henri Matisse, the dazzling light of the South was an important source of inspiration: lengthy stays in the French Riviera in 1904 and 1905 resulted in a lightening of his palette and the embrace of pure, glowing jewel tones. Vlaminck had already seen Matisse's large landscape painting *Luxury, Calm, and Voluptuousness* (fig. p. 36) in the spring of 1905 at the Salon des Indépendants in Paris, where he himself was represented with eight works, and soon thereafter he also encountered the works Derain and Matisse had created in the Riviera the same year. Presumably under the influence of these models, Vlaminck's choice of colors changed within a short period of time. Although he consistently worked in the cooler light of northern France, many of his Fauvist views of the Seine are characterized by a vivid palette that seems to echo his colleagues' landscape paintings from the South of France. In *Rueil, the Boathouse* (cat. 41), the color scheme is dominated by the cobalt blue of the river. The vermilion of the building in the background sets a pronounced accent, while the red-painted stripe of the boat along the shore provides a visual parenthesis. The bright green of the vegetation,

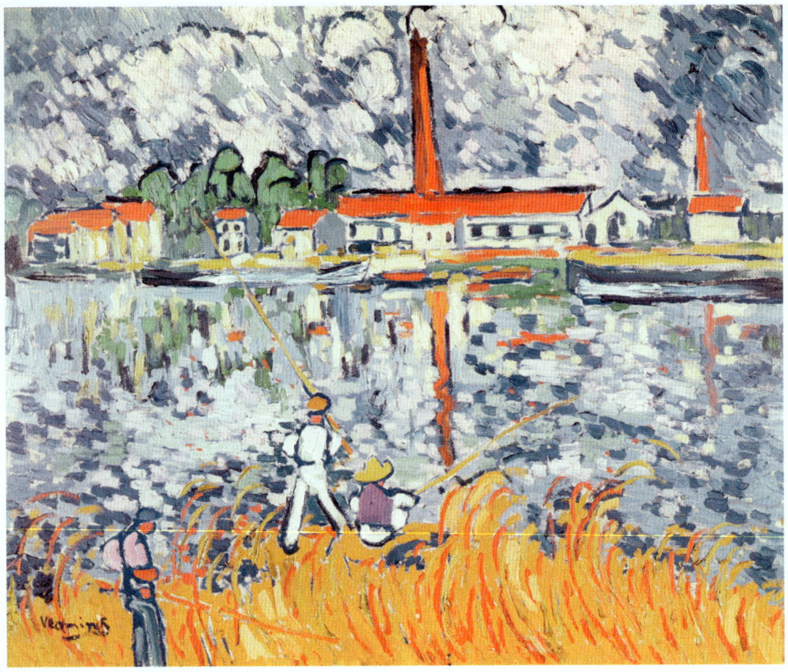

Maurice de Vlaminck,
Fishermen at Nanterre, 1906,
private collection

frequently heightened with flickering strokes of yellow-orange, establishes a complementary contrast that intensifies the radiance of the colors. Contrasting details are employed in a similar way in *The Fishermen* (cat. 56), where the blue and white of water and sky once again serve as a foil for pictorial elements in green and red.

Vlaminck grew up near Chatou, and as an enthusiastic cyclist he had thoroughly explored the surrounding landscape in his youth. In his paintings of the Seine Valley, he strove for topographical accuracy and represented his chosen scenes multiple times, experimenting with a wide variety of perspectives. His location while painting can often be identified quite precisely using sources such as old cadaster maps and historical postcards.[2] The names of towns or tracts of land associated with many of his pictures, however, are generally not the artist's own original titles, but later designations. Among Vlaminck's preferred motifs were the bridges across the Seine—including the Pont de Chatou, a railway bridge that had already been immortalized by Renoir in a painting from 1881 (Musée d'Orsay, Paris). Constructed in 1876, it spans both arms of the river on either side of the Île de Chatou and runs directly alongside Vlaminck's first studio at the former restaurant Levanneur. As with the river landscapes of the Impressionists, in Vlaminck's works the massive bridges also serve to structure the composition—whether as a visual axis lending dynamism to the image, or as a pictorial motif that functions as a frame. In *The Bridge at Chatou* (cat. 50), the artist painted the view from Rueil toward the bank of the island in the Seine, which is lined with poplars and fronted by a green wooden washing shed. The recession into depth along the three massive arches leads the viewer's eye into the center of the picture—a path-like axis that forms a stabilizing counterpoint to the diagonal of the river course. A fisherman standing on the embankment in the left foreground and a solitary sailboat to the right animate the otherwise uninhabited river landscape.

A number of Vlaminck's works show the importance of the Seine for modern water sports—a theme that also figured prominently in the painting of Impressionism (cats. 47–49, 52). *The Boats* (cat. 49), for example, recalls the motifs of Monet's pictures from Argenteuil and, appropriately enough, evinces a similarly sketch-like approach to brushwork that seems to echo the *taches* of Impressionist painting. Unlike Monet and other Impressionists, however, Vlaminck avoided the conventional association of the Seine Valley with urban tourism. Significantly, none of his landscapes show the well-heeled day-trippers who typically appear as staffage figures in the visual world of Impressionism. In Vlaminck's work, a focus on workers and the simple rural population goes hand in hand with motifs emphasizing the economic utilization of the Seine and highlighting its importance for the industrial infrastructure around Paris. One of Vlaminck's first landscape paintings was *The Banks of the Seine, Nanterre* from 1904 (fig. p. 25), which he exhibited the following year at the Salon des Indépendants in Paris. The painting shows the Papeterie de la Seine, a paper factory famous for its modern architecture; as an industrial landmark in Nanterre, it was popular as a postcard motif early on. Vlaminck seems interested above all in the red of the tile roofs and smokestack, which stand out dramatically against the fresh blue and white of the sky and river. In later compositions, as well, he used the juxtaposition of factory architecture and water to feature the interplay of vermilion and cobalt (cat. 38; fig. p. 116)—a tonal contrast he also employed in paintings such as *Tugboats on the Seine, Chatou* (cat. 37) and *Banks of the Seine at Bougival* (cat. 46).

In his autobiographical writings, Vlaminck repeatedly emphasized his pride in his autodidactic standing as well as his allegedly resolute rejection of art-historical tradition. Furthermore, he was at pains to characterize his Fauvist works as the result of an impetuous, instinctive approach to painting. His views of the Seine Valley, however, show that Vlaminck was highly strategic in his choice of motifs and perspectives. His plein-air painting was based on extensive, first-hand exploration of the landscape and combined a quest for immediacy and topographical authenticity with a cool eye for a formally appealing pictorial design. In addition, both thematically and stylistically, many of his works echo the painting of the Impressionists, whose artistic interest in the Seine Valley he emulated. In their motivic variety and brilliant color schemes, Vlaminck's Fauvist images of the Seine from 1904 to 1908 are among his most important paintings, works that helped further the liberation of color from its imitative function and paved the way for an art of pure expression.

Translated from German by Melissa M. Thorson

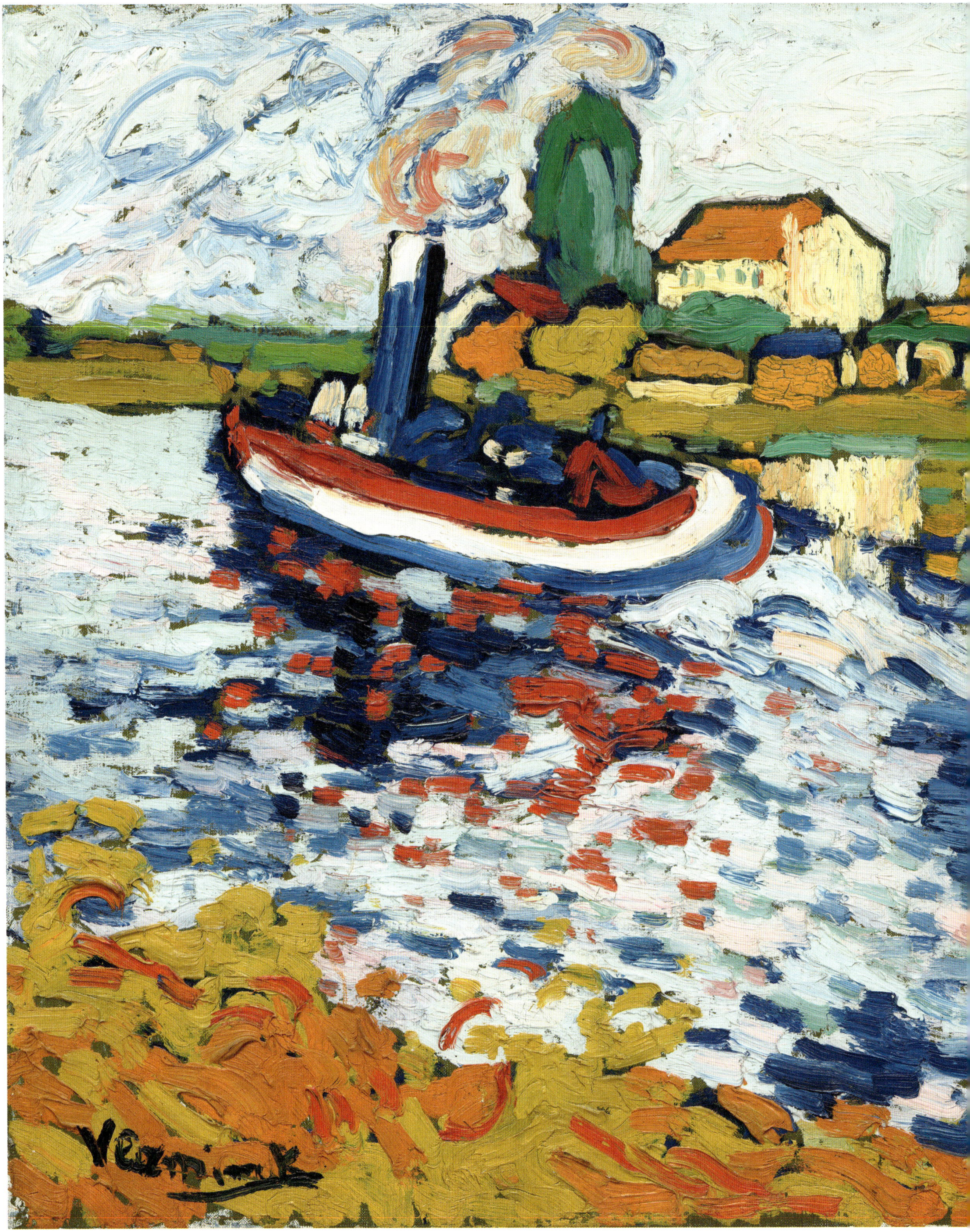

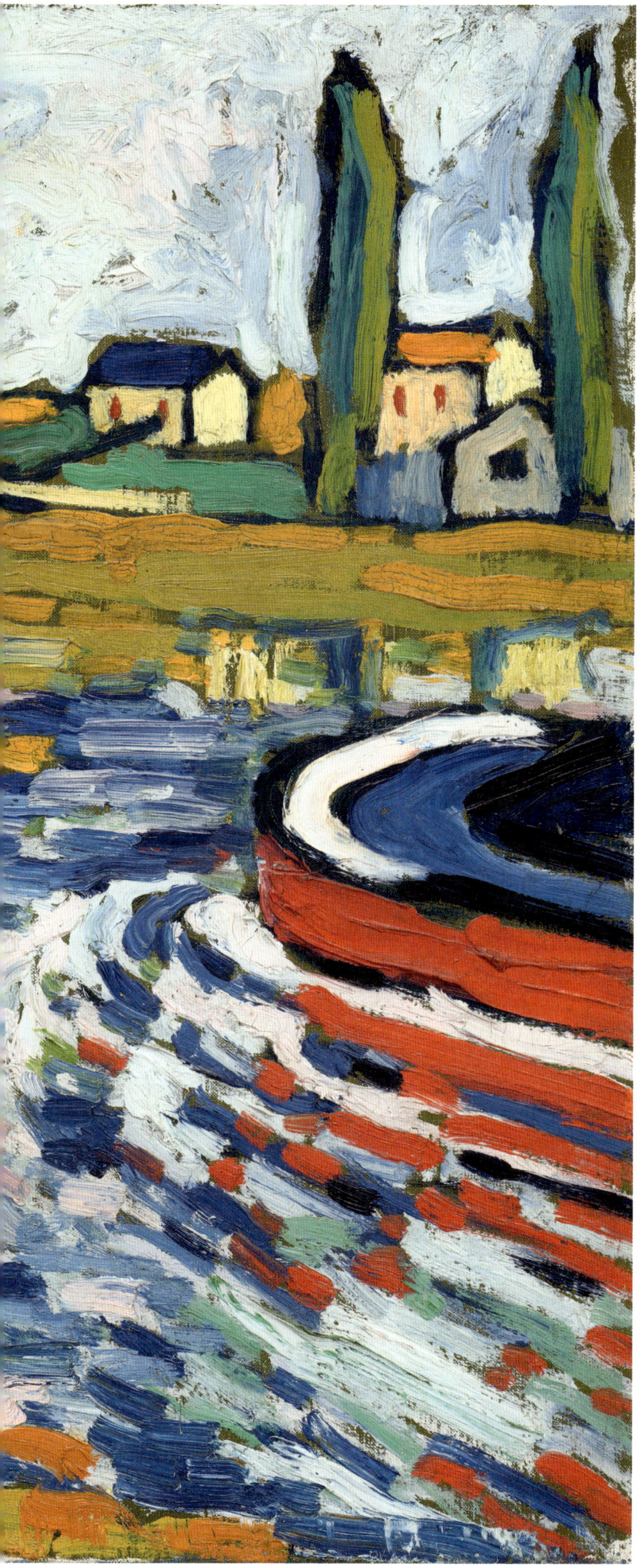

37
Tugboats on the Seine, Chatou, 1906

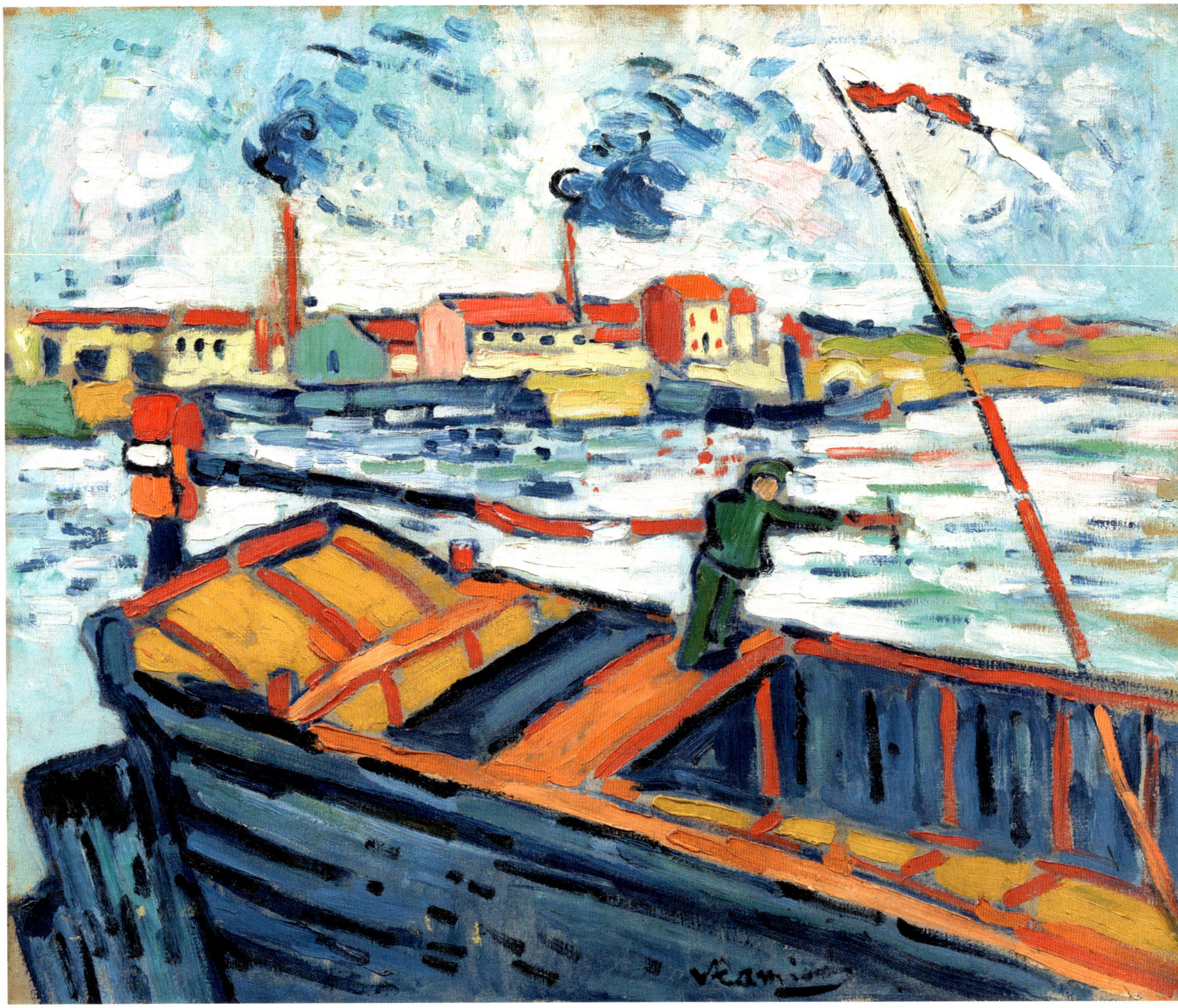

38
Canal Boat, 1905–06

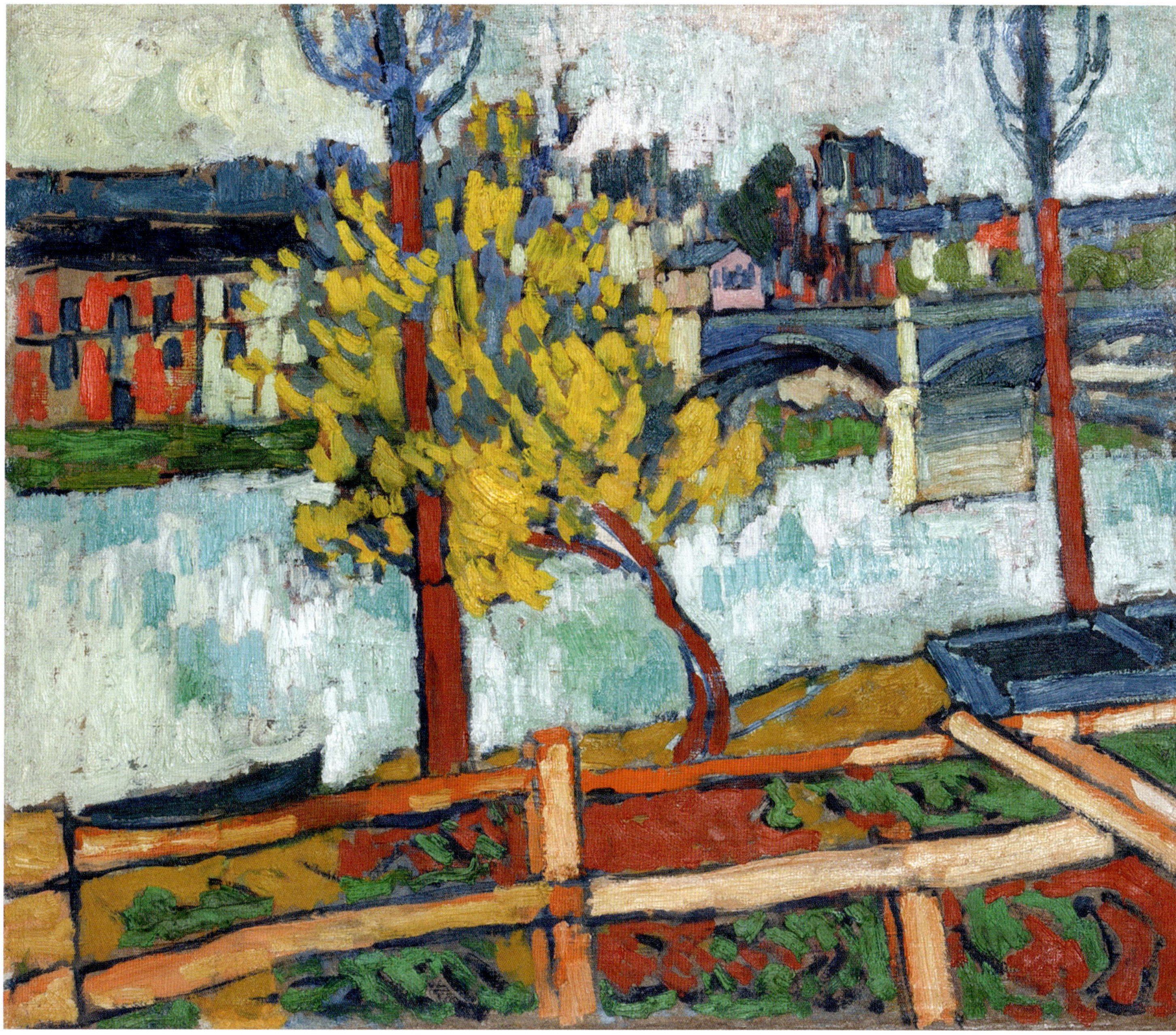

39
Banks of the Seine at Chatou, 1905

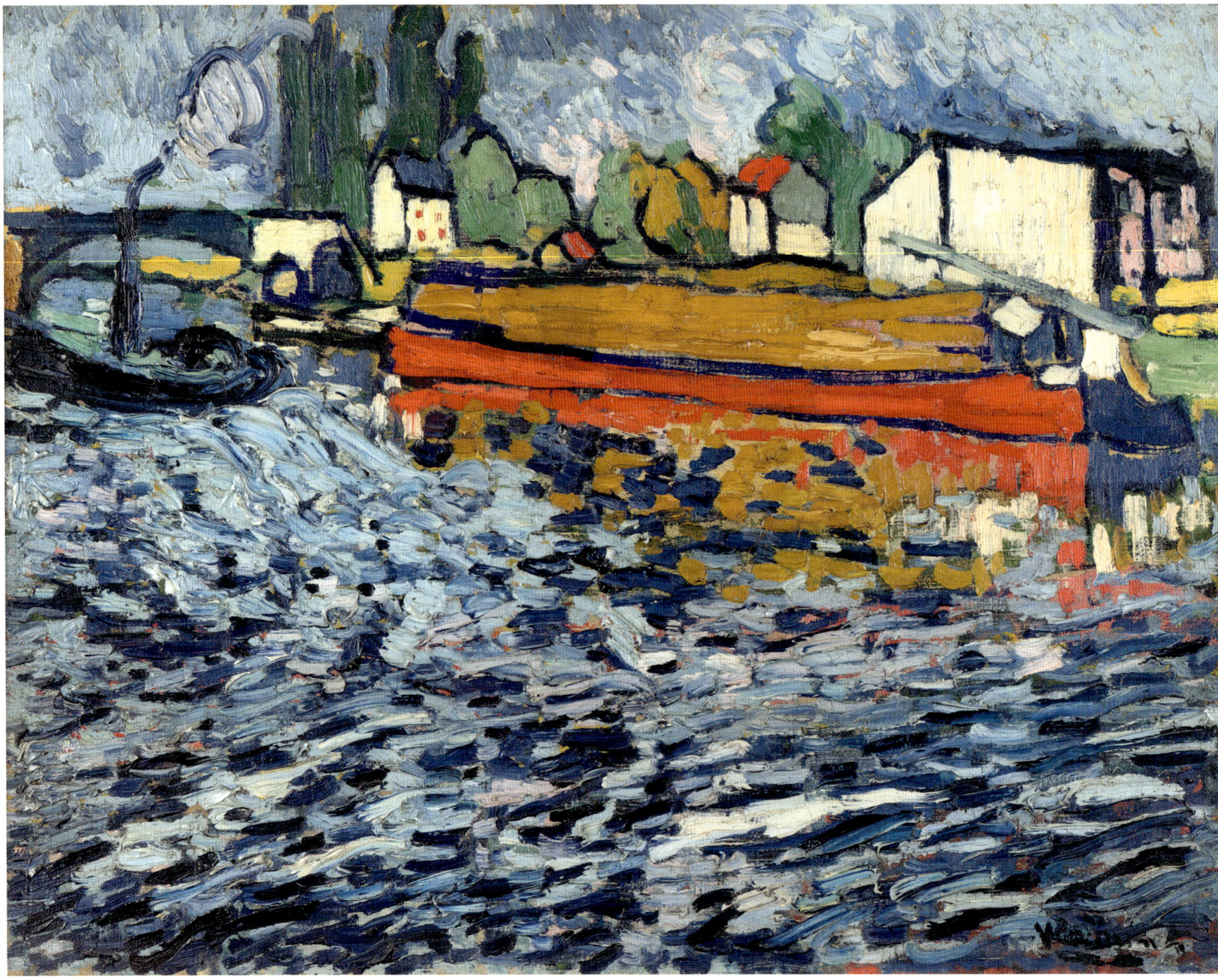

40
River Scene with Bridge, ca. 1905

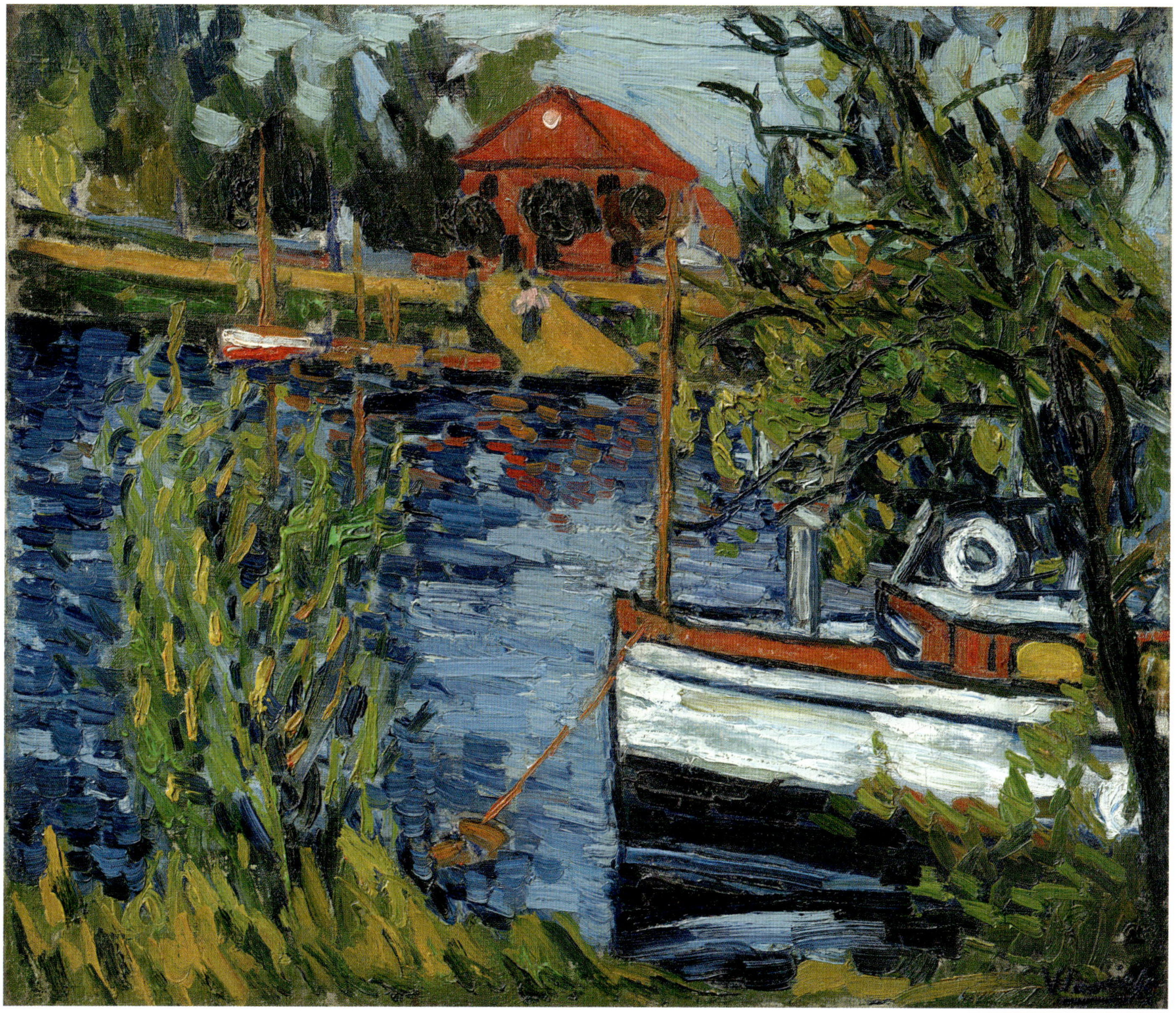

41
Rueil, the Boathouse, 1906

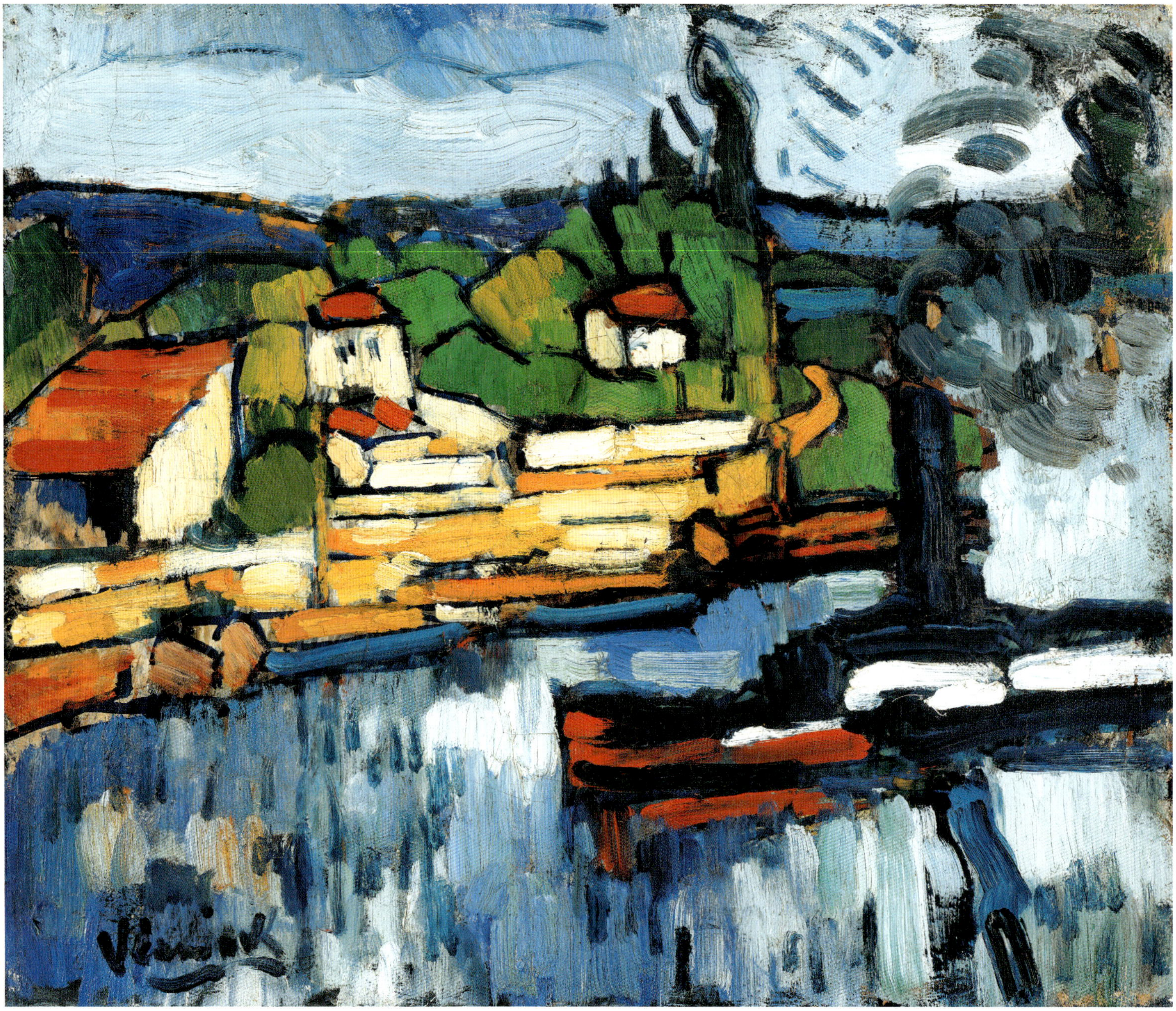

42
The Seine at Chatou, ca. 1906–07

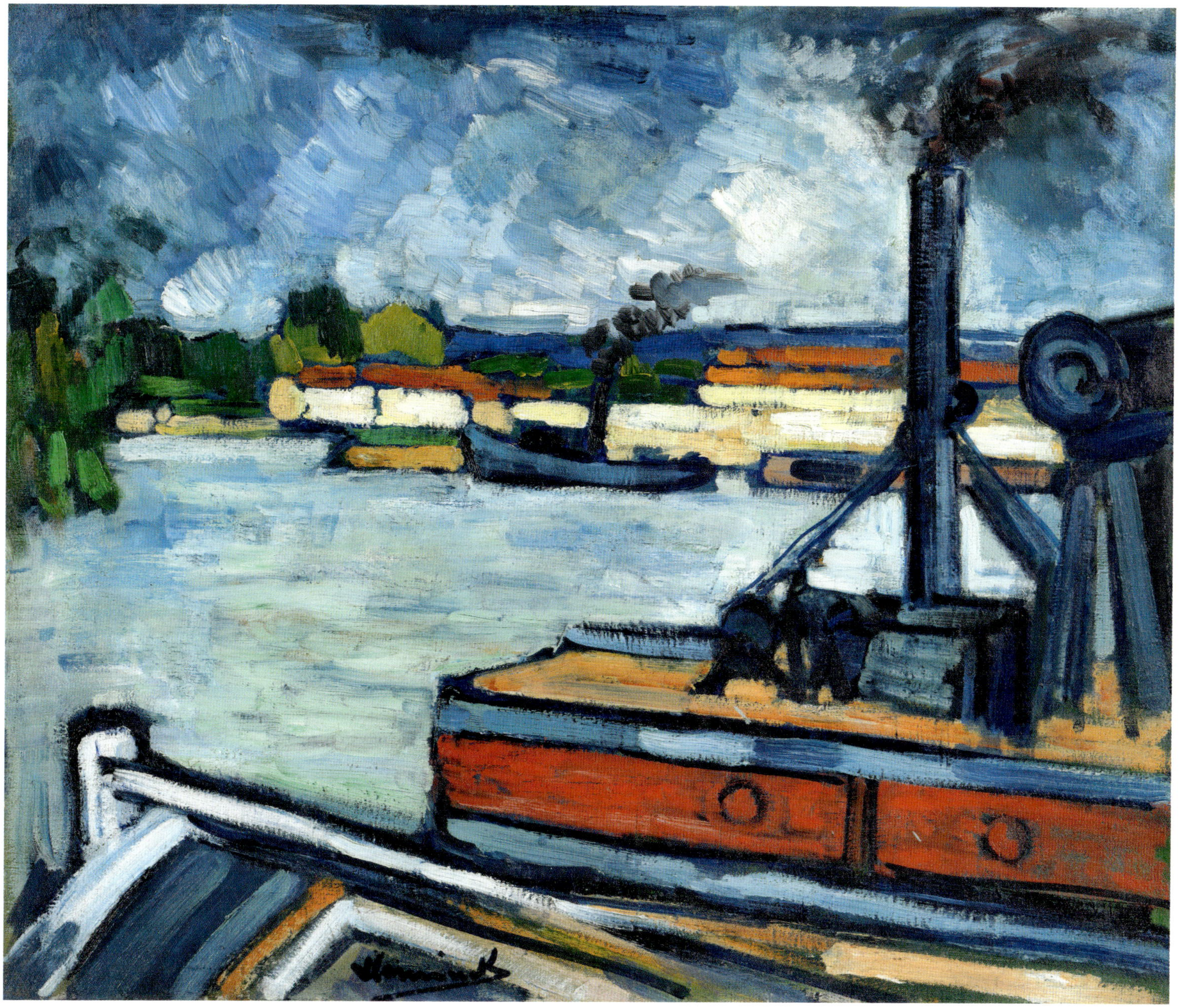

43
The Seine at Nanterre, 1906–07

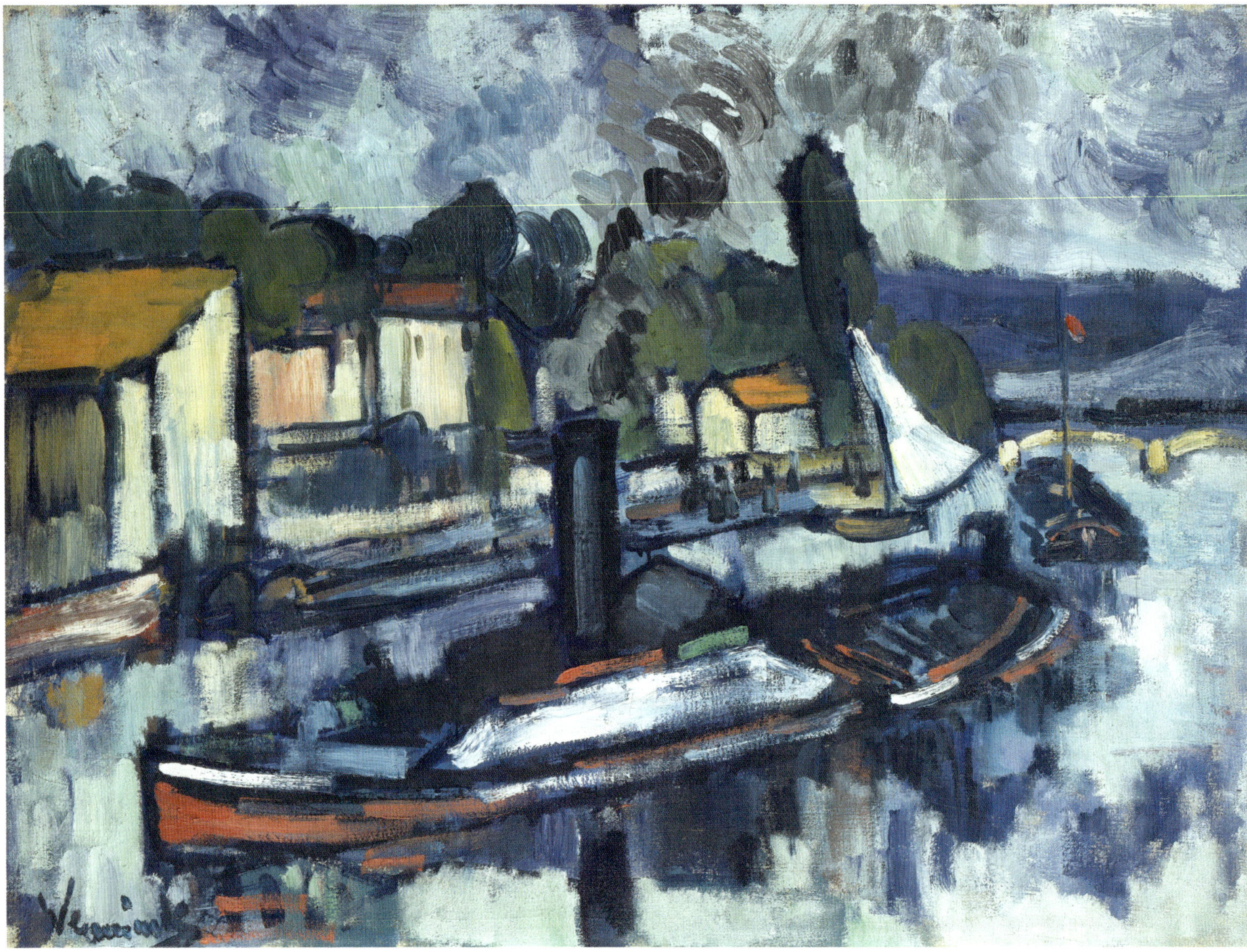

44
The Tugboat, 1908–10

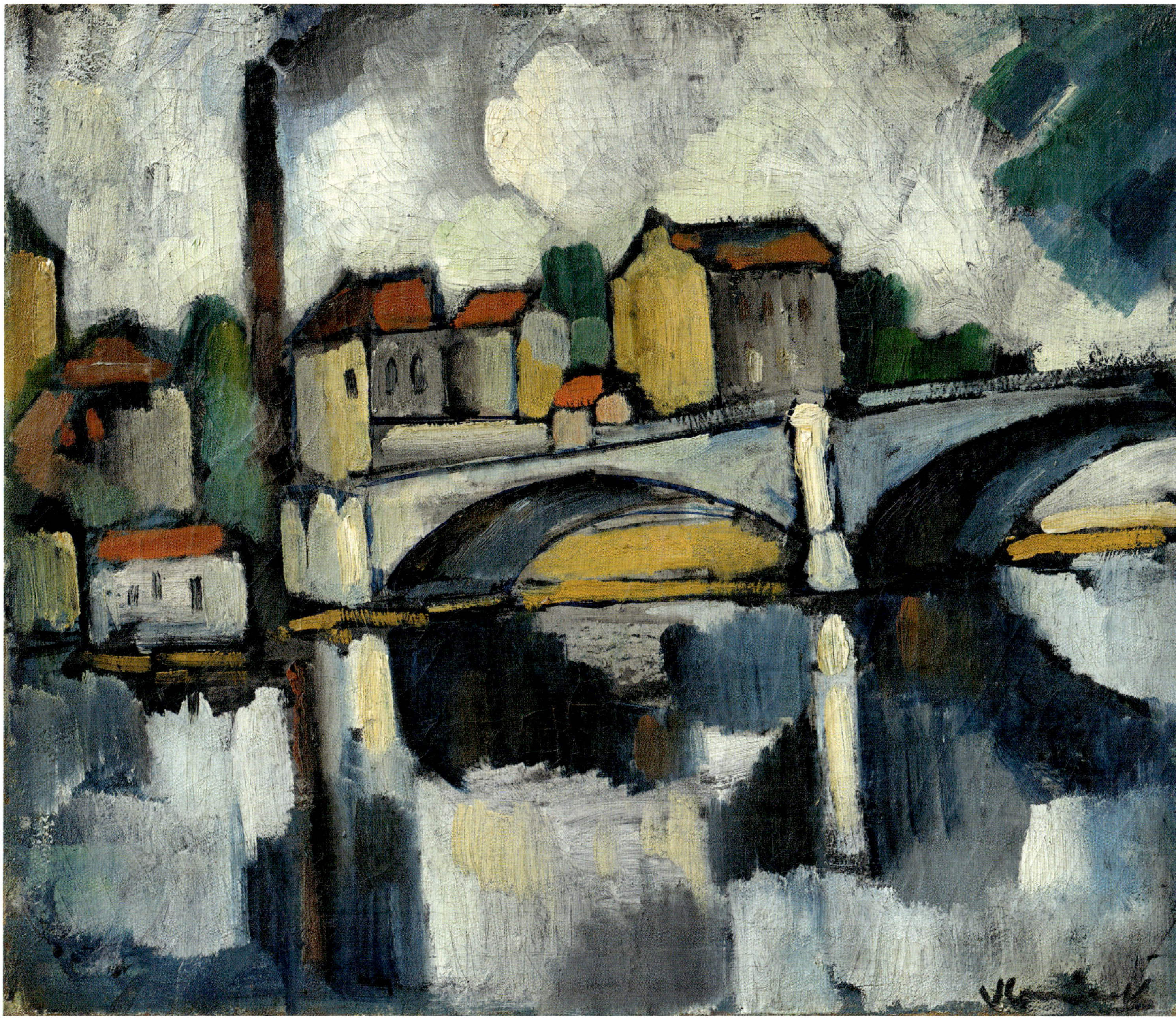

45
The Bridge, undated

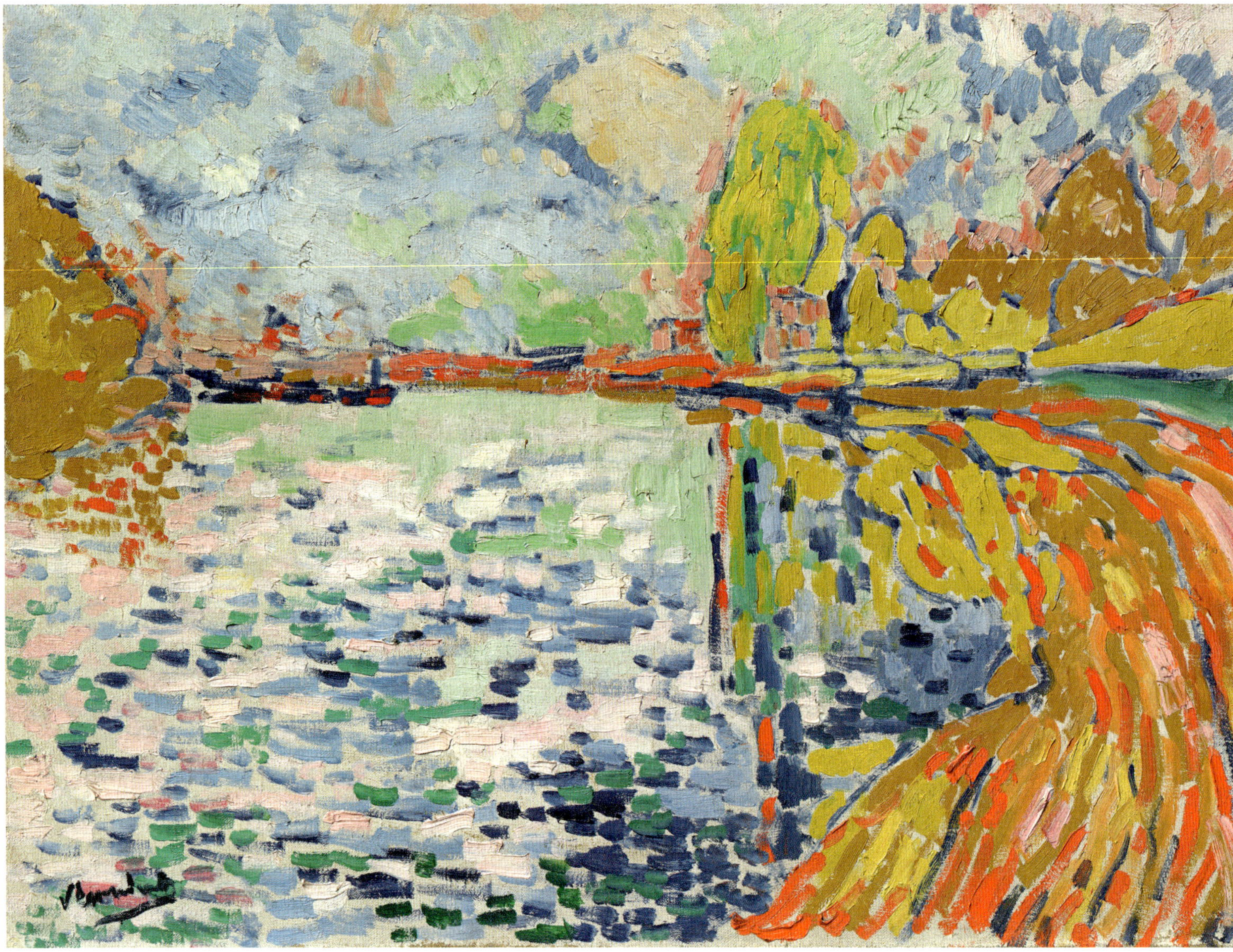

46
Banks of the Seine at Bougival, 1906

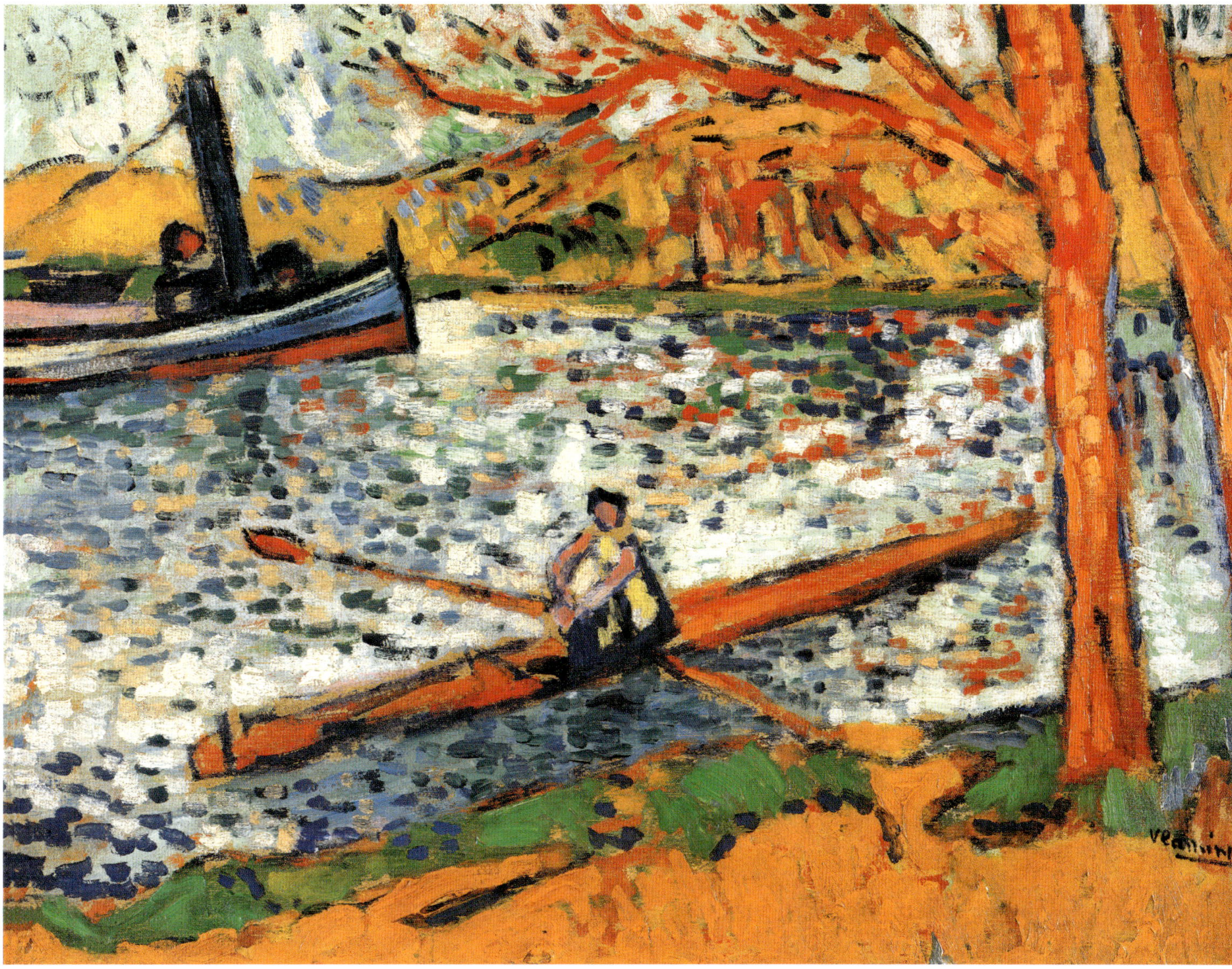

47
Rowboat at Chatou, ca. 1906

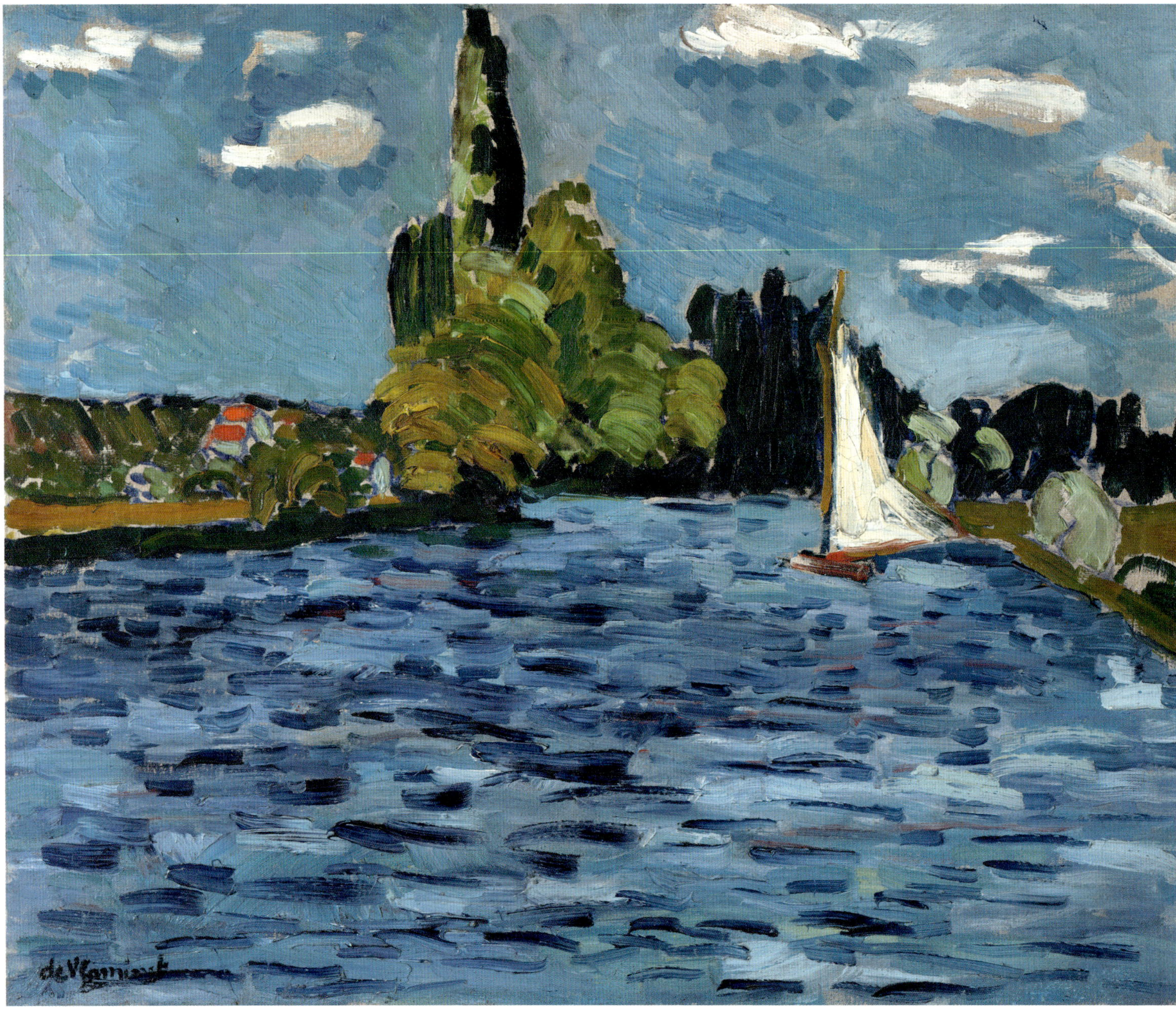

48
Sailing Boat, Chatou, ca. 1906

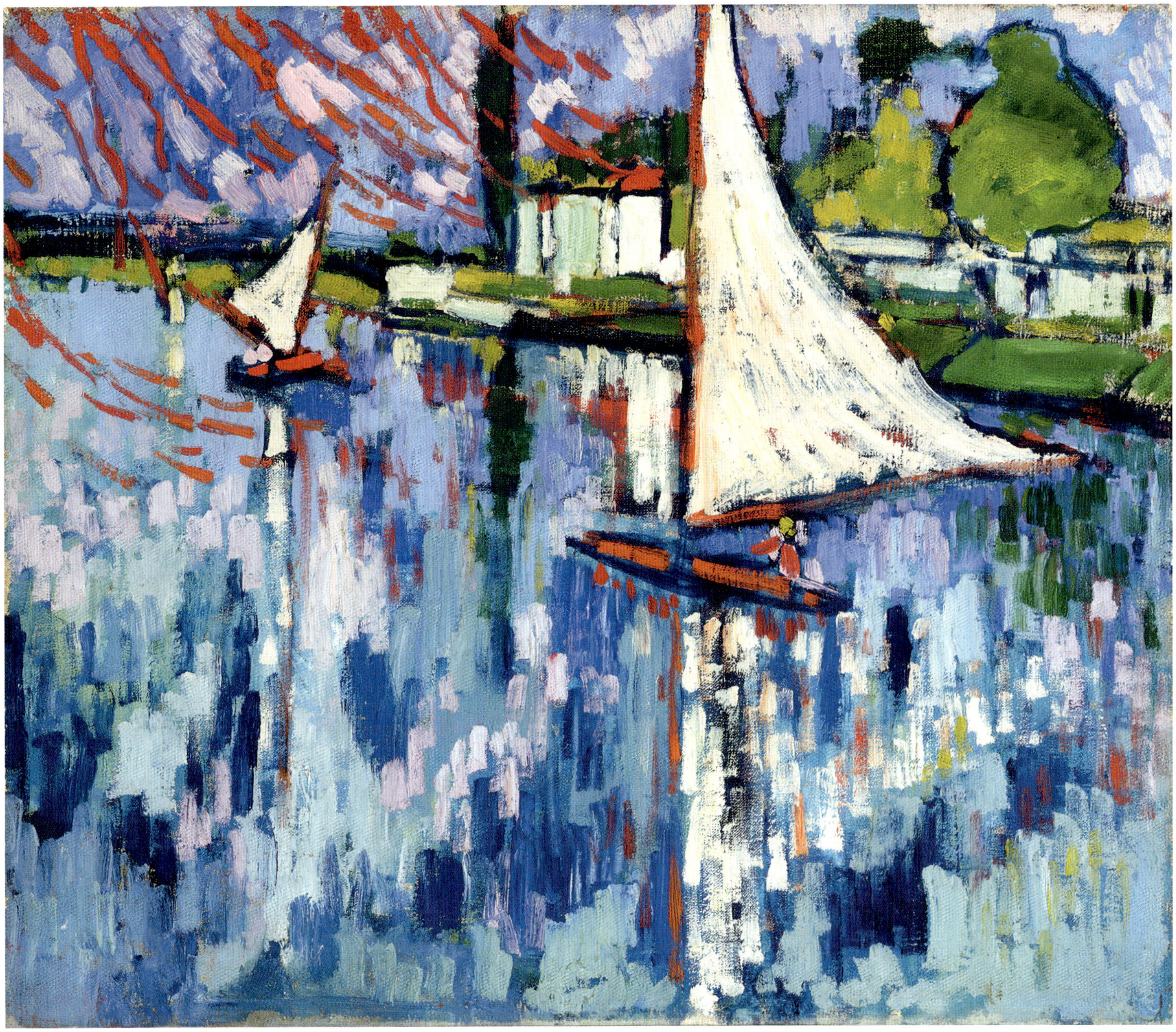

49
The Boats, 1905

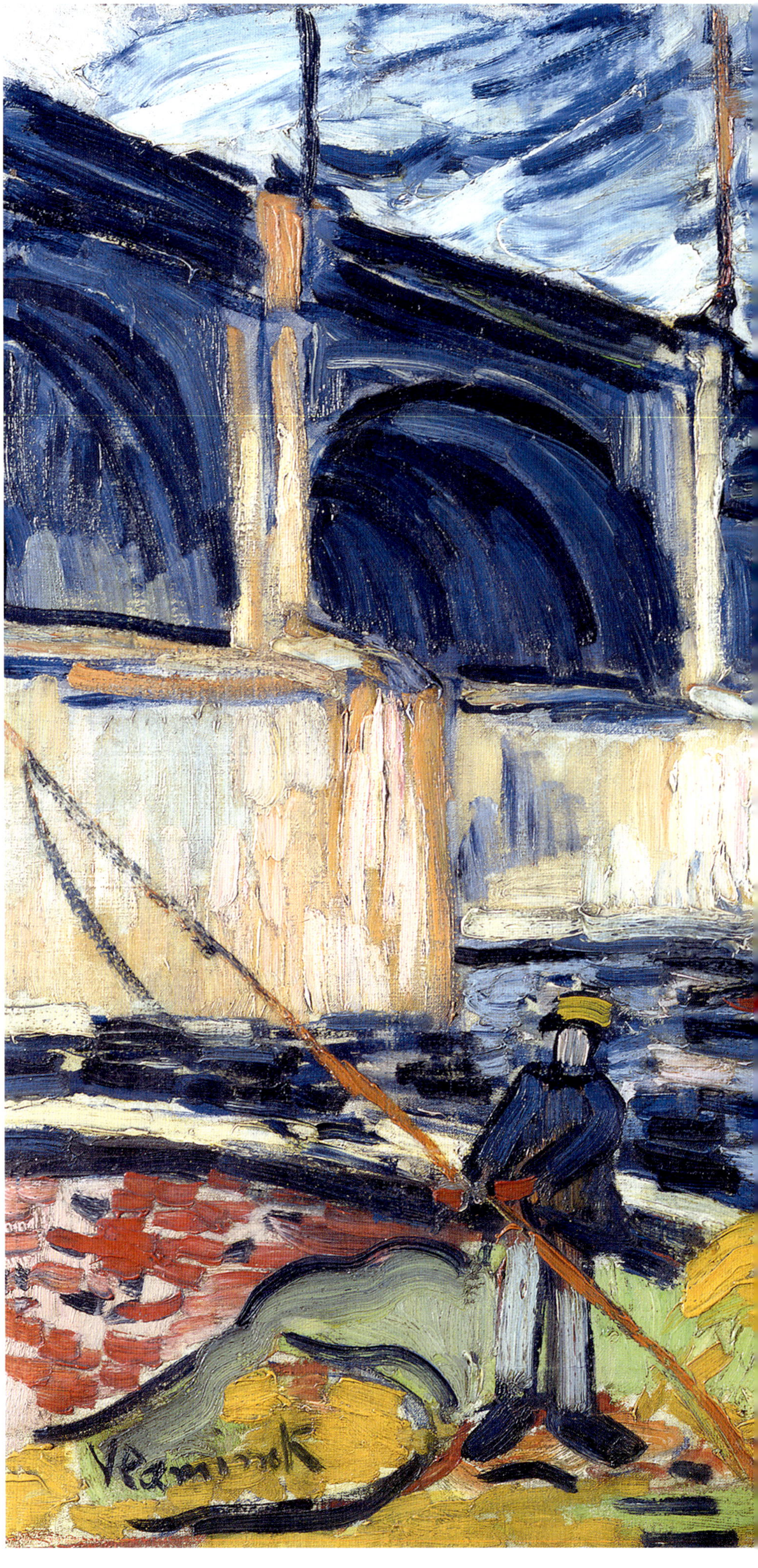

50
The Bridge at Chatou, 1905

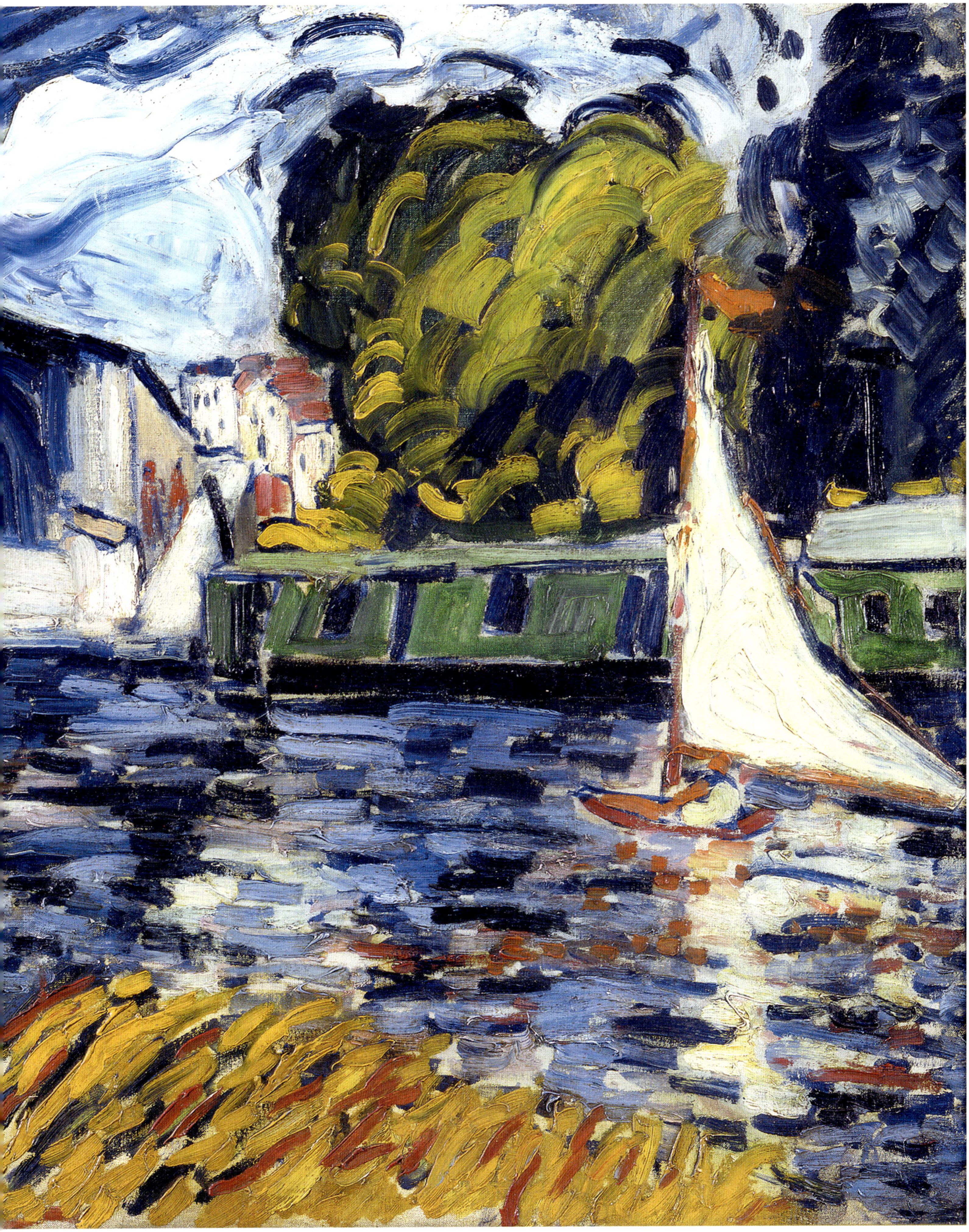

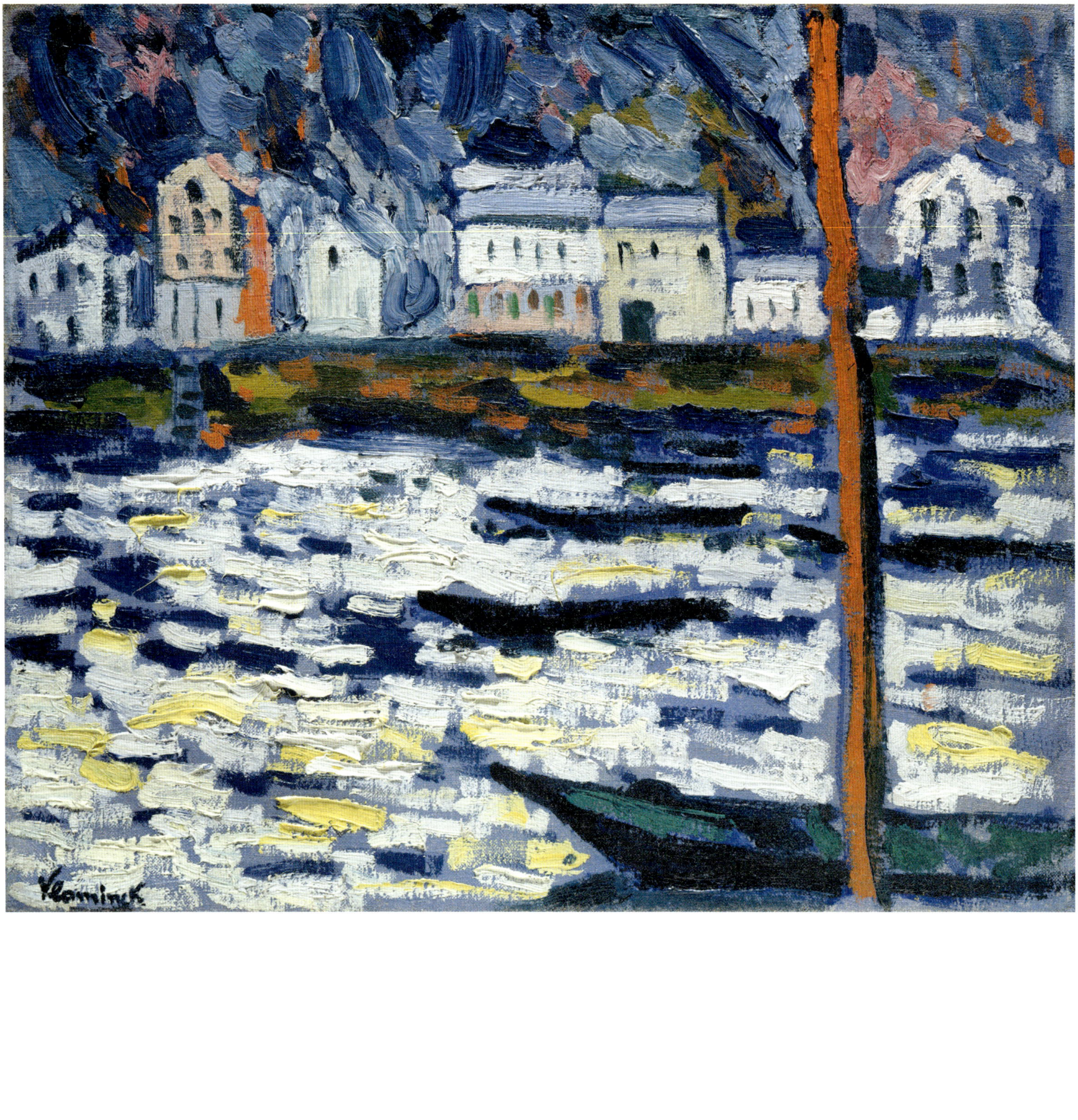

51
Sunlight on the Water, 1905

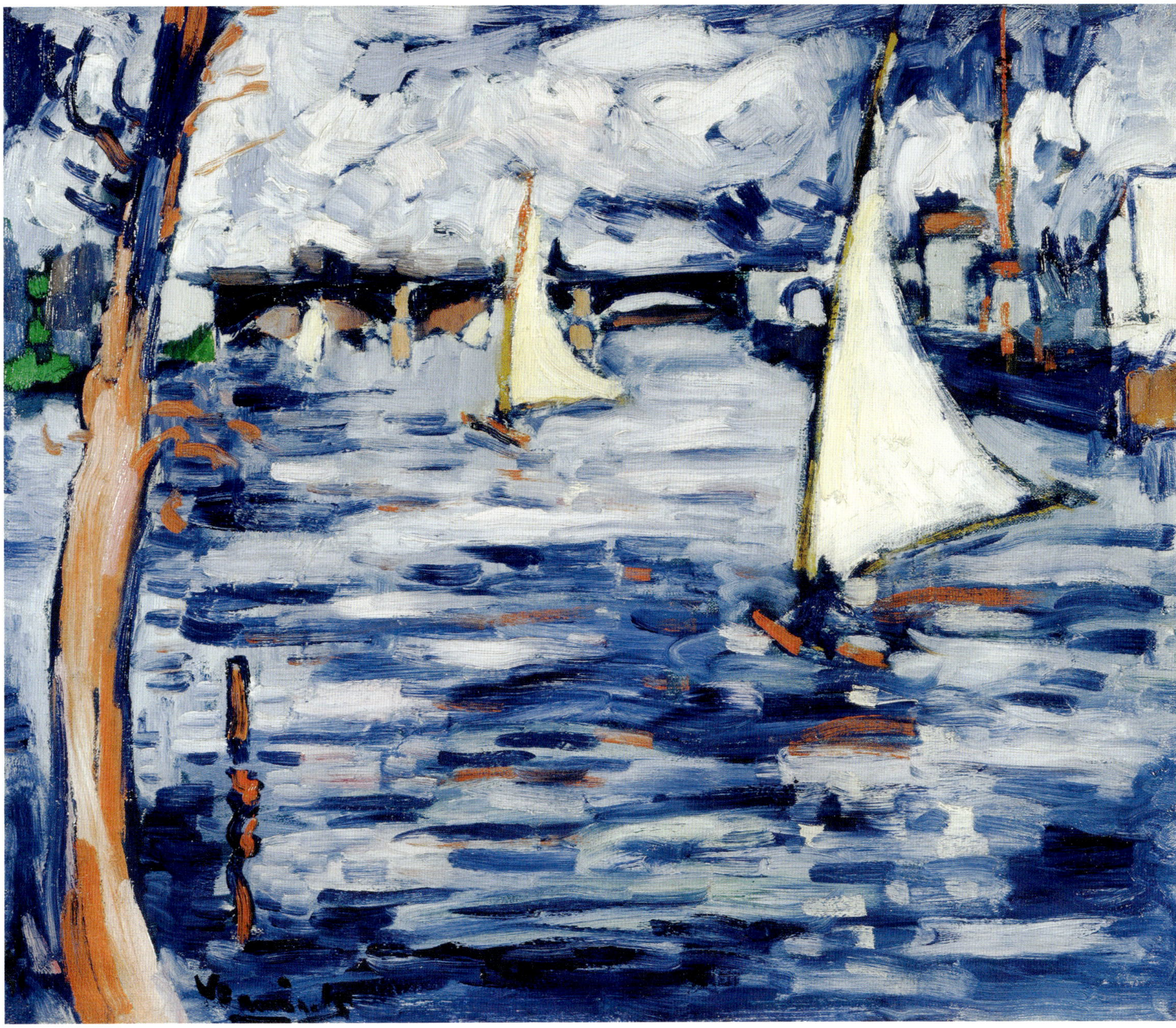

52
Sailing Boats at Chatou, 1907

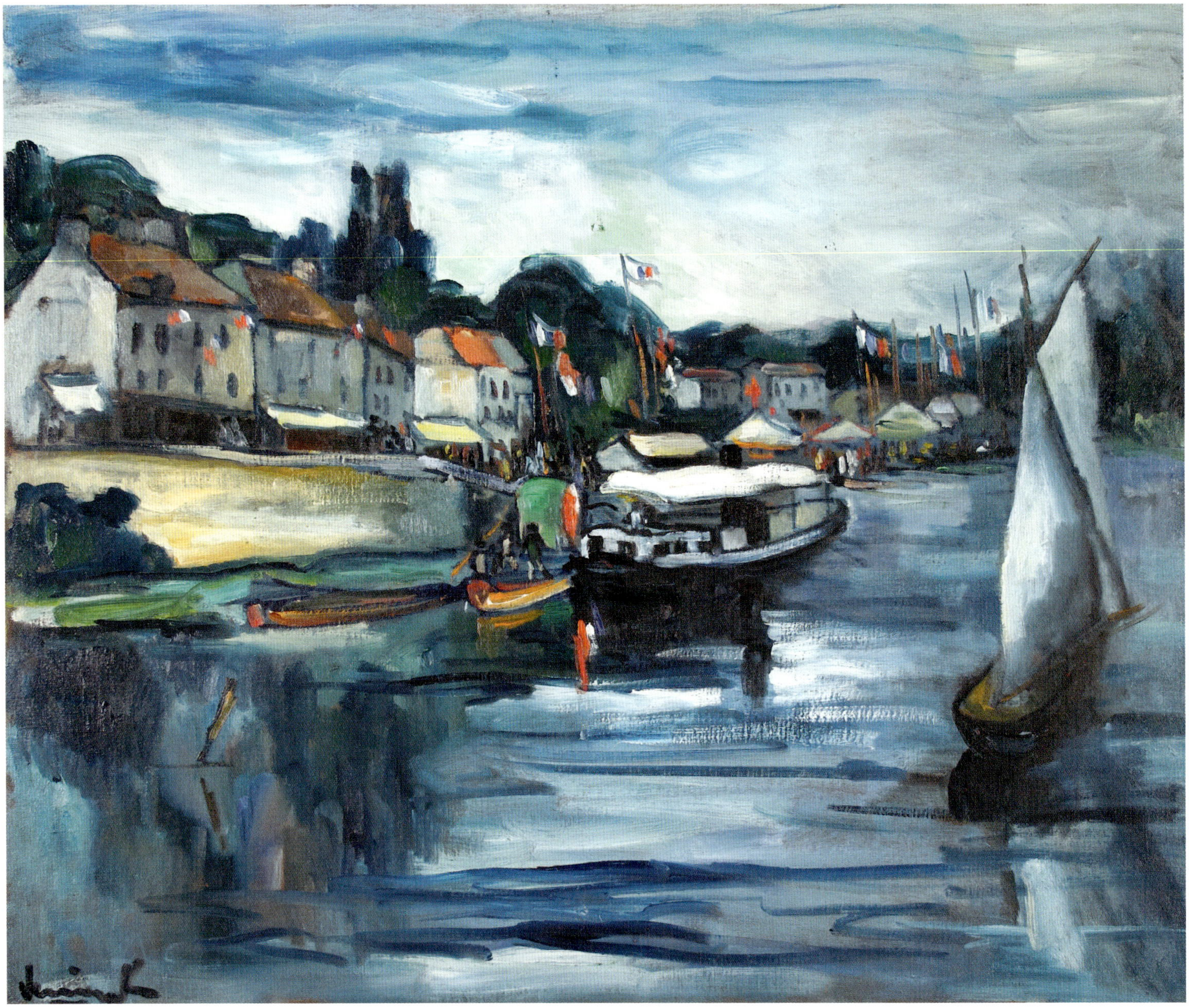

53
Riverbank, July 14, ca. 1908–09

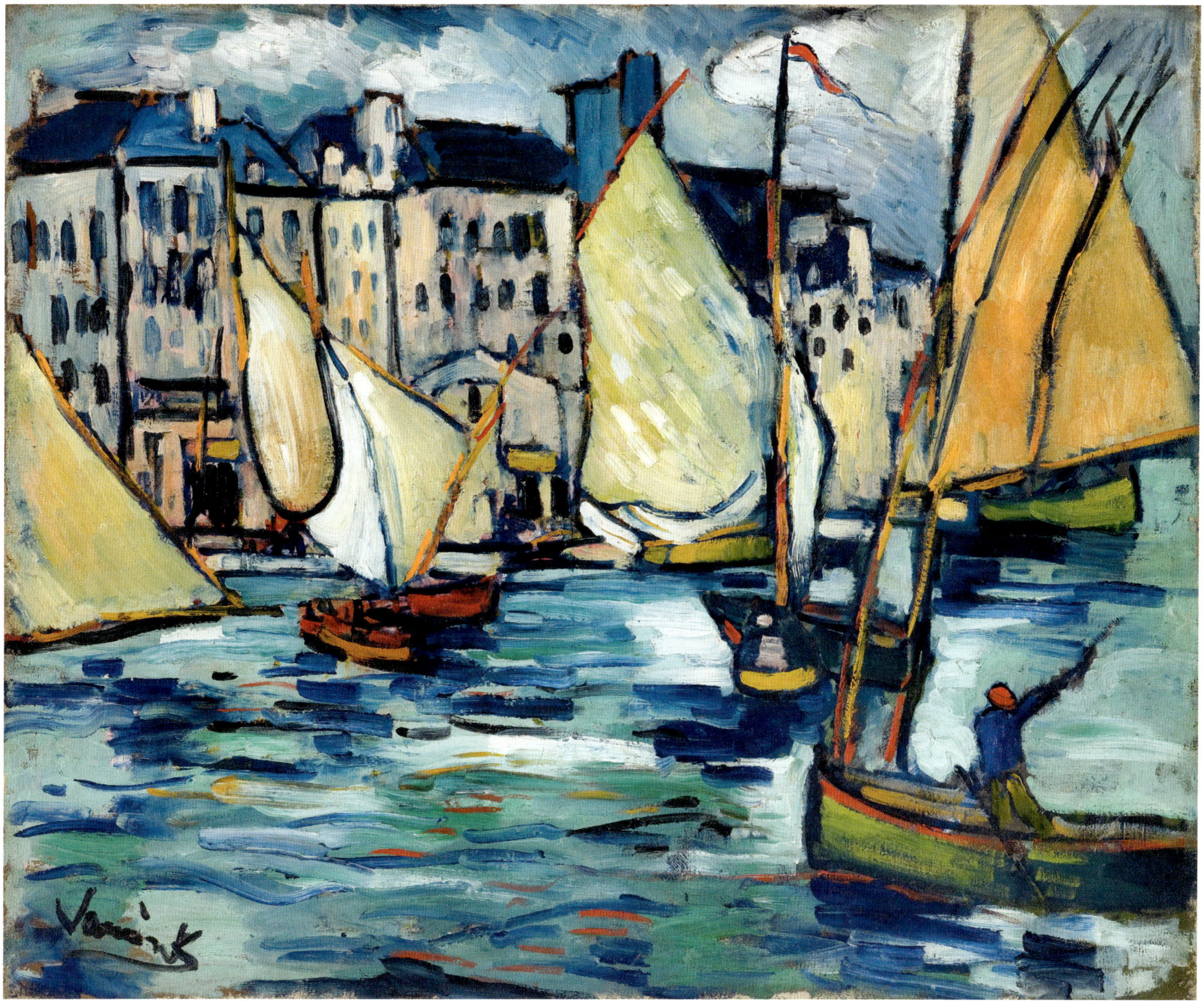

54
Le Havre, Grand Quai, 1906

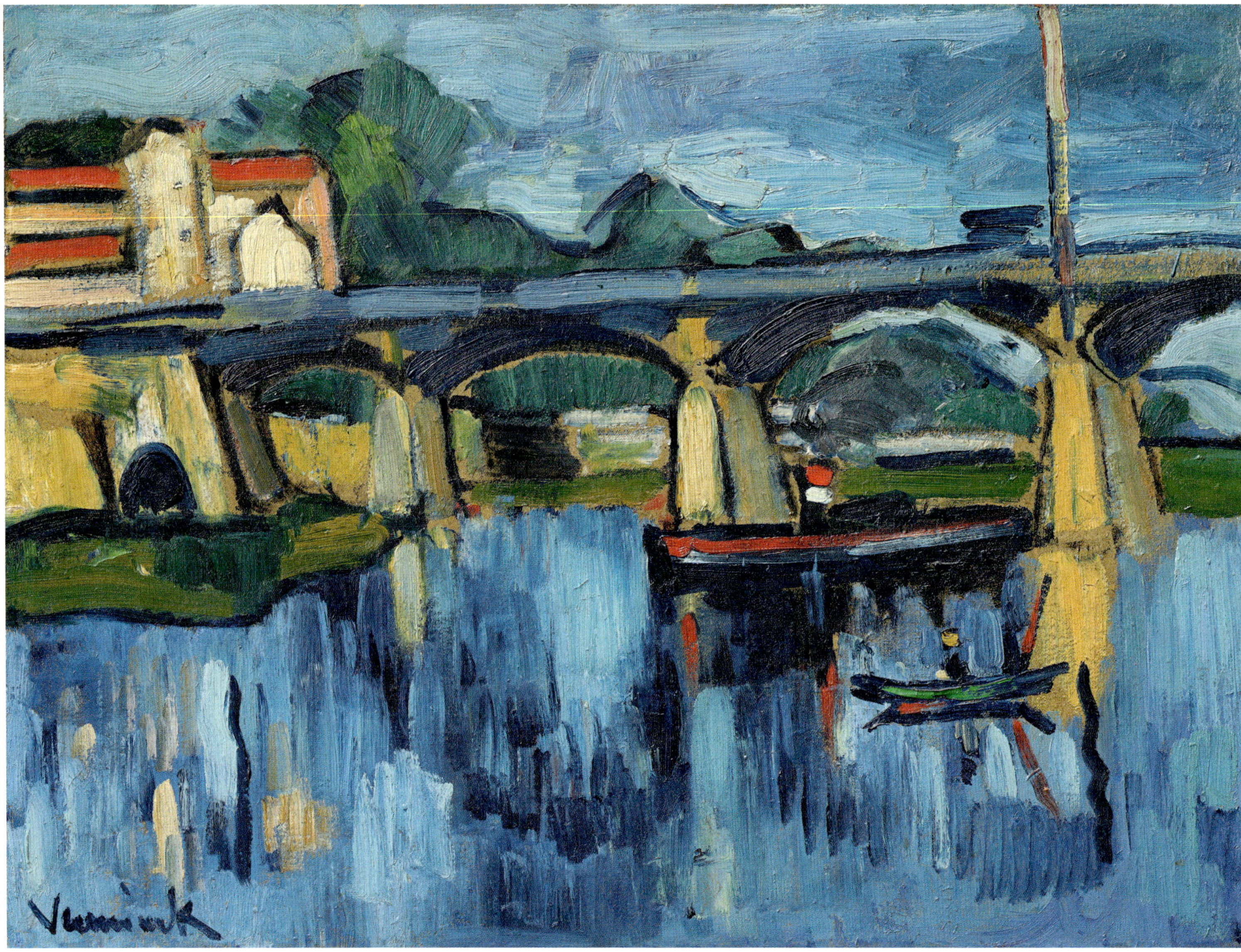

55
The Bridge at Chatou, 1906–07

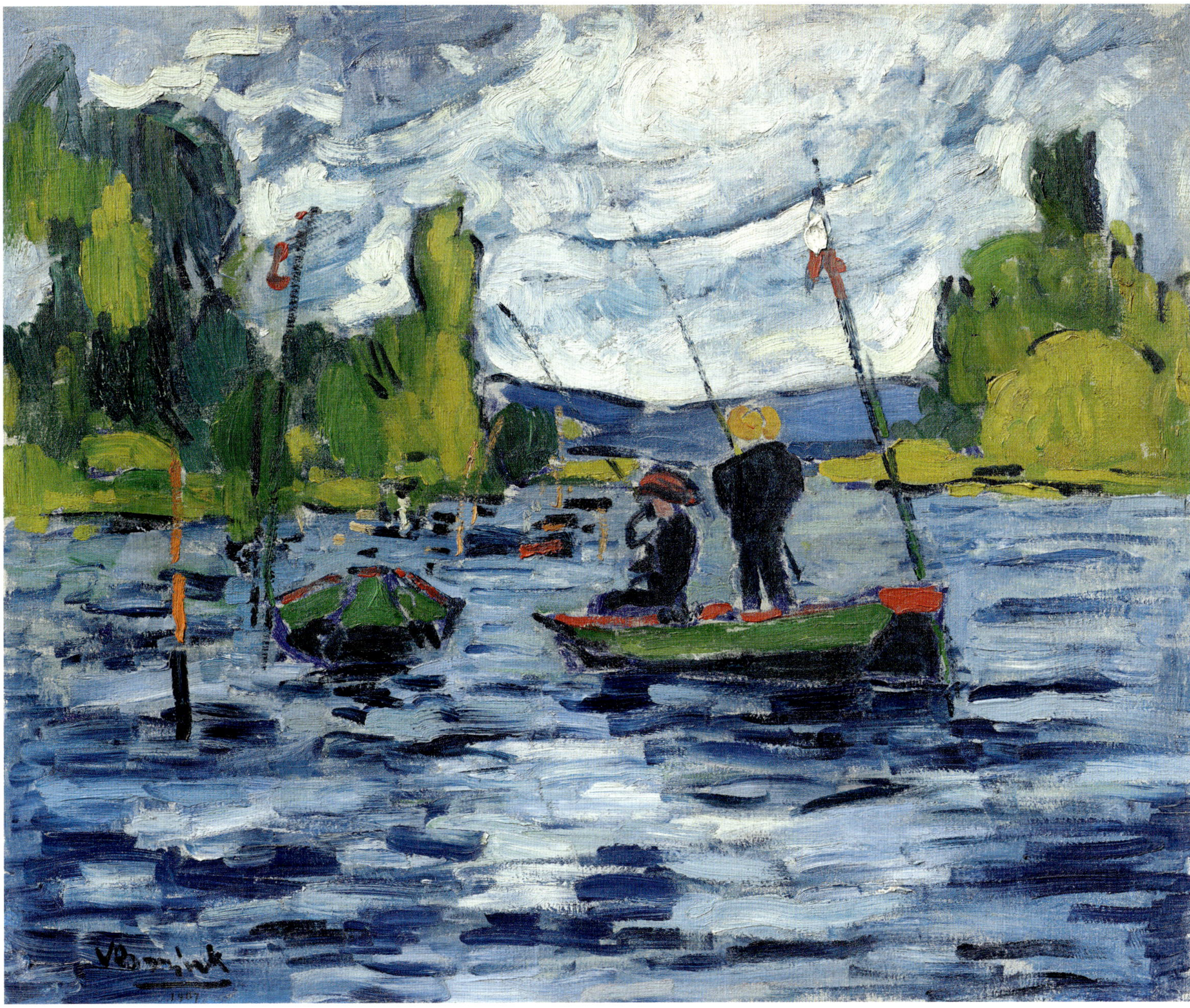

56
The Fishermen, 1907

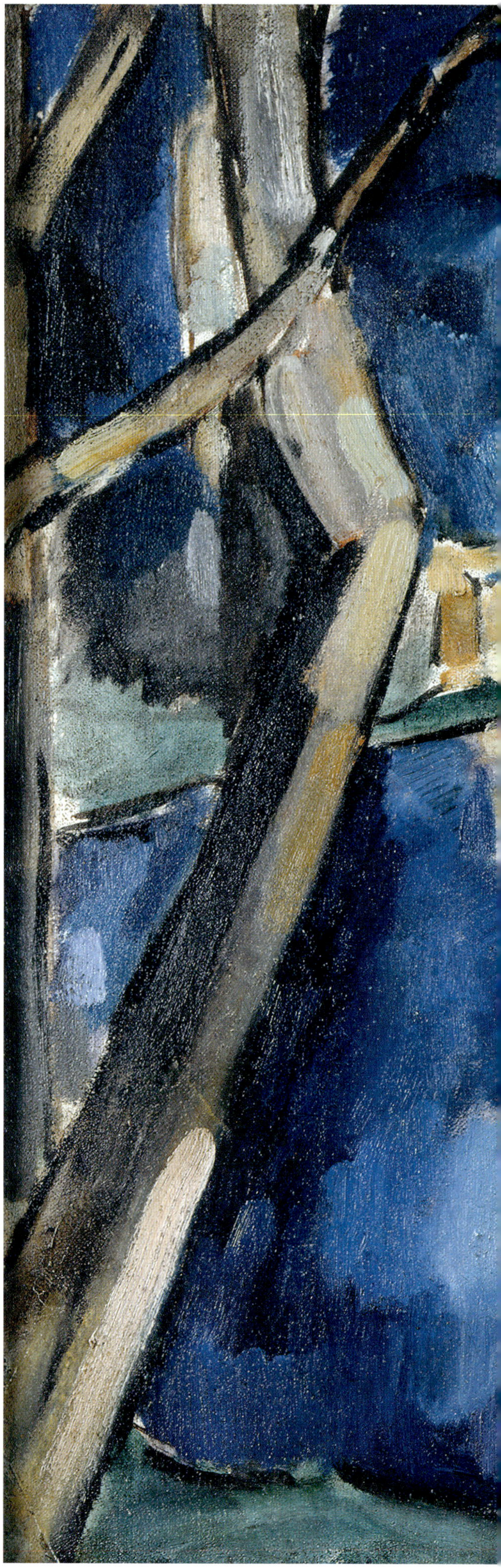

57
The Bridge at Chatou, ca. 1908

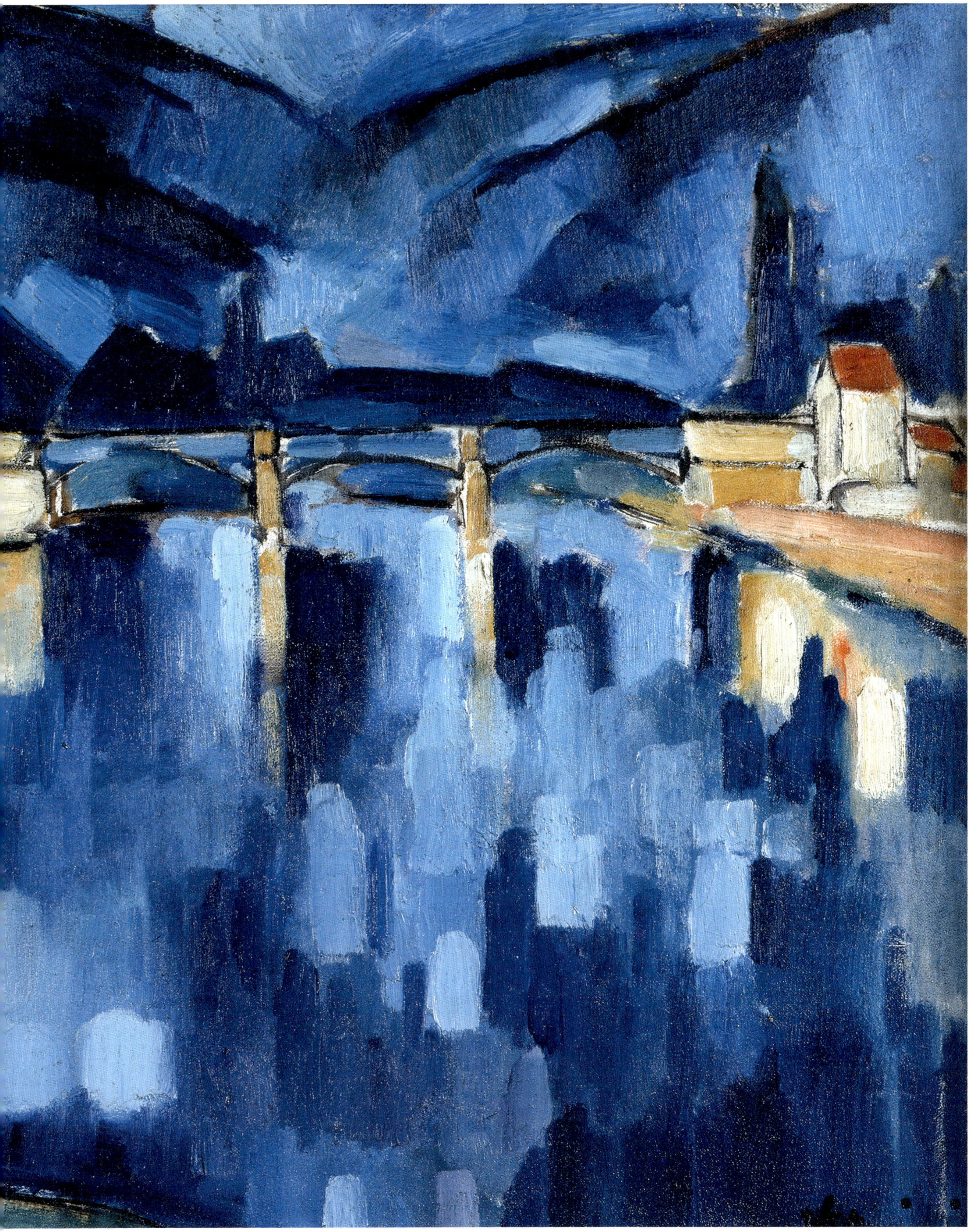

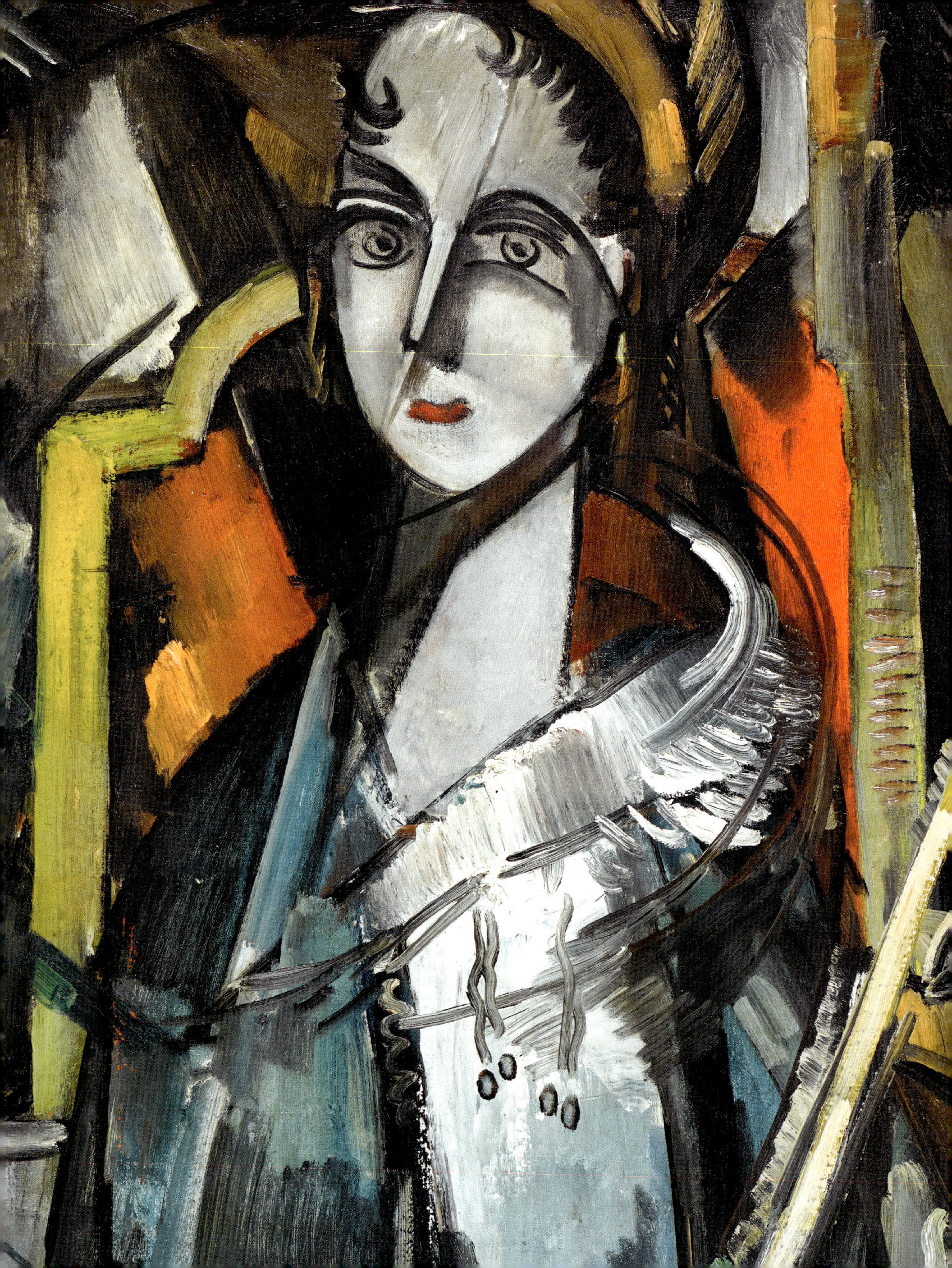

The Spirit of Cézanne Fragmentation of Forms

Anna Storm

In the winter of 1906–07, an ongoing process of change began to take place in the work of Maurice de Vlaminck. The first symptom of this new direction was an increasing rejection of the brilliant, garish colors that had characterized his Fauvist paintings. The intense contrasts of red and yellow or red and blue typical of his previous images appeared less frequently, and the agitated, impasto brushwork that had marked his painterly approach during the Fauvist phase began to change as well. During this period, Vlaminck primarily painted landscapes, a motif that would predominate throughout his entire oeuvre. But in the winter of 1906–07, when the weather made it difficult to work outside and the landscape along the Seine Valley was barren, Vlaminck also painted a number of still lifes in his studio (cats. 21–27, 65). In these carefully balanced compositions, he experimented with new formal means and explored alternative pictorial solutions. His growing interest in spatial effects and surface design is unmistakably manifested in these pictures. In many respects, these still lifes also show remarkable parallels to the work of Paul Cézanne, whose oeuvre was virtually omnipresent in early-twentieth-century Paris.[1]

Even before his death in 1906, Cézanne was considered a founding father of modern painting along with Vincent van Gogh and Paul Gauguin. At that time, art dealer Ambroise Vollard was the premier purveyor of works by Cézanne, who had left the capital and retreated to the country in the late nineteenth century. Vlaminck reported that he regularly went to Vollard's and sometimes accompanied him on visits to collectors to see works by Cézanne.[2] Other Fauve artists such as Henri Matisse and André Derain, as well as pioneers of Cubism such as Georges Braque and Pablo Picasso, also considered Cézanne a role model and inspiration. Matisse was especially close to Cézanne and had purchased a piece from his series of *Bathers* from Vollard in 1899.[3] In September 1907, a few months after Cézanne's death, a major retrospective in his honor opened at the Salon d'Automne. In total, four exhibitions with at least 146 works by the artist were on view that year,[4] giving rise to a genuine "Cézanne fever" that left its mark on the artistic development of many young painters. Not exclusively, but certainly in part due to the rediscovery and new reception of Cézanne, the brilliantly colored painting of Fauvism underwent a reorientation that would affect Vlaminck's work as well.

The stylistic affinity to Cézanne is especially apparent in the painting *Still Life* (cat. 65). Here Vlaminck arranged a few objects on a wooden table in the same close-up view typical of

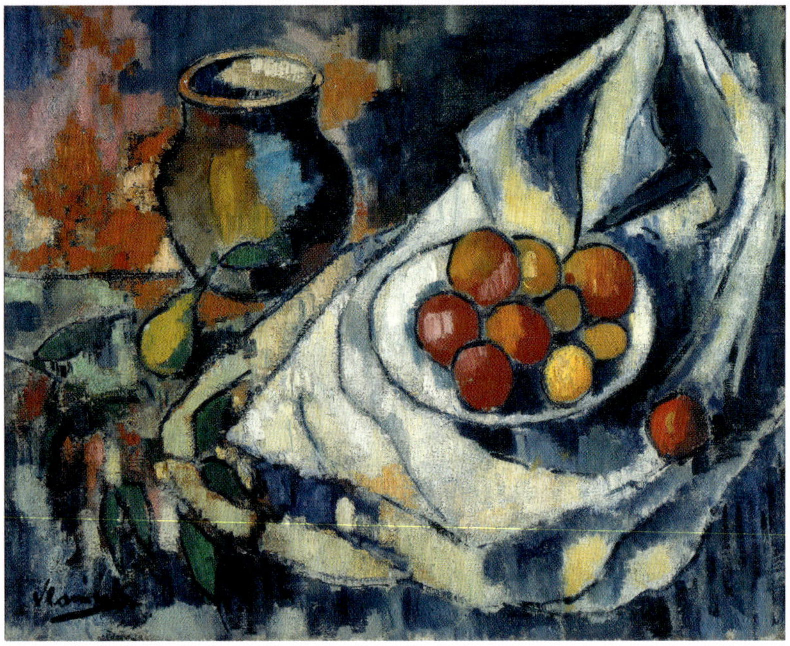

Maurice de Vlaminck,
Still Life with Fruit and Vase,
ca. 1906–07,
private collection

Cézanne: a shallow white dish with oranges and grapes on the left and a blue vase with a green bouquet on the right. The wooden table is positioned parallel to the picture plane and stands out against a blue background structured by short brushstrokes. At the top, a picture frame hangs down diagonally into the scene, echoing the color of the wooden table. Here, Vlaminck avoided strong complementary contrasts, choosing naturalistic colors instead. While the paint is still applied in broad strokes, it lacks the dynamism and energy of the Fauvist pictures of 1905–06. The scene has a cropped effect, with no compositional framing; the space seems flat and undefined. These spatial and formal elements are also characteristic of Cézanne's still lifes. An additional point of comparison is the white tablecloth, a feature typical of Cézanne that also occurs in many of Vlaminck's still lifes. For both painters, it is clear that the intent was not first and foremost to evoke the material qualities of the fabric; rather, the tablecloth functions as a compositional device and sometimes also as a metaphorical duplication of the canvas.

From 1908 on, Vlaminck began experimenting with Cubist forms that can be interpreted as a radicalization of Cézannesque impulses. The same year, Georges Braque, who had previously painted Fauvist landscapes, and his colleague Pablo Picasso created their first Cubist paintings. A pioneering example of Vlaminck's turn toward Cubism is the painting *Still Life* from 1910–11 (cat. 68). Here the palette is noticeably darker than that which had defined his Fauvist work. The application of paint appears smoother, the brushwork less agitated and dynamic, the individual brushstrokes less clearly legible. Viewed in close-up and slightly from above, a group of vessels is carefully arranged: a blue jug, an orange-red plate, a brown pitcher, and a white dish with a tall foot in which a number of fruits, presumably apples, are placed. There is only the suggestion of a red table, its edge visible to the left. As in many other still lifes by Vlaminck, the scene is composed of different planes and forms that negate both a unified perspective and a realistic sense of three-dimensional space.

Perhaps the most impressive example of Vlaminck's response to Cubism is the painting *Opium* (cat. 64), created in ca. 1910 and thus the height of the new movement. The figural image is composed of countless geometricizing surfaces and forms that produce an effect of fragmentation. At the same time, in a manner typical of Cubism, the painting lacks both a unified perspective and a sense of illusionistic space. Only on second glance do we recognize the opium pipe referenced in the title, held in the hand of the female figure sitting in a tall-backed chair with a yellow frame. The reduced palette consists of brown, ocher, gray, and black, with occasional contrasting accents in blue and orange. The figure's face is indicated with only a few lines and is strongly reminiscent of contemporaneous portraits by Picasso. While Vlaminck's early work includes a number of figural images, this portrait of a woman is unique for his Cubist phase and thus could conceivably be interpreted as an exercise, an experiment with a new method of painting in a genre otherwise unusual for his oeuvre.

Vlaminck's landscapes, on the other hand, show numerous borrowings from the art of Cubism and are frequently marked by affinities to the clearly structured space of Cézanne's depictions of nature. In *Landscape near Martigues* (cat. 59), which Vlaminck painted in the South of France in 1913, the hues are significantly earthier and more naturalistic than those he had employed in his earlier landscapes. The composition is organized in horizontal planes, which the artist developed using restless and at times energetically hatched brushstrokes. To the right, the landscape is open and can be continued in imagination, while on the left, dense vegetation in saturated tones of green serves as a frame. In contrast to the still lifes, which focus on the picture plane, here the painter chose a perspectival view into depth, as Cézanne had done in numerous landscapes from the early 1880s. The interest in Cézanne thus played a determinative role in Vlaminck's entire artistic development in the years following the zenith of Fauvism in 1905–06. Like the other Fauve painters, he turned away from his formerly bright-colored, expressive, and often tactile modeling approach to painting and instead experimented with new methods of design that reveal not only the influence of Cézanne, but also obvious parallels to Cubism. In this process, the genre of still life served Vlaminck particularly well as an arena for experimental reorientation, enabling him to develop formal and compositional means that would soon also translate into his figural and landscape images.

Translated from German by Melissa M. Thorson

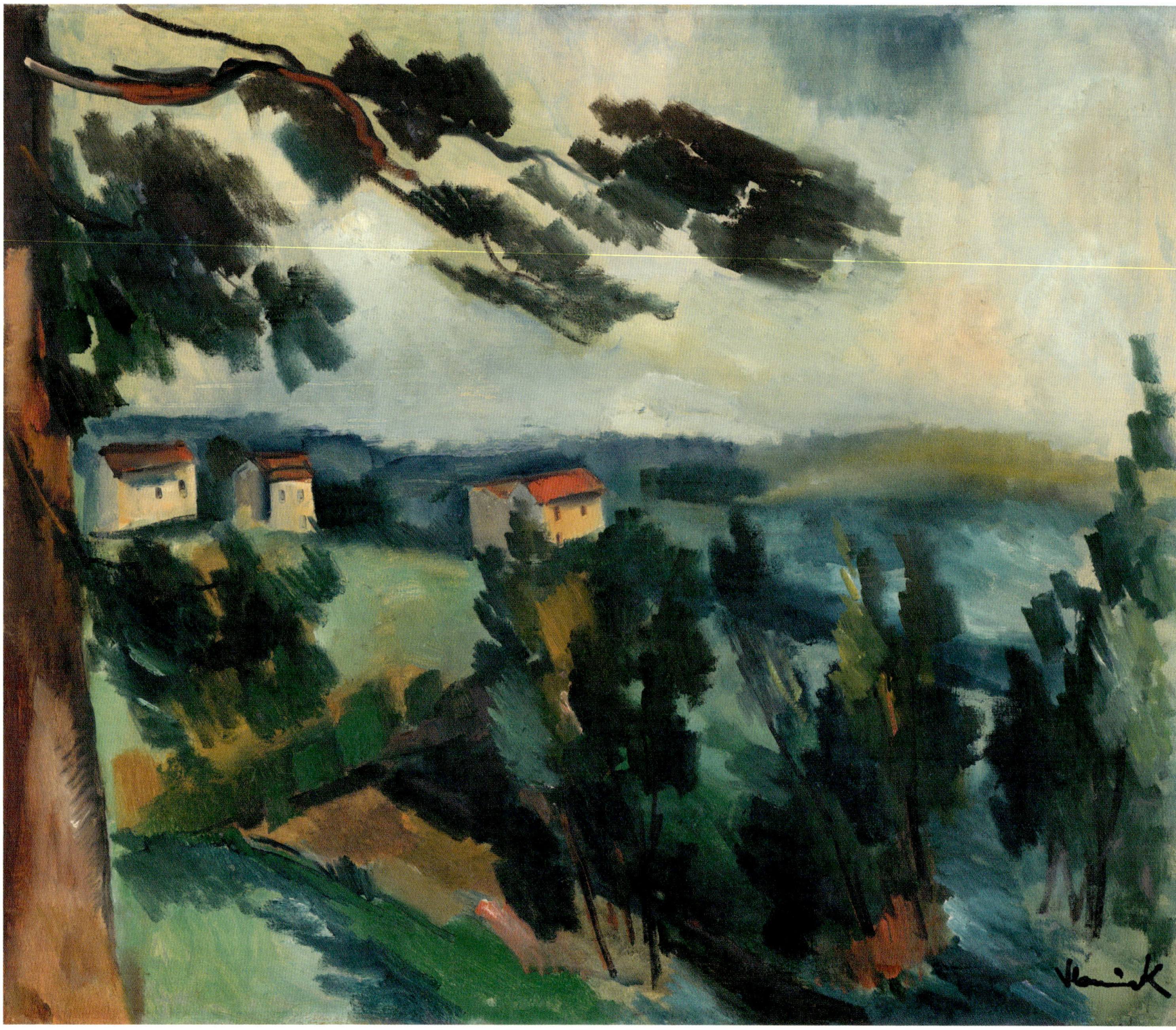

58
Three Houses, 1910

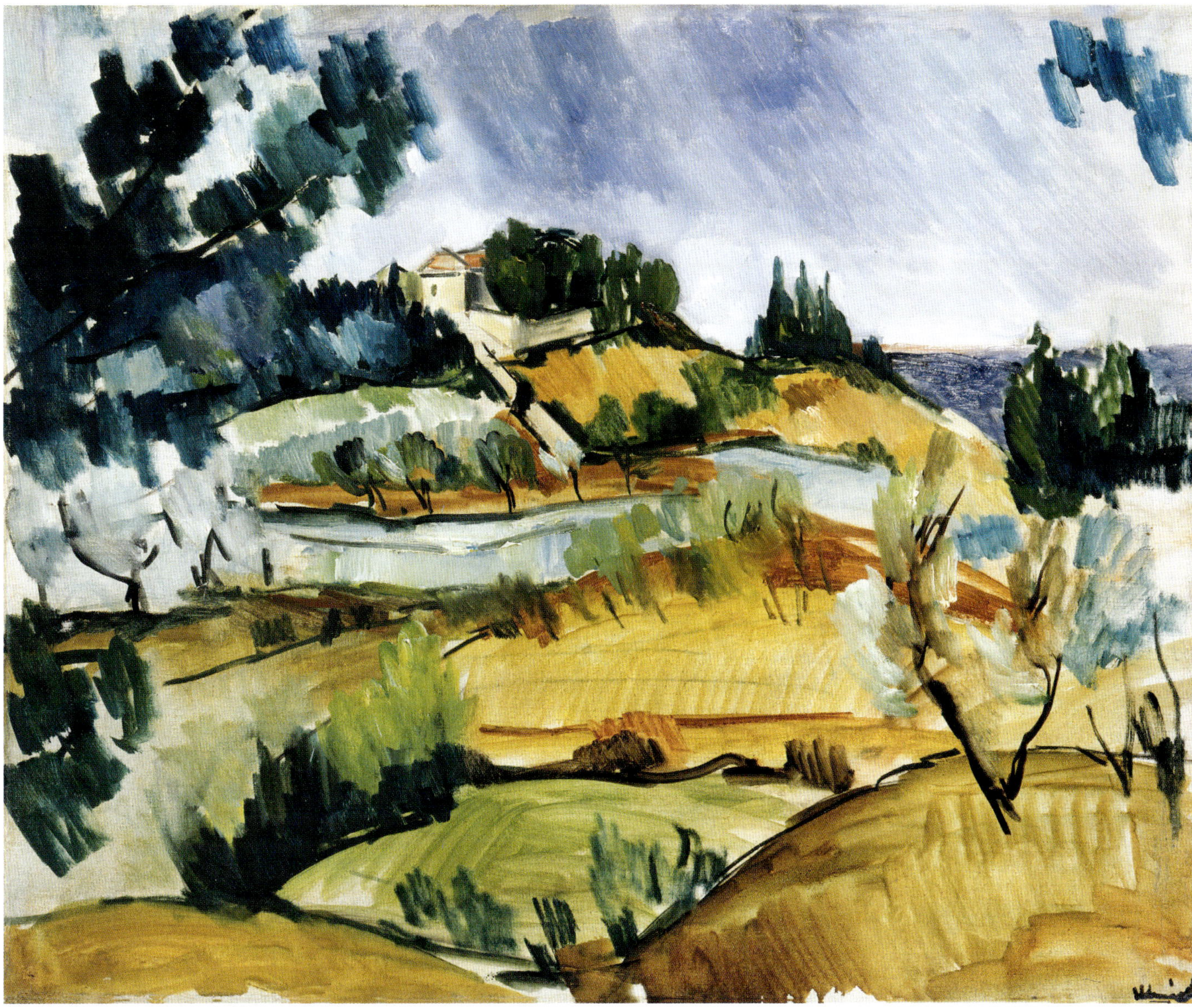

59
Landscape near Martigues, 1913

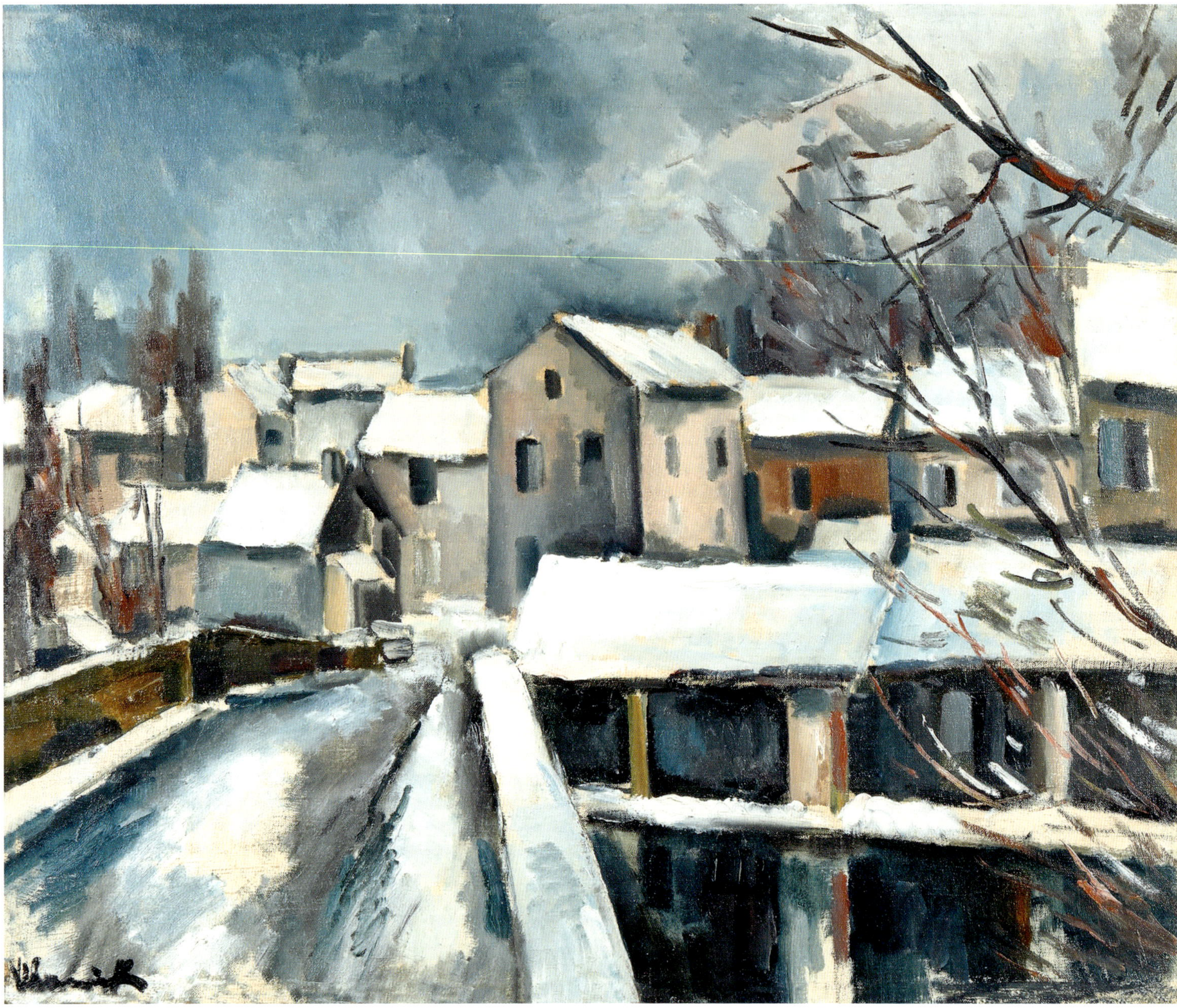

60
The Washhouse in the Snow, 1913

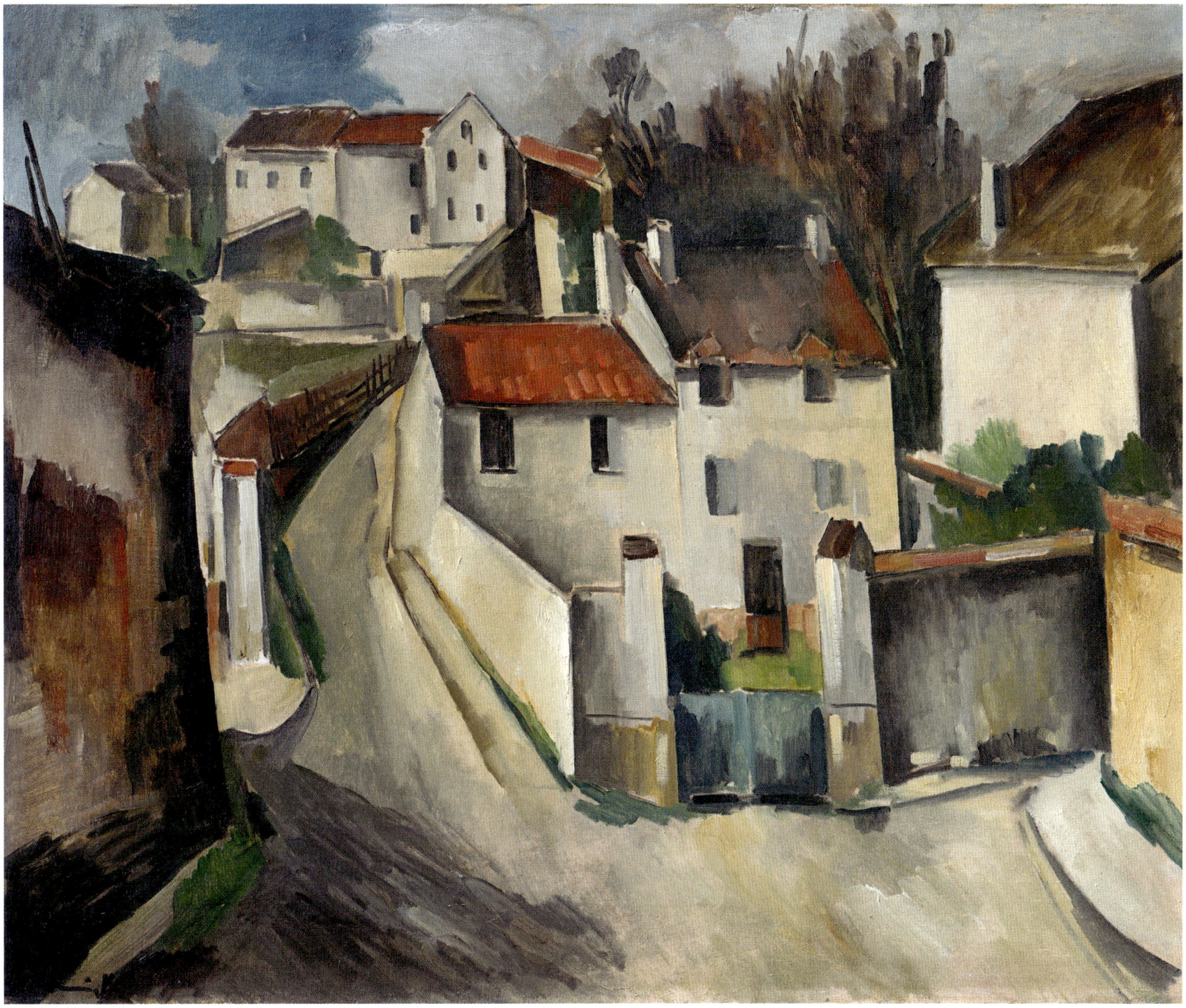

61
Saint-Michel District, Bougival, 1913

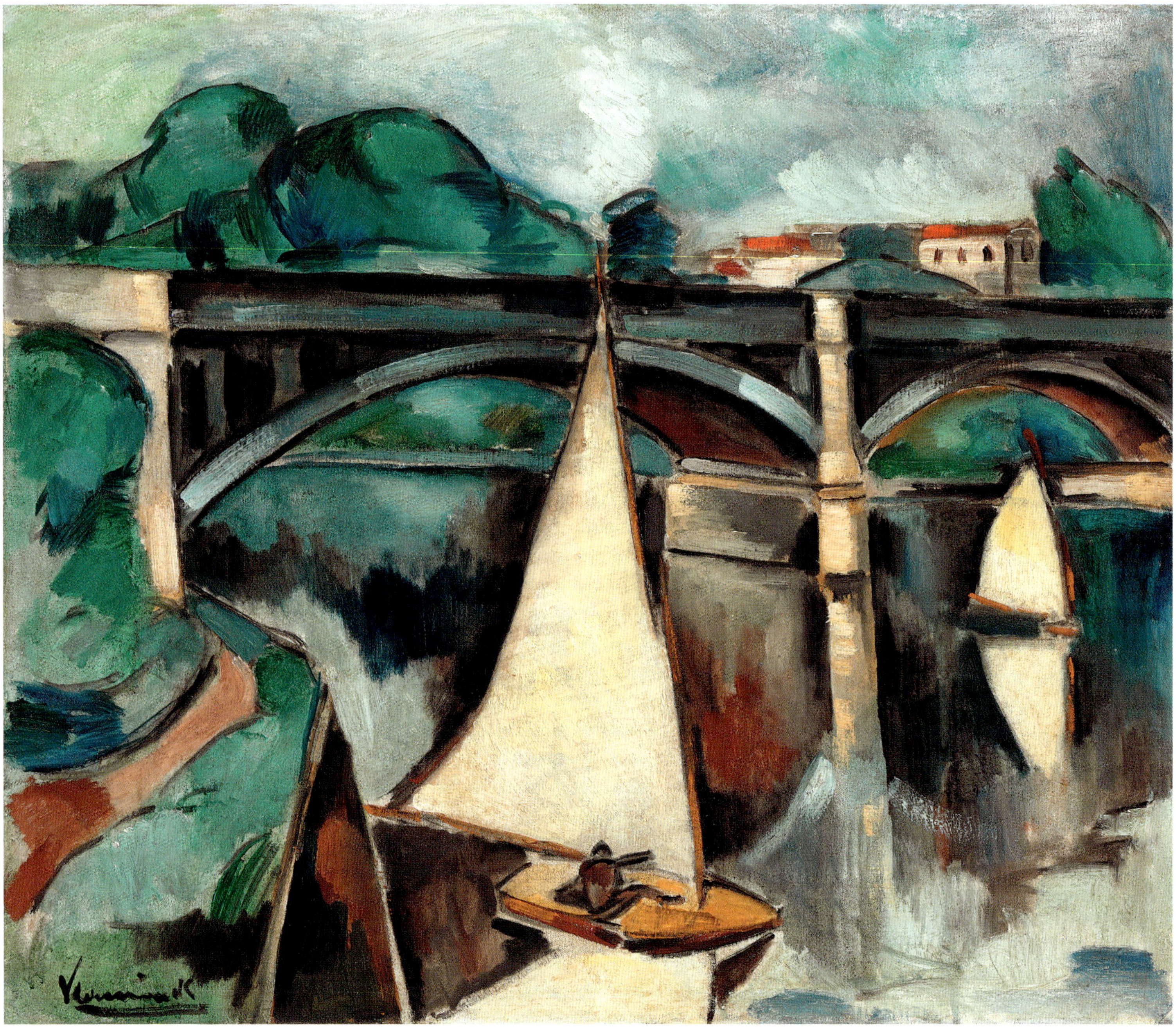

62
Sailboats at Chatou, ca. 1908

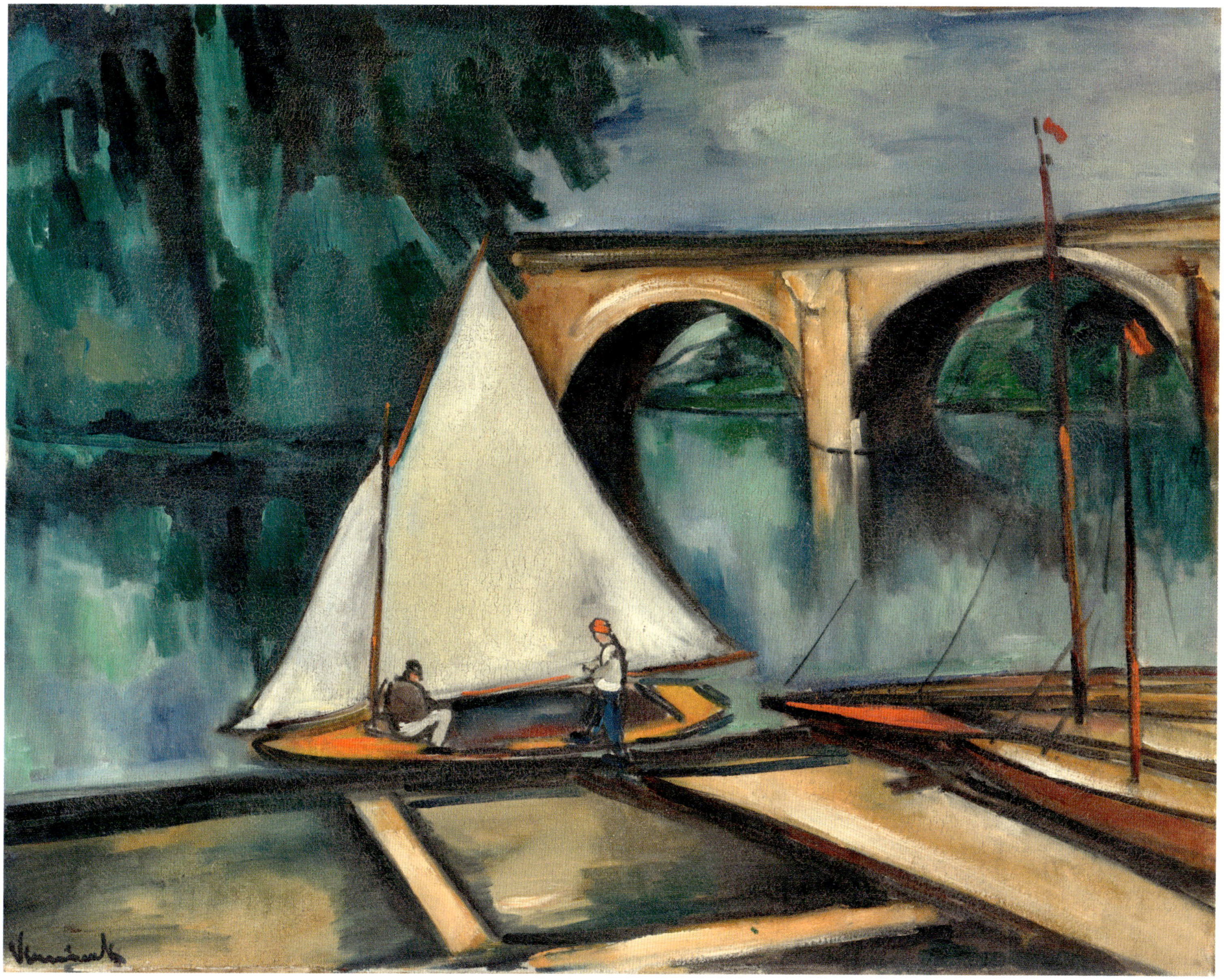

63
Sailboats, before 1918

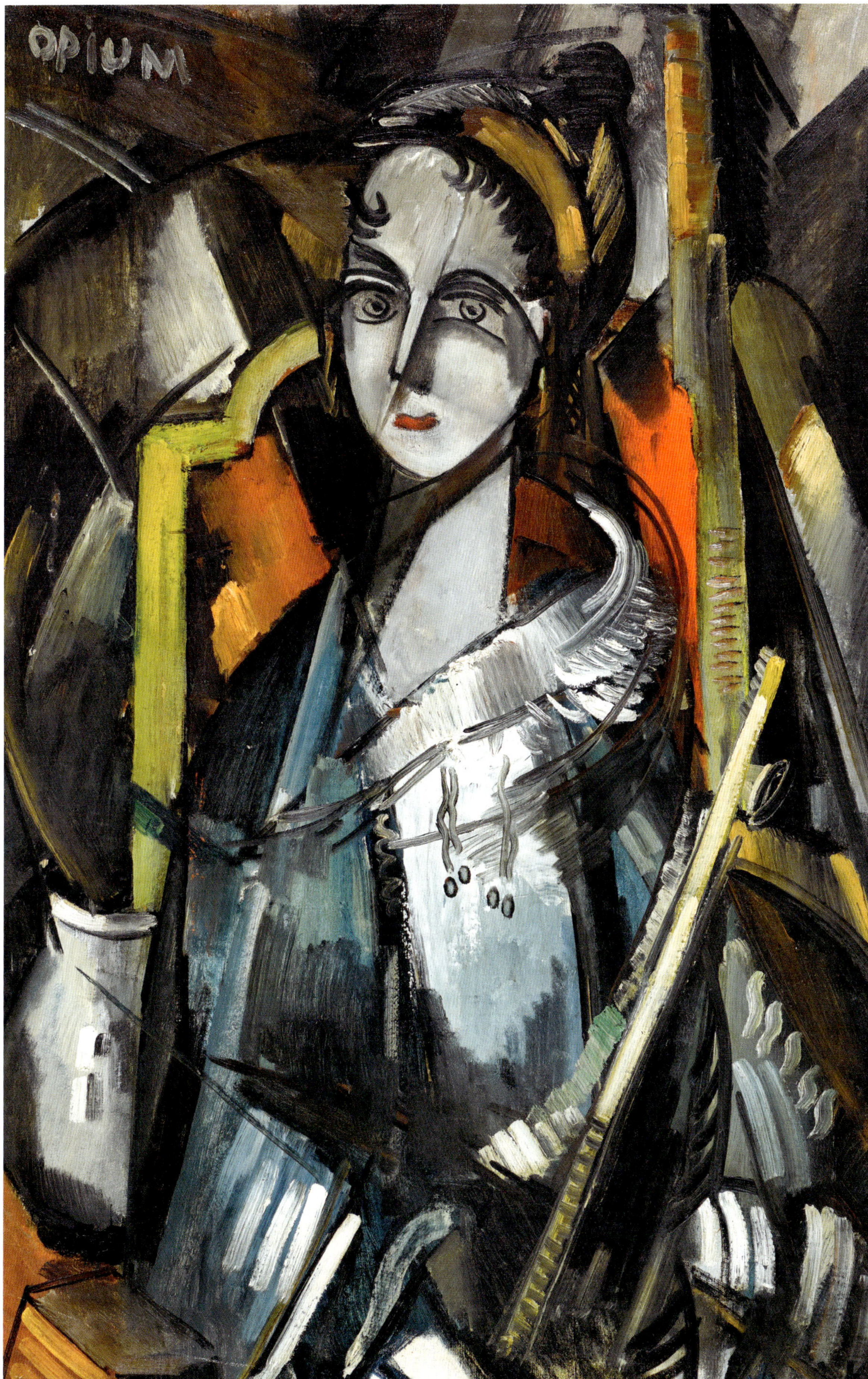

64
Opium, ca. 1910

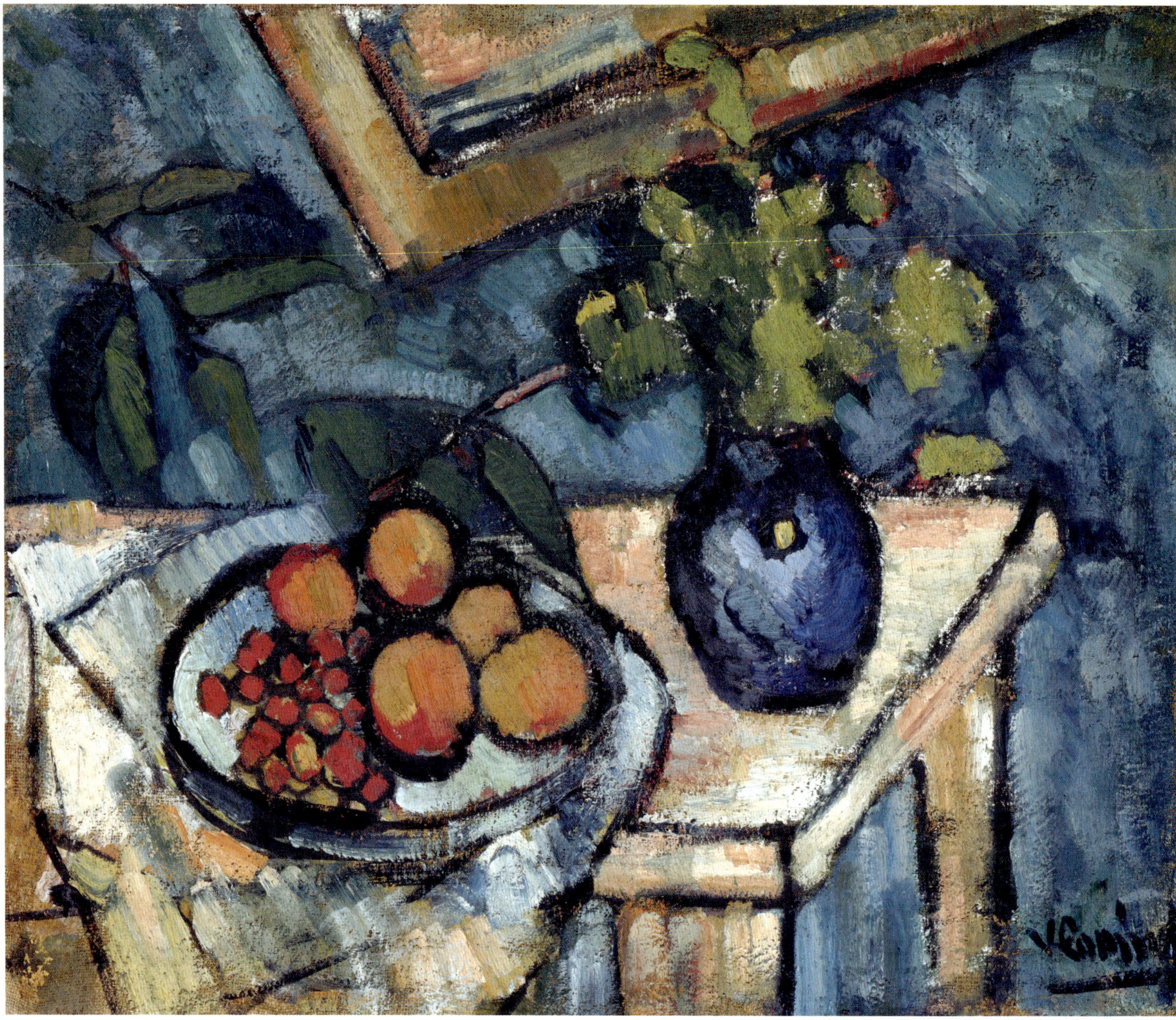

65
Still Life, 1907

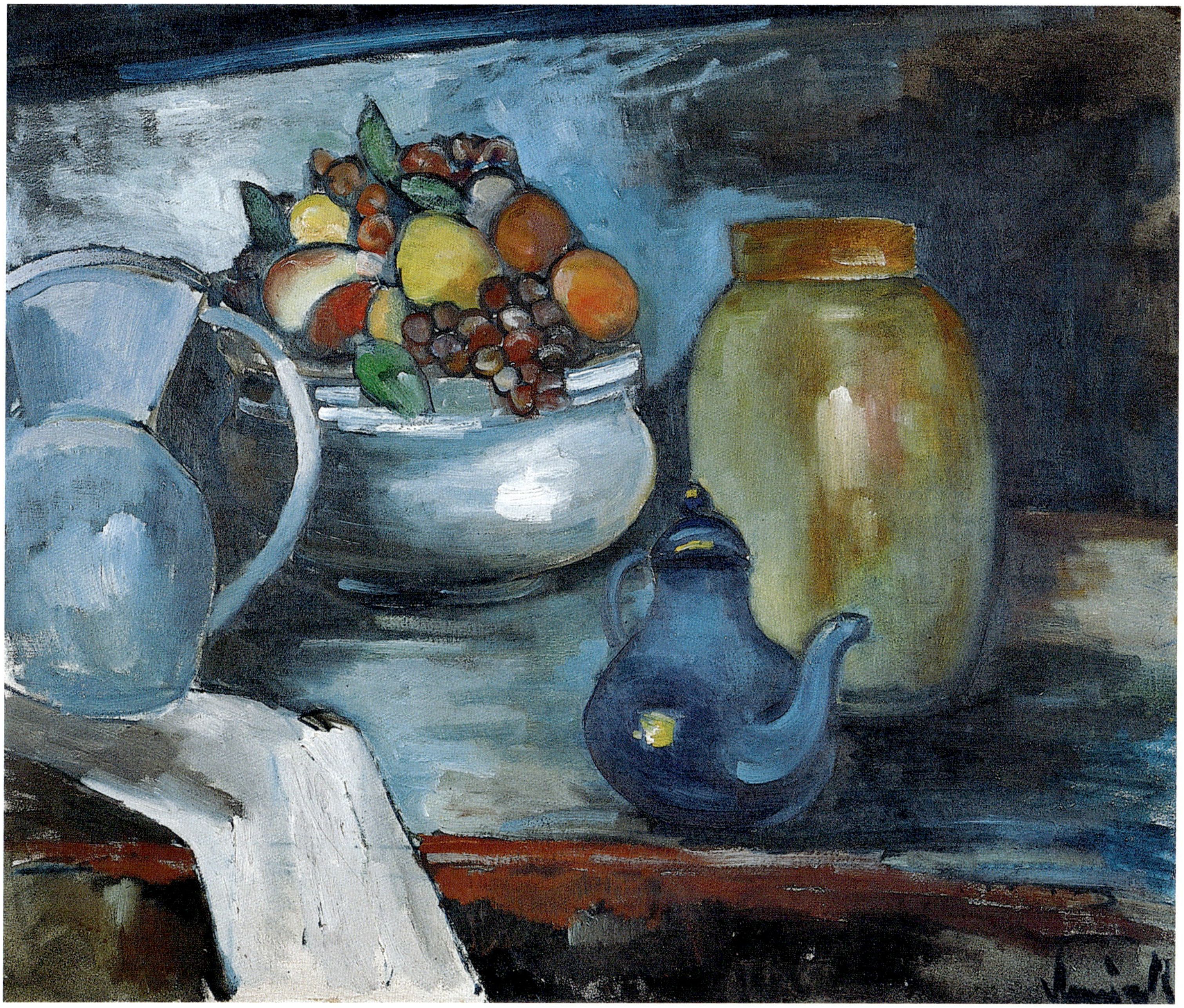

66
Still Life, before 1911

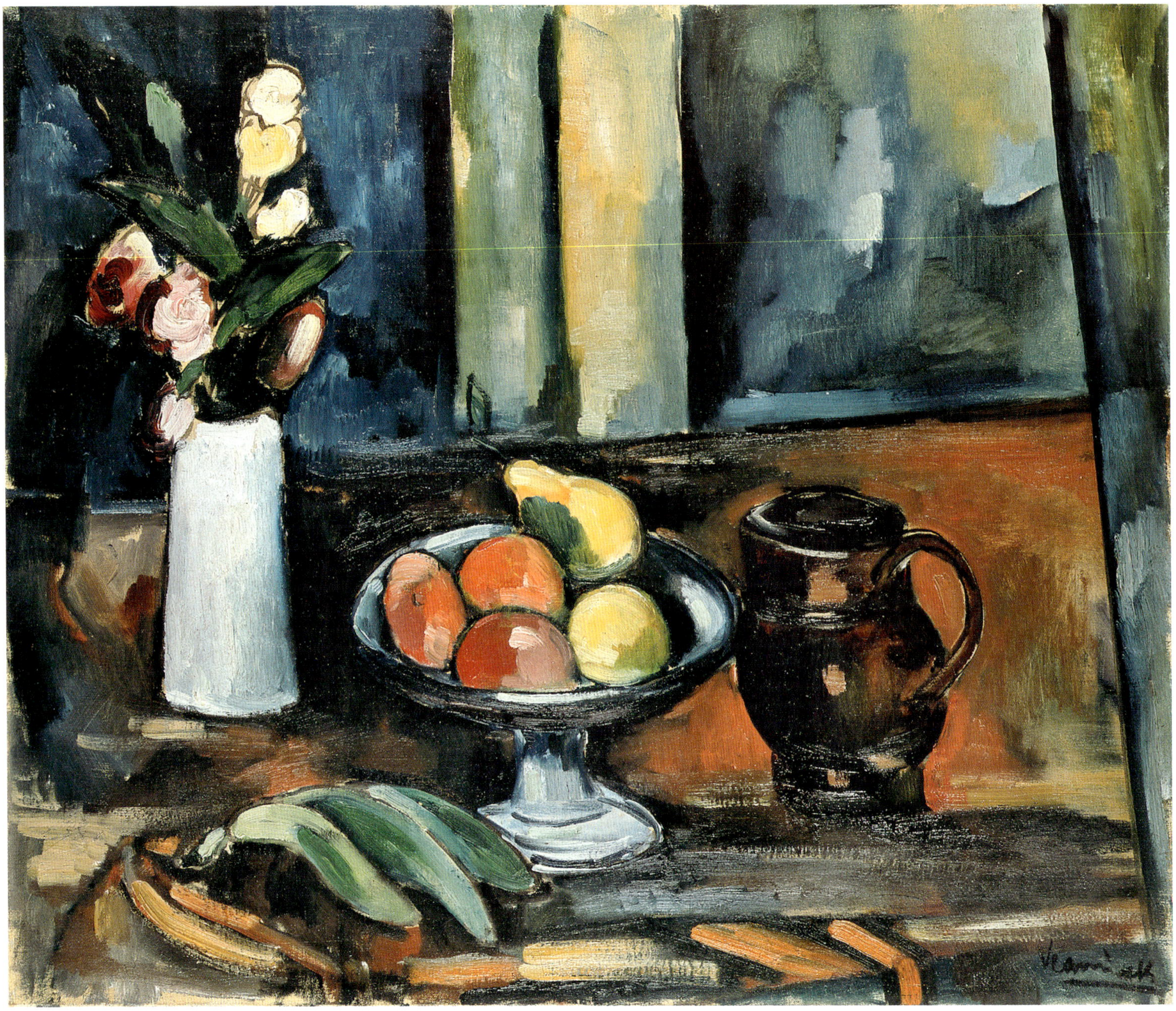

67
Still Life with Flowers and Fruit, 1911

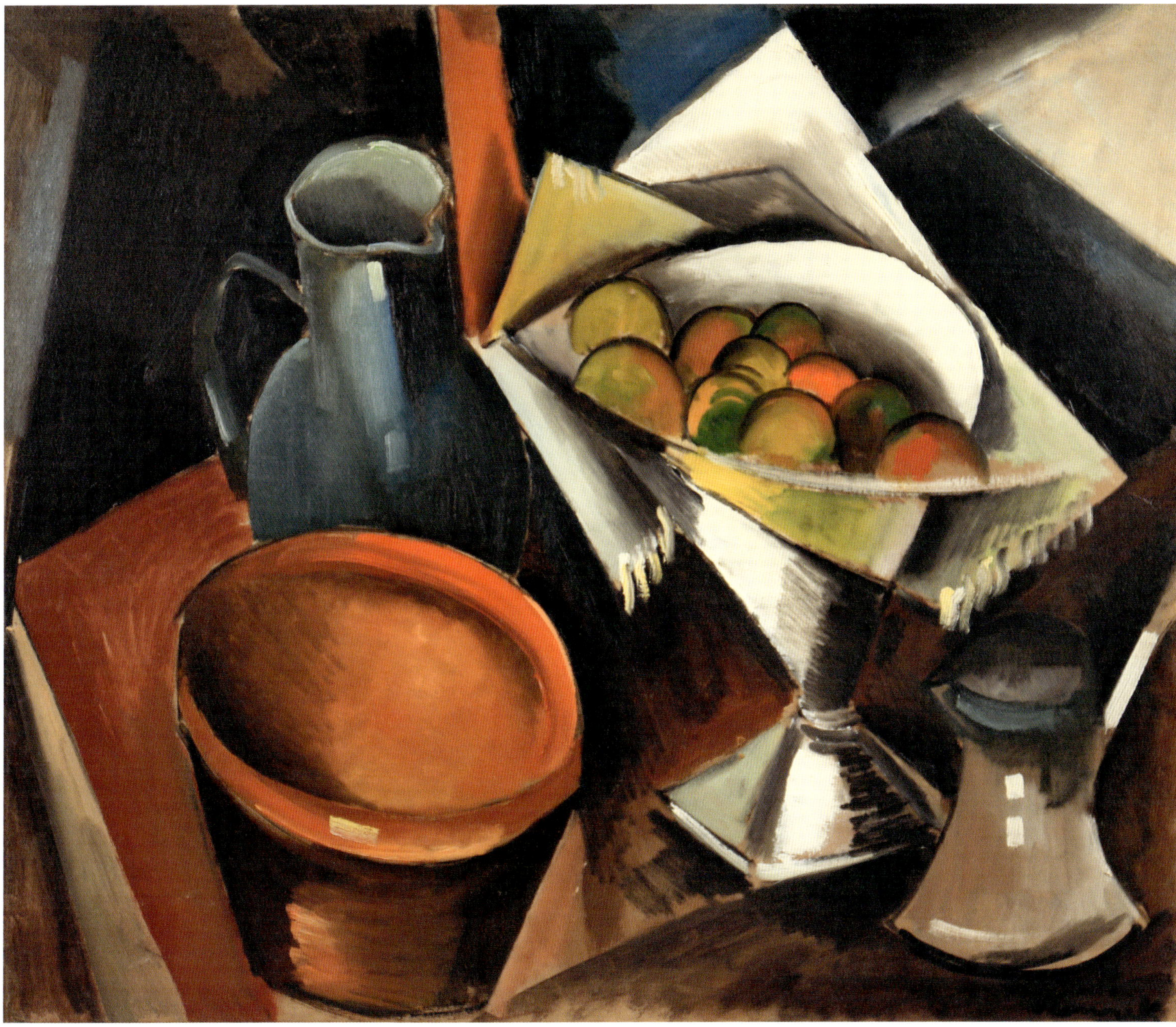

68
Still Life, 1910–11

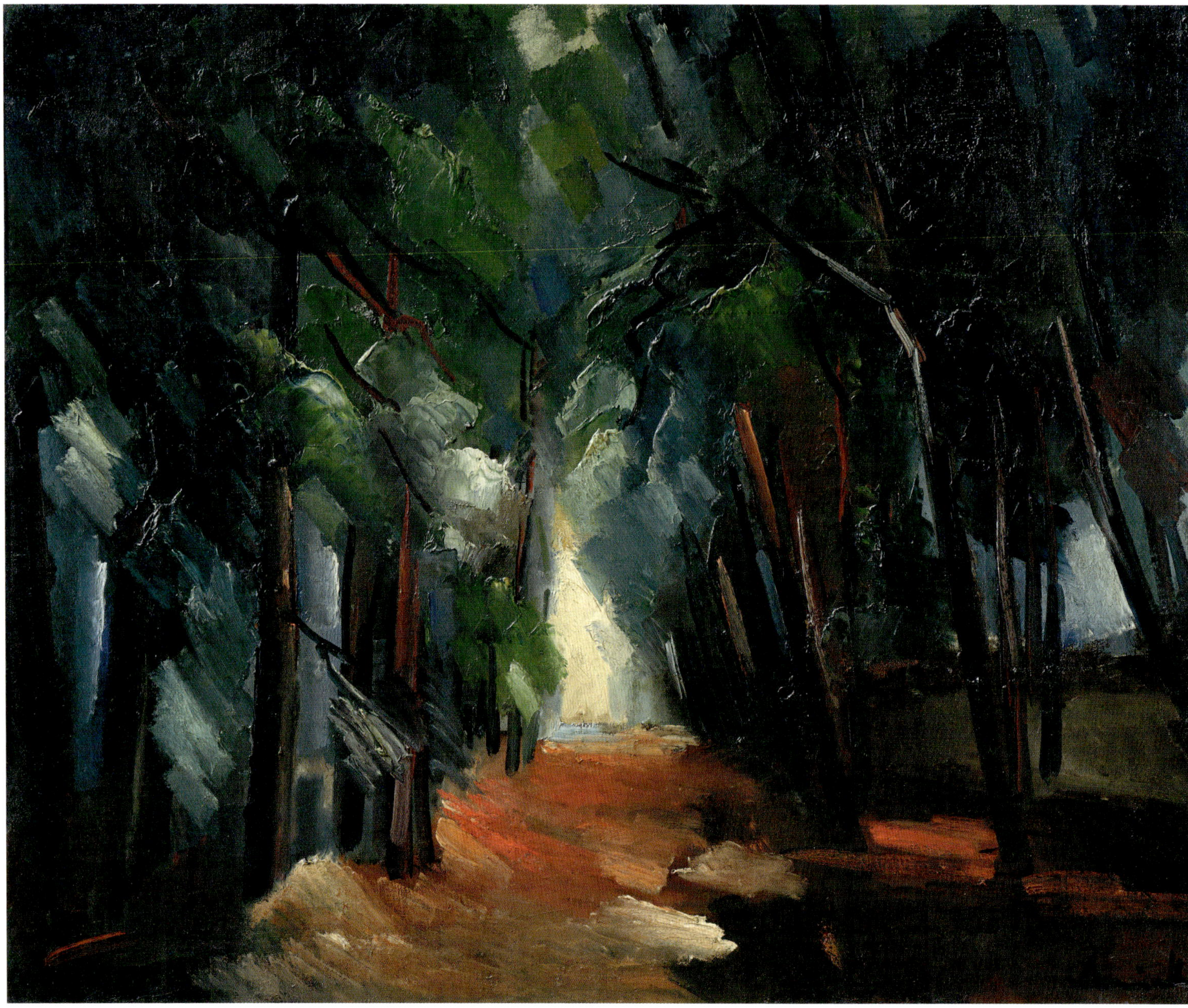

69
The Forest, 1914–18

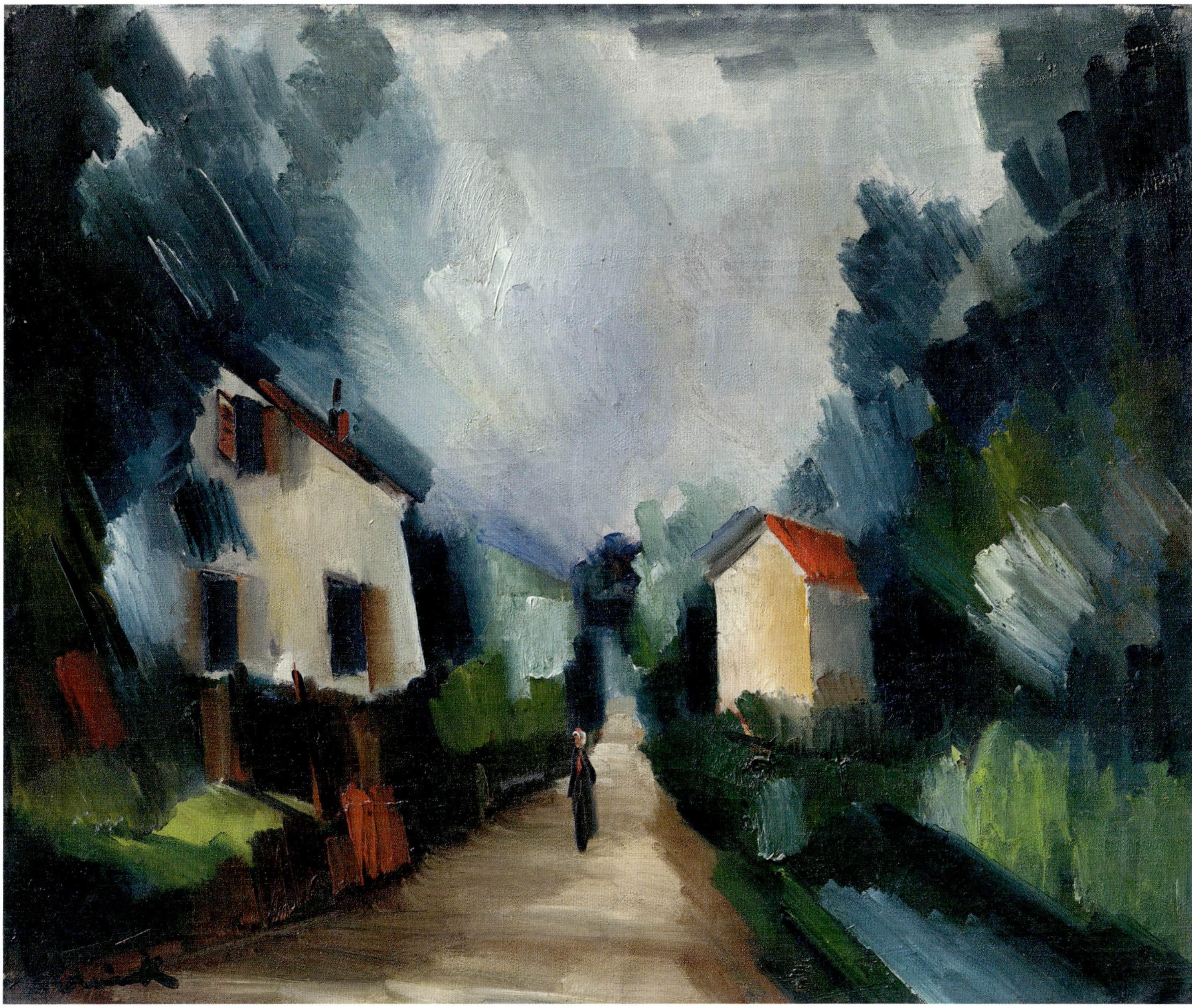

70
Village Road, 1911

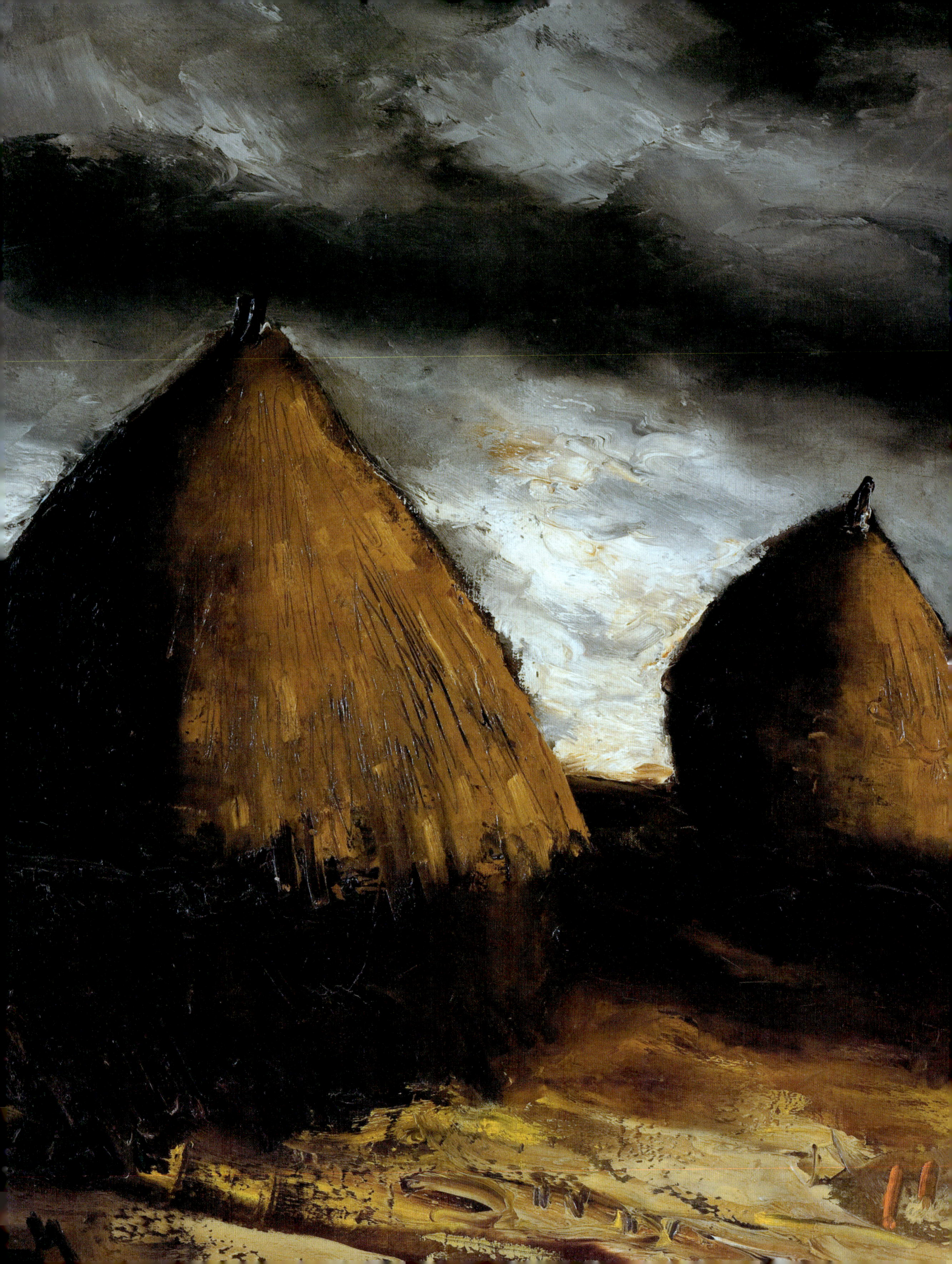

Bleak Landscapes

The Late Work

Daniel Zamani

As one of the most important proponents of Fauvism, Vlaminck had made an essential contribution to the development of modern painting between 1904 and 1908. Around 1910 he produced numerous works in which he experimented with increasingly abstract design processes and approximated the Cubist formal experiments of artists such as Pablo Picasso and Georges Braque. The outbreak of World War I brought an end to Vlaminck's dialogue with new tendencies in modern French art. While his former comrade-in-arms Henri Matisse remained one of the most important trendsetters both in France and abroad, Vlaminck's late work falls outside the bounds of all avant-garde currents. In a statement published in 1942, concerning the supposed impotence of French modernism under the influence of Picasso, there are striking parallels to the reactionary understanding of art that characterized National Socialist Germany.[1] Vlaminck's concurrent praise of the vitality of German culture under Hitler, published the previous year, may have contributed to the fact that his late work has hardly been researched in France either.[2] From a formal perspective, however, his works show no evidence whatsoever of a right-wing or even Fascist artistic ideology. Rather, his late and often extraordinarily bleak compositions can be stylistically interpreted as an idiosyncratic version of late Impressionism, combined with expressive elements. They are characterized by dynamic brushwork and sketch-like rendering of the subject matter, as well as a multifaceted play of textures and tonal contrasts.

From the 1920s on, snow-covered village landscapes and forests became one of Vlaminck's favorite motifs—a subject which, as *effet de neige,* had already played an important role in French Impressionism. But while the winter scenes of painters such as Claude Monet and Alfred Sisley evoke a fundamentally cheerful atmosphere, Vlaminck's landscapes, covered in ice and snow, often appear uninviting and threatening. Rather than bright, luminous areas enlivened by shadows vibrating with color, Vlaminck's images of winter are dominated by a dirty white that contrasts with accents in gray and black. In his 1920 painting *Village in the Snow* (cat. 72), Vlaminck adopted a pictorial formula echoing his earlier, Cubist-informed landscape *The Washhouse in the Snow* (cat. 60). The street in the middle of the scene leads the viewer's eye into the center of the composition. The effect of depth is intensified by the exaggerated diagonals of the two rows of houses that come together at the top of this triangular area. The two miniscule figures in the lower left, indicated only as black silhouettes, seem

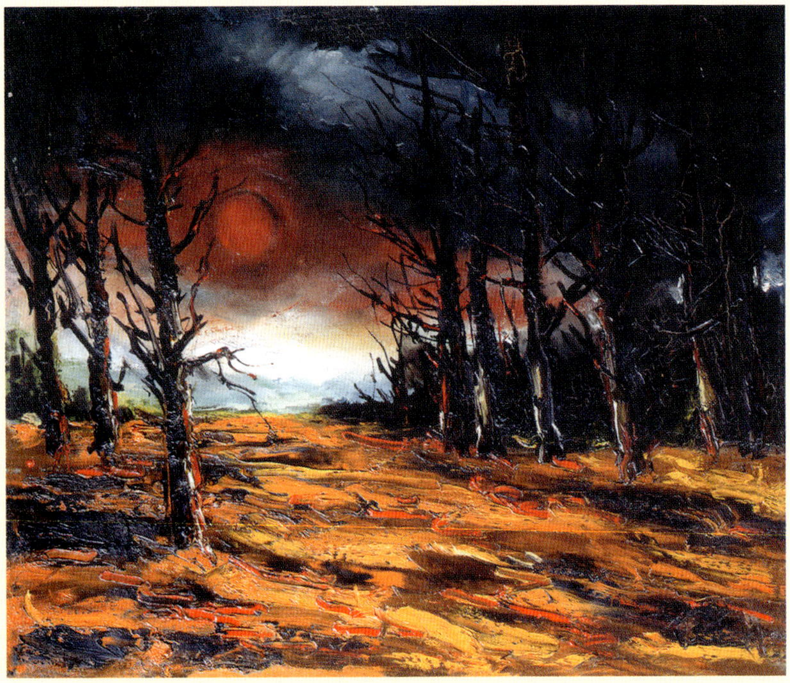

Maurice de Vlaminck,
Sunset, 1954–55,
private collection

lost against the bleak, menacing backdrop of the village. In his large-scale painting *View of Saint-Maurice-lès-Charencey in the Snow* (cat. 73), Vlaminck uses a dark, stormy landscape to further intensify the dissonance between man and nature, while isolated accents in bright red heighten the sense of imminent threat.

The impression of nature as a sublime, unfathomable, and potentially fearsome elemental force is characteristic of many of Vlaminck's late landscapes and bespeaks a return to images of nature in the Romantic tradition. A telling example of this tendency is the 1950 painting *Stormy Landscape* (cat. 74). The energetic brushwork and extremely loose articulation of the surface suggest a rapid rendering of the motif, while the closely cropped composition and unmistakable focus on atmospheric phenomena show striking affinities to late eighteenth- and nineteenth-century oil studies painted in the open air. Beneath a sky covered in thick, dark storm clouds, the middle ground, rendered entirely in dark colors, is scarcely legible; the deep black band that obstructs our gaze into the depths of the landscape is penetrated only by isolated strokes of red or earthy brown. In the foreground, streaks of impasto paint and energetic hatch marks in lurid yellow set a pronounced accent and produce a glaringly shrill effect.

The motif of a threatening, stormy landscape also occurs in numerous later paintings by Vlaminck depicting agrarian motifs such as haystacks or dramatically agitated wheat fields (cats. 78–81).[3] Many of these works show the continuing influence of Vincent van Gogh, whose oeuvre was of profound significance for Vlaminck's Fauve phase. While Vlaminck's early work *The Wheat Field (Champs de Blé)* (cat. 33) is rendered entirely in pure, luminous hues and recalls the brimming vitality of the sun-drenched harvest scenes of the Impressionists and Postimpressionists, his late versions of the same subject unmistakably allude to Van Gogh's somber *Wheatfield with Crows* (fig. p. 49). The latter, one of Van Gogh's most famous works, was shown in Paris in much-acclaimed gallery exhibitions such as those of 1908, 1925, and 1927. As in his Fauvist works, Vlaminck did not copy the model, but creatively interpreted it. In *Harvest during Approaching Thunderstorm* (cat. 79), he follows Van Gogh by dividing the composition into two parts, into the intense dark blue of the sky and the strongly textured yellow-orange of the field of wheat. Instead of a flock of crows flying threateningly toward the viewer, Vlaminck articulates the boundary between the sky and the vegetation in dark black—an intervention that suggests the imminent outbreak of a severe storm.

Other images of nature in Vlaminck's late work likewise occasionally quote nineteenth-century models: his *Landscape* of 1930 (cat. 77), for instance, where the reverent pose of the two figures on the right as well as the cart behind them alludes to the pair of peasants in Jean-François Millet's iconic painting *The Angelus* (1857–59, Musée d'Orsay, Paris). Scholars have often interpreted these references to traditional images of peasants as reflective of Vlaminck's love of the agrarian landscape of northern France, which was characterized by expansive wheat fields as well as the haystacks and grainstacks he frequently painted. The choice of such timeless motifs and the remarkably strong associations with the tradition of nineteenth-century French painting, however, may also signal a conscious rejection of progress and modernization and with it a clear, implicit refusal of the avant-garde of his day and its increasing interest in social and political themes.

Against this background, Vlaminck's 1945 painting *The Fire* (cat. 71) is especially difficult to interpret. The apocalyptic picture shows the dark silhouette of a ruined row of houses, presumably in a city, against a towering backdrop of blazing red flames. In front, a group of schematically rendered figures stands in the street, watching the horrifying drama as if transfixed. Depicted from the rear, they almost compel the viewer to identify with them. In the context of the many photographs that circulated in the French media in the 1940s showing bombed-out residents amid destroyed cityscapes, a political interpretation of Vlaminck's painting—perhaps as a metaphor for the horrors of World War II—seems almost unavoidable. Whether the work can also be read as a symbol of the casualties of France seems questionable, especially in light of Vlaminck's cultural and political affinities to Nazi Germany. That he was willing to cultivate such sympathies despite the branding of his own works as "degenerate" and their confiscation from German institutions in 1937 bespeaks the complexity both of the art-historical study of Nazi cultural politics and of the interpretation of contemporaneous paintings as clearly "legible," ideologically unequivocal documents.

Translated from German by Melissa M. Thorson

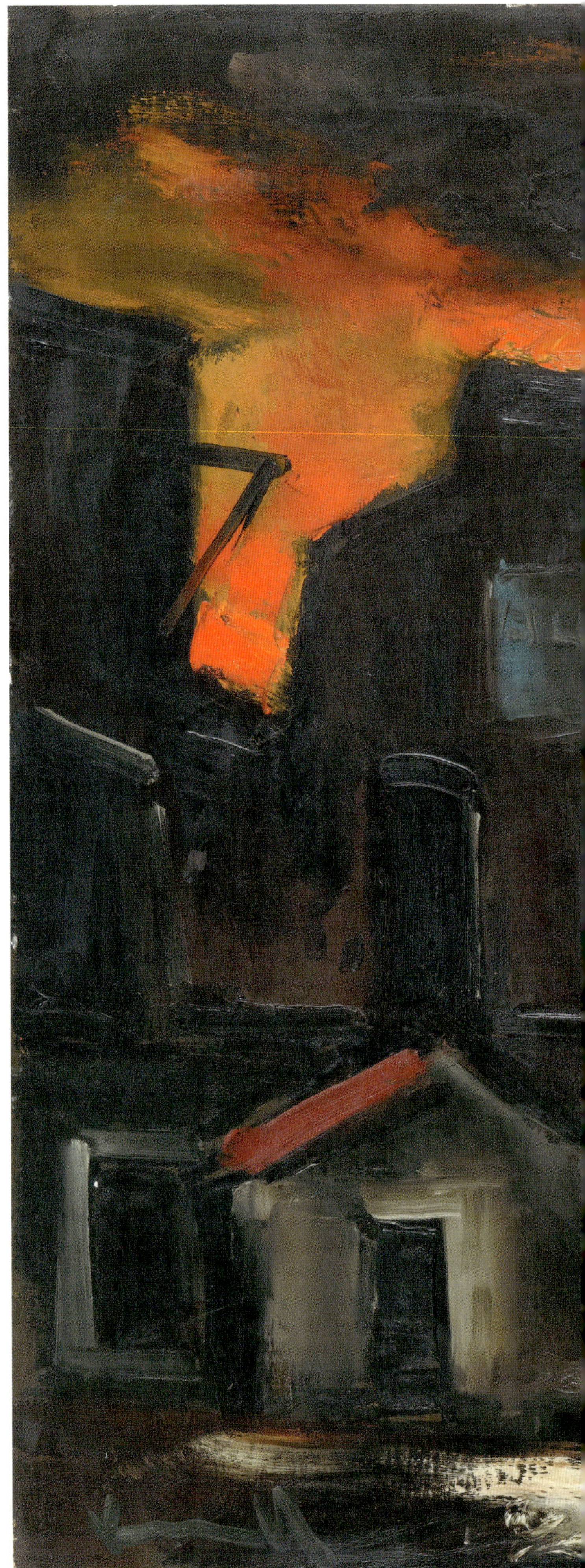

71
The Fire, 1945

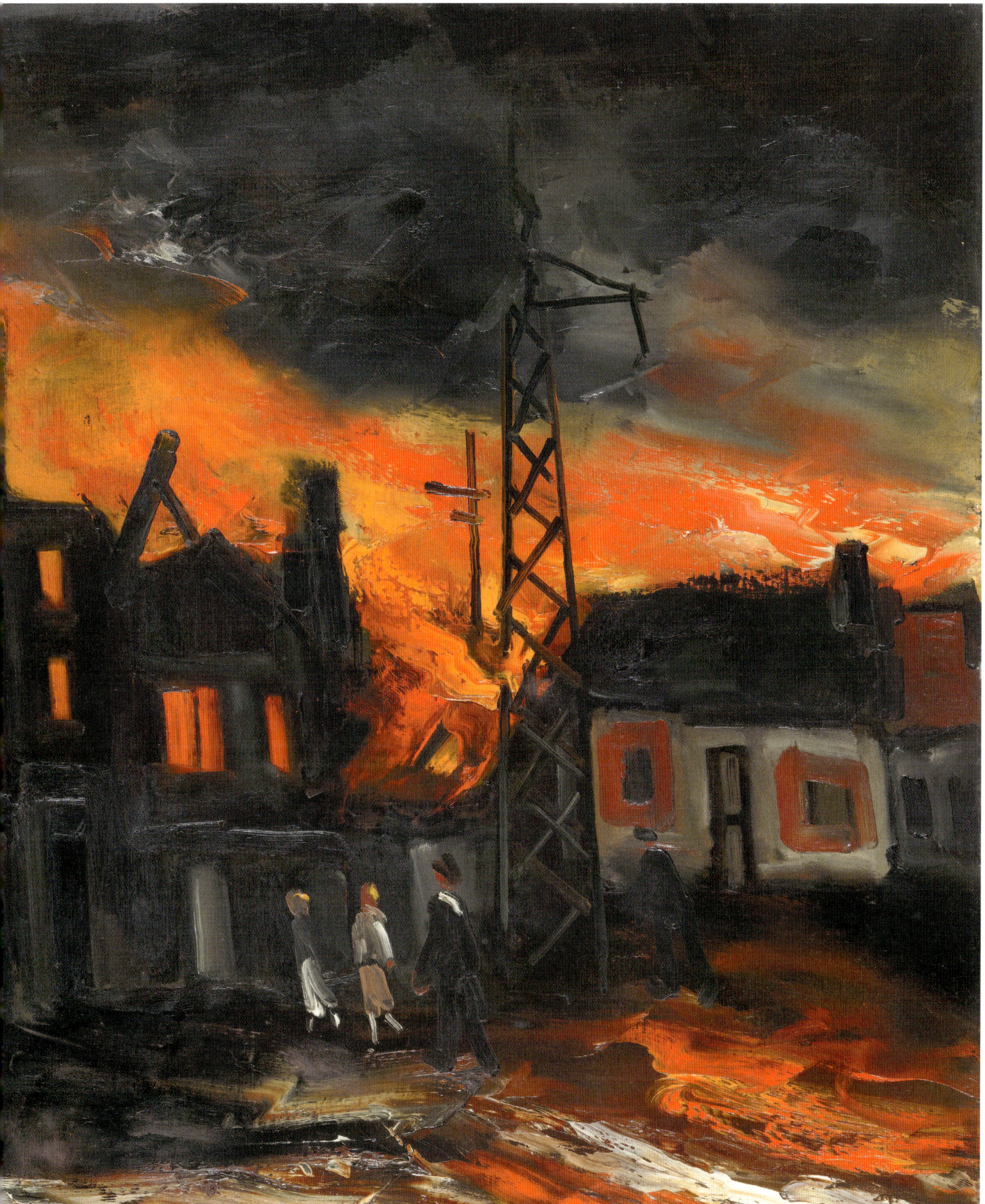

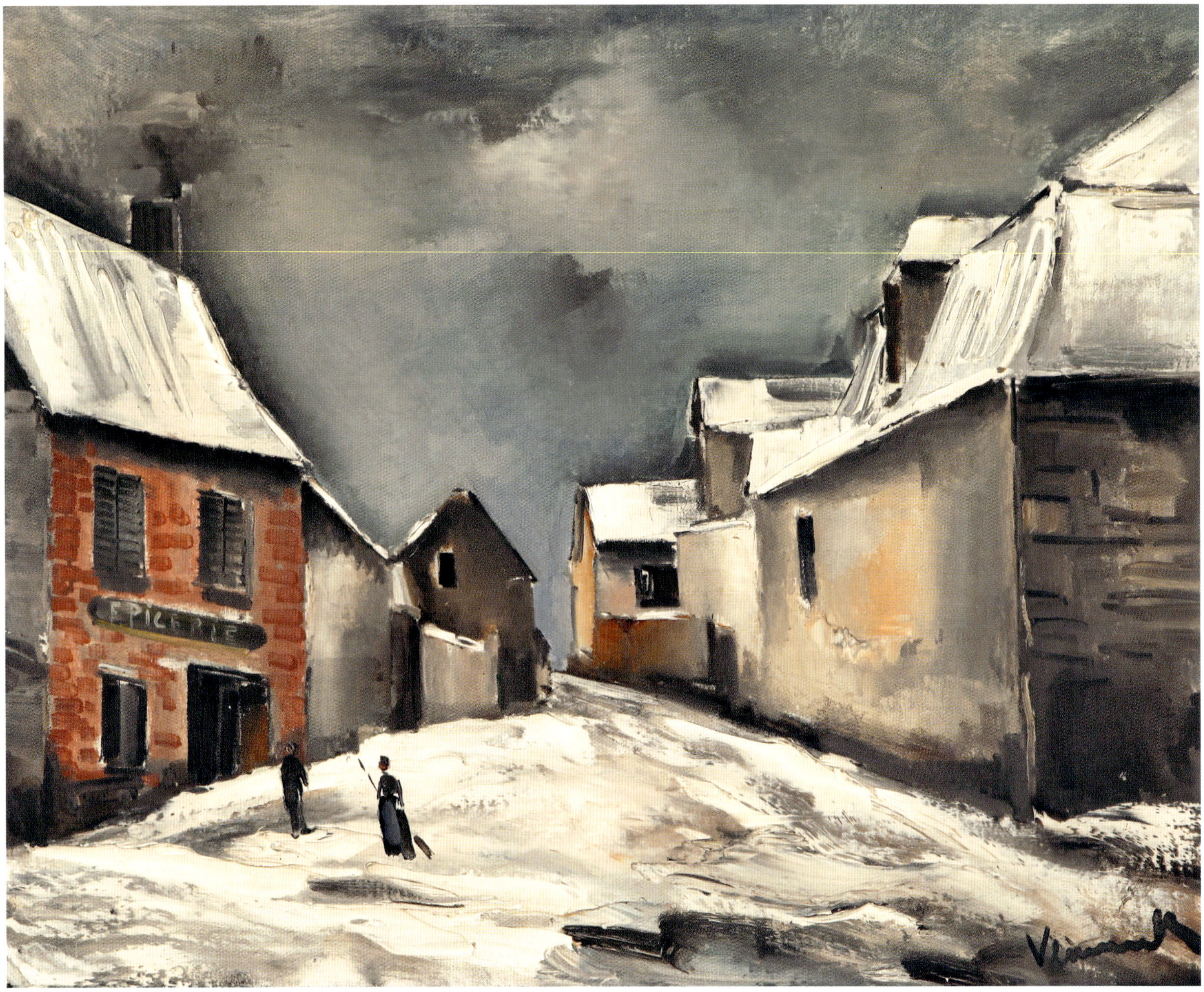

72
Village in the Snow, 1920

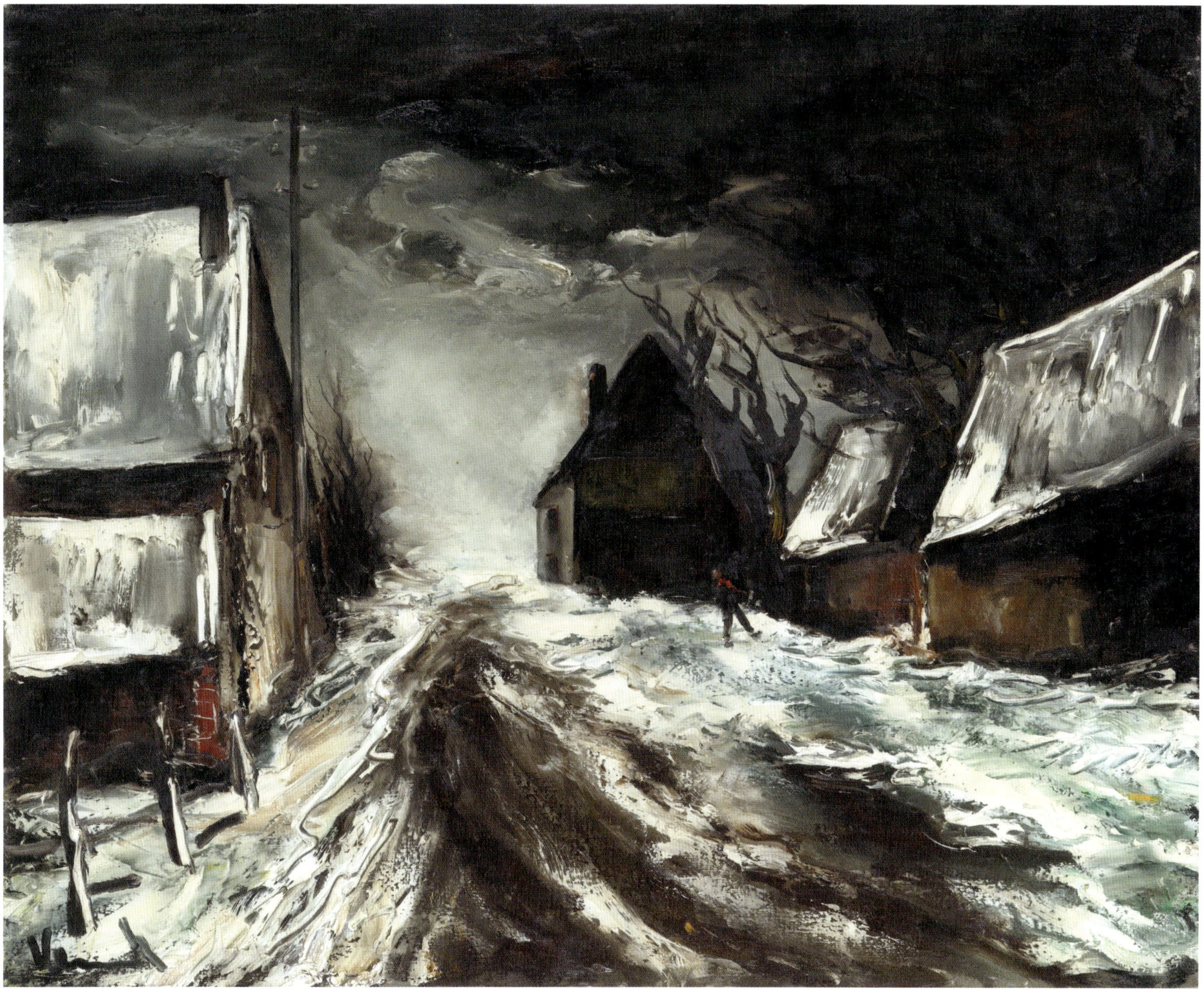

73
View of Saint-Maurice-lès-Charencey in the Snow, 1950

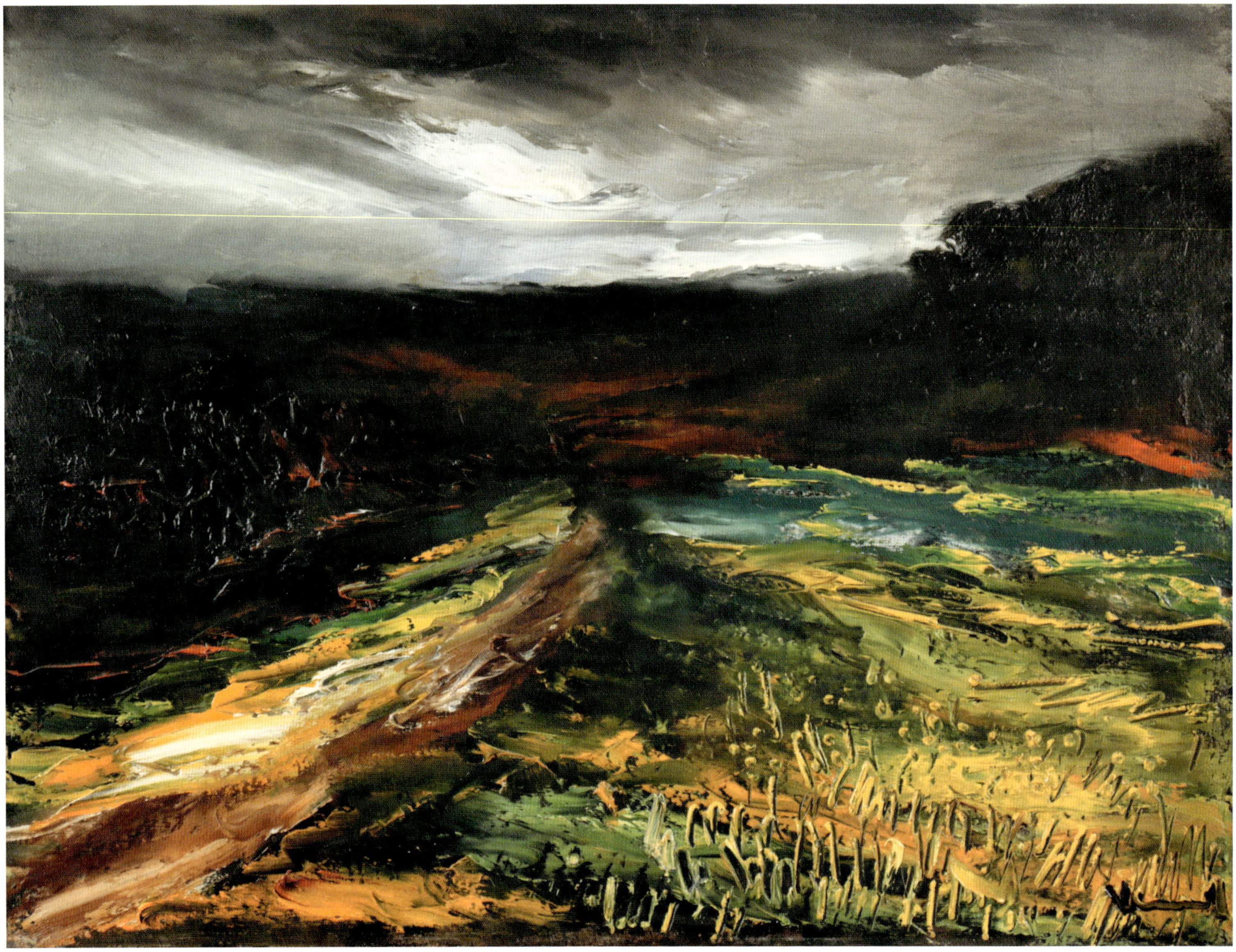

74
Stormy Landscape, 1950

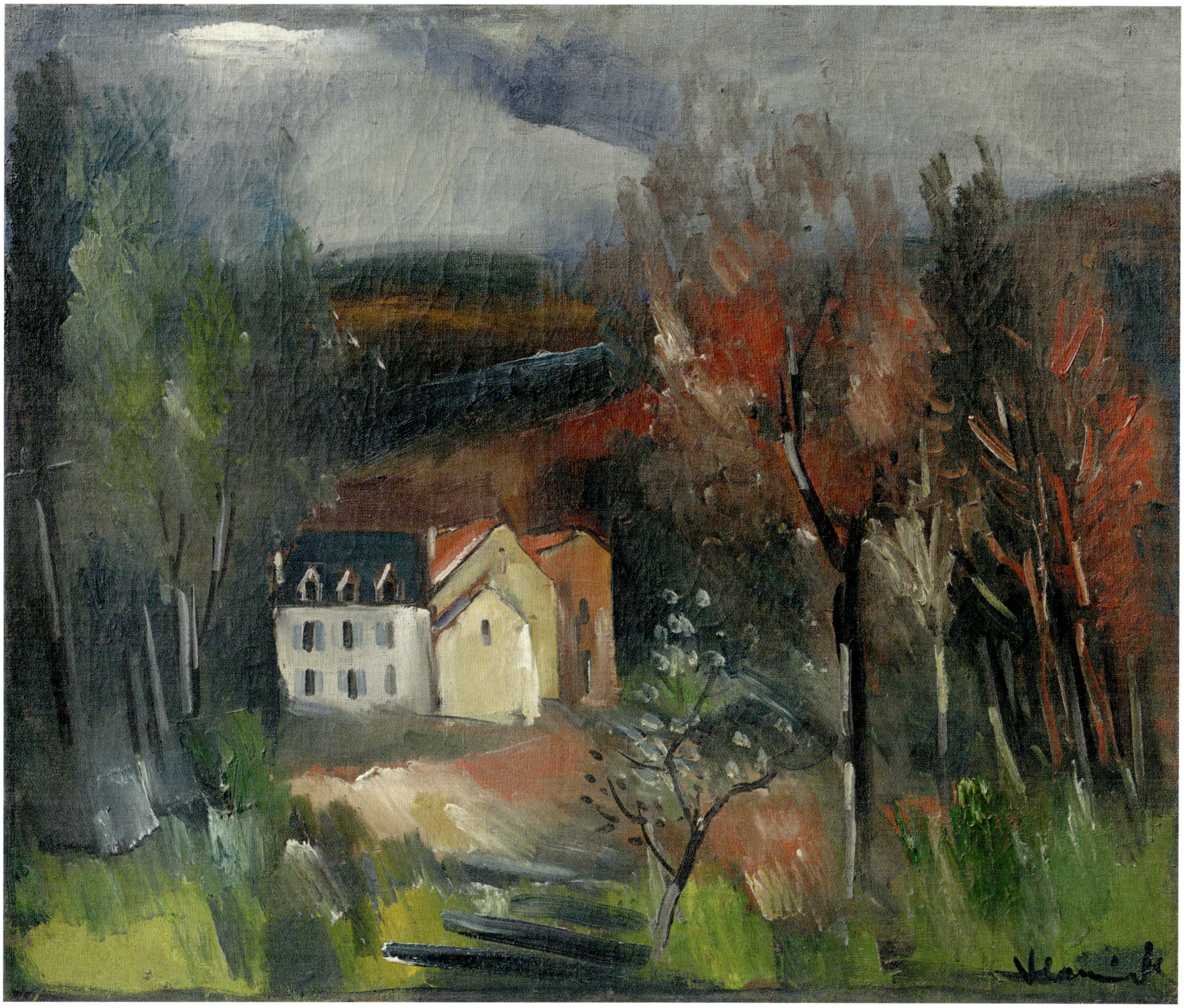

75
Landscape with Red Roofs, undated

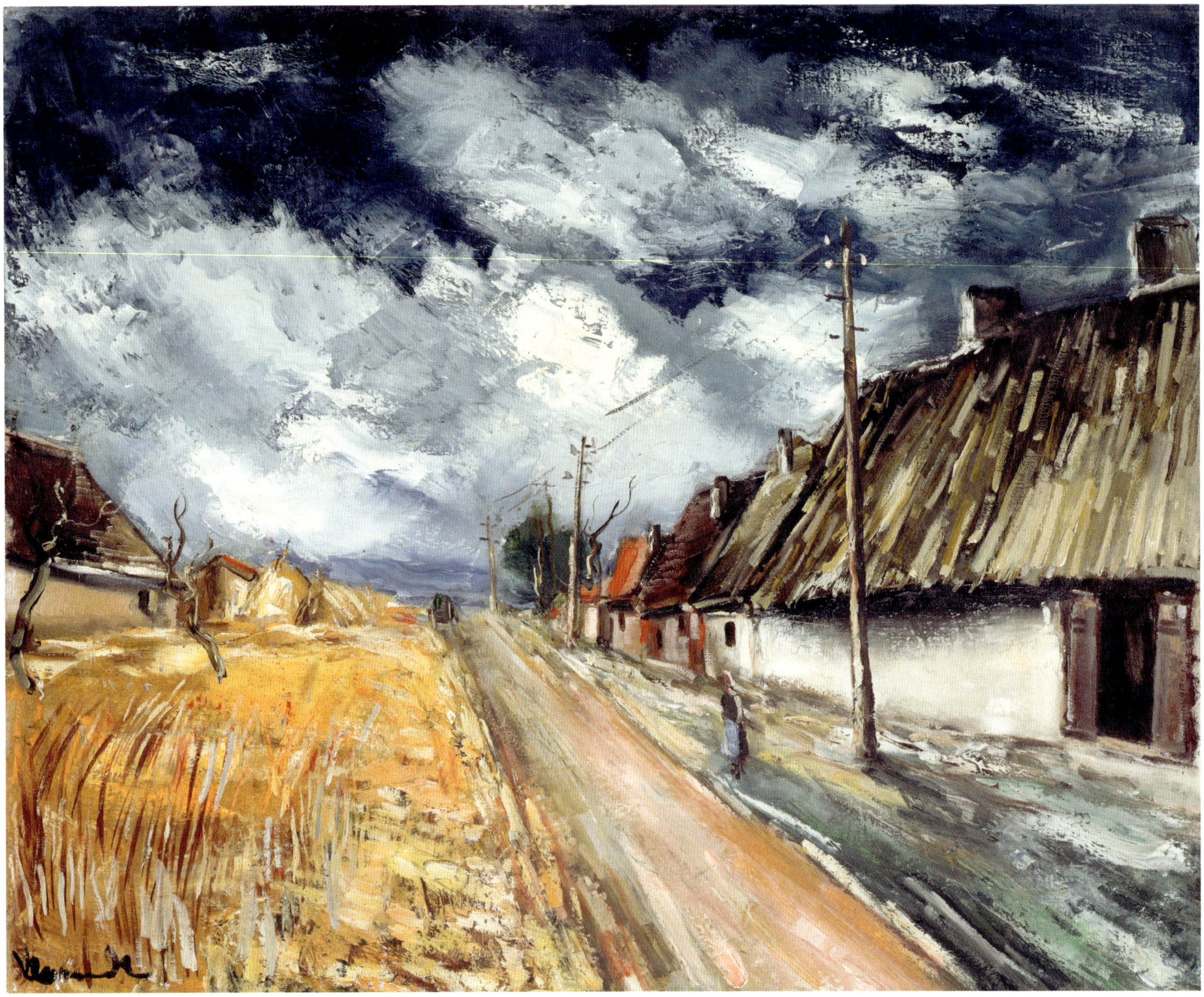

76
Houses with Thatched Roofs, 1933

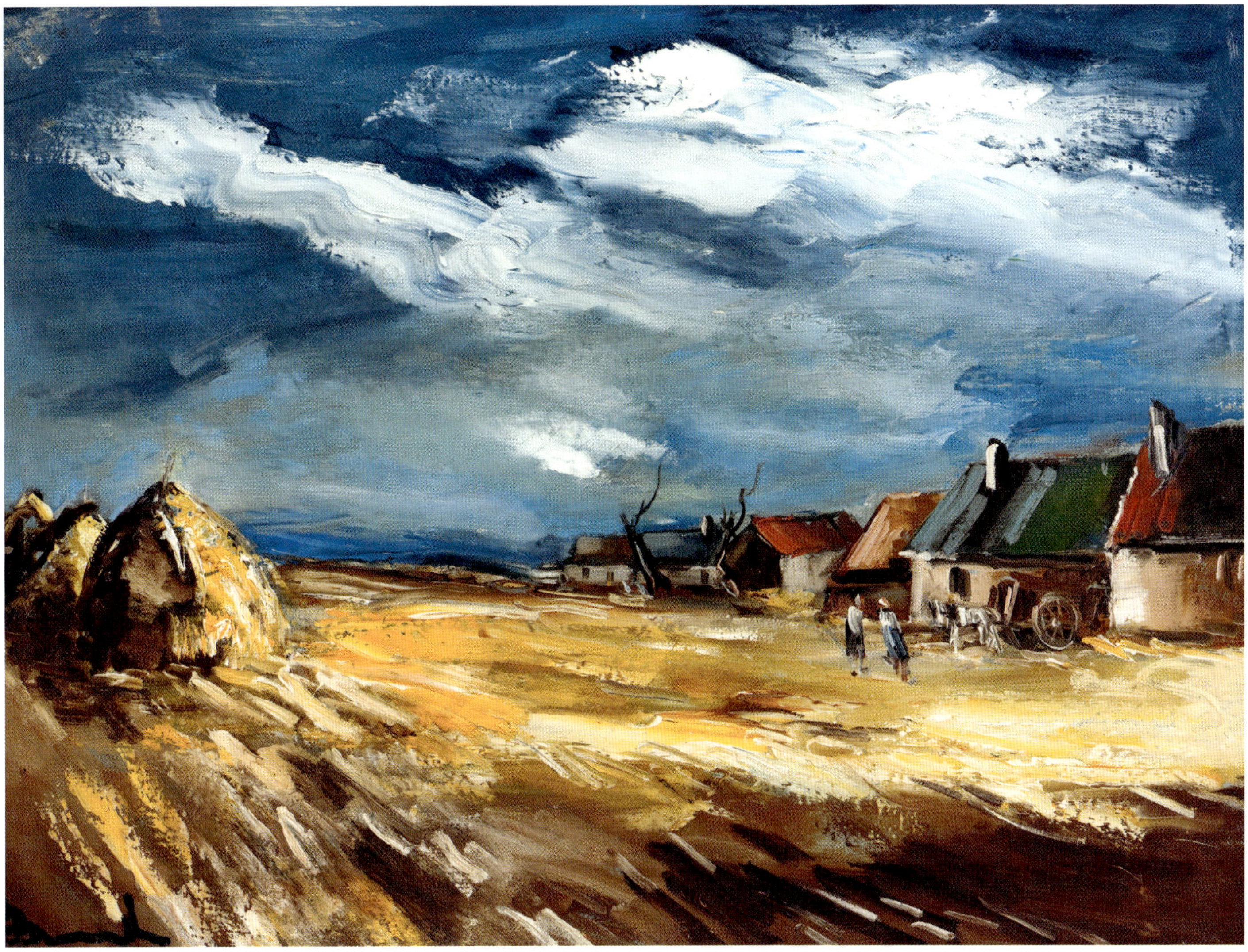

77
Landscape, 1930

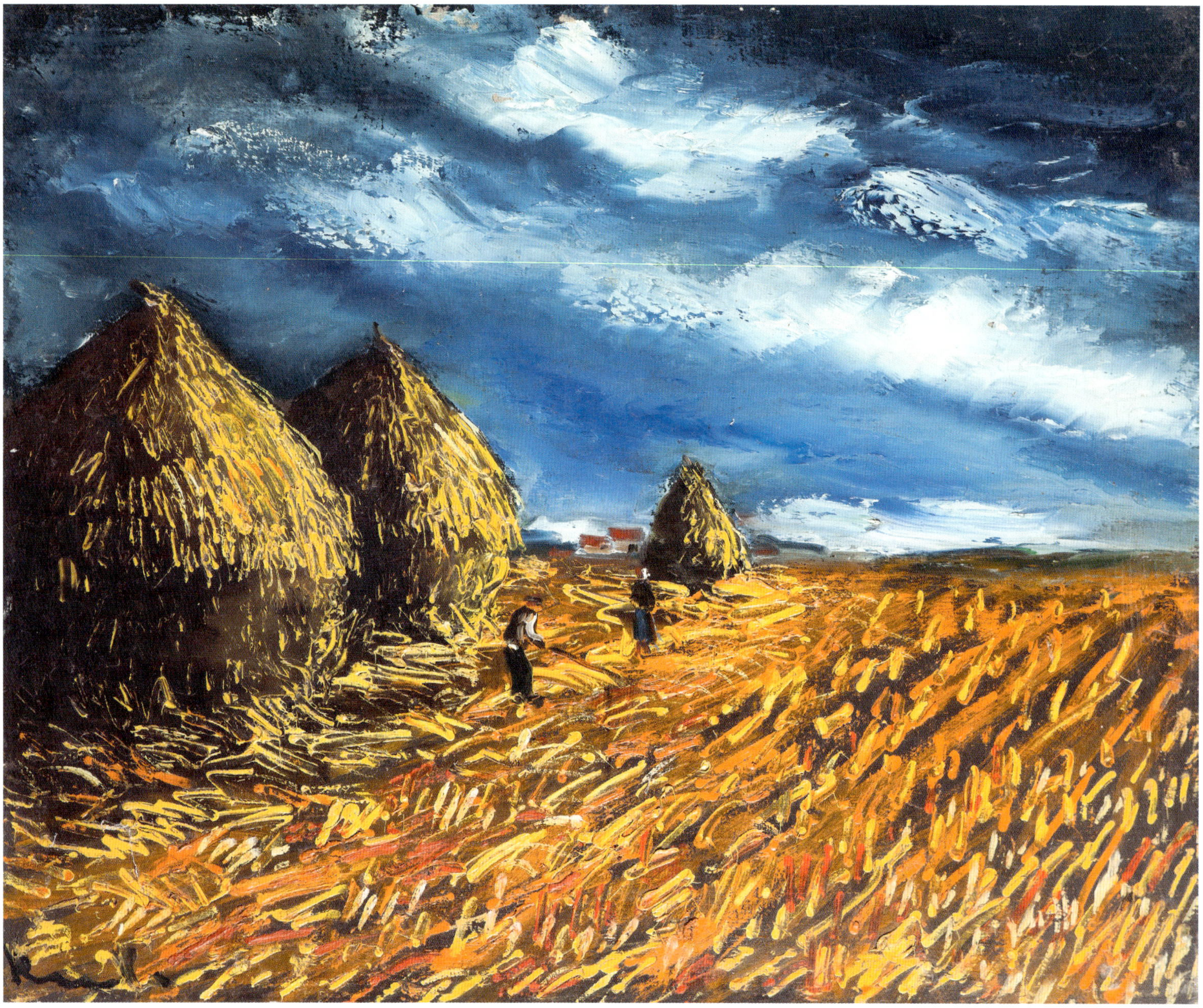

78
The Haystacks, ca. 1945–50

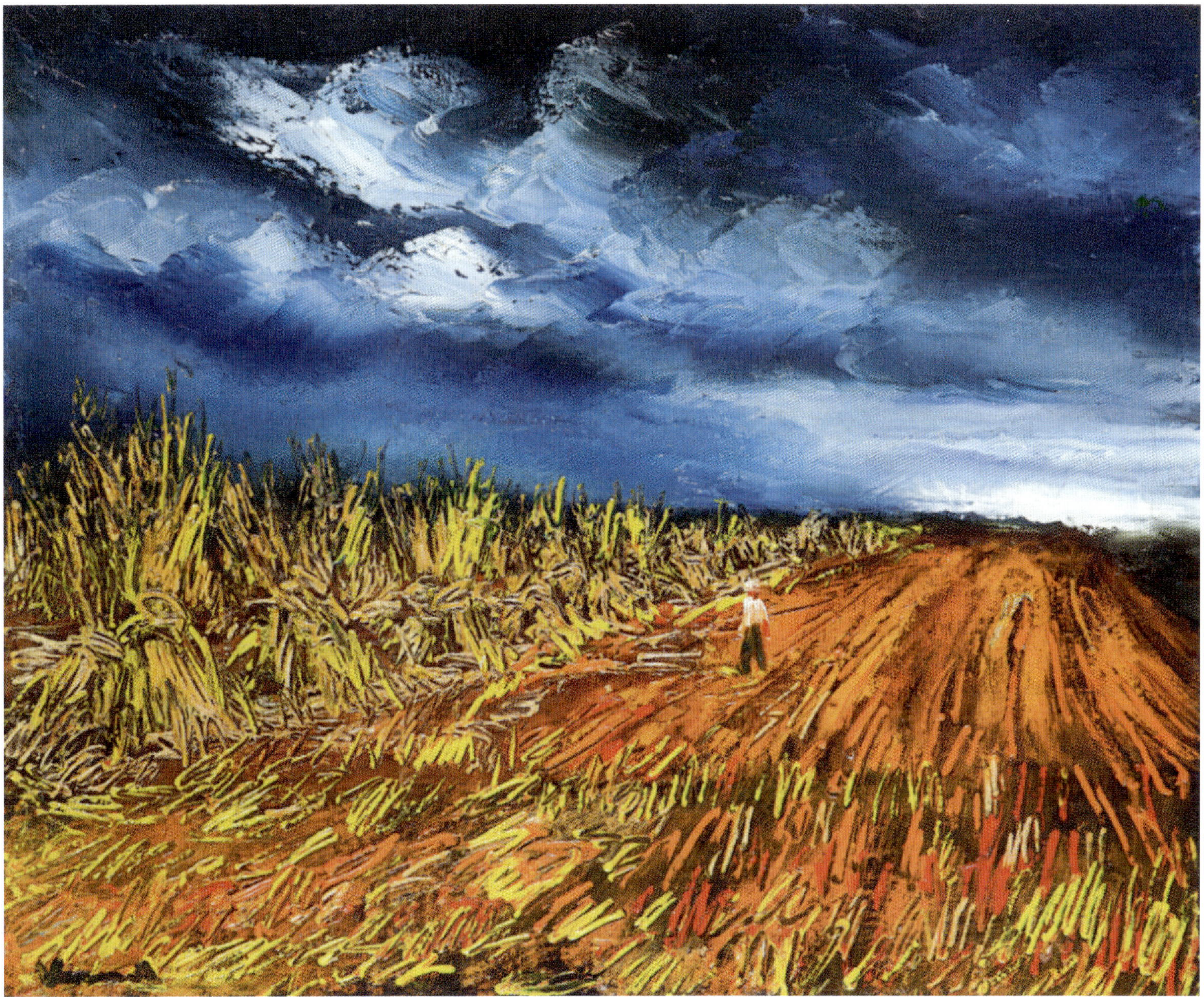

79
Harvest during Approaching Thunderstorm, 1950

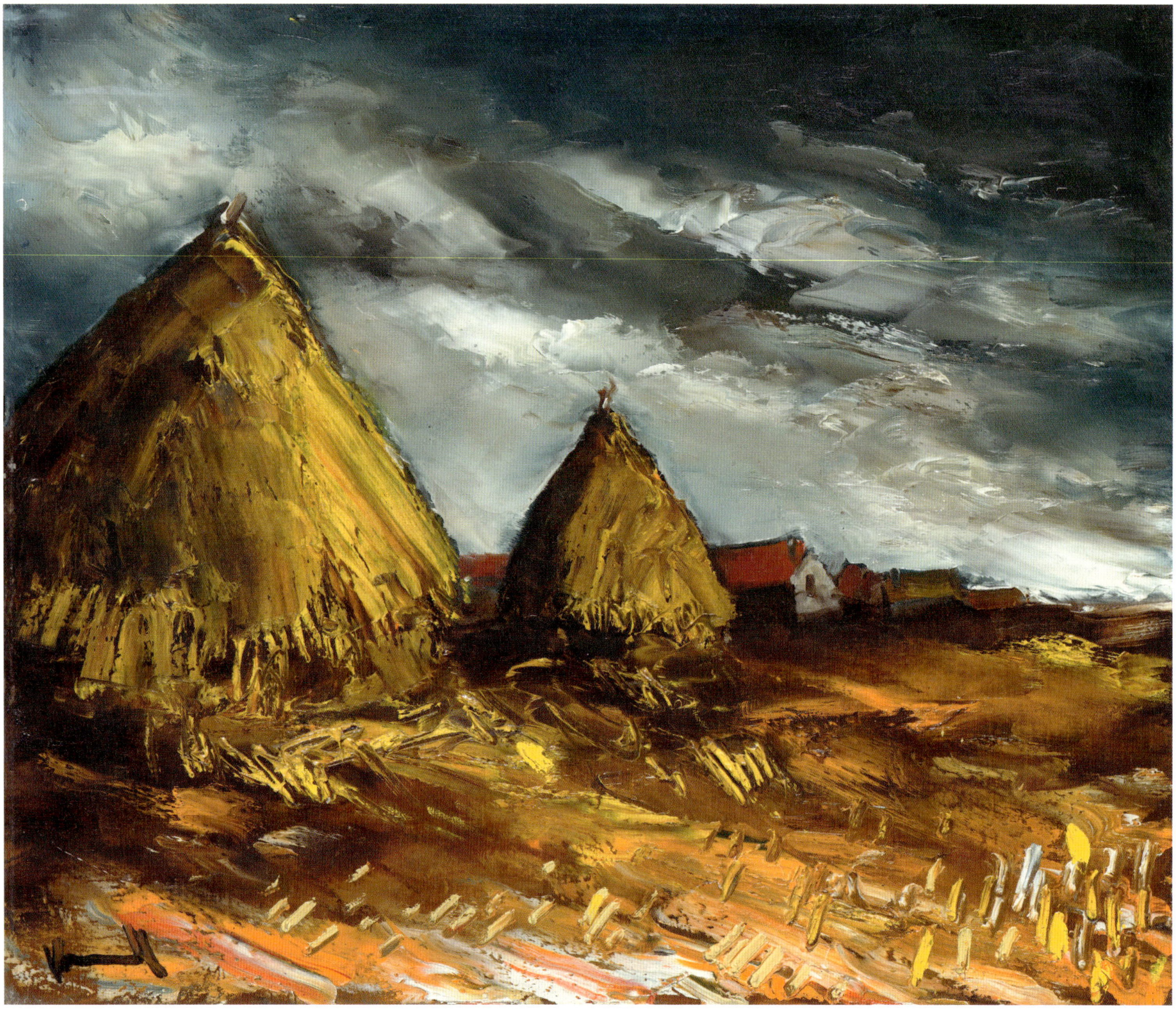

80
The Grainstacks, 1950

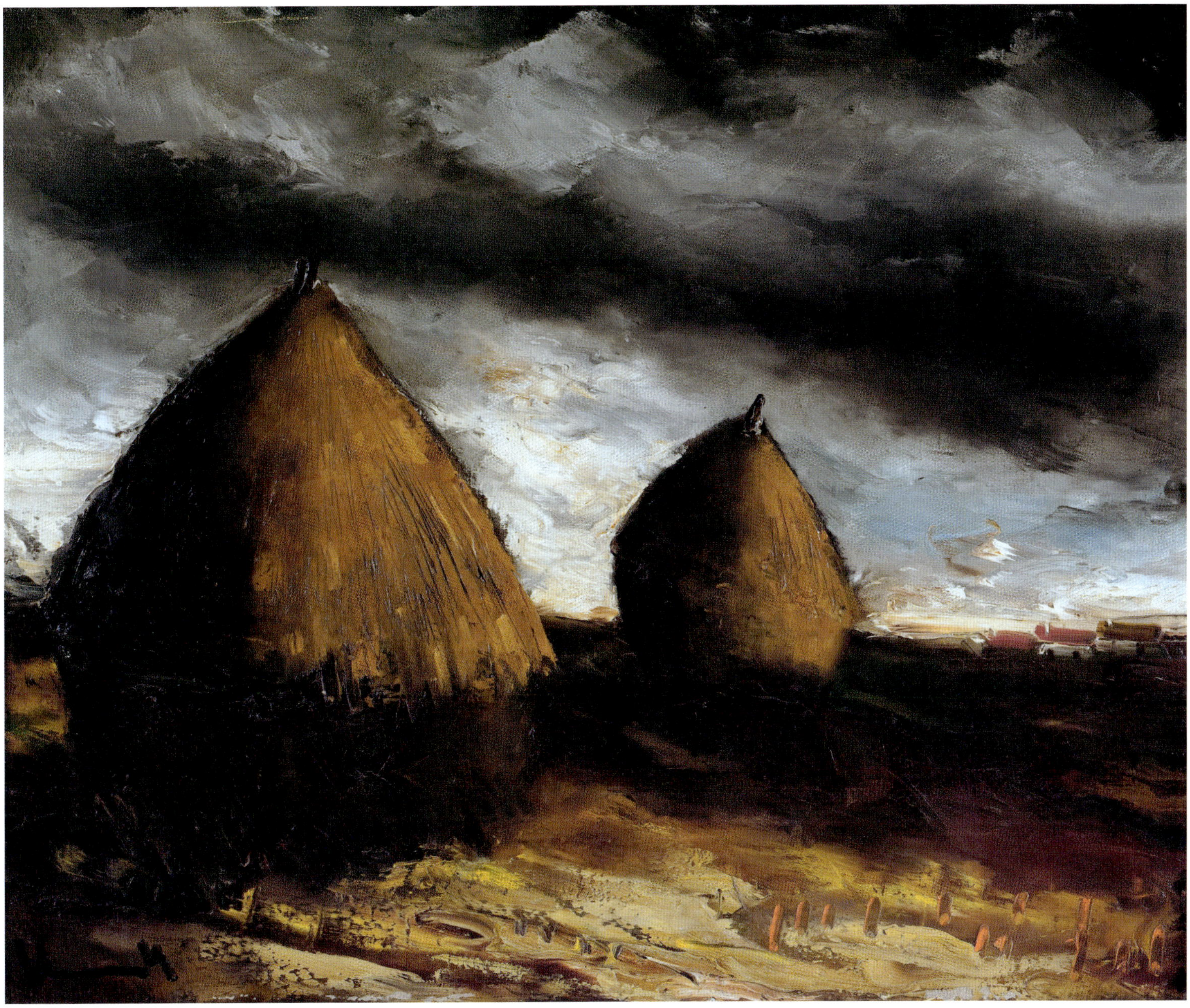

81
The Last Haystacks, 1952

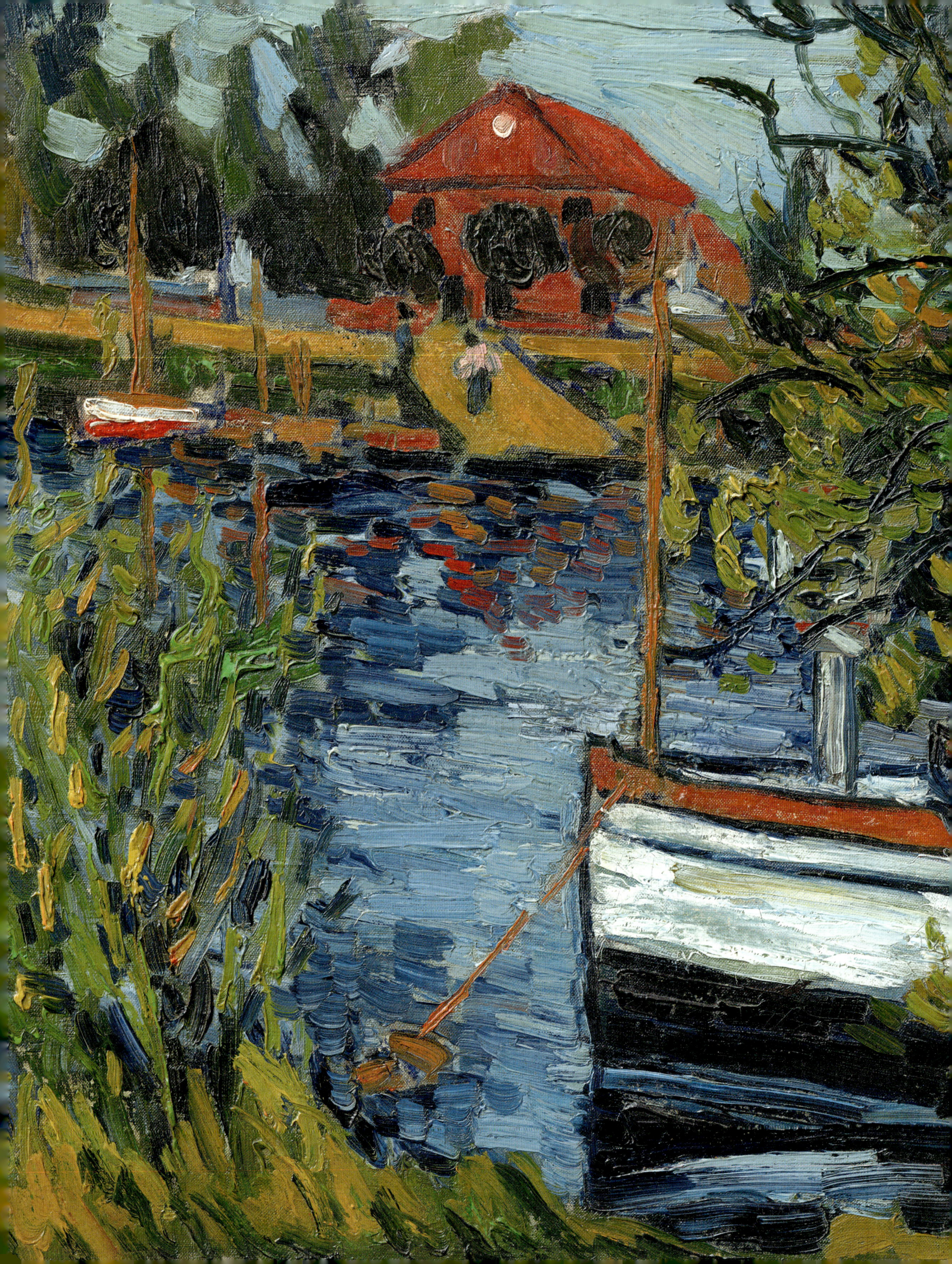

List of Exhibited Works

1
Portrait of Père Bouju, 1900
Oil on canvas, 72 × 48.5 cm
Centre Pompidou, Paris, Musée national d'art moderne/ Centre de création industrielle, Gift of Berthe de Vlaminck, 1959, on permanent loan to the Musée des Beaux-Arts de Chartres since 1995
Inv. AM 3689 P
Potsdam only

2
Young Girl with Doll, 1902
Oil on canvas, 104 × 53 cm
Musée des Beaux-Arts de Chartres
Potsdam only

3
On the Counter, 1900
Oil on canvas, 41 × 32 cm
Musée Calvet, Avignon, donated to the Fondation Calvet by Émile Joseph-Rignault, 1947
Inv. 22289
Potsdam only

4
La Grenouillère, ca. 1905
Oil on canvas, 41.9 × 34 cm
Brooklyn Museum, New York, Bequest of William K. Jacobs Jr.
Inv. 1992.107.39

5
Carrières-sur-Seine, or The Village, 1905
Oil on canvas, 89 × 116 cm
Museum Folkwang, Essen, acquired in 1963 with the support of the state of North Rhine–Westphalia
Inv. G 333

6
Chestnut Grove in Chatou, 1905
Oil on canvas, 60 × 73 cm
Musée d'Art moderne, Troyes, Collections nationales Pierre et Denise Lévy, Gift of Pierre and Denise Lévy, 1976
Inv. MNPL 333
Potsdam only

7
Twilight, 1904–05
Oil on canvas, 54 × 65.5 cm
Tel Aviv Museum of Art, Bequest of Max Bodner, New York
Inv. TAMA 86.707
Potsdam only

8
Park in Carrières-Saint-Denis, 1904
Oil on canvas, 54 × 62.9 cm
Private collection

9
A Street in Marly-le-Roi, 1905–06
Oil on canvas, 54 × 65 cm
Centre Pompidou, Paris, Musée national d'art moderne/ Centre de création industrielle
Inv. AM 2674 P

10
Suburban Landscape, 1905
Oil on canvas, 60.3 × 73 cm
Museum of Fine Arts, Boston, Gift and Bequest of David and Peggy Rockefeller
Inv. 1991.426
Potsdam only

11
The Red Trees, 1906
Oil on canvas, 65 × 81 cm
Centre Pompidou, Paris, Musée national d'art moderne/
Centre de création industrielle
Inv. AM 2673 P

12
Trees at the Blue House, 1906
Oil on canvas, 54.5 × 65.5 cm
Private collection
Potsdam only

13
The Hills at Rueil, 1906
Oil on canvas, 48 × 56 cm
Centre Pompidou, Paris, Musée national d'art moderne/
Centre de création industrielle
Inv. AM 2675 P

14
Route maraîchère, 1905
Oil on canvas, 60 × 73 cm
Kunst Museum Winterthur, gift of the Volkart Foundation,
2009
Inv. 958

15
View of Bougival, 1906
Oil on canvas, 46.5 × 55.5 cm
Tel Aviv Museum of Art, Bequest of Harry and
Leah Meklembourg, New York
Inv. TAMA 79.203
Potsdam only

16
Landscape at Bougival, 1906
Oil on canvas, 63.5 × 76.5 cm
Stedelijk Museum Amsterdam,
bequeathed by Helge Spechter-Höxbroe
Inv. A 22588
Not in the exhibition

17
Bougival, ca. 1905
Oil on canvas, 82.6 × 100.6 cm
Dallas Museum of Art,
The Wendy and Emery Reves Collection
Inv. 1985.R.82
Potsdam only

18
The Girl from the Rat mort, 1905
Oil on canvas, 32.1 × 46 cm
Private collection
Potsdam only

19
Woman with a Hat, 1905
Oil on canvas, 56.5 × 47.6 cm
National Gallery of Art, Washington, DC,
Donated by Lolo Sarnoff in memory of her parents,
Mr. and Mrs. Robert von Hirsch
Inv. 1981.84.1
Potsdam only

20
Reclining Nude, 1905
Oil on canvas, 28 × 42 cm
Private collection
Potsdam only

21
Still Life with Books and Fruit Bowl, 1906
Oil on canvas, 46.3 × 54.9 cm
Private collection

22
Blue Still Life, ca. 1907
Oil on canvas, 72.9 × 91.5 cm
Private collection
Potsdam only

23
Still Life with Vase, Pitcher, and Fruit Bowl, 1907
Oil on canvas, 73 × 60 cm
Staatsgalerie Stuttgart, acquired with lottery fund in 1959
Inv. 2569
Potsdam only

24
Still Life, 1907
Oil on canvas, 50.5 × 65 cm
Private collection

25
The Table (Still Life with Almonds), 1907
Oil on canvas, 54.3 × 65.4 cm
Private collection, Courtesy Beaumont Nathan Art Advisory
Potsdam only

26
Still Life, 1907
Oil on canvas, 60 × 73 cm
Centre Pompidou, Paris, Musée national d'art moderne/
Centre de création industrielle, Bequest of Georges
Grammont, 1959, on permanent loan to the
Musée de l'Annonciade, Saint-Tropez since 1972
Inv. AM 3845 P

27
Blue Vase with Flowers, ca. 1906
Oil on canvas, 81.5 × 45.7 cm
Carmen Thyssen Collection
Inv. CTB.1997.9
Wuppertal only

28
Fields, Rueil, ca. 1906–07
Oil on canvas, 55 × 65 cm
Carmen Thyssen Collection
Inv. CTB.1998.65
Potsdam only

29
Pond at Ursine near Chaville, 1905
Oil on canvas, 54 × 65 cm
Triton Collection Foundation, the Netherlands

30
The Blue House, 1906
Oil on canvas, 54.6 × 64.8 cm
Minneapolis Institute of Art,
Bequest of Putnam Dana McMillan
Inv. 61.36.17
Potsdam only

31
Houses at Chatou, ca. 1905
Oil on canvas, 81.3 × 101.6 cm
Art Institute of Chicago,
Gift of Mr. and Mrs. Maurice E. Culberg
Inv. 1951.19

32
Fisherman in Chatou, 1906
Oil on canvas, 46 × 55 cm
Private collection
Potsdam only

33
The Wheat Field (Champs de Blé), ca. 1906
Oil on canvas, 65.9 × 81.8 cm
Milwaukee Art Museum,
Gift of Mrs. Harry Lynde Bradley
Inv. M1953.12
Potsdam only

34
The Rural Luncheon, 1906
Oil on canvas, 65 × 80.9 cm
Private collection

35
Forest Scene with Deadwood (Deadwood Collectors), 1906
Oil on canvas, 64.5 × 80.5 cm
Private collection
Potsdam only

36
Underbrush, 1905
Oil on canvas, 60 × 72.5 cm
Private collection
Potsdam only

37
Tugboats on the Seine, Chatou, 1906
Oil on canvas, 50.2 × 65.1 cm
National Gallery of Art, Washington, DC,
Collection of Mr. and Mrs. John Hay Whitney
Inv. 1998.74.4
Potsdam only

38
Canal Boat, 1905–06
Oil on canvas, 60.2 × 73 cm
Artizon Museum, Ishibashi Foundation, Tokyo
Potsdam only

39
Banks of the Seine at Chatou, 1905
Oil on canvas, 53 × 65 cm
Private collection
Potsdam only

40
River Scene with Bridge, ca. 1905
Oil on canvas, 50 × 63.7 cm
Wadsworth Atheneum Museum of Art, Hartford, CT,
Gift of Mr. and Mrs. Robert Montgomery
Inv. 1972.13
Potsdam only

41
Rueil, the Boathouse, 1906
Oil on canvas, 54.7 × 65.7 cm
Hasso Plattner Collection
Inv. MB-Vla-02

42
The Seine at Chatou, ca. 1906–07
Oil on canvas, 38 × 46 cm
Albertina Museum, Vienna—Batliner Collection
Inv. GE130DL

43
The Seine at Nanterre, 1906–07
Oil on canvas, 60 × 73 cm
Van Gogh Museum, Amsterdam (purchased with support from the VriendenLoterij, the Mondriaan Fund and the Rembrandt Association, with the additional support from the Prins Bernhard Cultuurfonds, and the VSBfonds)
Inv. s0514S2007
Potsdam only

44
The Tugboat, 1908–10
Oil on canvas, 53 × 73.4 cm
Hamburger Kunsthalle, acquired 1949
Inv. HK-2866

45
The Bridge, undated
Oil on canvas on panel, 38.4 × 46.4 cm
Hasso Plattner Collection
Inv. MB-Vla-09

46
Banks of the Seine at Bougival, 1906
Oil on canvas, 54 × 73 cm
Hasso Plattner Collection
Inv. MB-Vla-01

47
Rowboat at Chatou, ca. 1906
Oil on canvas, 50 × 65 cm
Albertina Museum, Vienna—Batliner Collection
Inv. GE129DL

48
Sailing Boat, Chatou, ca. 1906
Oil on canvas, 57.8 × 71.1 cm
Virginia Museum of Fine Arts, Richmond,
Collection of Mr. and Mrs. Paul Mellon
Inv. 95.23
Potsdam only

49
The Boats, 1905
Oil on canvas, 46.2 × 54 cm
Private collection

50
The Bridge at Chatou, 1905
Oil on canvas, 68 × 96 cm
Staatliche Museen zu Berlin, Nationalgalerie,
acquired with funds from the Deutsche Klassenlotterie
Inv. NG17/62

51
Sunlight on the Water, 1905
Oil on canvas, 38.2 × 45.7 cm
Metropolitan Museum of Art, New York,
Robert Lehman Collection, 1975
Inv. 1975.1.220
Potsdam only

52
Sailing Boats at Chatou, 1907
Oil on canvas, 50 × 61 cm
Kunsthaus Zürich, Johanna and
Walter L. Wolf Collection, 1984
Inv. 1984/0017

53
Riverbank, July 14, ca. 1908–09
Oil on canvas, 60 × 73 cm
Private collection
Potsdam only

54
Le Havre, Grand Quai, 1906
Oil on canvas, 81.3 × 100.3 cm
Saint Louis Art Museum, Gift of Mr. and Mrs. Wilbur D. May
Inv. 527:1957
Potsdam only

55
The Bridge at Chatou, 1906–07
Oil on cardboard on panel, 52.5 × 71.5 cm
Hasso Plattner Collection
Inv. MB-Vla-03

56
The Fishermen, 1907
Oil on canvas, 60 × 73 cm
Hasso Plattner Collection
Inv. MB-Vla-04

57
The Bridge at Chatou, ca. 1908
Oil on canvas, 46.4 × 55.3 cm
Wallraf-Richartz-Museum & Fondation Corboud, Cologne
Inv. WRM Dep. FC 729

58
Three Houses, 1910
Oil on canvas, 80.5 × 100.5 cm
Von der Heydt-Museum, Wuppertal
Inv. G 1020
Wuppertal only

59
Landscape near Martigues, 1913
Oil on canvas, 65.1 × 81.9 cm
Tate, Bequeathed by Sir Robert Hart 1970
Inv. T01254

60
The Washhouse in the Snow, 1913
Oil on canvas, 60 × 73 cm
Private collection, Courtesy Galerie de la Présidence, Paris

61
Saint-Michel District, Bougival, 1913
Oil on canvas, 81 × 100 cm
Hasso Plattner Collection
Inv. MB-Vla-06

62
Sailboats at Chatou, ca. 1908
Oil on canvas, 55 × 65 cm
Nahmad Collection

63
Sailboats, before 1918
Oil on canvas, 64.5 × 80.5 cm
Von der Heydt-Museum, Wuppertal
Inv. G 0701

64
Opium, ca. 1910
Oil on canvas, 81.3 × 53.2 cm
Hugh Lane Gallery, Dublin, Donated by the Friends
of the National Collections of Ireland in memory of
Sarah Purser, 1944
Inv. 922

65
Still Life, 1907
Oil on canvas, 54.4 × 65 cm
Musée d'Orsay, Paris, donated by Max and Rosy Kaganovitch, 1973
Inv. RF 1973 27

66
Still Life, before 1911
Oil on canvas, 60 × 73 cm
Von der Heydt-Museum, Wuppertal
Inv. G 0255
Wuppertal only

67
Still Life with Flowers and Fruit, 1911
Oil on canvas, 60 × 73 cm
Museum Ludwig, Cologne, Transfer from the Wallraf-Richartz-Museum in 1976, Haubrich Donation, 1946
Inv. ML 76/2773

68
Still Life, 1910–11
Oil on canvas, 63 × 75 cm
Private collection, Courtesy Galerie de la Présidence, Paris

69
The Forest, 1914–18
Oil on canvas, 60 × 73 cm
Hasso Plattner Collection
Inv. MB-Vla-08

70
Village Road, 1911
Oil on canvas, 60 × 73 cm
Hasso Plattner Collection
Inv. MB-Vla-05

71
The Fire, 1945
Oil on canvas, 65 × 81 cm
RMN-Grand Palais (Musée d'Orsay), on permanent loan to the Musée des Beaux-Arts de Chartres, bequest of Maurice de Vlaminck's daughter, Solange Prével-Vlaminck, 1978
Inv. RF 1978 10

72
Village in the Snow, 1920
Oil on canvas, 74.2 × 92.7 cm
Kunsthalle Mannheim
Inv. M620

73
View of Saint-Maurice-lès-Charencey in the Snow, 1950
Oil on canvas, 80 × 100 cm
RMN-Grand Palais (Musée d'Orsay), on permanent loan to the Musée des Beaux-Arts de Chartres, bequest of Maurice de Vlaminck's daughter, Solange Prével-Vlaminck, 1978
Inv. RF 1978 3

74
Stormy Landscape, 1950
Oil on canvas, 50 × 65 cm
Private collection, Courtesy Galerie de la Présidence, Paris

75
Landscape with Red Roofs, undated
Oil on canvas, 60 × 73 cm
Hasso Plattner Collection
Inv. MB-Vla-07

76
Houses with Thatched Roofs, 1933
Oil on canvas, 73.3 × 92 cm
Centre Pompidou, Paris, Musée national d'art moderne/ Centre de création industrielle
Inv. AM 2330 P

77
Landscape, 1930
Oil on canvas, 54 × 73 cm
Musée d'Art Moderne de la Ville de Paris
Inv. AMVP 1176

78
The Haystacks, ca. 1945–50
Oil on canvas, 60 × 73 cm
Fonds de dotation Maison Vlaminck
Potsdam only

79
Harvest during Approaching Thunderstorm, 1950
Oil on canvas, 60 × 73 cm
Fonds de dotation Maison Vlaminck
Potsdam only

80
The Grainstacks, 1950
Oil on canvas, 55 × 65 cm
RMN-Grand Palais (Musée d'Orsay), on permanent loan to the Musée des Beaux-Arts de Chartres, bequest of Maurice de Vlaminck's daughter, Solange Prével-Vlaminck
Inv. RF 1978 5

81
The Last Haystacks, 1952
Oil on canvas, 60 × 73 cm
Musée d'Art Moderne de la Ville de Paris, Donation of Henry Thomas, 1984
Inv. AMVP 2681

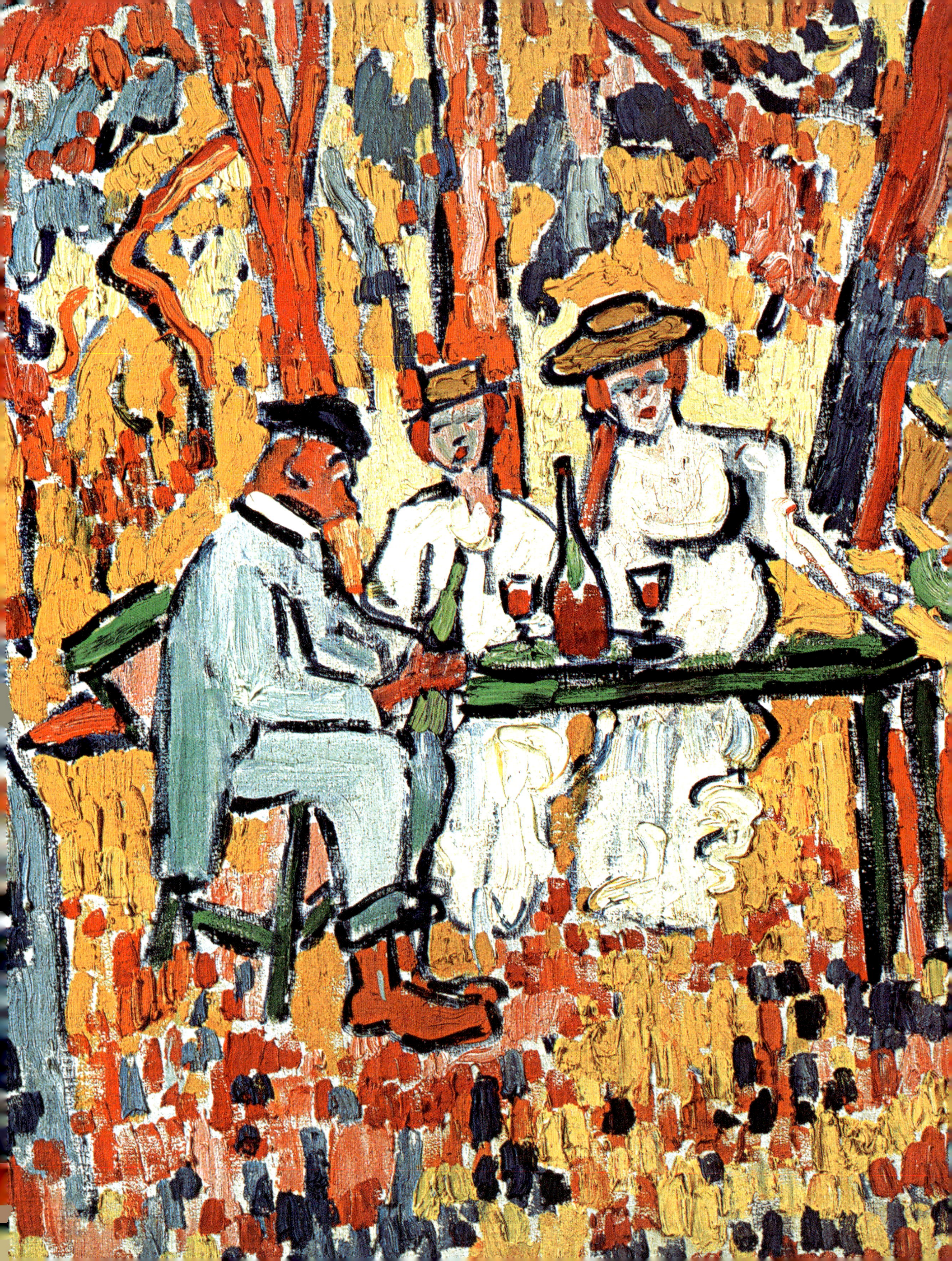

Chronology

Compiled by Valentina Plotnikova
and Daniel Zamani

1876

On April 4 Maurice de Vlaminck is born in Paris to a family of modest circumstances. His father runs a musical instrument shop, and his mother teaches piano. Vlaminck's youth is marked by an affinity for music; he begins playing the violin early on and at times will earn his living as a violinist. Significantly, a 1905 portrait by André Derain shows Vlaminck not as a painter but as a musician (fig. 2).

1879

The family moves to Vésinet west of Paris, where Vlaminck spends most of his childhood and youth. In 1893 the family settles in Chatou, a village on the Seine that is now a suburb of Paris, where Vlaminck later establishes his first studio. He explores the countryside around Chatou extensively as an enthusiastic cyclist.

1893

Vlaminck, who intends to pursue a career as a musician and composer, begins painting as a hobby. A local painter, Jules Robichon, introduces him to the fundamentals of drawing. Together with artist Henri Rigal, Vlaminck paints in the open air along the Seine Valley near Chatou. During excursions to Paris, he is exposed to the art of the Impressionists at venues including Galerie Le Barc de Bouteville.

1896

In early September Vlaminck marries Suzanne Berly, with whom he will have three daughters: Madeleine (b. 1896), Solange (b. 1898), and Yolande (b. 1905). The young father initially supports his family as a violinist as well as with prize money from cycling tournaments.

1897

In August Vlaminck suffers a severe bout of typhoid fever, bringing his career as a cyclist to a premature end. In September he begins three years of military service. In the officers' library of his regiment, he encounters communist and anarchist ideas in the writings of authors such as Karl Marx and Élisée Reclus. In the early twentieth century, he contributes a number of articles to anarchist magazines and later describes the intent of his Fauvist painting in rhetoric unmistakably informed by his political affinity for anarchism. In an interview from 1928, he states, "With my cobalts and vermilions, I wished to burn down the École des Beaux-Arts and to render my impressions without any thought for what has been achieved in the past. . . . life and I, I and life."[1]

1
Maurice de Vlaminck, ca. 1902–03

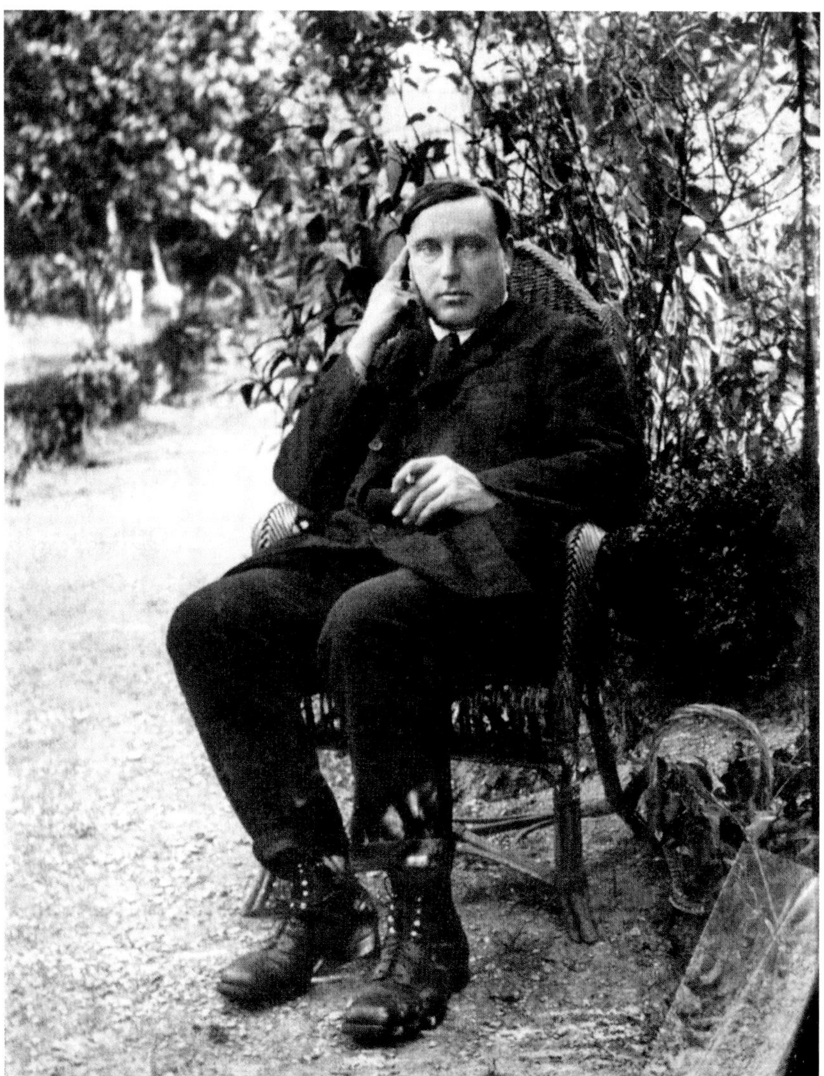

1900

During a two-week home leave, Vlaminck meets André Derain, who will become one of his closest friends. Their exchange strengthens his desire to pursue a career as a painter. Between December 1900 and September 1901, the two artists share a studio in the former restaurant Levanneur on Île de Chatou, an island in the Seine. The railway bridge next to the building will later become one of the Vlaminck's most frequent motifs (cats. 32, 50, 55, 57). His first documented paintings, the figural images *On the Counter* (cat. 3) and *Portrait of Père Bouju* (cat. 1), are created in 1900; in his subsequent oeuvre, portraits will play only a subordinate role in comparison to landscape painting and still life.

1901

Galerie Bernheim-Jeune shows the first Vincent van Gogh retrospective in Paris (March 15–31). The accompanying catalog lists seventy-one works, including what is perhaps now Van Gogh's most famous painting, *The Starry Night* (1889, Museum of Modern Art, New York). The exhibition features numerous major works from French private collections and inaugurates the canonization of Van Gogh as one of the founding fathers of modern art. Vlaminck is profoundly moved by this encounter with his work and in 1905 is able to immerse

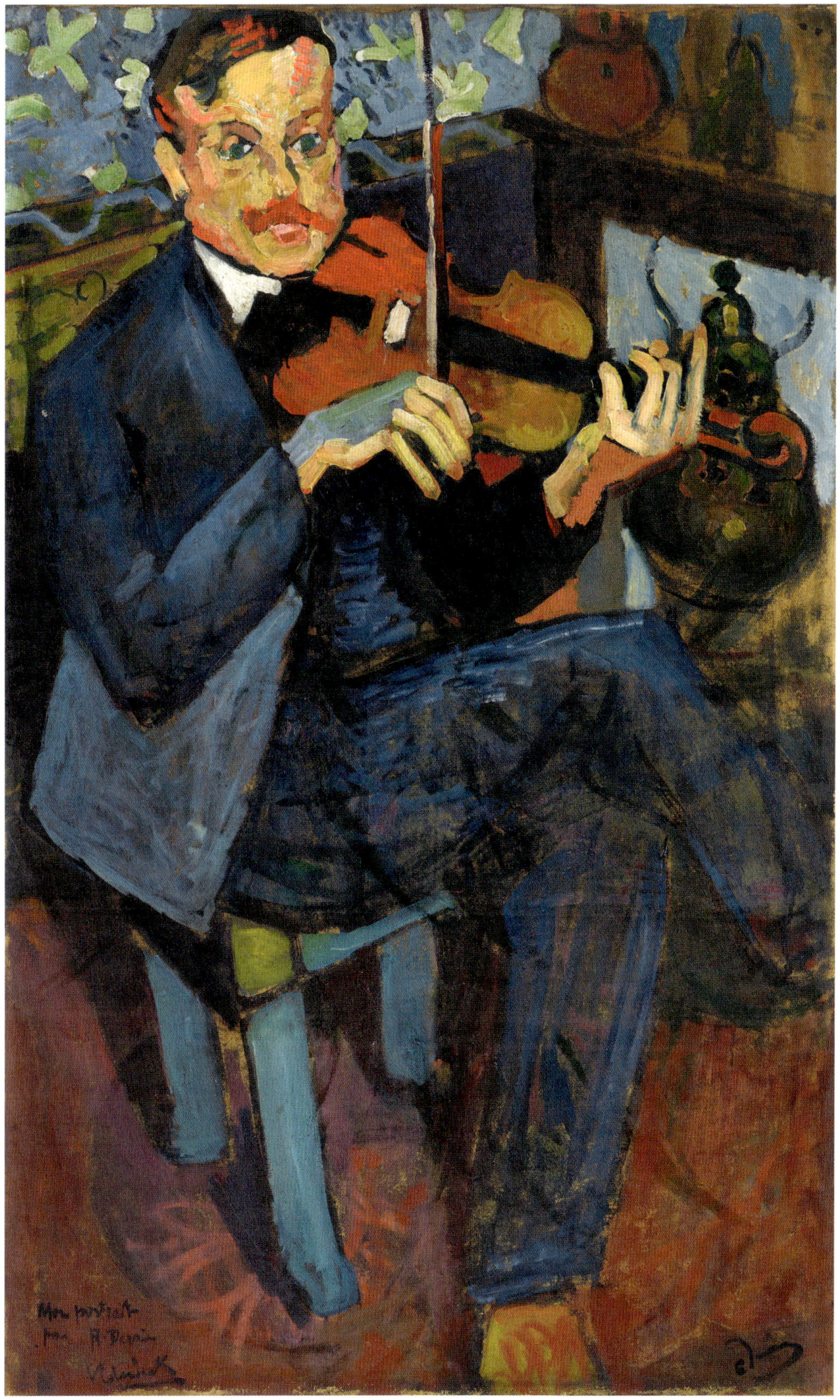

2
André Derain,
Portrait of Vlaminck Playing the Violin, 1905,
Artizon Museum,
Ishibashi Foundation,
Tokyo

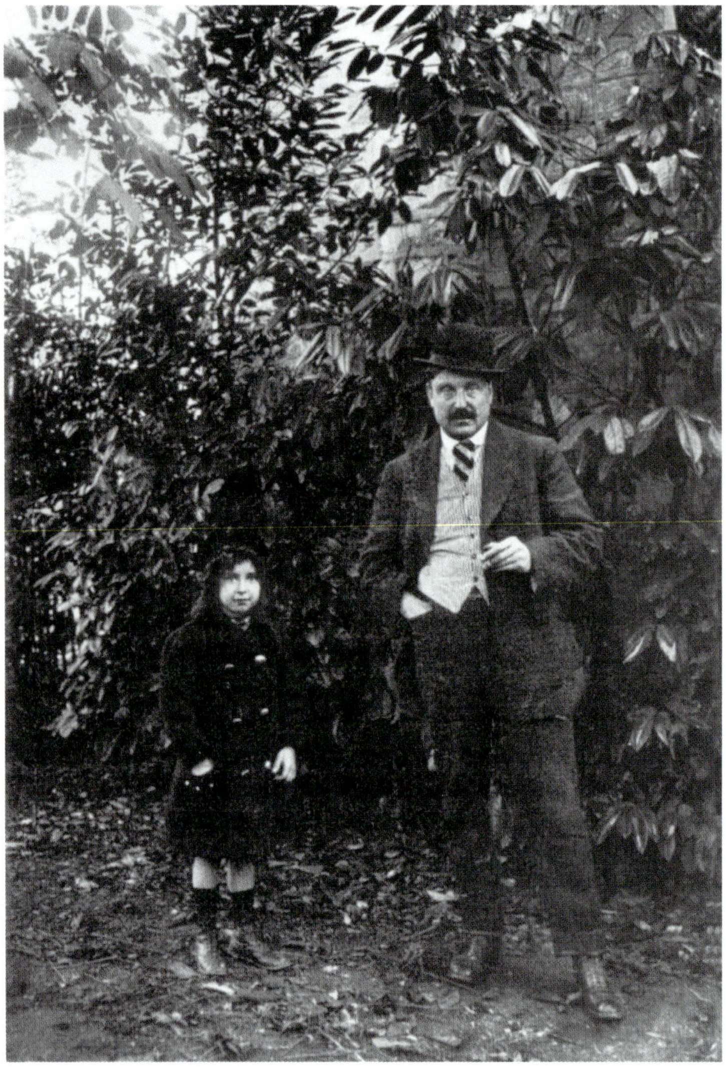

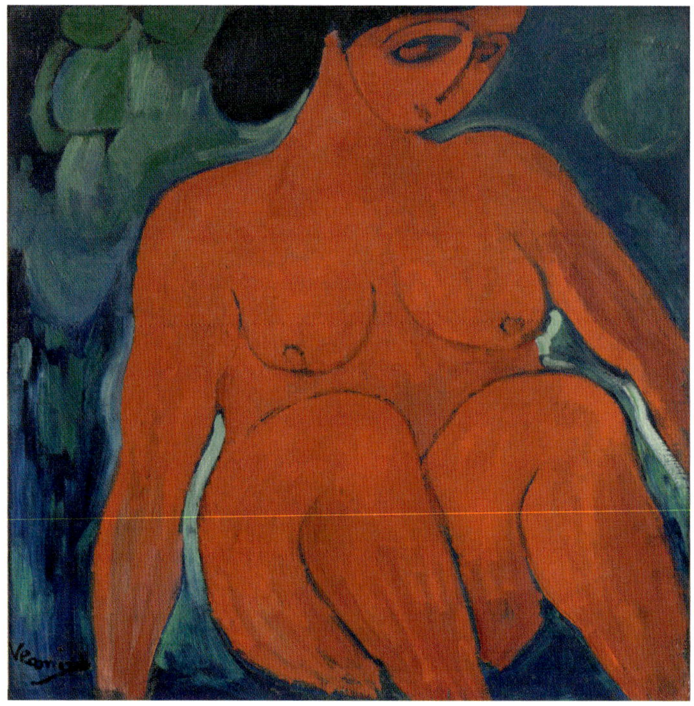

3
Vlaminck and his daughter Solange, ca. 1904

4
Maurice de Vlaminck, *Red Nude,* 1905, private collection

himself in Van Gogh's Postimpressionist painting once more at the Salon des Indépendants in Paris. The influence of Van Gogh on Vlaminck's work is especially apparent in 1905 and 1907, both in the choice of colors and in the brushwork and strongly textured surfaces; numerous paintings by Vlaminck also make obvious allusions to Van Gogh's motifs, such as *The Wheat Field (Champs de Blé)* (cat. 33) from around 1906. At the exhibition at Bernheim-Jeune, Vlaminck meets Henri Matisse, who later will become a leader of the Fauves.

1902

Vlaminck and Derain begin a regular correspondence that will continue until 1914.

1904

In the late summer, Matisse spends a number of weeks in the French Riviera, where the light inspires him to create the large painting *Luxury, Calm, and Voluptuousness* (fig. p. 36). The brilliantly colored composition reflects the influence of the Pointillism of Paul Signac, which also manifests itself in works such as Vlaminck's landscape *Underbrush* (cat. 36) from 1905. While Derain and Matisse later return to the Riviera to paint on multiple occasions, Vlaminck's images of nature concentrate entirely on the topography of his native Seine Valley.

1905

At Matisse's suggestion, Vlaminck submits eight paintings to the Salon des Indépendants in Paris (March 24–April 30), where 4,269 works by 669 artists are exhibited. The Salon also includes two retrospectives in honor of Georges Seurat and Vincent van Gogh, with forty-three and forty-five works respectively. In the fall Vlaminck participates in the Salon d'Automne (October 18–November 25), where five of his paintings, including *Twilight* (cat. 7) and *Park in Carrières-Saint-Denis* (cat. 8), are shown in a room together with works by artists such as Charles Camoin, Derain, Albert Marquet, and Matisse. The artists' brash approach to color prompts critic Louis Vauxcelles to describe them as *fauves* ("wild beasts"), a term that soon becomes established in art-historical parlance. The significant journalistic response to the exhibition gives the young painters their breakthrough, and soon their works are shown together on a regular basis. As a loose collective, the avant-garde Fauvist movement lasts for only a few years before beginning to wane around 1907–08, concurrently with the rise of Cubism. In November art dealer Ambroise Vollard acquires most of the works in Vlaminck's studio, and his financial support allows the artist to focus on painting from then on.

1907

The Salon des Indépendants (March 20–April 30) presents a retrospective in honor of Paul Cézanne, who had died the previous year—the first of many exhibitions in Paris that will give rise to a genuine "Cézanne fever."

5
Maurice de Vlaminck, *Rustic Setting, or Children in a Garden,* 1903, private collection

6
Maurice de Vlaminck, *Woman in the Country,* 1904, private collection

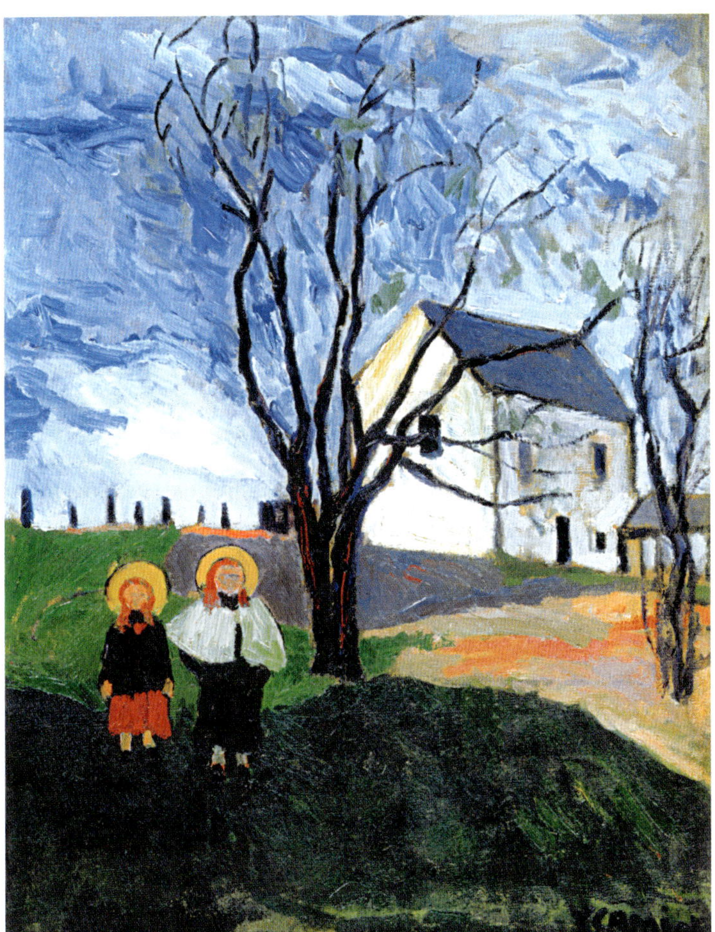

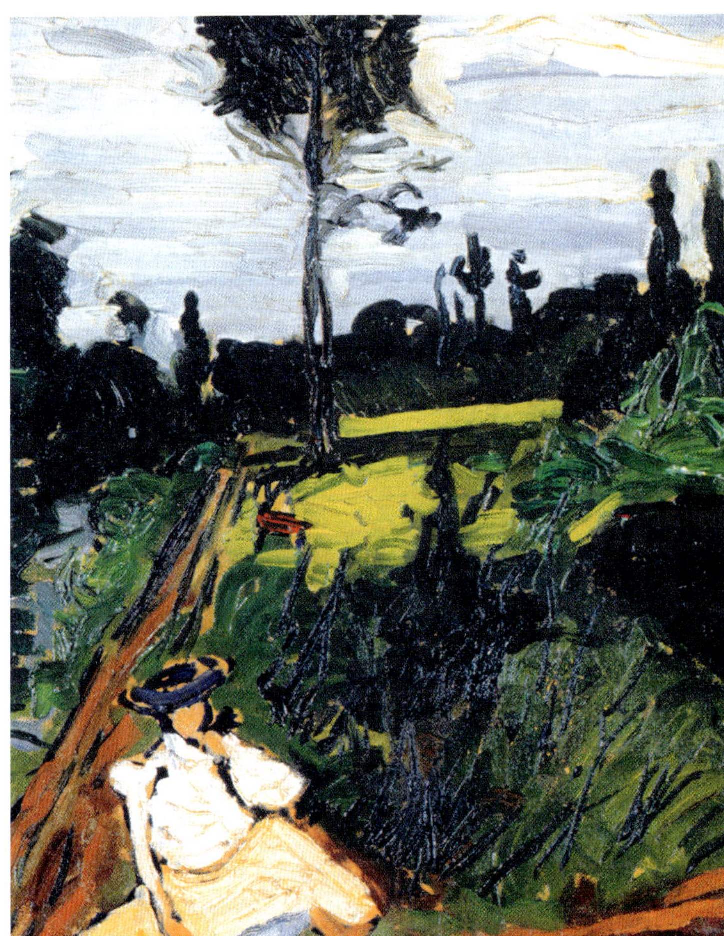

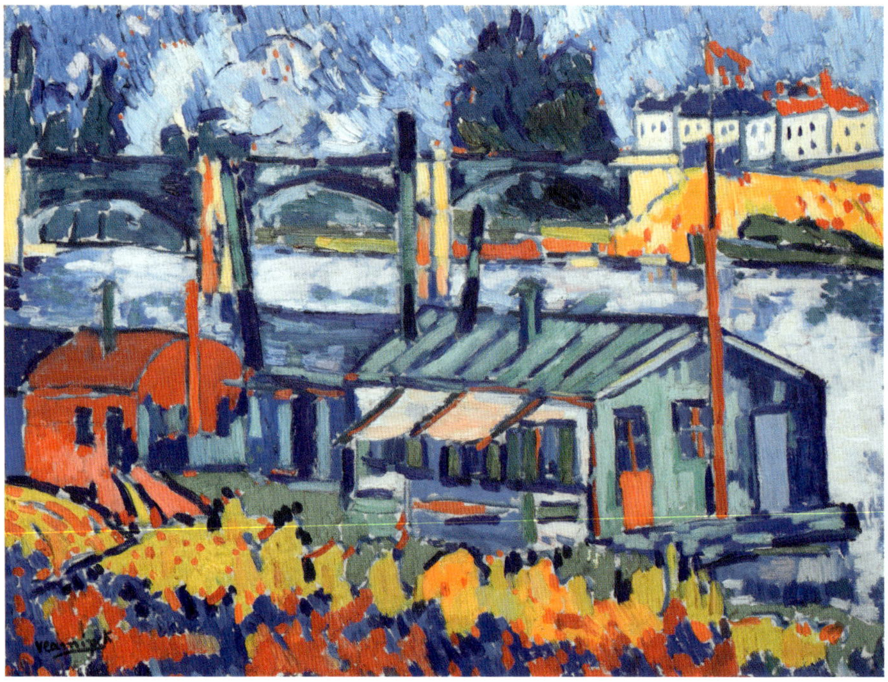

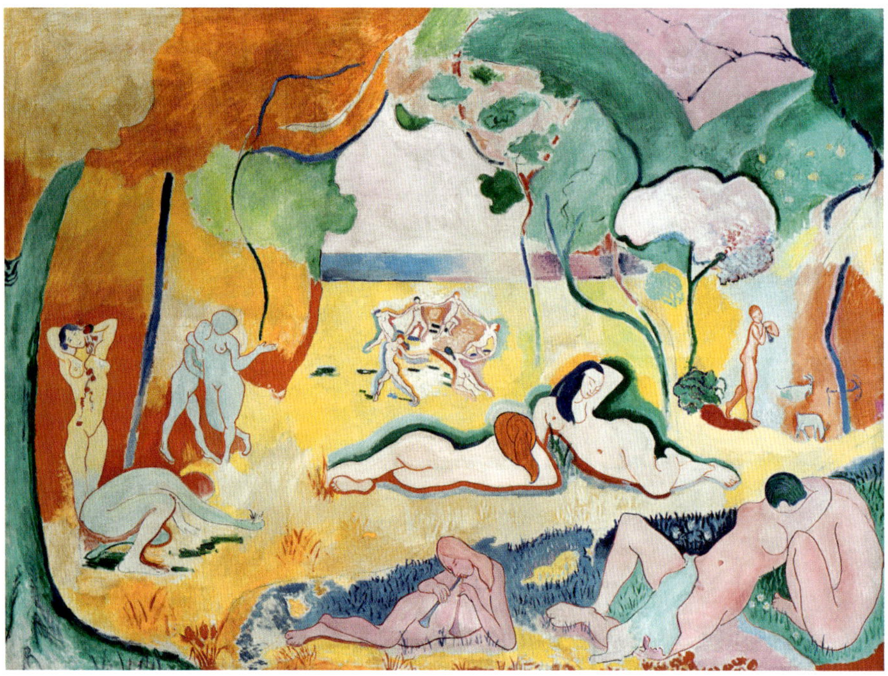

7
Maurice de Vlaminck,
The Bridge of Chatou, 1906,
Centre Pompidou, Paris

8
Henri Matisse,
The Joy of Life, 1905–06,
Barnes Foundation,
Philadelphia

Vlaminck's interest in the planar, geometricizing painting of Cézanne is manifested early on in his still lifes (cats. 21–27, 65) and from 1907–08 on will lead to a break with the garish colors and vehement brushwork of Fauvism.

1908–09

Georges Braque and Pablo Picasso paint their first works in the Cubist style, which is characterized by the fragmentation of individual objects into geometrically schematized planes. Many of Vlaminck's works created before 1914 suggest an interest in Cubism, a movement from which he will later resolutely distance himself.

1910

Around 1910 Vlaminck paints *Opium* (cat. 64), his only figural work in the Cubist style. The painting is likely created in response to the numerous images of women in Picasso's work.

1912

From May 25 to September 30, the *Internationale Kunstausstellung des Sonderbundes westdeutscher Kunstfreunde und Künstler* (International Art Exhibition of the Special League of West German Art Lovers and Artists) takes place in Cologne. The exhibition decisively contributes to the canonization of French modernism, giving pride of place to Vincent van Gogh and Paul Cézanne. Six works by Vlaminck are featured in the show, and former fellow Fauves such as Derain and Matisse are represented as well. Works by Vlaminck are also shown in the second exhibition of the avant-garde gallery Der Sturm in Berlin.

1913

Vlaminck signs an exclusive two-year contract with the influential art dealer Daniel-Henry Kahnweiler. From February 17 to March 15, he is represented at the Armory Show in New York, which then travels to Chicago and Boston and will decisively influence the American reception of French modern art. In December selected pieces by Vlaminck are included in a group exhibition at the Düsseldorf gallery of Alfred Flechtheim, who shows the artist frequently until March 1933. In 1929 he devotes an extensive solo exhibition to Vlaminck's work.

1914

In August Vlaminck is drafted into military service but is exempt from fighting on the front as a father of three daughters. World War I marks a turning point in his painting and brings with it a rejection of the Paris avant-garde. Vlaminck's subsequent works remain unswayed by the innovations of French modernism and instead resemble an idiosyncratic variation of Postimpressionism. Many late paintings show eerie, snow-covered landscapes (cats. 72, 73) or agrarian motifs such as wheat fields or grainstacks, a motivic echo of the visual world of Impressionism (cats. 77–81). Regarding the influence of the war years, Vlaminck later wrote, "The war taught me a great lesson. All my confidence in civilisation, science, progress, socialism has been destroyed. I don't believe in anything any longer. I only have confidence in myself."[2]

1919

Vlaminck acquires a small estate to the north of Paris in Valmondois, where he soon establishes a studio. The following year, he moves to Auvers-sur-Oise, where his great role model Van Gogh had spent the last days of his life. He is accompanied by his new partner, Berthe Combe, whom he will marry

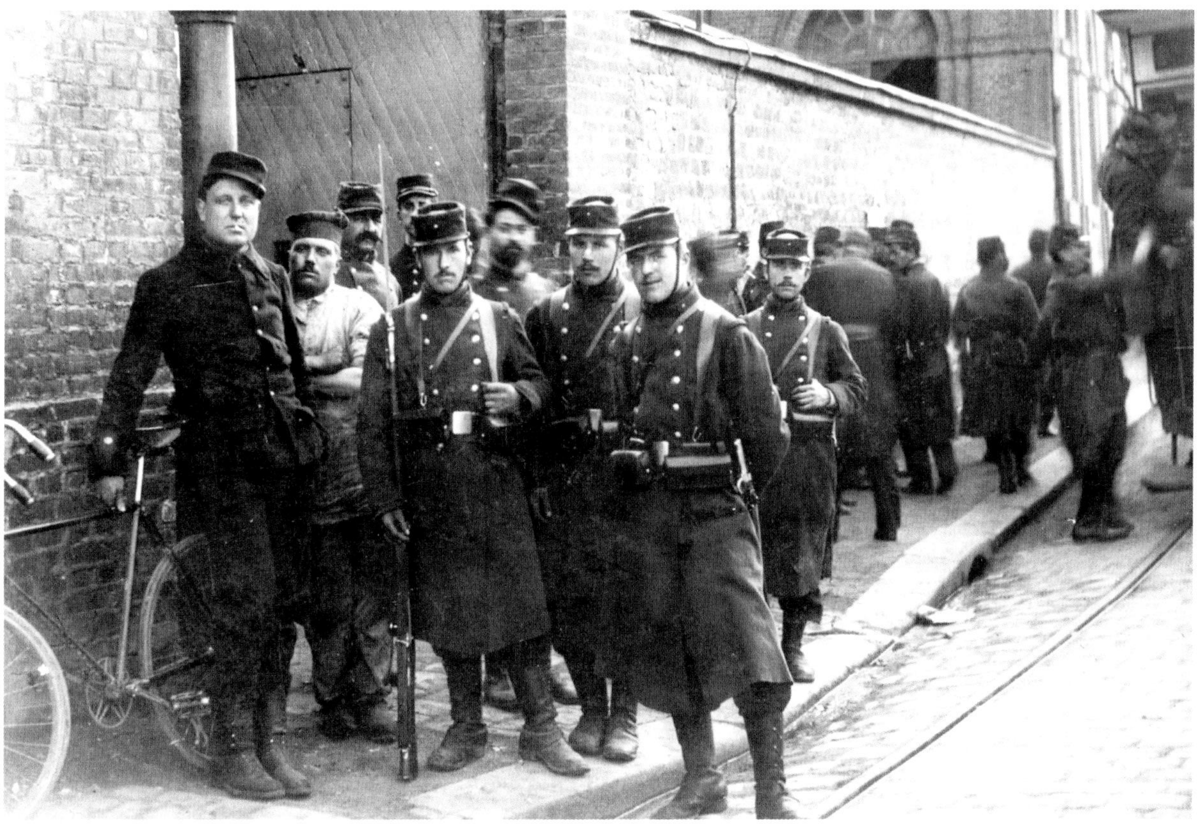

9
Vlaminck as a soldier during World War I (left), 1914

in April 1928, three years after his divorce from Suzanne Berly. The relationship produces two daughters: Edwige (b. 1920) and Godeliève (b. 1927).

1925

Vlaminck moves to the hamlet of La Tourillière near Rueil-la-Gladière, to the west of Paris. The following year, he undertakes extensive work on his new house, where he establishes a studio.

1929

Vlaminck has a large solo exhibition at Albert Flechtheim's gallery in Düsseldorf. He publishes *Tournant dangereux: Souvenirs de ma vie,* the first of several autobiographical texts that will influence the art-historical reception of his painting. Other later writings include *Poliment* (1931), *La Haute-Folie: Suivie de Cartes sur table* (1934), and *Portraits avant décès* (1943). In *Tournant dangereux* (Dangerous Corner), he retrospectively stylizes himself as the "wild" painter par excellence: "My enthusiasm allowed me to take all sorts of liberties. I did not want to follow a conventional way of painting; I wanted to revolutionise habits and contemporary life, to liberate nature, to free it from the authority of old theories and classicism, which I hated as much as I had hated the general or the colonel of my regiment. . . . I heightened all my tonal values and transposed into an orchestration of pure colour every single thing I felt. I was a tender barbarian . . . . I translated what I saw . . . without any method, and conveyed truth, not so much artistically as humanely."[3]

10
Maurice de Vlaminck
at home with his family,
1928

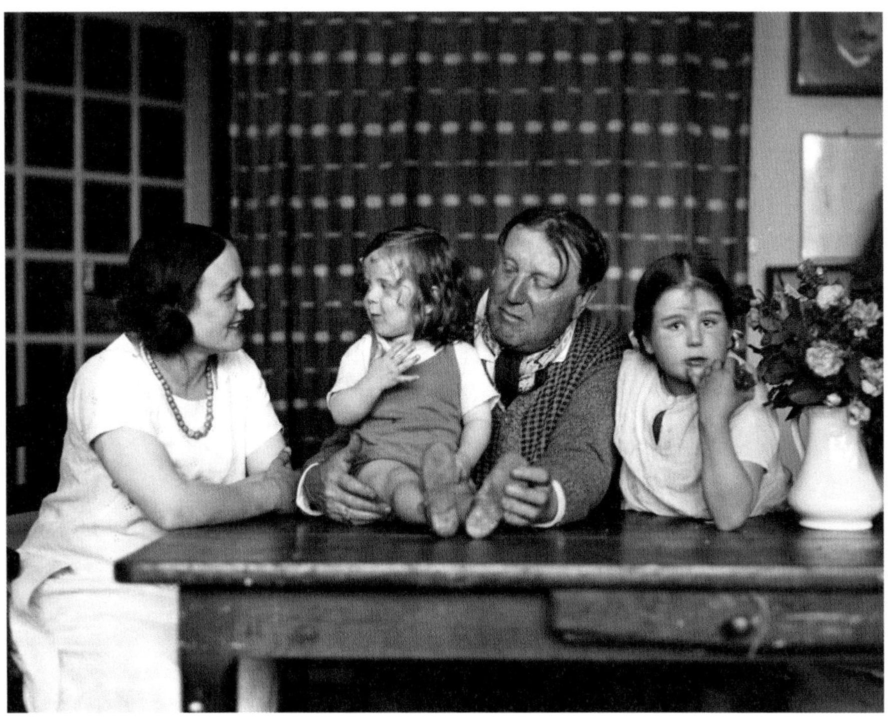

1937

In the course of the Nazi attack on modern art, a number of Vlaminck's works in German collections are confiscated as "degenerate," including paintings in Essen, Cologne, and Wuppertal.

1941

Vlaminck cultivates contact in occupied Paris with Arno Breker, a sculptor courted by Adolf Hitler, and writes a number of articles criticizing French avant-garde painting under the aegis of Picasso. He participates in a trip to Germany (October 30–November 16), which is organized by the German ministry of propaganda and will later be vehemently criticized. Following the trip, Vlaminck enthusiastically describes cultural politics under the Nazis in the *Pariser Zeitung:* "Along the whole route, in all the cities, museums, and exhibitions and in our visits to the artists' studios, I was impressed by the rebirth of

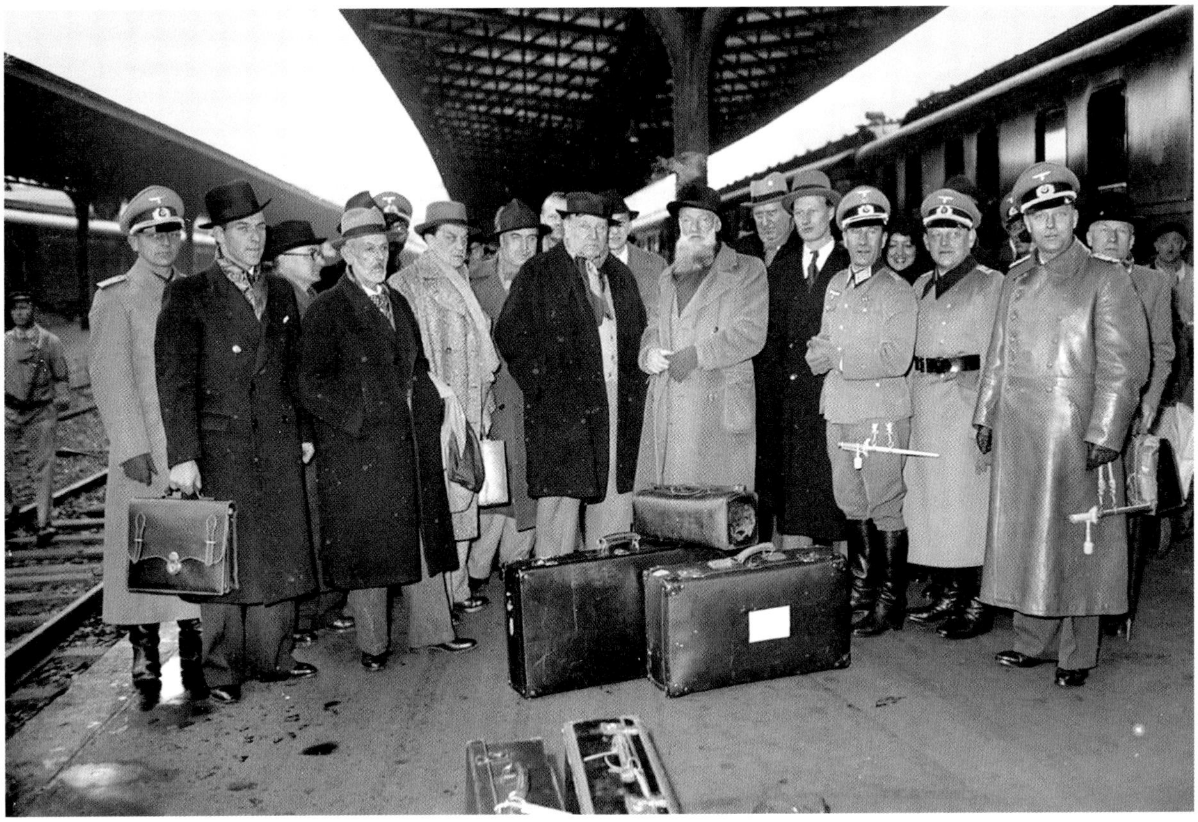

11
French artists on a trip to Germany organized by Arno Breker and Otto Abetz. From left to right: Charles Despiau, Othon Friesz, André Dunoyer de Segonzac, Maurice de Vlaminck, Kees van Dongen, and André Derain. Gare de l'Est, Paris, October 1941

architecture and sculpture. . . . The efforts of contemporary German painting are manifested in the return to the sources of Germanic inspiration. After its liberation from poorly assimilated foreign influences, German painting will once again find a national path that offers it greater freedom of expression."[4] In 1944, following the liberation of France, Vlaminck is prohibited from showing his work for one year due to his political stance during the occupation.

1947

Galerie Bing in Paris mounts a double exhibition of the Fauvist painting of Vlaminck and Derain.

1956

Vlaminck is honored with a major retrospective at Galerie Charpentier in Paris, which is enthusiastically received by the critics.

1958

Vlaminck dies on October 11 at La Tourillière.

Translated from German by Melissa M. Thorson

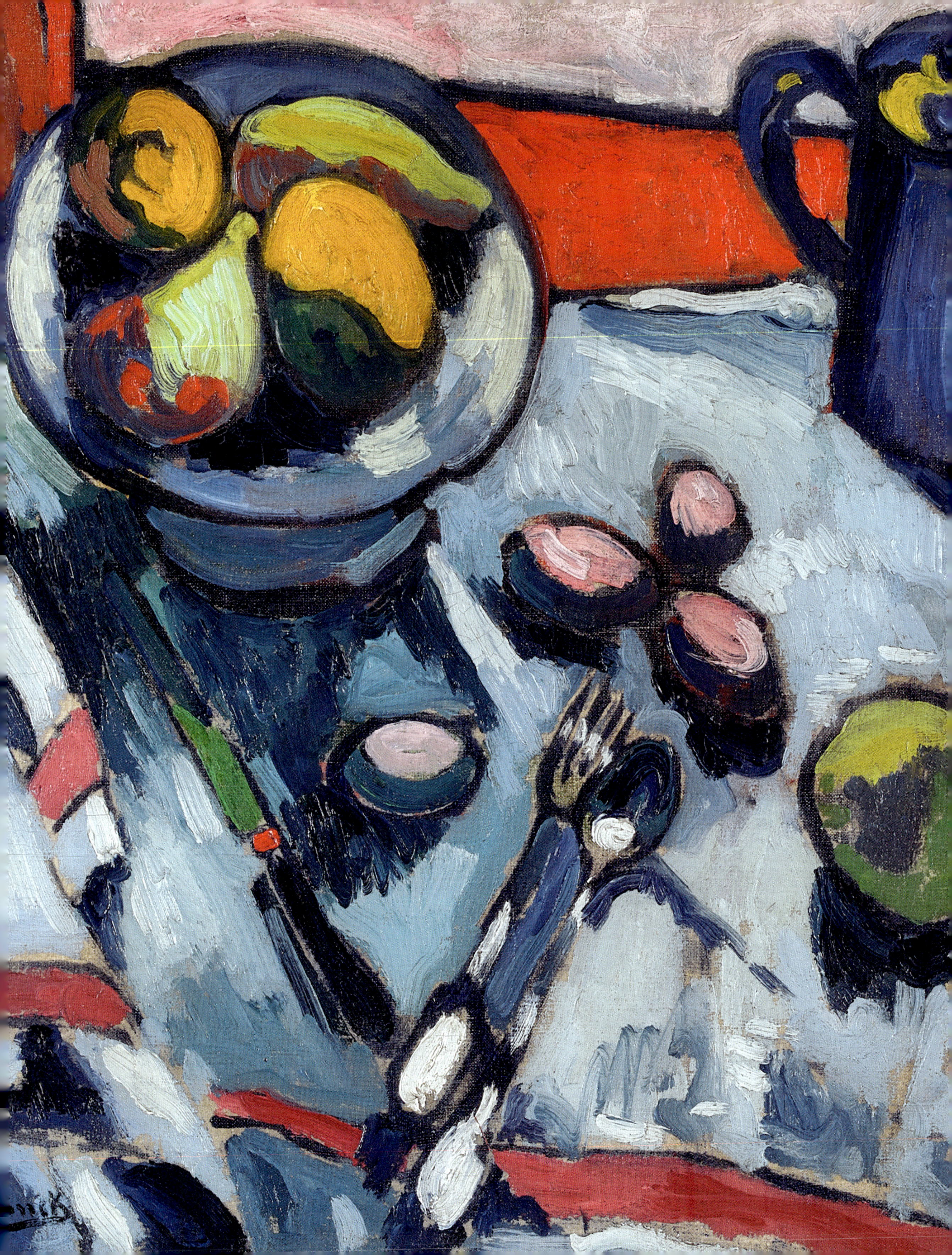

Notes

"Destined by Fate": Vlaminck and Fauvism pp. 22–29

1 Daniel-Henry Kahnweiler, *Mes galeries et mes peintres* [1961], Paris 1982, 125, quoted in *André Derain: An Outsider in French Art,* exh. cat., Statens Museum for Kunst, Copenhagen 2007, 81.
2 Guillaume Apollinaire, "De Vlaminck: Le Salon d'Automne [1907]," in Dagen 1994, 113–26, here 123.
3 Vollard 1936, 200–01.
4 Vauxcelles 1905.
5 See Rémi Labrusse, "'Fauvism': A Word and a Thing," in Vienna 2013, 250–65, here 253–54.
6 Christian Lassalle, "Note," in Louis Vauxcelles, *Le Fauvisme,* ed. Lasalle, Paris 1999 [new edition of Vauxcelles 1958], 21.
7 Ibid., 25.
8 Claudine Grammont, "L'Avant-garde comme stratégie: L'Exemple du scandale des fauves," in *Quel scandale!,* ed. Marie Dollé, Saint-Denis 2006, 67–75, here 70.
9 Henri Matisse, "On Modernism and Tradition, 1935," in *Matisse on Art,* ed. Jack D. Flam, New York 1973, 71–72, as well as the transcription by Tériade of a statement made by Matisse in July 1951, in ibid., 132.
10 Vlaminck 1965, 28.
11 New York 1976, 30.
12 Charles Morice, "Le XXIe Salon des Indépendants," in *Le Mercure de France* (April 15, 1905), quoted in Dagen 1994, 33.
13 Ibid., 35.
14 Vauxcelles 1905.
15 Quoted in Vallès-Bled 2008, no. 17.
16 Vlaminck 1965, 56.
17 Matisse 1973 (see note 9), 72.
18 Quoted in New York 1976, 30.
19 Vlaminck 1966, 74.
20 See Lisa Smit's contribution to this catalog, 40–49.
21 Vallès-Bled 2008, p. 569. Vallès-Bled identified seven of the eight works.
22 Ibid., no. 2.
23 Bernard Dorival, "La Vie des musées: Nouvelles acquisitions; Treize mois d'activité du Musée national d'art moderne," in *La Revue des arts* 4–5 (1959), 223.
24 Vallès-Bled 2008, no. 13.
25 Vlaminck 1965, 55–56; Maurice de Vlaminck, "Souvenirs et témoignages," in Dagen 1994, 209–15, here 211–12; on the identification of the buyer as Ernest Siegfried, see Vallès-Bled 2008, no. 17.
26 Grammont 2006 (see note 8), 67–75.
27 "Correspondance Havas" (October 22, 1905), in Dagen 1994, 214.
28 Vallès-Bled 2008, no. 21.
29 Vauxcelles 1905, 30; English translation from *Art of the Avant-Gardes*, ed. Steve Edwards and Paul Wood, New Haven 2004, 39.
30 Arsène Darmesteter, *La Vie des mots:* Étudiée dans leurs significations, 1886, par. 64, quoted in Edgar Wind, *Kunst und Anarchie: Die Reith Lectures 1960,* Frankfurt am Main 1979, 114n17.
31 See Jean-Paul Bouillon, "Maillol und Denis. Künstlerischer Bund und historischer Augenblick," in *Aristide Maillol,* exh. cat., Georg-Kolbe-Museum, Berlin 1996, 127–44, here 139.
32 François Monod, "Le Salon d'automne," in *Art et Décoration* XVIII (1905), 198–210; André Gide, "Promenade au Salon d'automne," in *Gazette des beaux-arts* XXXIV (1905), 475–85, quoted in Uwe Fleckner, *Jean-Auguste-Dominique Ingres, Das türkische Bad: Ein Klassizist auf dem Weg zur Moderne,* Frankfurt am Main 1996, 5.
33 See "Ingres," in Sauvage 1959, 63.
34 Vlaminck 1965, 108.
35 Ibid., 83.
36 Quoted in Vallès-Bled 2008, no. 90, after Sauvage 1956, 27.
37 Sauvage 1959, 65.
38 Joséphin Péladan, "Le Salon d'automne: Ingres et Manet [1905]," in Labrusse/Munck 2005, 244.
39 Teubner 2022, 111, 114.
40 The paintings *Region of Paris, View from Montmartre* and *Outskirts of Montmartre, Rue Championnet* by Maximilien Luce, both 1887, Kröller-Müller Museum, Otterlo, are reproduced in *Seurat, Signac, Van Gogh: Ways of Pointillism,* exh. cat., Albertina, Vienna 2016, cats. 42, 43.
41 Quoted in Robyn Roslak, *Neo-Impressionism and Anarchism in Fin-de-Siècle France: Painting, Politics and Landscape,* Aldershot 2007, 127–28.
42 Debray 2013, 298; Teubner 2022, 111.
43 Vlaminck 1965, 83.

Anarchy of Color: Vlaminck's Fauvist Painting pp. 30–39

1 See Vlaminck 1929 and Vlaminck 1966. On Vlaminck's interest in anarchism and social revolution, see Leighten 2007 and Teubner 2022.

2 On the influence of Van Gogh on the Fauves in general, see Giry 1990, esp. 282–88; and O'Laoghaire 1992. On the reception of Van Gogh by Vlaminck in particular, see Lisa Smit's contribution to this catalog, 40–49.

3 The following paintings by Vlaminck were shown at the exhibition: *The Valley at Port-Marly* (fig. p. 27), *Twilight* (cat. 7), *Park in Carrières-Saint-Denis* (cat. 8), *My Father's House* (fig. p. 27), and *The Pond at Saint-Cucufa* (1903, private collection)

4 For detailed analysis of the reaction of art critics to the Fauve exhibition at the Salon d'Automne in 1905, see Roger Benjamin, "Fauves in the Landscape of Criticism: Metaphor and Scandal at the Salon," in Los Angeles 1990, 241–68; Schieder 1999; and Ann Dumas, "The Salon d'Automne of 1905: A Baptism of Fire," in New York 2023, 49–60.

5 Vauxcelles 1905. Unless otherwise noted, all translations are by Daniel Zamani.

6 Vlaminck 1966, 66.

7 On the establishment of the Fauves in the Parisian art market, see Peter Kropmanns, "The Fauves and the Parisian Art Market," in Basel 2023, 17–26.

8 The extensive and heated debate over the relative preeminence of color or form that began in the sixteenth century has gone down in art history as *disegno e colore* and was intensively renegotiated in the nineteenth century. See, for example, Jonas Gavel, *Colour: A Study of Its Position in the Art Theory of the Quattrocento and Cinquecento,* PhD diss., Stockholm 1979; Maurice Poirier, "The Disegno-Colore Controversy Reconsidered," in *Explorations in Renaissance Culture* 13 (1987), 52–86; Thomas Puttfarken, "The Dispute about Disegno and Colorito in Venice: Paolo Pino, Lodovico Dolce and Titian," in *Kunst und Kunsttheorie, 1400–1900,* ed. Peter Ganz et al., Wiesbaden 1991, 75–99; John Gage, *Colour and Culture: Practice and Meaning from Antiquity to Abstraction,* London 1993; and Steffi Roettgen, "Venedig oder Rom—Disegno e Colore: Ein Topos der Kunstkritik und seine Folgen," in *zeitenblicke* 2, no. 3 (2003), https://www.zeitenblicke.de/2003/03/roettgen.htm (accessed on January 2, 2024).

9 André Derain, quoted in Duthuit 1929b, 268.

10 Vlaminck 1966, 74.

11 On nudes in Fauve painting, see Herbert 1992, esp. ch. 2 ("Mirroring the Nude"), 56–81. For the sociopolitical context of Fauvist bordel scenes, see Gabrielle Houbre, "With and without the Fauves: Perspectives on Prostitution in the 1900s," in Basel 2023, 37–44. For a more general study of prostitution in late-nineteenth- and early-twentieth-century French avant-garde painting, see *Bordell und Boudoir: Schauplätze der Moderne; Cézanne, Degas, Toulouse-Lautrec, Picasso,* exh. cat., Kunsthalle Tübingen, 2005; and *Splendeurs et misères: Images de la prostitution, 1850–1910,* exh. cat., Musée d'Orsay, Paris 2015.

12 On the scandal provoked by *Olympia* at the Salon of 1865, see Beatrice Farwell, *Manet and the Nude: A Study in Iconography in the Second Empire,* PhD diss., New York 1981; Hans Körner, "Anstößige Nacktheit: 'Das Frühstück im Freien' und die 'Olympia' von E. Manet," in *Streit um Bilder: Von Byzanz bis Duchamp,* ed. Karl Möseneder, Berlin 1997, 181–99; and Dino Heicker, *Manet, ein Streit und die Geburt der modernen Malerei: Ein Lesebuch zum Pariser Salon von 1865,* Berlin 2015.

13 On Fauvist "primitivism" inspired by African art, see Rolf Wedewer, *Form und Bedeutung: Primitivismus, Moderne, Fremdheit,* Cologne 2000; *Primitivism and Twentieth-Century Art: A Documentary History,* ed. Jack D. Flam, Berkeley 2003; Roger Benjamin, *Orientalist Aesthetics: Art, Colonialism, and French North Africa, 1880–1930,* Berkeley 2003; Joshua I. Cohen, "Rethinking Fauve 'Primitivism,'" in Cohen, *The "Black Art" Renaissance: African Sculpture and Modernism across Continents,* Oakland 2020, 23–54; and Maureen Murphy, "The Closeness of the Distant: A Plea for a 'More Balanced' History of Art," in Basel 2023, 51–60.

14 See Vlaminck 1966, 71.

15 On the importance of the South of France and the light of the French Riviera for Fauvist painting, see James D. Herbert, "Painters and Tourists: Matisse and Derain on the Mediterranean Shore," in Los Angeles 1990, 153–76; and Dita Amory, "Reinventing Color in Collioure (1905)," in New York 2023, 19–28.

16 "'To Paint Happiness'? Henri-Edmond Cross's Landscapes," in Potsdam 2018, 22–31, here 24–27.

17 On the significance of the Mediterranean for the Neo-Impressionists and the avant-garde allusion to the tradition of the pastorale, see Claudine Grammont, "Lux(e)," in *Le Grand Atelier du Midi: De Cézanne à Matisse,* exh. cat., Musée Granet, Aix-en-Provence 2013, 134–64.

18 On Vlaminck's painterly exploration of the Seine valley, see Jacqueline Hartwig's contribution to this catalog, 114–17.

19 On the role of the Seine landscape in French Impressionist and Postimpressionist painting, see *Impressionists on the Seine: A Celebration of Renoir's Luncheon of the Boating Party,* exh. cat., Phillips Collection, Washington, DC, 1996; *Monet: The Seine and the Sea,* exh. cat., National Galleries of Scotland, Edinburgh 2003; *Regardez, Monsieur Monet . . . comme la Seine a changé!,* exh. cat., Espace André Graillot, Le Havre 2013; *Monet and the Seine: Impressions of a River,* exh. cat., Philbrook Museum of Art, Tulsa 2014; and *Van Gogh and the Avant-Garde: Along the Seine,* exh. cat., Van Gogh Museum, Amsterdam 2023.

20 For a comparison of the works of Renoir and Vlaminck, see Herbert 1992, 20–21.

21 On Van Gogh's adaptation of traditional rural motifs such as wheat fields or sowers, see Monica Juneja, *Peindre le paysan: L'Image rurale dans la peinture française de Millet à Van Gogh,* Paris 1998; *Van Gogh's Sheaves of Wheat,* exh. cat., Dallas Museum of Art, 2006; *Jean-François Millet: Sowing the Seeds of Modern Art,* exh. cat., Van Gogh Museum, Amsterdam 2019; and *Ceux de la terre: La Figure du paysan, de Courbet à Van Gogh,* exh. cat., Musée Gustave Courbet, Ornans 2022.

22 Herbert 1992, 27–28.

23 Ibid.

24 Vlaminck 1966, 12.

25 André Derain, quoted in Duthuit 1929b, 268.

26 Vlaminck 1966, 11.

27 On Vlaminck's reception of Cézanne, see Anna Storm's contribution to this catalog, 50–57.

"My Inner Being Deeply Shaken": Vlaminck's Reception of Van Gogh's Art pp. 40–49

I am indebted to Brittney Annan, Teio Meedendorp, and Maïthé Vallès-Bled for their help in writing this essay. I am also grateful for the fruitful exchange with Bregje Gerritse, researcher at the Van Gogh Museum in Amsterdam, who is currently doing research for her dissertation "The Reception of Vincent van Gogh in Paris 1886–1914: Art Dealers, Collectors, and Critics."

1 Vlaminck 1929, 229; English translation in Vlaminck 1966, 147. Vlaminck also later recalled that "his inner being" had been "deeply shaken" by the emotional encounter with Van Gogh's painting. See Vlaminck 1943, 31; translated in Susan Alyson Stein, ed., *Van Gogh: A Retrospective,* New York 1986, 315. This essay frequently quotes from Vlaminck's autobiographical writings. It should be noted that these texts do not necessarily fully reflect reality and that Vlaminck strategically used them to influence the early art-historical reception of his work.

2 Vlaminck 1943, 13. Unless otherwise indicated, all translations are by Daniel Zamani.

3 *Exposition Vincent van Gogh,* exh. cat., Galerie Bernheim-Jeune, Paris 1901.

4 Vlaminck 1943, 30; English translation in Stein 1986 (see note 1), 315.

5 Marja Supinen, "Julien Leclercq: A Champion of the Unknown Vincent van Gogh," in *Jong Holland* 6,6 (1990), 5–14, here 12.

6 Julien Leclercq, "Vincent van Gogh," in Paris 1901 (see note 3), 2 and 10; English translation in Stein 1986 (see note 1), 310, 313.

7 Vlaminck 1929, 229; English translation in Vlaminck 1966, 147.

8 Vlaminck 1943, 31.

9 Vlaminck 1943, 31; English translation in Stein 1986 (see note 1), 315.

10 Vlaminck 1943, 32; English translation in Stein 1986 (see note 1), 316.

11 Vlaminck 1943, 35; English translation in Stein 1986 (see note 1), 317.

12 Letter from André Derain to Maurice de Vlaminck (undated), in Dagen 1994, 75.

13 Letter from André Derain to Maurice de Vlaminck (March 26, 1901) in Dagen 1994, 41.

14 See Carol M. Zemel, *The Formation of a Legend: Van Gogh Criticism, 1890-1920,* Ann Arbor 1980; and Nathalie Heinich, *The Glory of van Gogh: An Anthropology of Admiration*, Princeton 1997.

15 "Publication History: The Early Publications of the Letters," in *Vincent van Gogh: The Letters*, https://vangoghletters.org/vg/publications_2.html (accessed March 15, 2024).

16 Clement 1994, 337.

17 Julien Leclercq, "Vincent van Gogh," in Paris 1901 (see note 3); Octave Mirbeau, "Vincent Van Gogh," in *Le Journal,* March 17, 1901. Derain refers to Mirbeau's article and to Van Gogh's correspondence in letters to Vlaminck; see Dagen 1994, 41, 77. Vlaminck himself marvels at Van Gogh's correspondence in his autobiography of 1943 without implicating when he read this; see Vlaminck 1943, 192.

18 Vlaminck 1943, 29.

19 Vallès-Bled 2008. The catalogue raisonné lists twenty-four paintings created between 1900 and 1904–05, followed by no less than 187 paintings created between 1905 and 1907. It could very well be that more paintings existed at some point in the past, as it is not unusual for early work to be less well preserved. Moreover, the relatively low number is also explained by the fact that Vlaminck's lack of money in his early years as a painter prompted him to reuse his canvases multiple times. See Vallès-Bled 2008, 529.

20 *Société des artistes Indépendants: Catalogue de la 21ème exposition 1905; Exposition rétrospective Vincent van Gogh,* exh. cat., Grandes Serres de l'Alma, Paris 1905, 13–16.

21 Louis Vauxcelles, "Le Salon des Indépendants," in *Gil Blas,* March 23, 1905, 25–26.

22 Vallès-Bled 2008, 569. Vallès-Bled has identified seven of the eight works.

23 Vlaminck 1943, 74.

24 Dagen 1994, 24.

25 Vauxcelles 1905 (see note 21), 25–26.

26 Vallès-Bled 2008, 82–83; and Vlaminck 1943, 75.

27 Crespelle 1958, 85–86.

28 *Société du Salon d'Automne: Catalogue des ouvrages de peinture, sculpture, dessin, gravure, architecture et art décoratif: Catalogue de la 3ᵉ exposition,* exh. cat., Grand Palais des Champs-Élysées, Paris 1905.

29 Vauxcelles 1905.

30 Vallès-Bled 2008, 110.

31 Unpublished research by Teio Meedendorp, senior researcher at the Van Gogh Museum, Amsterdam.

32 Vlaminck 1943, 83–84.

33 Vollard 1936, 201.

34 Vlaminck 1943, 137.

35 Vollard 1936, 62–63; and Hans Luijten, *Jo Van Gogh-Bonger: The Woman Who Made Vincent Famous,* London 2023, 222–23.

36 Vlaminck 1943, 31; English translation in Stein 1986 (see note 1), 315.

37 Letter from Vincent van Gogh to Theo van Gogh, Arles (May 4, 1888), Amsterdam, Van Gogh Museum, inv. b0522.

38 Luijten 2023 (see note 35), 225–33. This breakthrough is primarily attributable to the exhibition at the Stedelijk Museum in Amsterdam in the summer of 1905, the largest Van Gogh exhibition ever held. From then on, his legacy would continue to grow to unparalleled heights.

39 Vlaminck 1929, 97; translation in Vlaminck 1966, 76.

40 Vlaminck 1943, 36.

41 *Wheatfield with Crows* was exhibited in Paris at monographic Van Gogh exhibitions at Galerie Bernheim-Jeune in 1908 and 1927, and at Galerie Marcel Bernheim in 1925. *Tree Roots* of July 27, 1890 (Van Gogh Museum, Amsterdam) is Van Gogh's last (and unfinished) painting.

42 Vlaminck 1943, 141.

Kinship of Forms: Cézanne, Picasso, Vlaminck pp. 50–57

1 Vlaminck 1966, 75.
2 On Vlaminck's reception of Van Gogh, see Lisa Smit's contribution to this catalog, 40–49.
3 *Les Fauves und die Zeitgenossen,* exh. cat., Kunsthalle Bern, 1950, unpaginated.
4 Maïthé Vallès-Bled, *Maurice de Vlaminck (1876–1958): La Période fauve/The Fauve Period, 1900–1907,* Paris 2008, 41.
5 Peter Geimer, "Vergleichendes Sehen oder Gleichheit aus Versehen? Analogie und Differenz in kunsthistorischen Bildvergleichen," in *Vergleichendes Sehen,* ed. Lena Bader, Munich 2010, 44–66, here 45–46.
6 Peter Kropmanns, "Matisse, the Fauves, and Cézanne," in Essen 2004, 194–203, here 194.
7 Ibid., 196.
8 Ibid.
9 Ibid., 197.
10 Clement Greenberg, "Cézanne and the Unity of Modern Art," in *Partisan Review* 18,3 (May–June 1951), 323–30, here 323; in addition to Cézanne, Greenberg also mentions Manet and Courbet.
11 Fred Leeman, "Painting 'after' Cézanne," in Essen 2004, 170–81, here 172.
12 Because of the painters' close friendship and artistic dialogue, Derain and Vlaminck have jointly been referred to as the "School of Chatou"; see Vallès-Bled 2008, 22.
13 Arthur Fink, "Testing Ground: Fauve Still Life," in Basel 2023, 45–49, here 45.
14 Ibid., 47.
15 Vallès-Bled 2008, 235.
16 Felix A. Baumann, "Still Life," in Essen 2004, 76–113, here 76.
17 The popularity of still life in the nineteenth century was due in part to the fact that as a genre, it was unencumbered by iconographical associations or disruptive implications; see ibid.
18 Ibid., 82.
19 Ibid., 86.
20 Ibid., 87.
21 Ibid.
22 Vallès-Bled 2008, 456.
23 In 1929 Vlaminck wrote, "Cubism became a veritable epidemic." Vlaminck 1966, 78.
24 Philip Hook, *Art of the Extreme: 1905–1914,* London 2021, 26.
25 Ibid.
26 Ibid., 28.
27 Brigitte Leal, "Cézanne's Cubism," in *The Cubist Cosmos: From Picasso to Léger,* exh. cat., Kunstmuseum Basel, 2019, 40.
28 Ariane Coulondre, "'It's Geometry in Spasm!": Cubism and the Press (1908–1919)," in Basel 2019 (see note 27), 244–50, here 244; Leeman 2004 (see note 11), 175.
29 Coulondre 2019 (see note 28), 244.
30 Hook 2021 (see note 24), 262.
31 Vlaminck's preferred motif was the landscape, although his early oeuvre also includes a significant number of portraits.
32 Maureen Murphy, "The Closeness of the Distant: A Plea for a More 'Balanced History' of Art," in Basel 2023, 51–59, here 52.
33 Ibid., 55.
34 See Leo Steinberg, "The Philosophical Brothel," *October* 44 (1988), 7–74; Lisa Florman, "Insistent, Resistant Cézanne: On Picasso's *Three Women* and *Les Demoiselles d'Avignon,*" in *Source: Notes in the History of Art* 31–32 (2012), 19–26.
35 Greenberg 1951 (see note 10), 326.
36 Ibid., 327.

The Expressive Power of Pure Color: Vlaminck and Painting from the Tube pp. 58–65

1 Maurice de Vlaminck, quoted in Genevoix 1954, vol. 1, 11; English translation in Brodskaya 2012, 85.
2 On Vlaminck's free thought, see Maïthé Vallès-Bled, "Le Peintre et la critique/Il pittore e la critica," in Aosta 1987, 22–95, here 42–51.
3 The notion that academic training was more detrimental than beneficial to a painter's aptitude is already found in the art discourse of the nineteenth century; see Krüger 2008, 167–70.
4 Vlaminck 1943, 37. Unless otherwise noted, all translations are by Daniel Zamani.
5 Duthuit 1929b, 262.
6 As recalled by Paul Sérusier and recorded in Maurice Denis, "L'Influence de Paul Gauguin [1903]," in Denis, *Théories, 1890–1910: Du symbolisme et de Gauguin vers un nouvel ordre classique,* Paris 1912, 160–66, here 161–62.
7 Munch even asserted that he had learned to squeeze the color directly onto the canvas from Van Gogh. See *Edvard Munchs brev,* ed. Max Linde, Oslo 1954, 46 (letter no. 483).
8 Vlaminck 1943, 72.
9 Elsewhere, Vlaminck even claimed that it was he who had prompted Derain to apply colors to the canvas "pure" and "as they come from the tube," thereby taking credit for his colleague's first Fauvist paintings; Vlaminck 1931, 137.
10 Henri Evenepoel, *Lettres à mon père, 1892–1899,* vol. 1, Brussels 1994, 197 (letter of July 27, 1893), 167 (letter of May 17, 1893).
11 On this development, see Michael Baxandall, *Painting and Experience in Fifteenth-Century Italy: A Primer in the Social History of Pictorial Style,* Oxford 1972, 1–27.
12 Paolo Pino, *Dialogo di pittura,* Venice 1548, 8; see Ludovico Dolce, "Dialogo della pittura [1557]," in *Trattati d'arte del Cinquecento fra manierismo e controriforma,* vol. 1, ed. Paola Barocchi, Bari 1960, 141–206, here 184.
13 Carlo Ridolfi, *Le maraviglie dell'arte ovvero le vite degli illustri pittori veneti e dello stato,* vol. 2, Venice 1648, 59; English translation in Carlo Ridolfi, *The Life of Tintoretto and of His Children Domenico and Marietta*, trans. Catherine Enggass and Robert Enggass, University Park and London 1984, 76.
14 Vlaminck probably used paints manufactured by Lefranc. See Benoît Noël, "Le Père Jary [avec un 'R']," in *La Gazette des amis de la Maison fournaise* 13 (2017), 9, https://www.amisfournaisechatou.com/wpcontent/uploads/2018/02/amis_maison_Fournaise_Chatou_Gazette_13.pdf (accessed on February 23, 2023).
15 Marcel Duchamp, "Apropos of 'Readymades' [1961]," in Duchamp, *The Writings of Marcel Duchamp,* ed. Michel Sanouillet and Elmer Peterson, New York 1973, 141–42.
16 Francis Roberts, "Interview with Marcel Duchamp: 'I Propose to Strain the Laws of Physics,'" in *ARTnews* 67 (December 1968), 46–47, 62–64, here 47. On Duchamp's thesis, see Thierry de Duve, *Kant after Duchamp,* Cambridge, MA, 1996, 159–66.

[17] Clement Greenberg, “Modernist Painting [1961],” in Greenberg, *The Collected Essays and Criticism,* vol. 4, *Modernism with a Vengeance, 1957–1969,* Chicago 1986, 85–93, here 86.
[18] “Questions to Stella and Judd: Interview by Bruce Glaser [1964],” in *ARTnews* 65 (September 1966), 55–61, here 58.
[19] Vlaminck 1929, 97; Vlaminck 1966, 76.
[20] See Anthea Callen, *The Art of Impressionism: Painting Technique and the Making of Modernity,* New Haven 2000, 106.
[21] See Anthea Callen, *The Work of Art: Plein-Air Painting and Artistic Identity in Nineteenth-Century France,* London 2015, 72; Knott 2015, 17–19.
[22] Frédéric Goupil, *Manuel générale de la peinture à l'huile,* Paris 1877, 132.
[23] A. P. Laurie, “The Artist His Own Colour-Maker: An Enquiry and a Suggestion,” in *The Art Magazine* 15 (1892), 115–16.
[24] Fels 1928, 39; Vlaminck 1966, 11.
[25] For a compilation of critical reviews of works exhibited by the Fauves at the Salon d'Automne, see Vallès-Bled 2008, 209–21.
[26] Marcel Nicolle, “Le Salon d'automne,” in *Le Journal de Rouen,* November 20, 1905, 4; quoted in Alfred H. Barr Jr., *Matisse: His Art and His Public,* New York 1951, 55.
[27] Henri Matisse, “Il faut regarder toute la vie avec des yeux d'enfants [1953],” in Matisse, *Écrits et propos sur l'art,* Paris 1972, 321–23.
[28] As late as 1930, a critic would assert that Vlaminck's method of painting revealed a lack of cultivation: allegedly, the artist first kneaded his tubes, then squeezed out the paint and flung it onto the canvas where he would spread it around with his fingers. Now, however, this behavior was viewed positively, as evidence of overflowing creativity. On this criticism, see Vallès-Bled 1987 (see note 2), 86.
[29] Alexander Liberman, *The Artist in His Studio,* New York 1960, 26.
[30] Vlaminck 1929, 94; Vlaminck 1966, 74.
[31] R. Jacobsen, “Une Exposition Van Gogh à Groningue,” in *L'Art flamand et hollandais* 1 (1904), vol. 2, 13–20, here 14.
[32] Werner Weisbach, *Impressionismus: Ein Problem der Malerei in der Antike und Neuzeit,* Berlin 1910, 227.
[33] Vlaminck 1943, 133–34.
[34] Herwarth Walden, “Fachmännchen,” in *Der Sturm* 8 (1917–18), 186–90, here 190.
[35] On the rapid painting of the Impressionists, see Richard Brettell, *Painting Quickly in France,* exh. cat., National Gallery, London 2000.
[36] Gerarda Hermina Marius, *De Hollandsche Schilderkunst in de Negentiende Eeuw* [1903], The Hague 1920, 268.
[37] Max Osborn, “Van Gogh,” in *Velhagen und Klasings Monatshefte* 1,23 (1908–09), 361–73, here 370.
[38] Jakob Wassermann, “Nimführ and Willenius,” in *Die Rheinlande* 19 (1910), 61–66, here 61.
[39] Vollard 1984, 240; English translation in Vollard 1936, 200.

Intoxicated with Color: Fauvist Painting pp. 68–71

[1] On the genesis of Fauvism, see Heinz Widauer's contribution to this catalog, 22–29.
[2] See Tamar Garb, *The Painted Face: Portraits of Women in France, 1814–1914* (New Haven 2007), 1–18.
[3] On Vlaminck's reception of Cézanne, see Anna Storm's contributions to this catalog, 50–57 and 142–45.

Impressionist Motifs: Painting along the Seine pp. 114–17

[1] On Vlaminck's turn to Impressionist motifs, see Daniel Zamani's contribution to this catalog, 30–39.
[2] Vallès-Bled 2008, 37.

The Spirit of Cézanne: Fragmentation of Forms pp. 142–45

[1] On Vlaminck's reception of Cézanne, see also my essay in this catalog, 50–57.
[2] Peter Kropmanns, “Matisse, the Fauves, and Cézanne,” in Essen 2004, 194–203, here 196.
[3] Fred Leeman, “Painting ‘after’ Cézanne,” in Essen 2004, 170–81, here 179.
[4] Kropmanns 2004 (see note 2), 196.

Bleak Landscapes: The Late Work pp. 160–63

[1] Maurice de Vlaminck, “Opinions libres sur la peinture,” in *Comoedia* (November 6, 1942), 188.
[2] See Maurice de Vlaminck, “Impressions d'un voyage artistique en Allemagne,” in *Pariser Zeitung,* November 18, 1941; “L'Effort du reich en faveur des artistes a émerveillé Despiau, Friesz et Vlaminck,” in *Aujourd'hui,* November 20, 1941; and “Des Artistes français donnent leurs impressions,” in *L'Œuvre,* November 20, 1941.
[3] On Vlaminck's reception of Van Gogh, see Lisa Smit's contribution to this catalog, 40–49.

Chronology pp. 183–91

[1] Vlaminck 1966, 11.
[2] Vlaminck 1966, 143 (translation slightly modified).
[3] Vlaminck 1966, 74.
[4] Maurice de Vlaminck, “Impressions d'un voyage artistique en Allemagne,” *Pariser Zeitung,* November 18, 1941. Vlaminck made similarly enthusiastic statements in two other articles published in November 1941; see “L'Effort du reich en faveur des artistes a émerveillé Despiau, Friesz et Vlaminck,” *Aujourd'hui,* November 20, 1941; and “Des Artistes français donnent leurs impressions,” *L'Œuvre,* November 20, 1941.

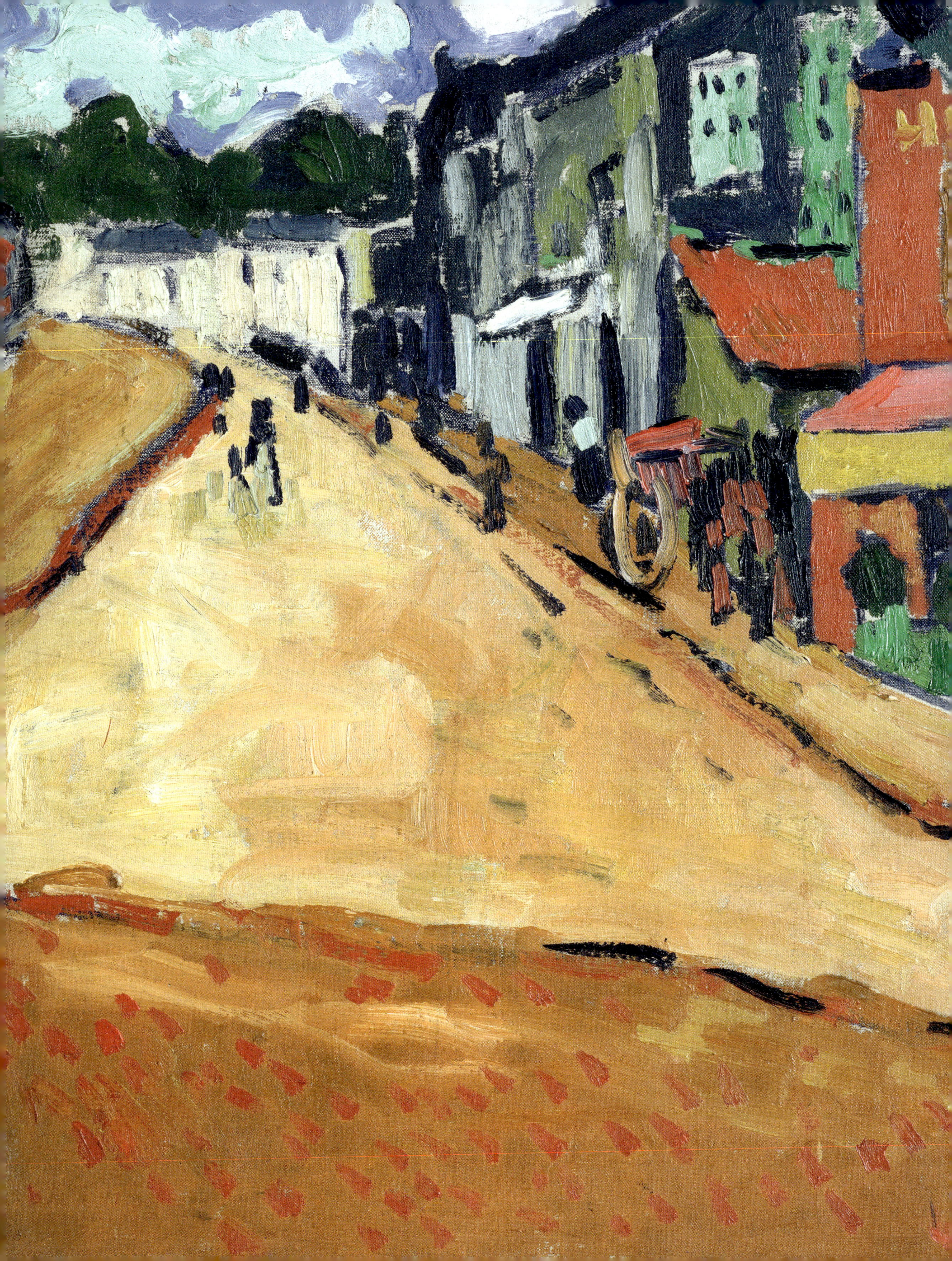

Selected Bibliography

Abe 2014
Tetsuo Abe, *Matisse, Vlaminck and Foujita in 1952,* Mishima 2014.

Aosta 1987
Vlaminck: Il pittore e la critica / Le Peintre et la critique, exh. cat., Centro Saint-Bénin, Aosta 1987.

Apollinaire 1907
Guillaume Apollinaire, "Le Salon d'Automne: Le Cas Maurice de Vlaminck," in *Je dis tout,* October 26, 1907.

Apollinaire 1910
Guillaume Apollinaire, "Exposition Maurice de Vlaminck," in *L'Intransigeant,* March 16, 1910.

Assouline 1990
Pierre Assouline, *An Artful Life: A Biography of D. H. Kahnweiler, 1881–1979,* trans. Charles Ruas, New York 1990.

Barcelona 2000
Les Années fauves, 1904–1908, exh. cat., Centre Cultural Caixa Catalunya, Barcelona 2000.

Barr 1977
Alfred H. Barr Jr., *Painting and Sculpture in the Museum of Modern Art, 1929–1967,* New York 1977.

Basel 2023
Matisse, Derain, and Their Friends: The Parisian Avant-Garde 1904–1908, exh. cat., Kunstmuseum Basel, 2023.

Bern 1961
Vlaminck, exh. cat., Kunstmuseum Bern, 1961.

Bertauld 1994
Suzanne Bertauld, "Les Fauves à Chatou: Regards sur Derain et Vlaminck," in *Association des Amis de la Maison Fournaise: Bulletin* 4 (1994), 2–11.

Boudaille 1968
Georges Boudaille, *Vlaminck,* Paris 1968.

Bouillot 1987
Roger Bouillot, "Hommage à Vlaminck," in *Œil* 383 (June 1987), 42–47.

Brian 1941
Doris Brian, "Les Fauves or Wild Beasts in Their Youth," in *Art News* 40,14 (November 1, 1941), 32.

Brodskaya 1987
Natalia Brodskaya, *Maurice de Vlaminck,* Leningrad 1987.

Brodskaya 2012
Natalia Brodskaya, *The Fauves,* New York 2012.

Cabanne 1966
Pierre Cabanne, *Vlaminck: Paysages,* Paris 1966.

Carco 1920
M. de Vlaminck: Trente et une reproductions de peintures et dessins, ed. Francis Carco, Paris 1920.

Carrà 1965
Massimo Carrà, *Maurice de Vlaminck,* Milan 1965.

Cartier 1958
Jean-Albert Cartier, "Rencontre avec Vlaminck," in *Le Jardin des arts* 49 (November 1958), 29–32.

Charensol 1956
Georges Charensol, "Beaux-arts: L'Œuvre de Vlaminck," in *Revue des deux mondes* 8 (April 15, 1956), 732–38.

Charensol 1958
Georges Charensol, "Beaux-arts: Vlaminck," in *Revue des deux mondes* 21 (November 1, 1958), 142–48.

Chassé 1963
Charles Chassé, *Les Fauves et leur temps,* Lausanne 1963.

Chassey 1996
Éric de Chassey, "Signac et les fauves," in *Signac et la libération de la couleur: De Matisse à Mondrian,* exh. cat., Musée de Grenoble, 1996, 143–76.

Cholet 1981
Peintres fauves et cubistes: Braque, Derain, Matisse, exh. cat., Musée des Arts, Cholet 1981.

Clement 1994
Russell T. Clement, *Les Fauves: A Sourcebook,* Westport, CT, 1994.

Clochard 1958
William Clochard, *Vlaminck à qui je dois . . . Souvenirs de 1907 à 1924,* Chartres 1958.

Cohen 2017
Joshua I. Cohen, "Fauve Masks: Rethinking Modern 'Primitivist' Uses of African and Oceanic Art, 1905–08," in *Art Bulletin* 99 (June 2017), 136–65.

Cone 1998
Michele C. Cone, "French Art of the Present in Hitler's Berlin," in *Art Bulletin* 80 (September 1998), 555–67.

Crespelle 1958
Jean-Paul Crespelle, *Vlaminck: Fauve de la peinture,* Paris 1958.

Crespelle 1963
Jean-Paul Crespelle, *Fauves und Expressionisten,* Munich 1963.

Crespelle 1964
Jean-Paul Crespelle, *Montmartre vivant,* Paris 1964.

Dagen 1994
Philippe Dagen, *Le Fauvisme: Textes de peintres, d'écrivains et de journalistes,* Pour ou contre 2, Paris 1994.

Dagen 1998
Philippe Dagen, *Le Peintre, le poète, le sauvage: Les Voies du primitivisme dans l'art français,* Paris 1998.

Debray 2013
Cécile Debray, *Le Fauvisme,* Paris 2013.

Derain 1994
André Derain, *Lettres à Vlaminck: Suivies de la correspondance de guerre,* Paris 1994.

Diehl 1948
Gaston Diehl, *Les Fauves: Œuvres de Braque, Derain, Dufy, Friesz, Marquet, Matisse, Van Dongen, Vlaminck,* Paris 1948.

Diehl 1971
Gaston Diehl, *Les Fauves,* Paris 1971.

Dorival 1943–46
Bernard Dorival, *Les Étapes de la peinture française contemporaine,* 3 vols., Paris 1943–46.

Dorival 1952
Bernard Dorival, "Fauves: The Wild Beasts Tamed," in *Art News Annual* 51,7 (November 1952), 98–129, 174–76.

Duhamel 1927a
Georges Duhamel, *Les Hommes abandonnés, illustré de lithographies par M. de Vlaminck,* Paris 1927.

Duhamel 1927b
Georges Duhamel, *Maurice de Vlaminck: Avec quatre cuivres originaux et vingt-quatre reproductions en phototypie,* Paris 1927.

Düsseldorf 1919
Wilhelm Kreis, Max Hünten, Manolo, De Vlaminck, exh. cat., Galerie Alfred Flechtheim, Düsseldorf 1919.

Düsseldorf 1929
Maurice de Vlaminck: Ölgemälde und Aquarelle aus den Jahren 1909 bis 1929, exh. cat., Galerie Flechtheim, Düsseldorf 1929.

Düsseldorf 1977
Vom Licht zur Farbe: Nachimpressionistische Malerei zwischen 1886 und 1912, exh. cat., Städtische Kunsthalle Düsseldorf, 1977.

Duthuit 1929a
Georges Duthuit, "Le Fauvisme (I)," in *Cahiers d'art* 4,5 (1929), 177–92.

Duthuit 1929b
Georges Duthuit, "Le Fauvisme (II)," in *Cahiers d'art* 4,6 (1929), 258–68.

Duthuit 1929c
Georges Duthuit, "Le Fauvisme (III)," in *Cahiers d'art* 4,10 (1929), 429–34.

Duthuit 1930
Georges Duthuit, "Le Fauvisme (IV)," in *Cahiers d'art* 5,3 (1930), 129–35.

Duthuit 1931
Georges Duthuit, "Le Fauvisme (V)," in *Cahiers d'art* 6,2 (1931), 78–82.

Duthuit 1949
Georges Duthuit, *Les Fauves: Braque, Derain, Van Dongen, Dufy, Friesz, Manguin, Marquet, Matisse, Puy, Vlaminck,* Geneva 1949.

Duthuit 1950
Georges Duthuit, *The Fauvist Painters,* trans. Ralph Manheim, New York 1950.

Essen 2004
Cézanne and the Dawn of Modern Art, exh. cat., Museum Folkwang, Essen 2004.

Essen 2012
Im Farbenrausch: Munch, Matisse und die Expressionisten, exh. cat., Museum Folkwang, Essen 2012.

Estienne 1947
Charles Estienne, "Vive la couleur!," in *Combat* 6,845 (March 26, 1947), 2.

Fels 1928
Florent Fels, *Vlaminck,* Paris 1928.

François 1958
Les Pensées et la voix de Vlaminck: Avec 5 dessins originaux de l'auteur, ed. Camille François, Paris 1958.

Freeman 1994
Judi Freeman, "Une association spirituelle ou l'histoire d'un dialogue entre Derain et Vlaminck," in Paris 1994, 59–65.

Galloyer 2000
Anne Galloyer, "L'Atelier commun Derain-Vlaminck," in *Cahiers André Derain* 2 (2000), 16–18.

Gautherie-Kampka 1995
Annette Gautherie-Kampka, *Les Allemands du Dôme: La Colonie allemande de Montparnasse dans les années 1903–1914,* Bern et al. 1995.

Gauthier 1949
Maximilien Gauthier, *Vlaminck,* Paris 1949.

Genevoix 1954
Maurice Genevoix, *Vlaminck,* Paris 1954.

Genevoix 1968
Maurice Genevoix, "Mon ami Vlaminck," in *Le Jardin des arts* 167 (October 1968), 34–37.

Giry 1976
Marcel Giry, "Le Curieux Achat fait à Derain et à Vlaminck au Salon des Indépendants de 1905 ou deux tableaux retrouvés," in *L'Œil* 254 (September 1976), 26–31.

Giry 1981
Marcel Giry, *Le Fauvisme: Ses origines, son évolution,* Neuchâtel 1981.

Giry 1990
Marcel Giry, "Van Gogh and the Fauves," in *Vincent van Gogh and the Modern Movement, 1890–1914,* exh. cat., Museum Folkwang, Essen 1990, 267–95.

Grammont 2000
Claudie Grammont, *La Genèse du fauvisme,* Paris 2000.

Green 1999
Christopher Green, "Roger Fry's Canon from African Sculpture to Vlaminck," in *Art Made Modern: Roger Fry's Vision of Art,* exh. cat., Courtauld Institute of Art, London 1999, 135–212.

Halle an der Saale 2017
Alexej von Jawlensky—Georges Rouault: Sehen mit geschlossenen Augen, exh. cat., Kunstmuseum Moritzburg, Halle an der Saale 2017.

Halperin 1988
Joan Ungersma Halperin, *Félix Fénéon: Aesthete and Anarchist in Fin-de-Siècle Paris,* New Haven 1988.

Hartlaub 1950
Gustav Friedrich Hartlaub, *Gemälde von Braque, Derain, Dufy, Friesz, Marquet, Matisse, van Dongen, Vlaminck,* Paris 1950.

Herbert 1989
James D. Herbert, *Fauvism and After: The Politics of French Cultural Unity,* New Haven 1989.

Herbert 1992
James D. Herbert, *Fauve Painting: The Making of Cultural Politics,* New Haven 1992.

Jedlicka 1961
Gotthard Jedlicka, *Der Fauvismus,* Zurich 1961.

Jolinon 1932
Joseph Jolinon, "La Rencontre de Vlaminck avec Derain," in *L'Art vivant* 158 (March 1932), 121.

Joubeaux 2000
Hervé Joubeaux, *Maurice de Vlaminck, 1876–1958: Peintures, estampes, céramiques, mobilier, broderie; Les Collections du Musée des Beaux-Arts de Chartres,* Chartres 2000.

Kahnweiler 1919
Daniel-Henry Kahnweiler, "Maurice de Vlaminck," in *Der Cicerone* 11 (1919), 757–61.

Kahnweiler 1920
Daniel-Henry Kahnweiler, *Maurice de Vlaminck: Mit einem Selbstbekenntnis des Künstlers,* Leipzig 1920.

Knott 2015
Stephen Knott, *Amateur Craft: History and Theory,* London 2015.

Kropmanns 2012
Peter Kropmanns, "Frankreich—die Säle 10 und 11: Nabis, Fauves, Kubisten und neuere Tendenzen," in *1912, Mission Moderne: Die Jahrhundertschau des Sonderbundes,* exh. cat., Wallraf-Richartz-Museum & Fondation Corboud, Cologne 2012, 140–50.

Krüger 2008
Matthias Krüger, *Das Relief der Farbe: Pastose Malerei in der französischen Kunstkritik, 1850–1890,* Munich and Berlin 2007.

L'Isle-Adam 2007
L'Oise de Dupré à Vlaminck: Bateliers, peintres et canotiers, exh. cat., Musée d'Art et d'Histoire Louis-Senlecq, L'Isle-Adam 2007.

Labrusse/Munck 2005
Matisse—Derain: La Vérité du fauvisme, ed. Rémi Labrusse and Jacqueline Munck, Paris 2005.

Lambert 2014
Jacques Lambert, *De Montmartre à Montparnasse: La Vraie Vie de bohème (1900–1939),* Paris 2014.

Laude 1968
Jean Laude, *La Peinture française (1905–1914) et "l'Art nègre": Contribution à l'étude des sources du fauvisme et du cubisme,* Paris 1968.

Léal 2006
Collection art moderne: La Collection du Centre Pompidou, Musée national d'art moderne, ed. Brigitte Léal, Paris 2006.

Leighten 2007
Patricia Leighten, *The Liberation of Painting: Modernism and Anarchism in Avant-Guerre Paris,* Chicago 2007.

Lesieur-Troupet 1977
Hélène Lesieur-Troupet, "Les Bois gravés de Vlaminck," in *Nouvelles de l'estampe* 31 (January–February 1977), 11–16.

Leymarie 1959
Jean Leymarie, *Le Fauvisme: Étude biographique et critique,* Geneva 1959.

Leymarie 1987
Jean Leymarie, *Fauves and Fauvism,* New York 1987.

Lodève 1999
Les Fauves et la critique: Matisse, Derain, Vlaminck, Van Dongen, Marquet, Braque, Dufy, Camoin, Friesz, Manguin, Puy, Valtat, exh. cat., Musée de Lodève, 1999.

Lodève 2001
Derain et Vlaminck, 1900–1915, exh. cat., Musée de Lodève, 2001.

London 1978
Les Fauves, exh. cat., Lefevre Gallery, London 1978.

Los Angeles 1990
The Fauve Landscape: Matisse, Derain, Braque, and Their Circle, 1904–1908, exh. cat., Los Angeles County Museum of Art, 1990.

Lucerne 1939
Gemälde und Plastiken moderner Meister aus deutschen Museen, exh. cat., Galerie Fischer, Lucerne 1939.

Mac Orlan 1947
Pierre Mac Orlan, *Vlaminck: Peintures 1900–1945,* Paris 1947.

Mac Orlan 1958
Pierre Mac Orlan, *Vlaminck,* Stuttgart 1958.

Mascheroni/Carrà 1993
Vlaminck, ed. Anna M. Mascheroni and Massimo Carrà, London 1993.

Mexico City 2018
Vlaminck: La expresión del color, exh. cat., Museo Soumaya, Mexico City 2018.

Montaigne 1929
André Montaigne, *Maurice Vlaminck,* Paris 1929.

Müller 1956
Joseph-Émile Müller, *Le Fauvisme,* Paris 1956.

Munck 2001
Jacqueline Munck, "Derain/Vlaminck: La Raison et la passion fauves," in Lodève 2001, 31–41.

Munck 2007
Jacqueline Munck, "Ambroise Vollard et les fauves; Derain, Vlaminck," in *De Cézanne à Picasso: Chefs d'œuvre de la galerie Vollard,* exh. cat., Musée d'Orsay, Paris 2007, 129–41.

Munck 2019
Jacqueline Munck, "Matisse, die Fauves und die 'Erprobung der Mittel,'" in *Inspiration Matisse,* exh. cat., Kunsthalle Mannheim 2019, 18–25.

Münster 2019
Im Rausch der Farbe: Von Gauguin bis Matisse; Meisterwerke aus dem Musée d'Art moderne de Troyes, exh. cat., Kunstmuseum Pablo Picasso Münster, 2019.

Nacenta/Sauvage 1966
Maurice de Vlaminck, ed. Raymond Nacenta and Marcel Sauvage, Paris 1966.

New York 1932
Derain, Vlaminck: Comparative Exhibition, exh. cat., Museum of French Art, New York 1932.

New York 1952
Les Fauves, exh. cat., Museum of Modern Art, New York 1952.

New York 1954
Maurice de Vlaminck: His Blue Period, 1908–1914, exh. cat., Perls Galleries, New York 1954.

New York 1968
Vlaminck: His Fauve Period, exh. cat., Perls Galleries, New York 1968.

New York 1976
The "Wild Beasts": Fauvism and Its Affinities, exh. cat., Museum of Modern Art, New York 1976.

New York 2023
Vertigo of Color: Matisse, Derain, and the Origins of Fauvism, exh. cat., Metropolitan Museum of Art, New York 2023.

Nguyen-Schoendorff/Widman 2019
Odile Nguyen-Schoendorff and Pierre Widman, *Je suis Maurice de Vlaminck*, La Bauche 2019.

Nice 1996
La Céramique fauve: André Metthey et les peintres, exh. cat., Musée Matisse, Nice 1996.

O'Laoghaire 1992
Niamh O'Laoghaire, *The Influence of Van Gogh on Matisse, Derain and Vlaminck, 1898–1908*, Toronto 1992.

Ochsé 1973
Madeleine Ochsé, "Les Voies secrètes de la peinture: Vlaminck, exacerbation de la nature," in *Le Jardin des arts* 217 (March–April 1973), 52–55.

Oppler 1976
Ellen Charlotte Oppler, *Fauvism Reexamined*, New York 1976.

Paris 1920
Trente Tableaux de Vlaminck, exh. cat., Galerie Bernheim-Jeune, Paris 1920.

Paris 1927
Les Fauves, 1904 à 1908, exh. cat., Galerie Bing, Paris 1927.

Paris 1942
Les Fauves, peintures de 1903 à 1908, exh. cat., Galerie de France, Paris 1942.

Paris 1956
L'Œuvre de Vlaminck: Du fauvisme à nos jours, exh. cat., Galerie Charpentier, Paris 1956.

Paris 1962
Les Fauves, exh. cat., Galerie Charpentier, Paris 1962.

Paris 1966
Le fauvisme français et les débuts de l'expressionnisme allemand, exh. cat., Musée national d'art moderne, Paris 1966.

Paris 1987
Maurice Vlaminck, exh. cat., Galerie de la Présidence, Paris 1987.

Paris 1994
André Derain: Le Peintre du "trouble moderne," exh. cat., Musée d'Art Moderne de la Ville de Paris, 1994.

Paris 1999
Le Fauvisme ou l'épreuve du feu: Éruption de la modernité en Europe, exh. cat., Musée d'Art Moderne de la Ville de Paris, 1999.

Paris 2008
Vlaminck: Un instinct fauve, exh. cat., Musée du Luxembourg, Paris 2008.

Paris 2012
Modigliani, Soutine et l'aventure de Montparnasse: La Collection Jonas Netter, exh. cat., Pinacothèque de Paris, 2012.

Paris 2015
Matisse en son temps, exh. cat., Centre Pompidou, Paris 2015.

Paris 2017
André Derain: 1904–1914, la décennie radicale, exh. cat., Centre Pompidou, Paris 2017.

Passuth 2006
Krisztina Passuth, "Wild Beasts of Hungary Meet Fauves in France," in *Fauves: Hungarian Fauves from Paris to Nagybánya, 1904–1914*, exh. cat., Hungarian National Gallery, Budapest 2006, 11–36.

Pernoud 1994
Emmanuel Pernoud, *L'Estampe des Fauves: Une esthétique du contraste*, Paris 1994.

Perry 1956
Jacques Perry, *Vlaminck: Images de Roger Hauert*, Geneva 1956.

Pollag 1968
Sigmund Pollag, *Mes souvenirs sur Vlaminck*, Geneva 1968.

Potsdam 2018
Color and Light: The Neo-Impressionist Henri-Edmond Cross, exh. cat., Museum Barberini, Potsdam 2018.

Queneau 1949
Raymond Queneau, *Vlaminck ou le vertige de la matière*, Paris 1949.

Raynal 1950
Maurice Raynal, *Matisse, Munch, Rouault, fauvisme et expressionnisme*, Histoire de la peinture moderne 2, Geneva 1950.

Rey 1955
Robert Rey, *Maurice de Vlaminck*, Paris 1955.

Rueil-Malmaison 2015
Maurice de Vlaminck, 1876–1958, exh. cat., Atelier Grognard, Rueil-Malmaison 2015.

Rueil-Malmaison 2016
Peindre la banlieue, de Corot à Vlaminck, 1850–1950, exh. cat, Atelier Grognard, Rueil-Malmaison 2016.

Saint-Tropez 2013
Vlaminck: Les Années décisives (1900–1914), exh. cat., Musée de Saint-Tropez, L'Annonciade 2013.

Salmon 1956
André Salmon, *Le Fauvisme*, Paris 1956.

São Paulo 2001
Vlaminck, 1876–1958, exh. cat, Museu de Arte Brasileira, São Paulo 2001.

Sauvage 1956
Marcel Sauvage, *Vlaminck: Sa vie et son message*, Geneva 1956.

Sauvage 1959
Vlaminck: Mein Testament, ed. Marcel Sauvage, Zurich 1959.

Schaffhausen 1959
Triumph der Farbe: Die europäischen Fauves, exh. cat., Museum zu Allerheiligen, Schaffhausen 1959.

Schieder 1999
Martin Schieder, "'Aucun rapport avec la peinture': Die Fauves im Salon d'Automne von 1905 und die Kunstkritik," in *Prenez garde à la peinture! Kunstkritik in Frankreich 1900–1945,* ed. Uwe Fleckner and Thomas W. Gaehtgens, Berlin 1999, 405–23.

Selz 1967
Jean Selz, *Vlaminck,* Munich 1967.

Shapiro 1976
Theda Shapiro, *Painters and Politics: The European Avant-Garde and Society, 1900–1925,* New York 1976.

Siemsen 1924
Hans P. Siemsen, "Maurice de Vlaminck," in *Deutsche Kunst und Dekoration* 54 (1924), 60–62.

Sotriffer 1972
Kristian Sotriffer, *Expressionism and Fauvism,* New York 1972.

Stuttgart 1961
Maurice de Vlaminck: Gemälde, Aquarelle, Holzschnitte, Radierungen, Lithographien, exh. cat., Galerie Valentin, Stuttgart 1961.

Stuttgart 2011
Louis Valtat (1869–1952): Ein Künstler aus dem Kreis der Fauves und seine Malerfreunde, exh. cat., Galerie Stuttgart Stadtmitte Maier & Co. Fine Art, 2011.

Ternovetz 1923
Boris Nikolaevitch Ternovetz, "Vlaminck et Derain," in *Sredi kollekstionerov* 3/4 (1923), 8–20.

Teubner 2022
Maike Teubner, "Farbe als Ventil: Neu aufgefundene Beiträge von Maurice de Vlaminck in der Zeitung *Le Libertaire* und die Idee der Anarchie im Fauvismus," in *Anarchie und Ästhetik: Fallbeispiele vom 19. Jahrhundert bis zur Gegenwart,* ed. Susanne Gramatzki, Berlin 2022, 99–118.

Turpin 1948
Georges Turpin, *Les Fauves, les cubistes et leurs contemporains,* Panorama de la peinture française au XXe siècle 1, Paris 1948.

Vallès-Bled 1991
Maïthé Vallès-Bled, *Maurice de Vlaminck: Œuvres 1900–1956,* Paris 1991.

Vallès-Bled 1996
Maïthé Vallès-Bled, "Vlaminck et l'expérience de la céramique," in Nice 1996, 109–17.

Vallès-Bled 2008
Maïthé Vallès-Bled, *Vlaminck: Catalogue critique des peintures et céramiques de la période fauve/Critical Catalogue of the Fauve Paintings and Ceramics,* Paris 2008.

Vauxcelles 1905
Louis Vauxcelles, "Le Salon d'Automne," in *Gil Blas* 15 (October 17, 1905), unpaginated.

Vauxcelles 1958
Louis Vauxcelles, *Le Fauvisme: Étude biographique et critique,* Geneva 1958.

Vienna 2013
Matisse and the Fauves, exh. cat., Albertina, Vienna 2013.

Vlaminck 1927
Maurice de Vlaminck, *Histoires et poèmes de mon époque,* Paris 1927.

Vlaminck 1929
Maurice de Vlaminck, *Tournant dangereux: Souvenirs de ma vie,* Paris 1929.

Vlaminck 1931
Maurice de Vlaminck, *Poliment,* Paris 1931.

Vlaminck 1934
Maurice de Vlaminck, *La Haute-Folie: Suivie de Cartes sur table,* Paris 1934.

Vlaminck 1937
Maurice de Vlaminck, *Le Ventre ouvert,* Paris 1937.

Vlaminck 1939
Maurice de Vlaminck, *Pour une peinture lisible, vivante, humaine,* Paris 1939.

Vlaminck 1941
Maurice de Vlaminck, *La Mort de Mindrais,* Paris 1941.

Vlaminck 1943
Maurice de Vlaminck, *Portraits avant décès,* Paris 1943.

Vlaminck 1952
Maurice de Vlaminck, *Moyen-âge sans cathédrale,* Monte-Carlo 1952.

Vlaminck 1953
Maurice de Vlaminck, *Paysages et personnages,* Paris 1953.

Vlaminck 1965
Maurice de Vlaminck, *Rückblick in letzter Stunde: Menschen und Zeiten* [1943], St. Gallen 1965.

Vlaminck 1966
Maurice de Vlaminck, *Dangerous Corner* [1929], trans. Michael Ross, New York 1966.

Vlaminck 2012
Godelieve de Vlaminck, *Vlaminck, la soif de liberté: Témoignage,* Illiers-Combray 2012.

Vollard 1936
Ambroise Vollard, *Recollections of a Picture Dealer*, trans. Violet M. Macdonald, Boston 1936.

Vollard 1984
Ambroise Vollard, *Souvenirs d'un marchand de tableaux* [1936], Paris 1984.

Walterskirchen/Pollag 1974
Maurice de Vlaminck: Verzeichnis des graphischen Werkes; Holzschnitte, Radierungen, Lithographien, ed. Katalin von Walterskirchen and Sigmund Pollag, Bern 1974.

Wedewer 1981
Rolf Wedewer, *Aquarelle und Zeichnungen des 20. Jahrhunderts,* Cologne 1981.

Werner 1959
Vlaminck: 16 Beautiful Full Color Prints, ed. Alfred Werner, New York 1959.

Werner 1968
Alfred Werner, "Vlaminck, Wildest of the 'Beasts,'" in *Arts Magazine* 5 (March 1968), 30–33.

Werner 1975
Alfred Werner, *Maurice Vlaminck,* New York 1975.

Werth 1925
Vlaminck: Vingt et une reproductions d'après ses tableaux, ed. Léon Werth, Paris 1925.

Westheider 2004
Ortrud Westheider, "Französische Expressionisten und Kubisten in Berlin: Kees van Dongen, Maurice de Vlaminck, Pablo Picasso," in *Die Brücke und die Moderne 1904–1914,* exh. cat., Bucerius Kunst Forum, Hamburg 2004, 190–99.

Whitfield 1996
Sarah Whitfield, *Fauvism,* London 1996.

Zürcher 1995
Bernard Zürcher, *Les Fauves,* Paris 1995.

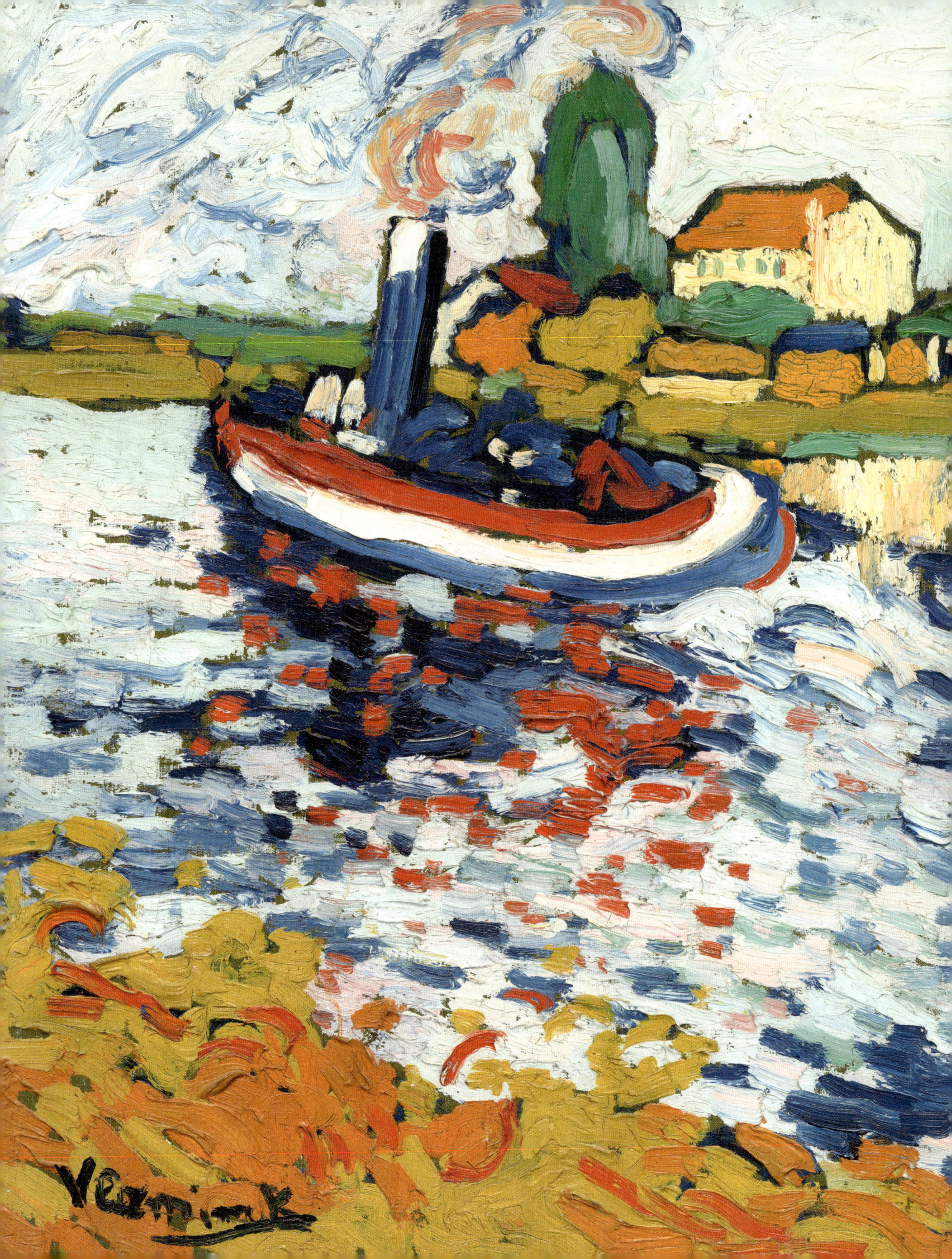
Vlaminck

Authors

Sterre Barentsen, assistant curator at the Museum Barberini in Potsdam since 2023, studied art history at the Courtauld Institute of Art in London and at the University of Oxford. She received her PhD from the Humboldt-Universität in Berlin with the dissertation *From Acid Lakes to Miningscapes: An Environmental Art History of the Late GDR* (2023). Barentsen was curator of the Moscow International Biennale for Young Art (2020) at the Moscow Museum of Modern Art and has contributed to the exhibition catalogs *Wolfgang Mattheuer/ Stan Douglas* (2022) and *Clouds and Light: Impressionism in Holland* (2023). She is currently preparing the exhibition *Kandinsky's Universe: Geometric Abstraction from Constructivism to Op-Art* (2025) at the Museum Barberini.

Jacqueline Hartwig, assistant curator at the Museum Barberini in Potsdam from 2022 to 2024, studied art history with a focus on curatorial studies and ethnology in Göttingen and Bari. She completed her master's thesis, "Spiel und Status: Zu Funktion und Auftraggeberschaft des Nürnberger Spieleteppichs," in 2021 and has contributed to the exhibition catalogs *Gilly—Weinbrenner—Schinkel: Baukunst auf Papier zwischen Gotik und Klassizismus* (2016), *Transformation of the World—Master Sheets by Hendrick Goltzius* (2020), and *Clouds and Light: Impressionism in Holland* (2023). At the Museum Barberini, she was assistant curator of the exhibition *Clouds and Light: Impressionism in Holland* (2023) and was involved in the preparations for *Edvard Munch: Trembling Earth* (2023) and *Unicorn: The Mythical Creature in Art* (2025).

Matthias Krüger, lecturer at the Ludwig-Maximilians-Universität (LMU) in Munich since 2019, received his PhD in 2004 with the dissertation *Das Relief der Farbe: Pastose Malerei in der französischen Kunstkritik 1850–1890* (2007). He completed his habilitation at LMU in 2019 on the topic of local color in regionalist and exoticist painting of the nineteenth and twentieth centuries. Krüger has held visiting professorships at the Universität Hamburg, Goethe-Universität Frankfurt am Main, and the LMU, and has been a guest professor at the Università Ca' Foscari in Venice and the Universität Graz. He has authored numerous publications on artistic techniques, materials, and utensils as well as on art theory and criticism. He is the editor of *Werkzeuge und Instrumente* (with Philippe Cordez, 2012), *Die Biologie der Kreativität: Ein produktionsästhetisches Denkmodell in der Moderne* (2013), and *Pro domo: Kunstgeschichte in eigener Sache* (with Léa Kuhn and Ulrich Pfisterer, 2021).

Valentina Plotnikova has been assistant curator at the Museum Barberini in Potsdam since 2024. From 2022 to 2024, she worked as a student assistant there. From 2020 to 2024, she was an assistant and then a curator at the Bode Gallery for Contemporary Art in Berlin. She studied art history and Italian at the Humboldt-Universität in Berlin. Her master's thesis, completed in 2024, is titled *Künstliches Licht als Protagonist der Malerei in den Großstadt-Nachtansichten von Lesser Ury.* From 2015 to 2019, she worked in international public relations, including a position at McKinsey & Company. From 2009 to 2015, Plotnikova studied international relations at the Freie Universität Berlin and the Moscow State Institute of International Relations. Her master's thesis, titled *Soft Power Index: Germany and Russia,* was completed in 2015.

Lisa Smit, curator for paintings at the Van Gogh Museum in Amsterdam since 2021, began her academic career there as a researcher in 2013, focusing on printmaking in fin de siècle France. She coordinated the project for cataloging the museum's collection and was involved in associated provenance research from 2018 to 2021. With a focus on the art of Van Gogh and his contemporaries as well as art in Vienna around 1900, Smit has curated the exhibitions *Choosing Vincent: Portrait of a Family History* (2023) and *In the Picture* (2020) and served as an exhibition researcher for the project *Golden Boy Gustav Klimt: Inspired by Van Gogh, Rodin, Matisse* (2022).

Anna Storm, deputy director of the Von der Heydt-Museum in Wuppertal since 2023, after working there as a curator since 2017. She studied art history and media studies at Ruhr-Universität Bochum and received her PhD from the Leuphana Universität Lüneburg with the dissertation *Aneignung und Eigensinn: Interpikturalität in der Malerei Helene Funkes.* Storm has served as curator or cocurator of numerous exhibitions, including *Bogomir Ecker: What the Photo Hides* (2018), *Vision and Terror of Modernity: Industry and Artistic Departure* (2021), *Brücke und Blauer Reiter* (2021), and *Strangers to Ourselves: Portraits from Paula Modersohn-Becker to Zanele Muholi* (2022).

Heinz Widauer, a freelance art historian since 2021, studied art history at the Universität Wien in Vienna and completed his PhD on the drawings and etchings of Sébastien Bourdon (1999). He worked as a research assistant in the graphic collection of the Albertina in Vienna from 1992, completed an internship in the drawings department of the J. Paul Getty Museum, Los Angeles, in 1995–96, and served as a collection curator of sixteenth- and seventeenth-century French drawings at the Albertina starting in 2000. Widauer has curated or cocurated numerous exhibitions, including *Vincent van Gogh: Drawn Pictures* (2008), *Matisse and the Fauves* (2013), *Seurat, Signac, Van Gogh: Ways of Pointillism* (2016), and *Claude Monet: A Floating World* (2018).

Daniel Zamani, artistic director at the Museum Frieder Burda in Baden-Baden since July 2024, received his PhD from the University of Cambridge on occult and medieval themes in the work of André Breton (2017). He was an assistant curator and then a research assistant at the Städel Museum in Frankfurt am Main from 2015 to 2017, and curator at the Museum Barberini in Potsdam from 2018 to 2024. He edited the books *Surrealism, Occultism, and Politics: In Search of the Marvellous* (with Tessel M. Bauduin and Victoria Ferentinou, 2018) and *Visions of Enchantment: Occultism, Magic and Visual Culture* (with Merlin Cox and Judith Noble, 2019). Zamani has curated or cocurated the exhibitions *Matisse—Bonnard: Long Live Painting!* (2017), *Color and Light: The Neo-Impressionist Henri-Edmond Cross* (2018), *Monet: Places* (2020), *The Shape of Freedom: International Abstraction after 1945* (2022), and *Surrealism and Magic: Enchanted Modernity* (2022).

Colophon

This catalog is published in conjunction with the exhibition

Maurice de Vlaminck: Modern Art Rebel

Museum Barberini, Potsdam
September 14, 2024–January 12, 2025

Von der Heydt-Museum, Wuppertal
February 16, 2025–May 18, 2025

Editors:
Roland Mönig, Michael Philipp,
Anna Storm, and Ortrud Westheider

Exhibition and Catalog:
Anna Storm and Daniel Zamani

Catalog Editing:
Daniel Zamani

Image Editing:
Valentina Plotnikova

Catalog

Editorial Direction, Prestel:
Markus Eisen
Graphic Design and Typesetting:
BrücknerAping, Büro für Gestaltung, Bremen
Copyediting:
Tas Skorupa, New York
Project Management:
Annette Krüger, Hamburg
Translation from English:
Melissa M. Thorson
Production Management, Prestel:
Cilly Klotz
Color Separations:
Reproline Genceller, Munich

Printing and Binding:
Printer Trento, Trento
Typeface:
Neue Haas Grotesk
Paper:
Garda Matt Ultra, 150 g/m²

MIX
Paper | Supporting responsible forestry
FSC® C015829

Penguin Random House Verlagsgruppe
FSC® N001967

Printed in Italy

A CIP catalog record for this book is available from the British Library.
Library of Congress Control Number is available.

ISBN 978-3-7913-7751-3
(German trade edition)
ISBN 978-3-7913-7752-0
(English trade edition)
ISBN 978-3-7913-9131-1
(German museum edition, Museum Barberini, Potsdam)
ISBN 978-3-7913-9132-8
(English museum edition, Museum Barberini, Potsdam)
ISBN 978-3-7913-9133-5
(German museum edition, Von der Heydt-Museum, Wuppertal)

www.prestel.de
www.prestel.com

Museum Barberini, Potsdam

Director:
Ortrud Westheider
Assistant to the Director:
Dorothee Entrup
Director Finance and Administration:
Janine Meyer
Chief Curator:
Michael Philipp
Research Associate
Provenance:
Linda Hacka
Assistant Curators:
Sterre Barentsen, Valentina Plotnikova
Registrars:
Sabine Pinkert, Nadine Vollmer
Student Assistants:
Anna Heling, Céline Veronique Marten
Communications and Marketing:
Achim Klapp, Marte Kräher, Valerie Maul, Carolin Stranz
Digitization and Information Security:
Stefan Scholze
IT-Administrators:
Andreas Papadimitriou, Sebastian Semmler
Educational Service:
Dorothee Entrup, Sophie Heldt, Andrea Schmidt
Events:
Deniz Lusch, Kaspar Winkler
Guest Management:
Frauke Herlyn, Angela Winkler
Accounting and Ticketing:
Yvonne Benesch, Heike Kraeft
Office Management and Ticketing:
Daniela Schaube
HR Administration:
Julia Pauline Nowak
Security:
Nikolaos Dokalis, Verena Daub
Building Services:
Carsten Loeper, Frank Altmann, Dennis Kokert

In collaboration with:

Conservation:
Felicitas Klein, Berlin
Friederike Beseler, Berlin
Exhibition Design:
Philipp Ricklefs, Berlin
BrücknerAping, Büro für Gestaltung, Bremen
Museum Shop:
Museum Barberini. Der Shop, Jörg Klambt
Transport:
Hasenkamp, Berlin

Von der Heydt-Museum, Wuppertal

Director:
Roland Mönig
Assistent to the Director:
Stefanie Masberg
Deputy Director:
Anna Storm
Curators:
Anna Baumberger, Anika Bruns, Beate Eickhoff, Henrike Stein
Digitization:
Philipp Gayer
Press and Communications, Marketing:
Marion Meyer
Education:
Julia Dürbeck, Karolina Bürger
Registrar/Reproduction and Image Rights:
Bettina Klecha
Conservation:
Andreas Iglhaut
Department of Prints and Drawings:
Stefanie Wachmann
Bookbinding:
Christoph Kolibabka
Library:
Anna Elbers
Assistant Press and Communications:
Mechthild Küster
Head of Museum Administration and Service:
Tanja Hormann
Head of Accounting, Von der Heydt-Museum gGmbH:
Katja Friedmann
Administration and Service:
Yvonne Heunatzki, Olesja Knodel
Guest Management:
Jean Oehm
Shipping Department:
Zdenka Hardi
Technical Services:
Marcel Körn, Marc Konstantin Wolferts, Heiko Stöcker
Switchboard:
Claudia Heer, Carsten Hinz
Shift Coordination:
Janina Nadja Otto, Stefan Wigge
Front Desk:
Gundula Pellegrini, Sandra Kingma-Sawer, Detlef Sommer
Security Service:
Dina Gradecak, Markus Christian Koch, Gundula Pellegrini,
Grigoritsa Samara, Sascha Schöning, Svenja Stöcker, Yeliz Topal

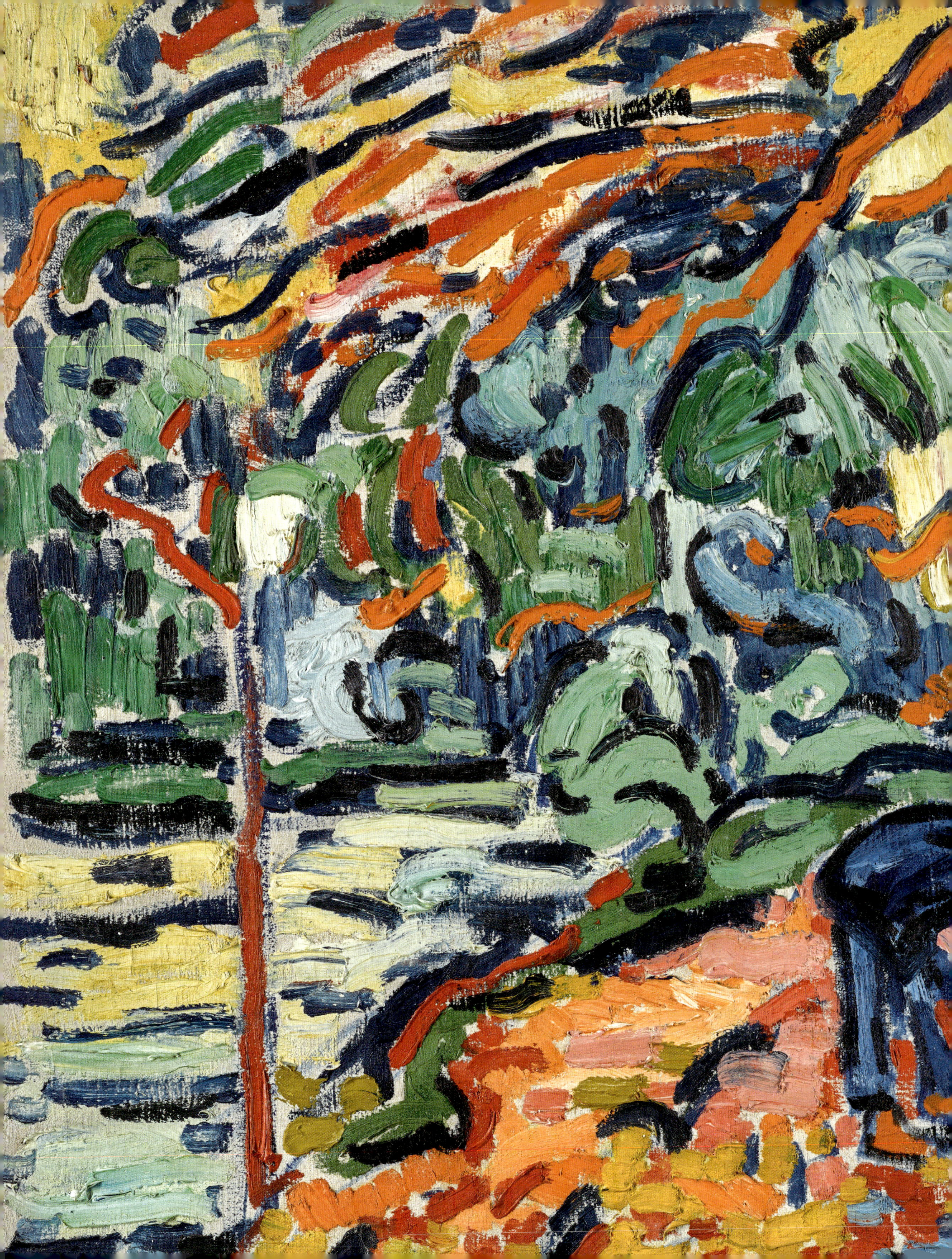

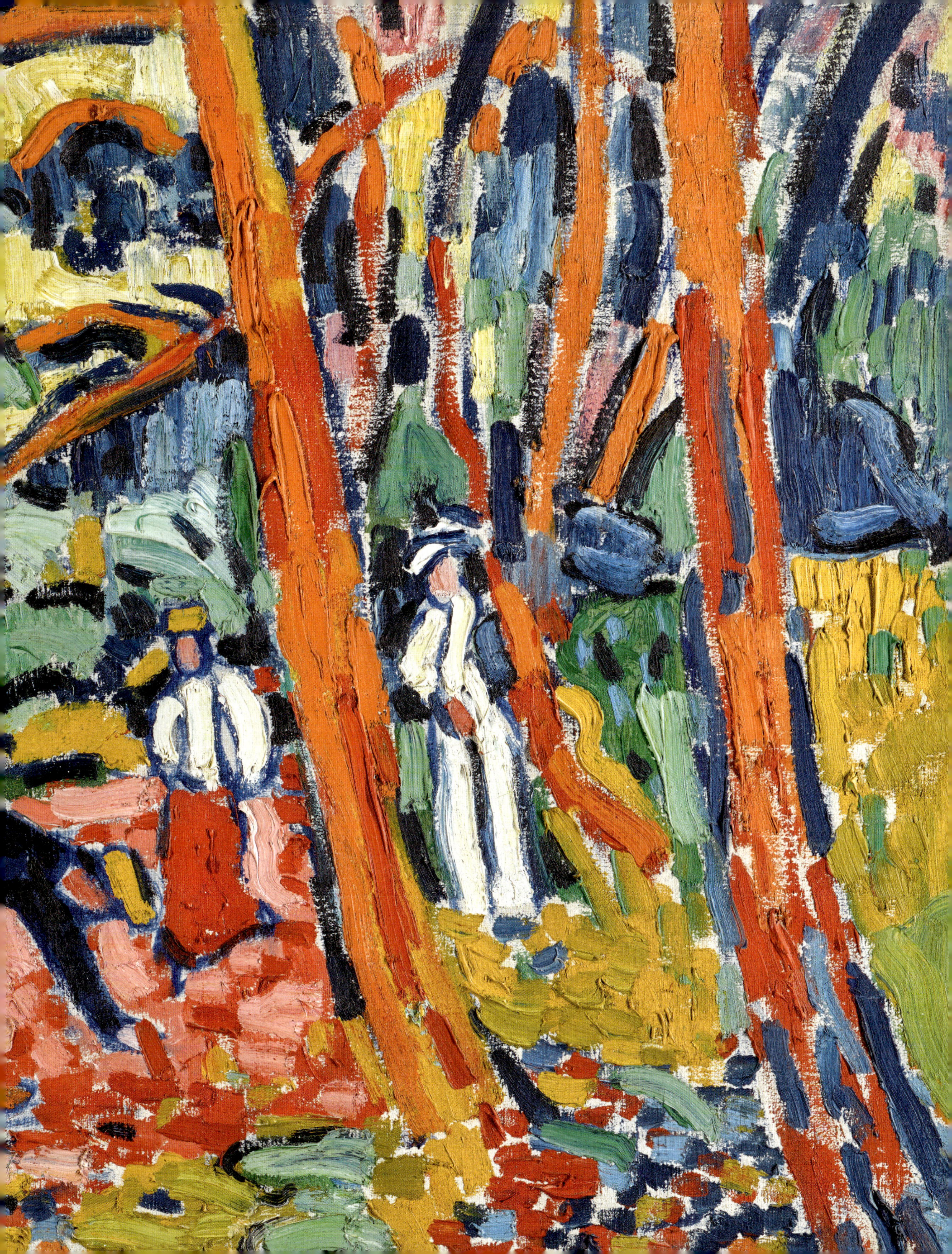

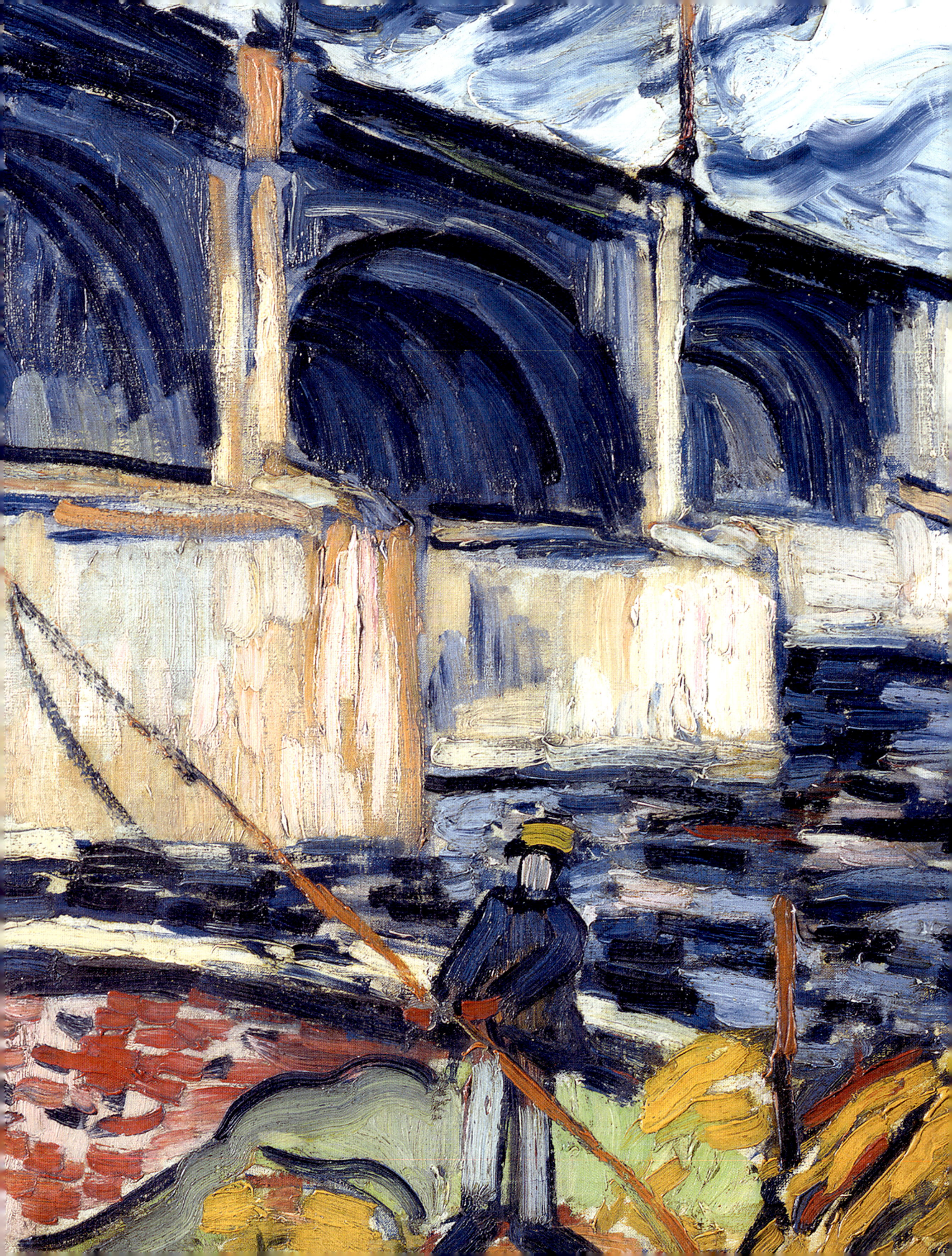

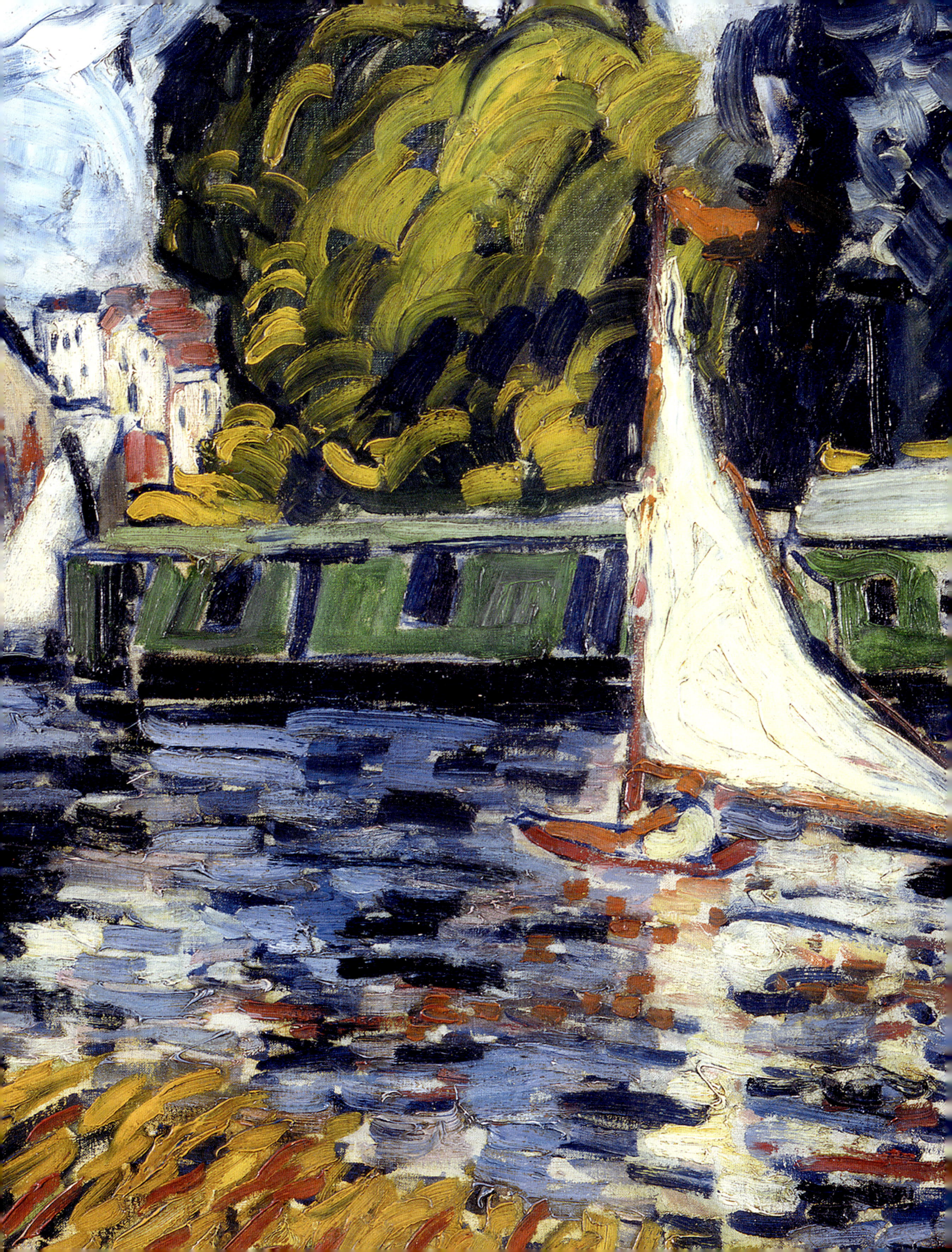

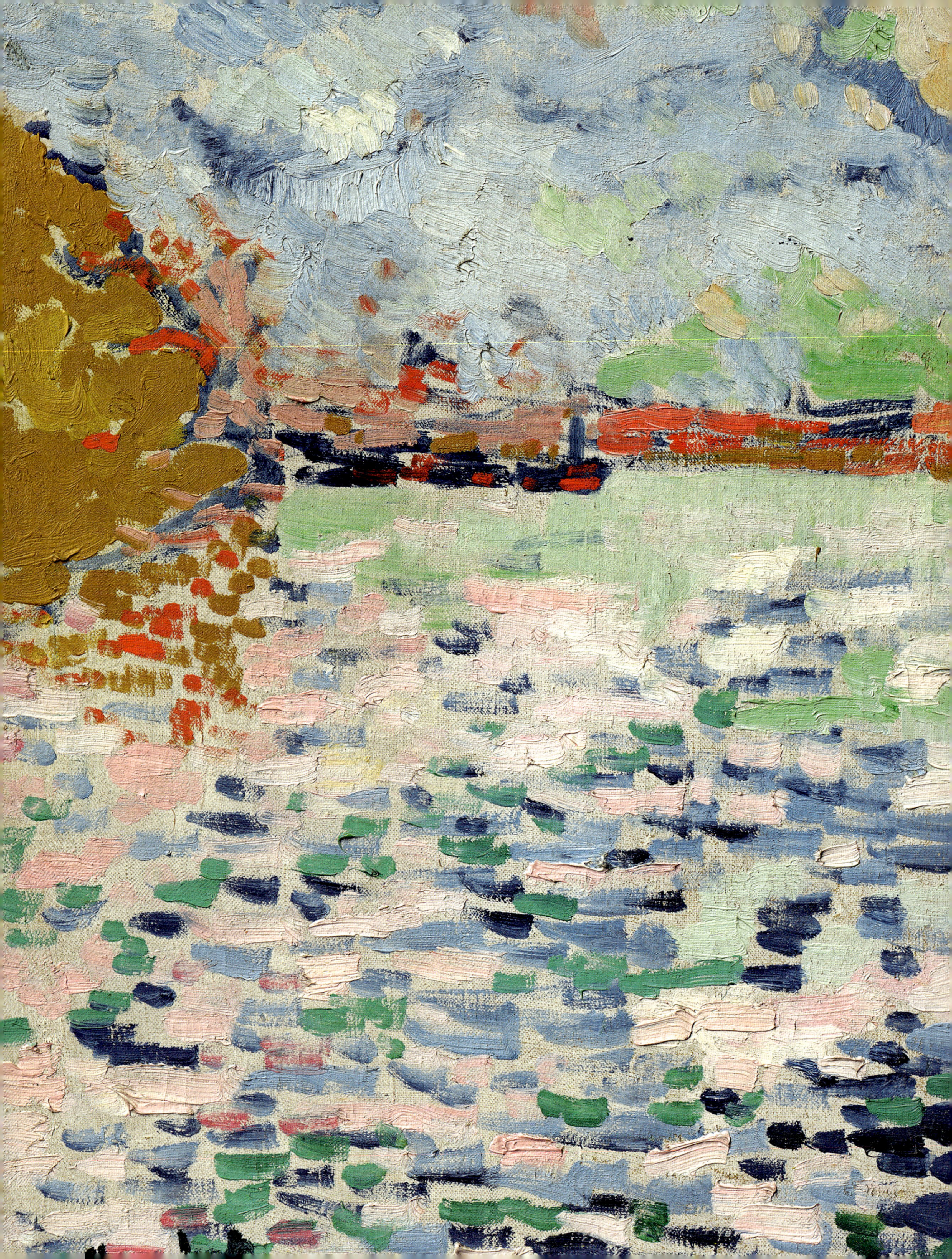

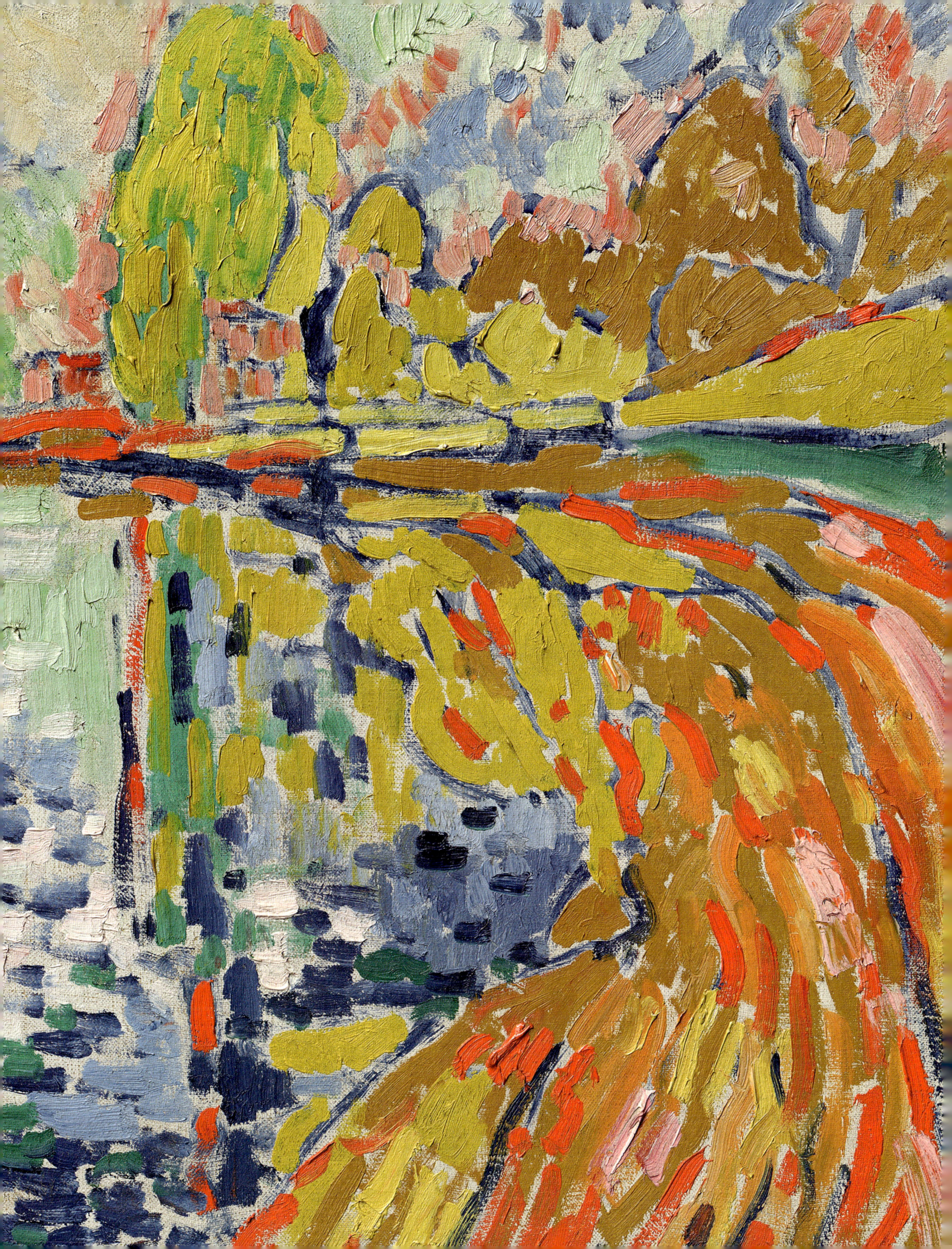

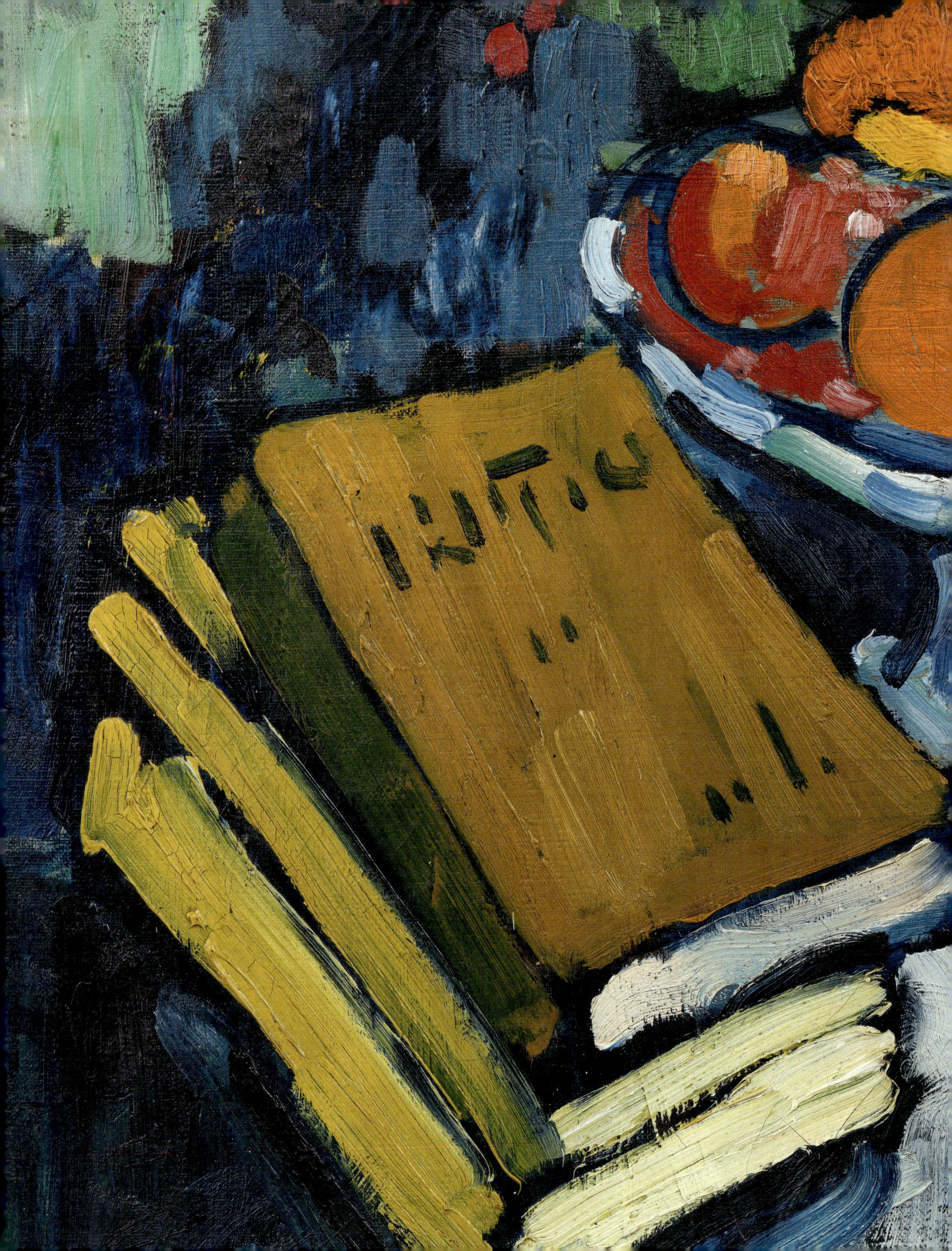

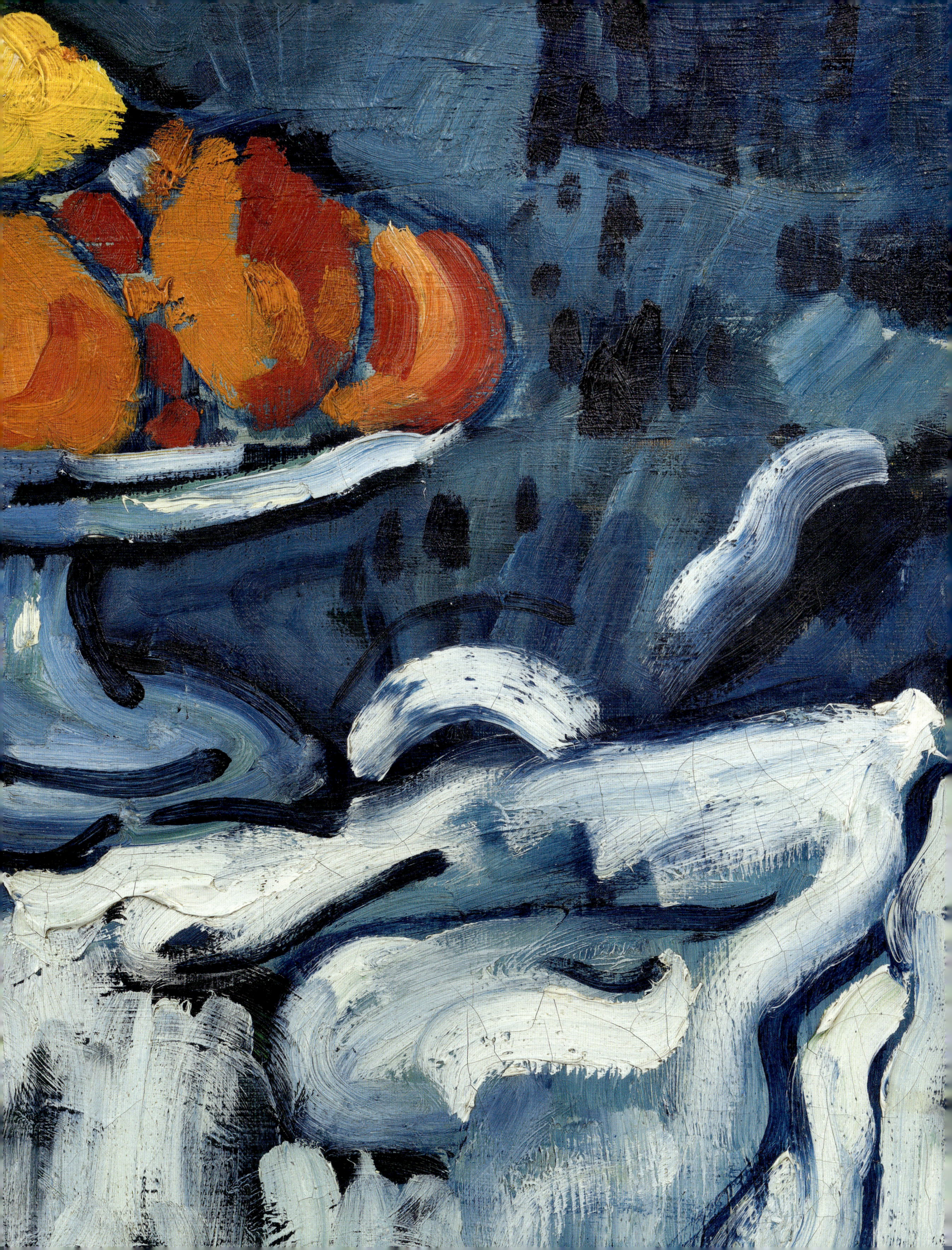

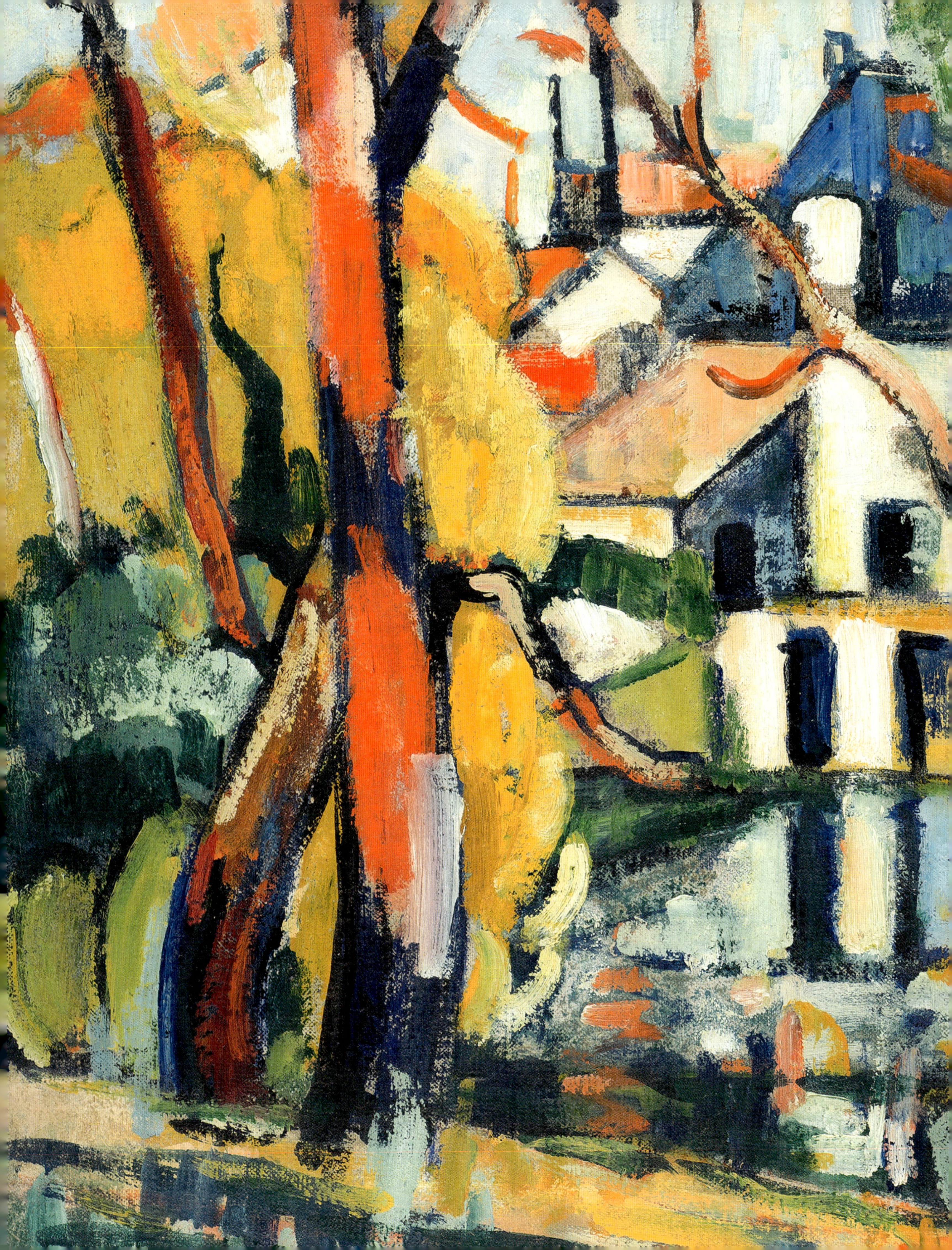

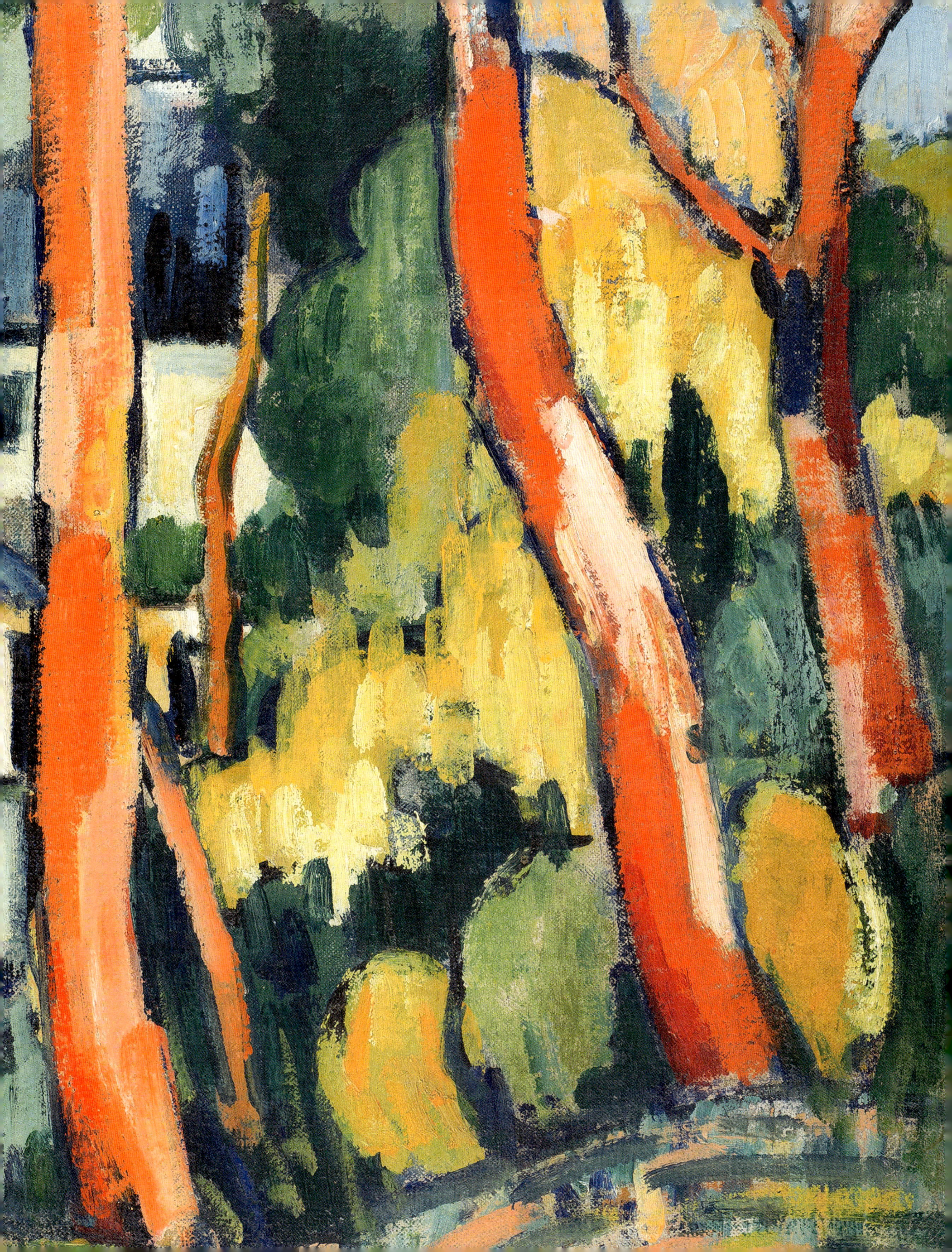

Image Credits

Stedelijk Museum Amsterdam: cat. 16
Van Gogh Museum, Amsterdam (Vincent van Gogh Foundation): cat. 43
Musée Calvet, Avignon (photo: Ville d'Avignon/Musée Calvet): cat. 3
bpk, Berlin: • CNAC-MNAM: cats. 1, 9 • CNAC-MNAM/Philippe Migeat: cats. 11, 13 • RMN-Grand Palais, Dépôt du Centre Pompidou/Gérard Blot: cat. 26 • Hamburger Kunsthalle (photo: Elke Walford): cat. 44 • Metropolitan Museum of Art: cat. 51 • RMN-Grand Palais (photo: Hervé Lewandowski): cats. 65, 71, 73, 80 • Kunsthalle Mannheim: cat. 72 • CNAC-MNAM (photo: Christian Bahier/Philippe Migeat): cat. 76 • RMN-Grand Palais (photo: Ville de Paris): cats. 77, 81
Staatliche Museen zu Berlin, Nationalgalerie (photo: Andres Kilger): cat. 50
Museum of Fine Arts, Boston: cat. 10
Art Institute of Chicago: cat. 31
Courtesy of Christie's: cats. 22, 49
Wallraf-Richartz-Museum & Fondation Corboud, Cologne (photo: © Rheinisches Bildarchiv, Cologne): cats. 57, 67
© DACS (photo: Tate): cat. 59
Dallas Museum of Art: cat. 17
Artothek, Fürth/Museum Folkwang, Essen: cat. 5
Wadsworth Atheneum Museum of Art, Hartford (photo: Allen Phillips): cat. 40
© Hugh Lane Gallery: cat. 64
Milwaukee Art Museum (photo: Efraim Lev-er): cat. 33
Minneapolis Institute of Art: cat. 30
Brooklyn Museum, New York: cat. 4
Triton Collection Foundation, the Netherlands: cat. 29
Artistica Art Collection Limited, Nicosia: cat. 21
Galerie de la Présidence, Paris: cats. 60, 68, 74
Photo: Christian Haas, Paris: cat. 53
Virginia Museum of Fine Arts, Richmond: cat. 48
Saint Louis Art Museum: cat. 54
Courtesy of Sotheby's: cats. 25, 32, 34–36
© Staatsgalerie Stuttgart: cat. 23
Tel Aviv Museum of Art: cat. 7 • photo: Margarita Perlin: cat. 15
© Carmen Thyssen Collection: cats. 27, 28
Artizon Museum, Ishibashi Foundation, Tokyo: cat. 38
Musée d'Art moderne, Troyes (photo: © Olivier Frajman): cat. 6
Albertina, Vienna—Batliner Collection: cats. 42, 47
National Gallery of Art, Washington, DC: cats. 19, 37
Kunst Museum Winterthur (photo: © Hans Humm, Zürich): cat. 14
Von der Heydt-Museum, Wuppertal (photo: Medienzentrum Wuppertal): cats. 58, 63, 66
Kunsthaus Zürich: cat. 52

Van Gogh Museum, Amsterdam (Vincent van Gogh Foundation): p. 49, fig. 9
akg-images, Berlin: p. 23, fig. 2; p. 29, fig. 9; p. 32, fig. 3; p. 35, fig. 6; p. 44, fig. 4; p. 188, fig. 8 • p. 36, fig. 7 (photo: Laurent Lecat) • p. 44, fig. 2 (photo: André Held) • Album/Joseph Martin/Fototeca H. Matisse: p. 31, fig. 1 • Album/Prisma: p. 57, fig. 10 • Hervé Champollion/akg-images: p. 37, fig. 8
bpk, Berlin: RMN-Grand Palais (photo: Benoît Touchard/Mathieu Rabeau): p. 38, fig. 9 • RMN-Grand Palais (photo: Hervé Lewandowski: p. 52, fig. 3 • CNAC-MNAM (photo: Philippe Migeat): p. 188, fig. 7 • Ministère de la Culture – Médiathèque du patrimoine et de la photographie, Dist. GrandPalaisRmn (photo: André Kertész): p. 190, fig. 10
Bridgeman Images, Berlin: p. 23, fig. 1; p. 55, fig. 8; p. 116; p. 25, fig. 5 (photo: © Christie's Images) • p. 34, fig. 5 (photo: Museum of Fine Arts, Houston) • p. 54, fig. 6 (photo: Philadelphia Museum of Art)
Ullstein Bild, Berlin (photo: Charlotte Rohrbach): p. 191, fig. 11
Scala, Florence: Digital Image, Museum of Modern Art, New York: p. 51, fig. 2
Pola Museum of Art, Hakone (photo: DNPartcom): p. 27, fig. 7
Metropolitan Museum of Art, New York: p. 46, fig. 6
© Kröller-Müller Museum, Otterlo (photo: Rik Klein Gotink): p. 39, fig. 11
Roger-Viollet, Paris: p. 189, fig. 9
Artizon Museum, Ishibashi Foundation, Tokyo: p. 185, fig. 2
National Gallery of Art, Washington, DC: p. 31, fig. 2; p. 52, fig. 4
Photo: Annik Wetter: p. 186, fig. 4
Emil Bührle Collection, long-term loan at the Kunsthaus Zürich: p. 24, figs. 3, 4

Images have been reproduced from the following publications: *Derain et Vlaminck, 1900–1915,* exh. cat., Musée de Lodève, 2001: p. 186, fig. 3 • *Van Gogh in Arles,* exh. cat., Metropolitan Museum of Art, New York 1984: p. 41, fig. 1 • Maïthé Vallès-Bled, *Vlaminck: Catalogue critique des peintures et céramiques de la période fauve/Critical Catalogue of the Fauve Paintings and Ceramics,* Paris 2008: cats. 2, 8, 24; p. 26, fig. 6; p. 27, fig. 8; p. 32, fig. 4; p. 38, fig. 10; p. 44, fig. 3; p. 187, figs. 5, 6 • *Vlaminck: Un instinct fauve,* exh. cat., Musée du Luxembourg, Paris 2008: cats. 18, 39; p. 39, fig. 12 • *Maurice de Vlaminck, 1876–1958,* exh. cat., Atelier Grognard, Rueil-Malmaison 2015: cats. 78, 79; p. 48, fig. 8; p. 162; p. 184, fig. 1

Image details have been used on the following pages: pp. 2–3 (cat. 56), pp. 4–5 (cat. 31), pp. 6–7 (cat. 55), pp. 8–9 (cat. 36), pp. 10–11 (cat. 54), p. 14 (cat. 19), p. 20 (cat. 32), pp. 66–67 (cat. 49), p. 68 (cat. 27), p. 114 (cat. 47), p. 142 (cat. 64), p. 160 (cat. 81), p. 176 (cat. 41), p. 182 (cat. 34), p. 192 (cat. 25), p. 198 (cat. 9), p. 204 (cat. 37), pp. 210–11 (cat. 35), pp. 212–13 (cat. 50), pp. 214–15 (cat. 46), pp. 216–17 (cat. 21), pp. 218–19 (cat. 12)